D1521301

The Tanner Lectures on Human Values

THE TANNER LECTURES

ON HUMAN VALUES

22

2001

Thomson, Warner, Vendler, Lepenies,
Lear, Hill, Ignatieff, Rosen, Diamond

Grethe B. Peterson, *Editor*

THE UNIVERSITY OF UTAH PRESS
Salt Lake City

THE TANNER LECTURES ON HUMAN VALUES
was set in Garamond by The Typeworks, Vancouver, BC, Canada

THE TANNER LECTURES ON HUMAN VALUES

The purpose of the Tanner Lectures is to advance and reflect upon scholarly and scientific learning that relates to human values.

To receive an appointment as a Tanner lecturer is a recognition of uncommon capabilities and outstanding scholarly or leadership achievement in the field of human values. The lecturers may be drawn from philosophy, religion, the humanities and sciences, the creative arts and learned professions, or from leadership in public or private affairs. The lectureships are international and intercultural and transcend ethnic, national, religious, or ideological distinctions.

The Tanner Lectures were formally founded on July 1, 1978, at Clare Hall, Cambridge University. They were established by the American scholar, industrialist, and philanthropist, Obert Clark Tanner. In creating the lectureships, Professor Tanner said, "I hope these lectures will contribute to the intellectual and moral life of mankind. I see them simply as a search for a better understanding of human behavior and human values. This understanding may be pursued for its own intrinsic worth, but it may also eventually have practical consequences for the quality of personal and social life."

Permanent Tanner lectureships, with lectures given annually, are established at nine institutions: Clare Hall, Cambridge University; Harvard University; Brasenose College, Oxford University; Princeton University; Stanford University; the University of California; the University of Michigan; the University of Utah; and Yale University. Other international lectureships occasionally take place. The institutions are selected by the Trustees.

The sponsoring institutions have full autonomy in the appointment of their lecturers. A major part of the lecture program is the publication and distribution of the Lectures in an annual volume.

The Tanner Lectures on Human Values is a nonprofit corporation administered at the University of Utah under the direction of a self-perpetuating, international Board of Trustees. The Trustees meet annually to enact policies that will ensure the quality of the lectureships.

The entire lecture program, including the costs of administration, is fully and generously funded in perpetuity by an endowment to the University of Utah by Professor Tanner and Mrs. Grace Adams Tanner.

Obert C. Tanner was born in Farmington, Utah, in 1904. He was educated at the University of Utah, Harvard University, and Stanford University. He served on the faculty at Stanford University and was a professor of philosophy at the University of Utah for twenty-eight years. Mr. Tanner was also the founder and chairman of the O. C. Tanner Company, the world's largest manufacturer of recognition award products.

Harvard University's former president Derek Bok once spoke of Obert Tanner as a "Renaissance Man," citing his remarkable achievements in three of life's major pursuits: business, education, and public service.

Obert C. Tanner died in Palm Springs, California, on October 14, 1993, at the age of eighty-nine.

GRETHE B. PETERSON
University of Utah

CONTENTS

PREFACE TO VOLUME 22

Volume 22 of the Tanner Lectures on Human Values includes lectures delivered during the academic year 1999–2000.

The Tanner Lectures are published in an annual volume.

In addition to the Lectures on Human Values, the Trustees of the Tanner Lectures have funded special international lectureships at selected colleges and universities which are administered independently of the permanent lectures.

Goodness and Advice

JUDITH JARVIS THOMSON

THE TANNER LECTURES ON HUMAN VALUES

Delivered at

Princeton University
March 24 and 25, 1999

JUDITH JARVIS THOMSON is professor of philosophy at the Massachusetts Institute of Technology. She was educated at Barnard College and at Cambridge University, and she received her Ph.D. from Columbia University. She is a fellow of the American Academy of Arts and Sciences and has also been a fellow at the Centre for Advanced Study, Oslo, Norway. She has been a visiting fellow or professor at the Australian National University, the University of Pittsburgh, the University of California at Berkeley, and Yale Law School. She is a member of the American Philosophical Association and is the recipient of a Guggenheim Fellowship. She has published in numerous philosophical journals, including *Philosophy and Public Affairs,* the *Journal of Philosophy,* and *Nous,* is the author of *Acts and Other Events* (1977); *Rights, Restitution, and Risk* (1986); *The Realm of Rights* (1990); and co-author of *Moral Relativism and Moral Objectivity* (1996, with Gilbert Harman).

PART ONE: GOODNESS

I.

Twentieth-century Anglo-American moral philosophy has been dominated by concern about the fact-value gap. Or at least about what appears to be a gap, indeed, an unbridgeable gap, between fact and value. Matters of fact seem to be epistemologically intelligible: we find out about them by the familiar methods of observation and experiment. Matters of value seem to be quite different. If we can't learn about them by reasoning to them from matters of fact, then there seems to be no way at all by which we can come to learn about them. But what reasoning could possibly take a person from a matter of fact to a matter of value? It is hard to see how any reasoning could. Are we therefore to conclude that nobody has good reason to believe about any judgment of value that it is true? Many moral philosophers regard that as an appalling conclusion, and try to show that it is unwarranted. Others think it the correct conclusion, and try to show that we should not be troubled by it. In any case, all start from the apparent fact-value gap; responding to the threat it seems to pose became the central task of Anglo-American moral philosophy in the century just past.

That there does not merely seem to be, that there really is a fact-value gap, is by now part of the culture. Or at least, part of a certain culture, that of the middle-class literate public. I don't need to *introduce* my freshmen to the fact-value gap: they bring it to college with them.

I do not mean that members of the public at large, and my college freshmen, do not have moral beliefs. Their acceptance of the idea that there is a fact-value gap shows itself in more subtle ways. If I ask my students whether it is morally permissible for people to lie and cheat whenever it would profit them to do so, they reply, "No, of course not."

Delivered as a Tanner Lecture on Human Values at Princeton University, 1999. What follows is a revised and expanded version of the lectures. I am grateful to my four commentators, and to the participants in the discussions following the lectures, for very helpful comments and criticism. Some of their comments have been taken into consideration in revising the text.

Material in Part I, sections 9–14, was part of a paper presented in a symposium with Dennis Stampe at the meeting of the American Philosophical Division, Central Division, in May 1999. I thank Stampe and the other participants for their comments and criticism.

If I go on to ask what they would say if a man disagreed, they do not reply, "He's mistaken, for the following reason: . . . "—giving a reason. What emerges is rather: "It's all just a matter of opinion. I have mine and he has his, and they differ." Or: "It's all just a matter of how you feel. I feel one way, he feels another."

We might describe the situation in this way. People have a great many beliefs about what it is good or bad, right or wrong to do; these are their first-order moral beliefs. What many people lack nowadays is the second-order belief that they have good reason to believe that their first-order moral beliefs are true.

I suppose that in some people, lack of this second-order belief shows itself in lack of confidence in their first-order moral beliefs. I doubt that this is true of many people, however. For the most part, I think, people who think that there is an unbridgeable fact-value gap, and therefore conclude that nobody has good reason to believe about any value judgment that it is true, feel entirely confident that lying and cheating are wrong. In most people, I think, lack of the second-order belief shows itself only on occasions on which they step back from ordinary life and reflect on their first-order moral beliefs—as, for example, in classrooms that say "Philosophy" on the door.

So where's the harm in it? I said just above that many moral philosophers regard the conclusion that nobody has good reason to believe about any judgment of value that it is true as appalling. Why so?—if accepting that conclusion is compatible with feeling entirely confident that lying and cheating are wrong.

That these are compatible is something that moral philosophers who accept the conclusion try to demonstrate. Perhaps they are right. Presumably it is not literally inconsistent in a man to feel entirely confident that a certain number will win tomorrow's lottery while believing that he has no good reason to believe it will. At best, however, he has a divided consciousness. And it would plainly be silly in him to stake much on that number.

Do those who accept the conclusion that nobody has good reason to believe about any judgment of value that it is true, while nevertheless feeling entirely confident that lying and cheating are wrong, have a divided consciousness? And would it be silly in them to stake much on its being the case that lying and cheating are wrong? These are good questions. But the prior question is surely whether anyone should accept that conclusion.

We should go back further, in fact. *Is* there really an unbridgeable gap between fact and value?

The prevalence of the idea that there is such a gap must have deep sources outside philosophy. That there is such a gap is a philosophical thesis, and no philosophical thesis becomes part of the culture unless there are other ideas in the culture that it reinforces and is reinforced by.

The prevalence of the idea that there is an unbridgeable gap between fact and value is overdetermined; in addition to sources outside philosophy, it has sources in other areas of philosophy as well as within moral philosophy. What I refer to are the grounds for a quite general skepticism that were laid out so strikingly by Descartes. My freshmen bring that too to college with them: they say that of course they believe they have fingers and toes, but they also say "That's just my opinion" and "That's just how I feel."

What I will fix on in Part I is one of the considerations within moral philosophy itself that has led moral philosophers to regard the idea as at a minimum having to be taken seriously. I will suggest that the consideration I discuss is a product of illegitimate abstraction.

2.

Since well before the twentieth century, moral philosophers have taken it to be their task to produce a theory about what we ought to do and why. That "why" is important: moralizers are happy to tell you what you ought to do—moral philosophers differ in that they aim to tell you also what makes it the case that you ought to do the things they say you ought to do. Moral philosophy, in other words, responds to the desire that moral requirement be 'rationalized,' that is, shown to be a requirement.

Very well: what might be thought to make it the case that Alfred in particular, or people generally, ought to do this or that?

Suppose that Alfred acted in a certain way—he took off his hat, or pressed a certain doorbell, or what you will. Let us say he pressed a doorbell. For him to do that was for an event to occur, namely, the event that consisted in his pressing the doorbell.

We may suppose that Alfred's pressing the doorbell caused many other events to occur. Thus, his pressing the doorbell caused a circuit to close, a bell to ring, a person inside the house to feel pleased, and so on

and on. These events—Alfred's pressing the doorbell, the circuit's closing, the bell's ringing, and so on—are all of them events that would not
have occurred if Alfred had not pressed the doorbell.

More generally, for a person to act is for a battery of events to occur,
events that would not have occurred if he had not acted. We could put it
more grandly: for a person to act is for the world to go in a way that it
otherwise would not.

If that is what it is for a person to act, then it is very natural to think
that the question whether he ought to act in such and such a way must
turn on a comparison between what the world will be like if he acts in
that way and what the world will be like if he acts in any of the other
ways in which it is open to him to act. So, for example, that the question
whether Alfred ought to press the doorbell turns on a comparison between what the world will be like if he presses it and what the world will
be like if he instead stamps his feet, or dances a jig, or stands stock still,
or . . . . There seems to be nothing else for it to turn on.

And what are the terms of the required comparison? An answer that
all but suggests itself is this: we need to settle whether what the world
will be like if he acts in such and such a way is *better or worse than* what
the world will be like if he acts in any of the other ways in which it is
open to him to act. Thus if the world will be better if Alfred presses the
doorbell than it will be if he instead stamps his feet, and better than it
will be if he instead dances a jig, and so on, then he ought to press the
doorbell. And if the world will not be better if Alfred presses the doorbell than it will be if he instead does one of those other things, then it is
not the case that he ought to press the doorbell.

In sum, a person ought to do a thing if and only if the world will be
better if he does it than if he does any of the other things it is open to
him to do at the time. Similarly, a person ought not do a thing if and
only if the world will be worse if he does it than if he does any of the
other things it is open to him to do at the time.

What if there is a tie? For example, what if the world will be equally
good whether Alfred presses the doorbell or dances a jig, but better if he
does either than if he does anything else it is open to him to do? The idea
we are looking at yields that it is not the case that Alfred ought to press
the doorbell and that it is not the case that he ought to dance a jig (since
the world will not be better if he does either). But the idea also yields
that it is not the case that Alfred ought not press the doorbell, and that
it is not the case that Alfred ought not dance a jig (since the world will
not be worse if he does either). So the idea yields that he need not, but

may, do either. It also yields, however, that he ought not do anything other than either.[1] These conclusions are plausible enough, and the possibility of ties therefore does not constitute a difficulty for those who are attracted by this idea.

Following current usage, I will call the idea Consequentialism.[2] It is, I think, deeply satisfying. How *could* it be perfectly all right to do a thing if the world will be worse if you do it than if you do something else instead? Moreover, given that for a person to act just is for the world to go in a way that it otherwise would not go, surely the question whether he ought to act had better turn on a comparison between how it will go if he acts and how it will go if he does something else—to repeat, there seems to be nothing else for it to turn on. And how is that comparison to be made if not by settling on which way of going would be better? Down the road from this idea lies the fact-value gap, among other serious difficulties. I have wanted first to bring out the idea's attractions. It is not surprising that so many people have found it attractive, and that those who reject it do not merely dismiss it, but feel the need to make a case against it.

I stress that Consequentialism says nothing at all about what would make the world be better or worse than it otherwise would be. The idea itself leaves that open.

But a moral philosopher needs to arrive at a view about this, so let us turn to it.

3.

What would make it the case that the world will be better if a person does one thing than it will be if he does another? "Better" is just the comparative of "good," so we can re-put our question as follows: what

---

[1] These are G. E. Moore's conclusions about ties; see his *Ethics* (London: Oxford University Press, 1949), 22–25. I thank Martha Nussbaum for reminding me of the need to mention ties.

[2] The idea was first given this name by G. E. M. Anscombe, in "Modern Moral Philosophy," *Philosophy* 33 (1958). Her article was reprinted in G. E. M. Anscombe, *Collected Philosophical Papers*, vol. 3 (Oxford: Basil Blackwell, 1981). The name is unfortunate, and more's the pity that it has become common usage, since it is so very likely to mislead. A Consequentialist does not believe that what fixes whether a person ought to do a thing is a comparison between the consequences of his doing it with the consequences of his doing anything else, if "consequences" is understood in the most natural way, namely as "effects." A Consequentialist believes that what fixes whether a person ought to do a thing is rather a comparison between what the world will be like if he does it with what the world will be like if he does anything else. These are very different ideas. For more on the difference, see note 3 below.

would make it the case that the world will be more good if a person does one thing than it will be if he does another? It is very natural to think that the world will be more good if it contains more of what is good or less of what is bad or both. Consider Alfred again. I invited you to suppose that if Alfred presses the doorbell, a great many events will occur that otherwise would not, namely, his pressing the doorbell, the circuit's closing, the bell's ringing, someone's feeling pleased, and so on. We may similarly suppose that if Alfred instead dances a jig, a great many events will occur that otherwise would not. Will the world be better, that is, more good, if he presses the doorbell than if he dances a jig? That—it is very natural to think—turns on whether some or other of the events that will occur if he presses the doorbell, and some that will occur if he instead dances a jig, will be good or bad, and if so, on how good or bad they will be.

Which events are good and which bad? A familiar idea says that an event is good just in case it consists in someone's feeling pleased, and bad just in case it consists in someone's feeling pain. This idea comes down to us from Bentham and John Stuart Mill.

It is certainly possible for Jones to be more pleased than Smith is. Suppose that is now the case. If an event is good if and only if it consists in someone's feeling pleased, then presumably the event that consists in Jones's being pleased is better than the event that consists in Smith's being pleased. Similarly for pains: if Jones's pain is more severe than Smith's, then the event that consists in Jones's feeling pain is worse than the event that consists in Smith's feeling pain.

I will call this idea about which events are good or bad, and about how good or bad they are, Hedonism About Goodness. Many people have found it a very attractive idea.

To return to Alfred, then. If he presses the doorbell, a battery of events will occur. If he instead dances a jig, a different battery of events will occur. Hedonism About Goodness tells us which of those events are good and which bad, and how good or bad they are. I mentioned that if Alfred presses the doorbell, a person inside the house will be pleased. Suppose that if Alfred instead dances a jig, then Alfred will be pleased. Suppose that Alfred will be less pleased if he dances a jig than the person inside the house will be if Alfred presses the doorbell. That counts in favor of its being the case that the world will be better if he presses the doorbell than if he dances a jig. But of course we would need to know a good deal more if we were to arrive at a conclusion on this matter: we would need to know whether anyone else will be pleased if Alfred acts in each way, and moreover, whether anyone will feel pain if he does, taking into consideration everyone who would be affected by Alfred's pressing the doorbell and by Alfred's instead dancing a jig.

Still, if we conjoin Hedonism About Goodness with Consequentialism, we have produced a theory about what a person ought to do and why. A person ought to do a thing if and only if—and if so, *because*—the balance of pleasure and pain that ensues if he does it is greater than that which ensues if he does any of the other things it is open to him to do instead.

The idea we have reached is, of course, Utilitarianism. Utilitarianism is one version of Consequentialism: a Consequentialist is also a Utilitarian if and only if he accepts Hedonism About Goodness.[3] I have laid out the process of reasoning by which it may be reached at some length, in order to bring out that it relies on two ideas, which it is important to distinguish from each other. One is Consequentialism, the other is Hedonism About Goodness. The contemporary literature of moral philosophy is full of objections to Utilitarianism; it is important, however, to be clear which of those two ideas a given objection to Utilitarianism is an objection to.

I am going to focus on an objection to Consequentialism that I think has not been taken seriously enough. But let us begin with Hedonism About Goodness.

I tried to make Hedonism About Goodness seem plausible when I presented it, which from this vantage point—the end of the twentieth century—is not easy to do. I know of no moral philosophers nowadays

---

[3]I said in note 2 above that the following two ideas are very different: (i) what fixes whether a person ought to do a thing is a comparison between the effects of his doing it with the effects of his doing anything else, and (ii) what fixes whether a person ought to do a thing is a comparison between what the world will be like if he does it with what the world will be like if he does anything else. And I said that it is (ii), not (i), that a Consequentialist opts for.

The difference between those ideas emerges clearly only if a Consequentialist rejects Hedonism About Goodness. Suppose a Consequentialist accepts Hedonism About Goodness. Then on his view, what matters to the question whether Alfred ought (as it might be) to press the doorbell is only the effects of Alfred's doing so and the effects of Alfred's acting otherwise. For example, while if Alfred presses the doorbell, then the world will contain the event that consists in his pressing the doorbell, that is morally irrelevant, since the event that consists in his pressing the doorbell is not itself, but at most has among its effects, events that consists in someone's being pleased or feeling pain.

But a Consequentialist might reject Hedonism About Goodness. In particular, he might instead say that some acts are themselves good or bad. On his view, then, it is not only events that are the effects of an act that matter morally, and opting for (ii) may yield a moral conclusion that is different from the moral outcome yielded by (i).

who accept it. Among many other objections, it has often been pointed out that a man might be pleased at someone else's feeling pain. Is his feeling pleased really to be thought a good event? We are surely inclined to think it positively vicious in a person to take pleasure in the pains of others. Insofar as we have intuitions about what counts as a good event—and I will return to this caveat shortly—it strikes us, intuitively, that a man's feeling pleased at the pain of another is not a good event.

Moreover, there is an interplay between Hedonism About Goodness and Consequentialism. Suppose we accept Consequentialism. If we were also to accept Hedonism About Goodness, then we would be committed to supposing that it counts in favor of the conclusion that we ought to do a thing that our doing it will cause a man to feel pleased at the pain of another—and indeed, counts the more strongly in favor of this conclusion, the more pleased he will be. We may well think that must be wrong.

Well, I will be suggesting that we should reject Consequentialism, so the fact that if you accept it, you had really better not also accept Hedonism About Goodness does not strike me as a serious objection to Hedonism About Goodness. What is objectionable about Hedonism About Goodness is internal to it. Feeling pleased is feeling pleased *by* something, and there is a world of difference between pleasures according as their objects differ from each other.

So suppose we reject Hedonism About Goodness. If we wish to retain Consequentialism, we now have a problem on our hands.

4.

A serious problem. For which events are good and which bad? What answer to this question is to replace Hedonism About Goodness? Suppose my team plays your team in the football finals, and that my team wins. "That's good," I say. "That's bad," you say. Which of us is right? How on earth is that question to be answered?

It might be suggested that neither of us is right—that is, that the event of my team's winning is not itself either good or bad, that, as some philosophers would say, the event of my team's winning is not *intrinsically* good or bad. Rather, it is at most *instrumentally* good or bad, good or bad only insofar as the events it will cause are intrinsically good or bad. Which, then, are the intrinsically good or bad events?

We might try to construct some examples. Suppose Alfred aims a gun at Bertha and fires it; Alfred misses, however, so Bertha survives. Perhaps we can say that Bertha's survival is an intrinsically good event. Bertha's death, had that occurred, would have been an intrinsically bad event; fortunately, her death did not occur.

There is a difficulty here, however, analogous to the one I pointed to when we looked at Hedonism About Goodness. For what if the reason why Alfred was aiming his gun at Bertha is that Bertha was villainously trying to kill Alfred? Let us suppose that Bertha, having survived, now kills Alfred, just as she had been villainously trying to. Are you still sure that Bertha's survival was an intrinsically good event? And that her death would have been an intrinsically bad one?

We might well want to say that a person's surviving—whether or not the person is a villain—is good for him, and that his death would be bad for him. But we need to remember that an event that is good or bad for one person can be the opposite, namely bad or good, for another person.

It has to be remembered also that what is in question here is not whether an event is good *for* or bad *for* a person, but rather whether it is just plain good or just plain bad. That is our question. And it is not in the least clear how it is to be answered.

5.

But what is good or bad for people must surely be in some way relevant to whether a person ought to act. Perhaps what is good or bad for people itself fixes what is just plain good or just plain bad? Perhaps a Consequentialist should therefore opt for the following idea about goodness: one event is better than another if and only if the first is 'more better for more' than the other. Consider again the event that consists in my team's winning its game with yours. "That's good," I say. "That's bad," you say. I asked: which of us is right? Perhaps the answer to this question is to be found out by finding out how many people the event is good for and how many it is bad for, and how good it is for those it is good for, and how bad it is for those it is bad for—the answer to the question being an appropriate function of those facts.

A Consequentialist who likes this idea could then say: the world will be better if a person does such and such than it will be if he does anything it is open to him to do instead just in case his doing the such and such will be more better for more. And if it will be, then it follows that that is what he ought to do.

There is a difficulty for this view that is a first cousin of one we have met twice before. Suppose it would profit me a lot to make you suffer a minor loss; suppose also that no one else would be affected by my act. It follows on this view that I ought to make you suffer the loss. That can't be right. There may well be cases in which it is permissible, even morally required, that one person cause another a loss. But it can't at all plausibly be thought that the mere fact that I would gain more by acting than you would lose counts in favor of its being the case that I ought to act.

The Consequentialist who rejects this idea about goodness can of course reject this outcome. He can remind us that he did not say that what matters morally is what is more good for more: what he said is that what matters morally is what is more good. And he can declare that some events that are more good for more may perfectly well be bad events. In particular, an event that consists in taking advantage of another for one's own profit may well be a bad event even if it is more better for more than any alternative open to the agent at the time.

It pays to stress this point. It seems nigh on a necessary truth that what a person ought to do is what would make the world be best—more good—than any alternative. That is why Consequentialism seems so attractive. It takes only a moment's reflection to see that it is not only not a necessary truth but false that what a person ought to do is what would make the world be more better for more than any alternative.

Of course a Consequentialist who rejects this idea about goodness owes us a better one. And what might that be?

6.

To summarize where we have come so far. I drew attention in section 4 to the attractiveness of Consequentialism, which is the idea that a person ought to do a thing if and only if the world will be better if he does it than if he does anything else it is open to him to do instead. And we were supposing that whether the world will be better turns on a comparison between the goodness or badness of the events that will occur if he does or does not choose the option. But which events are good and which bad? Once we have cut ourselves loose from Hedonism About Goodness, and from the idea I described in the preceding section, we are out at sea, adrift. It would be no surprise if people found themselves wondering how anyone could be supposed to have good reason for believing that a person ought to act in this way or that.

The point may be put another way. According to Consequentialism, the concept 'ought' reduces to the concept 'good.' If you want to know whether someone ought to do a thing, you need to ask what events will occur if he does it and what events will occur if he does anything else, and whether those events will be good or bad, and if so, how good or how bad. Let us now distinguish between two ways in which it can seem that we are at risk of having to become skeptics about morality. The first is this: it may be said that we just can't find out what all the events are that will occur if a person does or does not do a thing. Consider again Alfred's pressing the doorbell. I mentioned some of the events that that event will cause, but there are surely indefinitely many others that it will also cause. If we don't know which they all are, we can't even begin to assess the goodness or badness of all of them, and therefore can't find out whether Alfred ought to press the doorbell. I will call this shallow skepticism about morality. It is skepticism *about morality* because it is skepticism about the possibility of finding out what Consequentialism says must be found out if we are to find out whether judgments about what people ought to do are true. But it is shallow skepticism about morality because it is ultimately skepticism about matters of fact. The shallow skeptic says that if we could find out about the relevant matters of fact, then finding out about what people ought to do would be no problem.

Some Consequentialists have been shallow skeptics about morality, and contentedly so. I have G. E. Moore in mind in particular. According to Moore, we must just hope for the best: if we manage to do what we ought to do, that is just good luck for us. Other Consequentialists have not been contented at the prospect of having to become shallow skeptics about morality. No matter for our purposes.

For what we have in fact reached is the prospect of something markedly more worrisome, namely deep skepticism about morality. What we have reached is that even if we knew about all the events that will occur if a person acts and all that will occur if he does not, we are still in epistemological trouble because we have found no satisfactory way of settling which of those events would be good and which bad. What looms is the fact-value gap, and it looks unbridgeable.

So what's to be done?

7.

I suggest that the reason why we find no satisfactory way of answering the question which events are good and which are bad is that there is no such question. Consequentialism requires that there be such a question, and that we be able to answer it if we are to be able to tell whether a person ought to do a thing. That, I suggest, is itself a conclusive objection to Consequentialism.

If someone draws our attention to a certain event—say, Alfred's pressing a certain doorbell—and asks us whether that was or would be a good event, or a bad event, or neither, we should not think "Ah, what a hard question"; we should instead ask ourselves whether we so much as understand what we have been asked.

Why do we think we do understand? Or anyway, why do so many moral philosophers think they do? One answer emerges clearly in G. E. Moore's *Principia Ethica*, with which twentieth-century Anglo-American moral philosophy began.

Moore said it is clear that some things are good, some are bad, and some are neither. Goodness, he said, is the property that all and only the good things have in common. That is the property that we would be ascribing to a thing—whether an event or anything else—if we said of it "That's good"; and that is the property such that we are asking whether a thing possesses it when we ask about the thing "Is it good?"

This idea seems to issue from nothing better than an oversimplified conception of the way in which the adjective "good" functions in English. When people say about a thing "That's good," what they mean is always that the thing is *good in some way*. Perhaps they mean that the thing is a good fountain pen. Or a good book. Or a good apple. If so, what they mean is that the thing is good of a kind.

There is more too. A person might say "That's good," not meaning that the thing is good of a kind, but that it is good for use in doing this or that. Perhaps that the thing is good for use in making cheesecake. Or they may mean that the thing is good *for* such and such or so and so. Perhaps that the thing is or would be good for Alfred, or for England, or for the tree in my backyard. Or they may mean that the thing tastes good or looks good.

When talking about a person, they may say "He's good," meaning by this that he's good at playing chess, or that he is morally good—just or honorable or generous. When talking about an experience or an activity, they may say "It's good," meaning by this that it's pleasant or enjoyable.

What people *say* is the words "That's good," or "He's good," or "It's good," but what they mean—what *they*, but not their words, mean—is that the thing is good in one or other of the kinds of ways I have indicated.[4] It is the context in which they assert those words that makes clear what they meant by the words, that is, what, perhaps given their preceding remarks, their hearers are entitled to suppose they mean. If the context does not make this clear, then their hearers are at a loss.

We should be clear that the ways in which a thing can be good that I have been indicating are not *grounds* for thinking a thing is good. St. Francis was good. How so? Well, he was a morally good person—he was just and kind. Chocolate is good. How so? Well, it tastes good. If what I have supplied you with are grounds for thinking that St. Francis and chocolate are good, that is, grounds for thinking that they both possess the property goodness, then it ought to be in order to ask which is better, for the adjective "good" has a comparative. But do you make sense of the question whether St. Francis was better than chocolate?

I think we had better conclude that there is no such property as goodness. All goodness, as we can put it, is goodness in a way. When it is asked whether a thing is good—whether the thing is a book or pie tin, or a person or an event—the context, or the speaker, needs to let us in on what the relevant way of being good is, or we not only can't answer the question, we don't even know what question was asked.

Consider events in particular. Suppose someone asks whether Alfred's pressing the doorbell is or would be a good event. We should reply "How do you mean? Do you mean 'Would it be good *for* somebody?'" And we had better be told whether that is what is meant, or whether something else is meant. We had better not be told that what is in question is instead whether the event is just plain, pure good, for there is no such thing.

---

[4] This is a point I have made in a number of other places, most recently in "The Right and the Good," *Journal of Philosophy* 94, no. 6 (June 1997).

8.

Consequentialism, then, has to go. What is to replace it is a hard question, the harder in that Consequentialism rests on ideas that are very attractive. I will concentrate on it in Part II. Meanwhile, however, it pays to take note of some things we gain if we reject the question whether or not a thing is plain, pure good.

Most important, we are not now confronted with an unbridgeable fact-value gap.

For in the first place, there is no one fact-value gap: if there is one, there are many. Suppose we know a lot of facts about a certain fountain pen: how much ink it will hold, that it does not leak, how smooth its nib is, and so on. Ah, but is it a *good fountain pen*? Again, suppose we know a lot of facts about what a certain event would cause. Let it be the event that consists in Alfred's drinking some hot lemonade. Suppose, then, that we know, in particular, what that event would cause, given the condition Alfred is currently in—as it might be, that he has a sore throat. Ah, but would Alfred's drinking some hot lemonade be *good for him*? Again, suppose we know a lot of facts about how a certain brandy tastes: austere and delicate. (I take this description from a *New York Times* article on brandies.) Ah, but does the brandy *taste good*? If there are fact-value gaps, then I have drawn attention to three of them, for it is not at all plausible to think that what we have here are three cases in which we have facts in hand, and need to be told what consideration—the same in all three—would take us from the facts to the values. Whatever it is, if anything, that would entitle us to pass from those facts about the fountain pen to the conclusion that it is a good fountain pen is not at all plausibly thought to be the same as what would entitle us to pass from facts about Alfred and hot lemonade to the conclusion that his drinking some would be good for him, or the same as what would entitle us to pass from facts about how the brandy tastes to the conclusion that it tastes good.

Second, we should ask whether there really are unbridgeable fact-value gaps in the cases I mentioned.

What facts about a fountain pen warrant concluding that it is a good fountain pen? Well, some things are clear. It mustn't leak, it must be sturdy, it must hold enough ink to write several pages before filling, its nib must be smooth so as not to tear the paper being written on. A good fountain pen is one that would serve well the typical purposes of those who want fountain pens. And whether a pen would serve those purposes well is something we can and do find out all the time.

If Alfred has a sore throat, then it is very likely that the event that consists in his drinking some hot lemonade would be good for him. Why so? Well, it is very likely that his drinking some will make him feel better. Of course, that might be mistaken. Perhaps he has an ulcer as well as a sore throat; then, perhaps, drinking hot lemonade would not make him feel better, and would in fact be bad for him. We know perfectly well what *kinds* of consideration bear on the question whether that event would be good for him. There certainly are cases in which it is hard to find out whether an event would be good for a person, and among them are cases in which we may have to conclude that we cannot find this out. Perhaps we are unable to attach weights to the various considerations that bear on whether the event would be good for him, as, for example, where the event consists in his making this or that choice among possible careers. Still, there are limits to what counts as a consideration in such cases.

Whether something tastes good is a messier matter. That is partly due to the fact that we have so little in the way of phenomenological characterizations of tastes—getting past "sweet," "sour," "bitter," and "salty" is, for most of us, rather a stretch. It takes a professional to describe a brandy as austere and delicate. Moreover, most of us do not really attend to tastes very closely, and do not notice in them what a professional notices.[5] When you think on how important the tastes of things are to us, that can seem very surprising. The questions that arise here are interesting and, I think, insufficiently studied by philosophers. For our purposes, however, it is perhaps enough to draw attention to the fact that there is a difference, which is plain to all of us, between a person's *liking* the taste of something and its tasting good. Lots of people like the taste of strawberry Kool-Aid: it sells very well indeed. For all that, strawberry Kool-Aid does not taste good.[6]

There are ways of being good that are of particular interest to the

---

[5] More from the *Times* article about another brandy: it is "round and notably spicy in flavor, with hints of nutmeg, cinnamon and hazelnuts." J. L. Austin asked—in *Sense and Sensibilia*, ed. G. J. Warnock (Oxford: Oxford University Press, 1962)—"What sort of reception would I be likely to get from a professional tea-taster, if I were to say to him, 'But there can't be any difference between the flavors of these two brands of tea, for I regularly fail to distinguish between them'?" He left it to us to supply the answer.

[6] There is a term that I think appropriate here. Lots of people like what can best be described as kitsch. Kool-Aid is kitsch in the realm of taste.

moral philosopher, and I will be returning to them in Part II. Meanwhile, it just is not in general true that our intellectual lives are everywhere crisscrossed by unbridgeable fact-value gaps. The adjective "good" is among the most commonly used in the English language. What we should have been doing is to look at how it is in fact used, and at what does in fact settle that it is or is not applicable.

9.

A further benefit can be got by attending to the ways of being good. There is a concept which has been much leaned on by many contemporary moral philosophers, but which has seemed very dark to others. What I refer to is the concept 'reason for a person to do such and such.' It has been thought to have an intimate connection with the concept 'ought.' Some philosophers hold that it is not the case that a person ought to do a thing unless there is a reason for him to do it. Or even more strongly: what a person ought to do is precisely what there is most reason for him to do. I leave aside for the time being the question how the concept 'ought' connects with the concept 'reason for acting.' Let us ask instead what must surely be the prior question: what *is* a reason for a person to do such and such?

It is easy enough to begin: a reason for a person to do a thing is something that counts in favor of his doing it. But what is that?[7] There are a number of answers in the literature—I will discuss two of them.

Before we turn to them, however, we need to adopt two regimentations. The need for the first issues from the existence of a scatter of locutions in which the term "reason" appears: we need to decide how to connect the most common of them.

The weakest is the kind I started with, an example of which is:

(1) There is a reason for Alfred to press the doorbell, namely X.

I take it that (1) is consistent with Alfred's not believing that X is a rea-

---

[7] T. M. Scanlon says, "Any attempt to explain what it is to be a reason for something seems to me to lead back to the same idea: a consideration that counts in favor of it. 'Counts in favor how?' one might ask. 'By providing a reason for it' seems to be the only answer."

And Scanlon therefore says he will take the concept of a reason as primitive. See his *What We Owe to Each Other* (Cambridge: Harvard University Press, 1998), 17. As will emerge in section 12 below, I think there is another, better because more informative, answer to the question what it is for X to count in favor of a person's doing a thing than that X is a reason for the person to do it.

son for him to press the doorbell. Indeed, I take (1) to be consistent with Alfred's believing that there is no reason at all for him to press the doorbell.

There is room for dispute about what is the actual, or anyway the most common use of

(2) Alfred has a reason for pressing the doorbell, namely X.

For simplicity, I bypass arguments about usage. I will take it that Alfred can't have a reason for pressing the doorbell unless there really is one. Thus I will take it that (2) entails (1). On the other hand, I will also take it that it can't be the case that Alfred has a reason for pressing the door-bell, namely X, unless Alfred believes that X is a reason for him to press the doorbell. Thus I will take it that although (2) entails (1), (2) is not entailed by (1). I think that this decision does capture the most common use of (2), but whether it does does not matter for our purposes.

Suppose Alfred is now in process of pressing the doorbell. We may say:

(3) Alfred's reason for pressing the doorbell is X.

I take (3) to be stronger than (2). Alfred can have a reason for pressing the doorbell, namely X, and nevertheless not press it. (Perhaps he has a better reason for not pressing it.) By contrast, X can't be Alfred's reason for pressing the doorbell unless he is pressing it for that reason, and thus unless he is in fact pressing it. So (3) entails (2), but (3) is not entailed by (2).

So (3) is stronger than (2), and (2) is stronger than (1). I think that no theoretical issue turns on these decisions about (1), (2), and (3); that is why I say that what is in question here is (mere) regimentation.

Similarly for reasons for believing, or wanting, or expecting, or re-gretting, or hoping for, or feeling angry at, or . . . a thing; thus for any-thing for which there might be, and a person might have, a reason.

The need for a second regimentation is due to the fact that we need to fix on a general characterization of what a reason *is*. What, after all, might X be?

A reason is something one might reason *from*. What might a person reason from? Suppose that Alfred believes that Bertha's pig can fly. Why? Suppose the situation is this: Alfred believes that all pigs can fly, and therefore concludes that Bertha's pig can. We have three options.

(i) We can say that Alfred's reason for believing that Bertha's pig can fly is the fact that he, Alfred, believes that all pigs can fly. While pigs can't fly, Alfred does anyway believe that they can.

I think it plain that this option is not a happy one. Alfred does not reason that Bertha's pig can fly from the fact that he, Alfred, believes that all pigs can. His reasoning, we are supposing, went like this: "All pigs can fly, therefore Bertha's pig can." His premise was not that he, Alfred, believes that all pigs can fly, but rather that all pigs can fly.

I am not suggesting that a person couldn't reason to a certain conclusion from the fact that he believes this or that. That does seem to be possible. Suppose that Charles has loved Dora for years, but his suit had always seemed hopeless. He is now suddenly struck by the thought that Dora loves him too. He concludes—from the very fact that he now believes she does—that there must have been some evidence of her love for him in her past behavior, evidence that was unrecognized by him at the time, and is still unclear to him now. Cases in which a person reasons to a conclusion from the fact that he believes this or that must surely be rare, however: normally, we reason not from our believing something, but rather from what we believe.

I did not spend time on option (i) because I think it a plausible description of Alfred: I did so because an analogue of the point I make here will reappear later.

A second possible description of Alfred, (ii), is that his reason for believing that Bertha's pig can fly is the proposition that all pigs can fly. That proposition is false, but we could say never mind: Alfred thinks it true, and reasons from it to his conclusion. More generally, we can say that a reason is always a proposition, true or false, which someone who thinks it true might reason from; and where a person thinks a proposition is true and reasons from it, *it* is *his* reason.

The third possible description of Alfred, (iii), is that Alfred has no reason for believing that Bertha's pig can fly. This is what we say if we take it that a reason is always a fact. Alfred might himself say "My reason for believing that Bertha's pig can fly is the fact that all pigs can fly." If that is what he says, then it is clear that although he thinks he has a reason for believing that Bertha's pig can fly, he doesn't actually have one, since there is no such fact as the fact that all pigs can fly.

It should be noticed that opting for (iii) is compatible with supposing that there is an answer to the question why Alfred believes that Bertha's pig can fly. We can say that he believes that Bertha's pig can fly because he believes that all pigs can. In other words, we can explain his believing that Bertha's pig can fly. We cannot explain his believing that Bertha's pig can fly by giving his reason for believing it, since, according to (iii), he hasn't any; but he believes that all pigs can fly, and though that belief of his is false, the fact that he has it, we can say, is why he believes that Bertha's pig can fly.

I think that no deep theoretical issue turns on a decision between (ii) and (iii), for I think that any interesting claim we make about reasons on the supposition that they are propositions has an equally correct or incorrect analogue about reasons on the supposition that they are facts. That is why I take it, once again, that what is in question here is (mere) regimentation. Since taking reasons to be facts seems to me to square with usage better than taking them to be propositions, I will take them to be facts.

It should perhaps be stressed: I will be taking it that a reason is a fact not merely where it is a reason for believing something, but also where it is a reason for doing something. Indeed, also where it is a reason for feeling something or for wanting something and so on—that is, for whatever it is that a reason might be a reason for.

So much for regimentation. I said at the beginning of this section that a reason for a person to do a thing is something that counts in favor of his doing it. Given our second regimentation, we can re-put this point as follows: a reason for a person to do a thing is a fact that counts in favor of his doing it. Which facts are those? I said I would discuss two answers that may be found in the literature.

10.

According to the first answer, every reason for action is a desire, or want.[8] Suppose that Alfred wants to please Bertha. Suppose also that his pressing a certain doorbell would please her. Then, on this view, there is a reason for Alfred to press the doorbell, namely his wanting to please Bertha. What makes his wanting to please her a reason for him to press the doorbell is the fact that his pressing it would please her; but that being a fact, his wanting to please her *is* a reason for him to press it.

Given our first regimentation, it can of course be the case that although

---

[8] What I describe here is a simplified version of the theory argued for by Dennis Stampe in "The Authority of Desire," *Philosophical Review* (July 1987).

(1) There is a reason for Alfred to press the doorbell, namely his wanting to please Bertha,

is true,

(2) Alfred has a reason for pressing the doorbell, namely his wanting to please Bertha,

is false—after all, he may not know that his pressing the doorbell would please Bertha, and therefore not know that his wanting to please Bertha is a reason for pressing it. But if he does know that his pressing the doorbell would please her, and therefore believes that his wanting to please her is a reason for pressing the doorbell, then (2) is true. And we can understand how that reason counts in favor of his ringing the doorbell: it makes his ringing the doorbell be attractive to him.

This view is entirely compatible with our having bad reasons for action. Suppose instead that Alfred wants to annoy Bertha, and that his pressing the doorbell would in fact annoy her. Then there is a reason for him to ring the doorbell, namely his wanting to annoy Bertha. If he knows these things, then he has a reason for pressing the doorbell—and the reason counts in favor of his pressing the doorbell in that it makes his pressing the doorbell be attractive to him. That outcome is as it should be, for any theory of reasons for action must allow for the possibility of, indeed the fact of, there being bad reasons for action as well as good ones.

The theory also allows for there being stronger or weaker reasons for action: this difference (it says) turns on the strength or weakness of the want.

Given our second regimentation, however, this won't quite do as it stands. A desire is presumably a mental state. For example, and more precisely: Alfred's wanting to please Bertha consists in his being in a certain mental state. Alfred's wanting to annoy Bertha consists in his being in a different mental state. Is his being in a mental state a fact? Surely not: that idea seems to be a category mistake.

If a person's wanting something consists in the person's being in a certain mental state, then it looks as if no desire is a reason for action, since no desire is a fact.

An emendation all but suggests itself. A friend of this first theory could say that a reason for action is not itself a desire, but is instead the fact that consists in the person's having the desire.[9] Thus the reason there is for Alfred to press the doorbell is the fact that Alfred wants to

---

[9] Stampe agrees that a reason is a fact, and he tells us that when he says that a desire is a

please (or annoy) Bertha. And it is that—that fact—that makes his pressing the doorbell be attractive to him.

But the theory still won't do. As I said earlier, a reason is something a person might reason *from*. There surely are cases in which a person reasons to something from the fact that he wants something. In particular, there are cases in which a person takes the fact that he wants something to be a reason for doing something. Suppose Carol has always disliked milk in the past. She now finds herself wanting to drink some. There is a theory according to which people's wants in food often issue from a nutritional deficiency, thus, for example, that wanting to drink some milk might issue from a need for calcium. Let's suppose that theory is true, and that Carol believes it is. Then she might think: "Here is an interesting fact I have just noticed about myself: I want to drink some milk. Wanting to drink milk sometimes issues from a need for calcium. Therefore I may well need some calcium (which milk supplies). So my wanting to drink some milk is a reason for me to drink some." This is probably a relatively rare kind of case, however: normally, we reason not from the fact that we want something, but rather from facts about what we want and how it might be got.

Carol, who takes the fact that she wants to do something to be a reason for doing it, should remind us of Charles, who takes the fact that he believes one thing to be a reason for believing another. Both kinds of case are surely rare.

If so, then we cannot suppose that every reason for action is a desire. At most some are.

II.

I said that I would discuss two answers to the question what facts are reasons for action. Fortunately we can be brief about the second.

On this second view, every reason for action is a combination (a pair? a conjunction?) of a desire and a belief.[10] Suppose that Alfred wants to please Bertha and believes that his pressing a certain doorbell would

---

reason for action, what he really means is this: the fact that the person wants something is a reason for the person to act accordingly. See ibid.

[10] An influential example is Donald Davidson's account of reasons for action in "Actions, Reasons, and Causes," *Journal of Philosophy* 60 (1963). That article was reprinted in his *Essays on Actions and Events* (Oxford: Oxford University Press, 1980). According to Davidson, any pro-attitude can play the role of the required desire. Friends of this theory, and it has a great many, do not typically trouble themselves over the question what the mode of combination is, and I leave it open.

please her. Then, on this view, there is a reason for Alfred to press the doorbell, namely the combination consisting of his wanting to please Bertha and his belief that his pressing it would please her. Moreover, Alfred has a reason for pressing the doorbell, namely that want/belief combination—which counts in favor of his pressing the doorbell since it makes doing so be attractive to him.

We can, as I said, be brief about this theory. Given our second regimentation, a reason is a fact, so we had better reconstrue the theory to say that a reason for acting is not a want/belief combination but rather a combination consisting of the fact that a person wants this and the fact that he believes that. A reason, however, is something that one might reason from. But as we know, it is rare for a person to reason to something from the fact of his wanting this, and rare for a person to reason to something from the fact of his believing that—remember the cases of Carol and Charles—and presumably therefore at least as rare for a person to reason to something from the fact of his wanting this *and* believing that.

Why are so many philosophers inclined to say that a reason for acting is a want/belief combination? I think it pretty clear why they do. First, they think that a person's reason for doing a thing explains his doing of it.[11] Why so? It seems very plausible to think that if Alfred is pressing a doorbell for a reason, then when we have found out what his reason was, we have found out why he pressed it. That is, we have found an explanation of his pressing it. Indeed, what we have found, namely his reason for pressing the doorbell, itself explains his pressing it.

Following Hume, as many contemporary philosophers do, we may well believe, second, that something explains a person's doing a thing only if it contains a want and a belief. Something explains Alfred's pressing the doorbell only if it contains a want and a belief, in particular, the want and belief because of which he pressed it.[12]

---

[11] That this motivates the theory emerges clearly in Davidson, "Action, Reasons, and Causes." I hazard a guess that it also motivates the theory offered in Stampe, "The Authority of Desire."

[12] Hume did not, and contemporary philosophers also do not, say that something explains just anyone's doing just anything only if it contains a want and a belief: on their view, this holds only of doings that are intentional. (If a man is nervously and unwittingly tapping his fingers, then it may be that there is no want and belief out of which he is doing it; and his doing of it is presumably explainable by appeal to something else, perhaps in a case such as this, to anxiety.) On the other hand, a person who does a thing for a reason does do it intentionally, and it is only doings of things for reasons that concern us here. I therefore omit the qualification.

It follows that a person's reason for acting contains a want and a belief: a reason for acting is a want/belief combination.

This won't do, however. Following Hume, what explains a person's doing a thing is his wanting this and believing that. But the fact that he wants this and believes that is not likely to be his reason for doing the thing: such cases are rare. The more usual case is like this. We ask Alfred why he is pressing the doorbell, and he replies: "to please Bertha." We find out from his saying this that he wants to please Bertha, and believes that his pressing the doorbell will please her. And that—the compound fact that he wants to please Bertha and believes that his pressing the doorbell will please her—does explain his pressing the doorbell. But that compound fact is not his reason for pressing it.

This is why we can find out why a person does a thing even if he has no reason for doing it, but only thinks he does. Consider, first, reasons for belief. I invited you to imagine that Alfred believes that Bertha's pig can fly. We ask him why he believes this, and he says "All pigs can fly." According to our second regimentation, Alfred has no reason for believing that Bertha's pig can fly since there is no such fact as the fact that all pigs can fly. But we can nevertheless explain his believing that Bertha's pig can fly: he believes this because he believes that all pigs can.

So similarly for reasons for action. Suppose we ask Alfred why he is pressing a certain doorbell, and he replies: "to please Bertha." But suppose that his pressing the doorbell will not in fact please Bertha; suppose it will instead annoy her. Then Alfred has no reason for pressing the doorbell. But we can nevertheless explain his pressing it: he is doing so because he wants to please Bertha, and believes that his doing so will please her.

12.

So what is a reason for doing a thing? It is something that counts in favor of doing it. Given our second regimentation, we can re-put this point as follows: a reason for a person to do a thing is a fact that counts in favor of his doing it. Which facts are those? We have now rejected two answers that may be found in the literature.

I suggest that it would pay us to help ourselves to the fact that all goodness is goodness in a way, and to consider the following sufficient condition for a fact to be a reason for a person to do a thing: a fact is a reason for a person to do a thing if it is a fact to the effect that his doing the thing would be good in some way.[13] There is a reason for Alfred to press that doorbell if his pressing it would be good for him. Or good for Bertha or Charles. Or would be enjoyable. (I suppose a person might like pressing doorbells.) And so on. And I suggest that it is clear that a fact to the effect that Alfred's pressing the doorbell would be good in some way counts in favor of his pressing it.

The fact that Alfred's pressing the doorbell would be good in some way may not everywhere count very strongly in favor of his pressing it: its being enjoyable to ring doorbells does not count very strongly in favor of pressing yours or mine. But the fact that doing so would be enjoyable does count in favor of doing so.

Moreover, Alfred has a reason for pressing the doorbell if, for some way of being good, W, he knows that his pressing the doorbell would be good in way W. His knowing that pressing it would be good in way W is, of course, entirely compatible with his not pressing it. For example, he might not care in the least about the fact that his pressing the doorbell would be good in way W. But suppose he does care: suppose, in particular, that he wants to do something that is good in way W, and, in fact that he wants to do something that is good in way W more than he now wants to do anything else. Then given that he also believes that his pressing the doorbell would be good in way W, he may be expected to press it.[14] If he does press it, then his reason for pressing it is the fact that his doing so would be good in way W; and his wanting to do something good in way W, together with his believing that pressing the doorbell is good in way W, explains his pressing the doorbell.

It is perhaps worth stressing that Alfred can believe that his pressing the doorbell would be good in a way W compatibly with (i) his not wanting to press it, and (ii) his not wanting to do something good in way W. That his believing that his pressing the doorbell would be good in way W is compatible with (i), his not wanting to press it, is probably obvious enough. Even if his belief is that his pressing the doorbell would be good for him. I may know that my taking a certain nasty-

---

[13] G. E. M. Anscombe said that a bit of practical reasoning must be understood to have a major premise that attributes what she called a "desirability characterization" to the act contemplated. See her *Intention* (Oxford: Basil Blackwell, 1957). I suggest that we can interpret her as meaning that the major premise must assert that the act would be good in some way.

[14] I do not say that he will press it: I say only that he may be expected to do so, since I wish to leave room for the possibility of weakness of will.

tasting medicine would be good for me without wanting to take it. If I do take it, then that is presumably because, given that taking it would be good for me, I am willing to take it; but being willing to take it is not the same as wanting to take it. I hope it is also obvious that Alfred's believing that his pressing the doorbell would be good in way *W* is compatible with (ii) his not wanting to do something good in way *W*. Even if the way of being good is goodness for him. I may refrain from taking the nasty-tasting medicine, not merely because it tastes bad, but because I do not now want to do what is good for me.

The fact that one can know that doing a thing would be good in a certain way compatibly with wanting neither to do the thing nor to do something good in that way is due to the fact that it is *goodness in a way* that we are dealing with. A number of philosophers have held that believing a thing would be pure good, intrinsically good, motivates the believer to try to bring it about.[15] In particular, then, they have held that believing that one's doing a thing would be good motivates one to do it. Other philosophers have disagreed. Given the illegitimate abstraction that issued in the idea that there is such a property as goodness, and the consequent unclarity about what the property is, it is perhaps no surprise that this disagreement resists resolution.

In sum, I suggest that it would pay us to consider the following sufficient condition for a fact to be a reason for a person to do a thing: a fact is a reason for a person to do a thing if it is a fact to the effect that his doing the thing would be good in some way. Indeed, I think it a very plausible idea.

13.

There is a possible objection: accepting that sufficient condition yields that for each of the many things you might now do, there probably is at least one reason for you to do it. That is because there are many ways of being good, and for each of the many things you might now do, there

---

[15] See, for example, Charles L. Stevenson, "The Emotive Meaning of Ethical Terms," *Mind* 46 (1937), reprinted in his *Facts and Values* (New Haven: Yale University Press, 1963). J. L. Mackie's reason for suspicion of the property goodness is the very fact—he takes it to be a fact—that if there were such a property, it would have to be a property such that believing that a thing would have it motivates the believer to try to bring the thing about. See his *Ethics: Inventing Right and Wrong* (London: Penguin Books, 1977).

probably is at least one way in which your doing it would be good. Your mowing my lawn would be good for me. Your watering my lawn would be good for me and it would also be good for my lawn. Suppose your neighbor is doing something illegal; your helping him to hide the traces might be good for him. Again, your going out to dance a jig in the street might be good for use in a list (currently being compiled) of eccentric behaviors in the suburbs. And so on. But (so the objection goes): that many reasons for doing that many things is too many.[16]

My own impression is that this is not a worrisome objection. A reason for doing a thing counts in favor of doing it; but there being a fact that counts in favor of your doing a thing is entirely compatible with its being of no interest to you that there is. There being such a fact is also compatible with its being wrong for you to do the thing.

Moreover, any of the facts to the effect that your doing a thing would be good in a way might be your reason for doing it. As I say, you might not care that your doing a thing would be good in way W. But you might care; and it might be that you therefore do the thing for that reason.

It could of course be insisted that a fact to the effect that your doing a thing would be good in way W is a reason for you to do it only if you want to do what would be good in way W. Thus suppose you don't care that your watering my lawn would be good for me; suppose what you care about is lawns—what you want is that *they* be in good condition. Then it might be said that the fact that your watering my lawn would be good for me is not a reason for you to water my lawn; rather, it is only the fact that your watering my lawn would be good for the lawn that is a reason for you to water it.

If we accept this idea, then we have to say that the fact that your doing a thing would be good in way W is a reason for you to do it only if you want to do what would be good in way W. Moreover, that such a fact might be a reason for you to do a thing at one time and not another. That would be the case if at the earlier time you did not want to do what would be good in way W and then came to want to do so at a later time. Perhaps some people would find this narrow construal of reasons for action attractive.

I see no theoretically important reason for rejecting this narrow construal. Or for accepting it. Whatever we wish to accomplish in moral theory can be—indeed, had better be—accomplishable whether we opt

---

[16] I thank Sarah Stroud for making this objection: she said that on this view, reasons for action "come too cheap."

for this narrow construal of reasons for action or the broad construal of them that I have recommended.[17] I will return to this matter in Part II.

Meanwhile, I think it clear that the broad construal that I have recommended is more squarely in accord with our ideas about reasons for action. Consider a man who is standing by, watching a child drown. He has a life preserver, and could easily throw it to the child. His doing so would be good for the child. On the other hand, he cares not the least about the child, and does not want to do what would be good for it. I am inclined to think it simply false to say that there is no reason for him to throw the life preserver. There is a reason for him to do this, lying in the fact that his doing it would be good for the child. His not wanting to do what would be good for the child does not mean that there is no reason for him to do it; it means merely that he is a thoroughly bad person.

In sum, I suggest that we should reject this objection. We should agree that a fact is a reason for a person to do a thing if it is a fact to the effect that his doing it would be good in a way. Whether the person will do a thing there is reason for him to do, or ought to or must do it, are quite other matters, fixed by quite other considerations.

14.

Is the condition I have offered necessary as well as sufficient? One option is to say that it is, thus to say:

> (i) A fact is a reason for a person to do a thing if and only if it is a fact to the effect that his doing it would be good in a way.

Should we agree? No. It is surely plain that the fact that your *not* doing a thing would be bad in a way is a reason for you to do the thing. (The fact that your not doing the thing would be bad in a way certainly counts in favor of your doing it.) But the fact that your not doing the thing would be bad in a way is not itself a fact to the effect that your doing it would be good in a way.

Second, we should also allow that the fact that your doing a thing

---

[17] The narrow construal is recommended by Bernard Williams; see his "Internal and External Reasons," which first appeared in *Rational Action*, ed. Ross Harrison (Cambridge: Cambridge University Press, 1980), and was reprinted in Bernard Williams, *Moral Luck* (Cambridge: Cambridge University Press, 1981). See also T. M. Scanlon's careful discussion of Williams's arguments in Scanlon *What We Owe to Each Other,* App. Scanlon prefers the broad construal, as do I, but I take him to agree that there is no theoretically important reason for preferring it to the narrow one.

would be better in a way than your doing anything else is a reason for
you to do the thing. (This fact too counts in favor of your doing the
thing.) But this fact is not itself a fact to the effect that your doing the
thing would be good in a way.

Third, we should also allow that the fact that someone has a right
that you do the thing is a reason for you to do it. But this fact too is not
in itself a fact to the effect that your doing the thing would be good in a
way.

These facts are all evaluative, or normative, and no doubt there are
other examples that could be added. I suggest that what we should say
is this:

> (ii) A fact is a reason for a person to do a thing if and only if it is a
> fact to the effect that
> > his doing it would be good in a way, or
> > his not doing it would be bad in a way, or
> > his doing it would be better in a way than his doing anything
> > else, or
> > someone has a right that he do it, or . . .

leaving room for other evaluative facts to be added.

But only other evaluative facts. For if we suppose that a reason for a
person to do a thing is *itself* something that counts in favor of his doing
it, then we should limit reasons for action to evaluative facts, as (ii) is intended to do. It is their being evaluative that marks these facts as reasons
for action—since it is in virtue of their being evaluative that they count
in favor of an action.

But perhaps we do not use the term "reason for action" as strictly as
option (ii) requires? Suppose that Cora reasons to herself as follows: "My
drinking some milk would increase my calcium intake, so I'll drink
some."[18] And suppose that her premise is true, thus that her drinking
some milk really would increase her calcium intake. Let us call that the
Calcium Fact:

> (The Calcium Fact) Cora's drinking some milk would increase her
> calcium intake.

She takes the Calcium Fact to be a reason for her to drink some milk;
isn't it plausible to think that it is? If it is, then—since the Calcium Fact
is not evaluative—there are facts that are reasons for action that are not
evaluative, and option (ii) must be rejected.

[18] Notice how Cora differs from Carol of section 10, whose reasoning rested on the
premise that she wanted to drink some milk.

On the other hand, there is an assumption that Cora is making, namely, that her increasing her calcium intake would be good for her. (Else she would not take the Calcium Fact to be a reason for drinking some milk.) And if that assumption is false, then the Calcium Fact is not a reason for her to drink some milk. Thus, if her increasing her calcium intake would not be good for her, or would be positively bad for her, then the Calcium Fact is no reason at all for her to drink some milk.

We could say that the Calcium Fact is a reason for her to drink some milk if, but only if, her increasing her calcium intake would be good for her. If we do, we must reject the relatively simple option (ii). Alternatively, we could say that the Calcium Fact is not *itself* a reason for her to drink some milk. (It does not *itself* count in favor of her drinking some milk.) No doubt the Calcium Fact is a reason for believing that her drinking some milk would be good for her; after all, most of us really would benefit from increasing our calcium intake. We could therefore conclude that the Calcium Fact is (merely) a reason for believing that there is a reason for her to drink some milk. And we would therefore be able to retain the relatively simple option (ii).

My own impression is that nothing theoretically important turns on which of these options we choose, and I therefore recommend that we choose the relatively simple option (ii).

15.

My main concern in sections 9 through 14 has been the concept 'reason for action.' I have wished to bring out that we have an answer to the question "What is a reason for a person to do such and such?" if we help ourselves to the fact that all goodness is goodness in a way, and attend to the ways of being good.

I want to say a few things about desires by way of conclusion to Part I. I think it pays us to do so because here too it pays us to attend to the ways of being good.

We typically have a reason for wanting something, and I suggest that we should take reasons for wanting something to be similar to reasons for doing something. Thus I recommend that we say first: a fact F is a reason for a person to want a state of affairs S to obtain just in case F counts in favor of S's obtaining. And that we say second: F counts in favor of S's obtaining just in case F is a fact to the effect that S's obtaining would be good in a way, or *S*'s not obtaining would be bad in a way, or . . . , where the continuation is analogous to that in (ii) of section 14.[19] If there is no such fact, then though the wanter may think there is a reason for him to want *S* to obtain, he is mistaken: there isn't.

So a person can want something and there be no reason for him to want it. Can a person want something without even believing there is a reason for him to want it? G. E. M. Anscombe invites us to imagine a man who tells us he wants a saucer of mud. "How so?" we ask. "What would be good about your getting a saucer of mud?" "Nothing," he replies; "I just happen to want to get one." Anscombe suggests that this is unintelligible, and I think she is right.[20] I think that you can't want something without thinking there is a reason for you to want it—just as (I should think) you can't expect or regret something without thinking there is a reason for you to expect or regret it.

If these ideas are right, then—even apart from the considerations I drew attention to in section 10 above—it would be no surprise if some philosophers thought that the fact that a person wants something is a reason for him to try to get it. For suppose that you want a state of affairs *S* to obtain. Suppose that you have a reason for that want, namely the fact that *S*'s obtaining would be good in a certain way *W*. A little piece of reasoning takes you from that fact to the conclusion that your trying to get *S* to obtain would also be good in way *W*; and *that* is a reason for you to try to get *S* to obtain. So your reason for wanting lends weight to a reason for acting, and it is therefore easy to think that the wanting is itself a reason for acting. Easy, but I suggest mistaken.

16.

I have argued in Part I that Consequentialism must be rejected on the ground that it reduces what a person ought to do to the maximizing of goodness, whereas there is no such thing as goodness. All goodness, I said, is goodness in a way. I then said that we gain more from attending to the fact that all goodness is goodness in a way than merely a refuta-

---

[19] Note the availability of a more complicated condition on reasons for wanting a thing, analogous to the one available for reasons for acting; that is, one that allows for the possibility that nonevaluative facts may be reasons for wanting a thing.

[20] Anscombe, *Intention*. Warren Quinn makes a similar point in "Putting Rationality in Its Place," *Morality and Action* (Cambridge: Cambridge University Press, 1993). See also Richard Kraut, "Desire and the Human Good," *Proceedings and Addresses of the American Philosophical Association* 68; no. 2.

tion of Consequentialism: we are able to give an account of what it is for something to be a reason for acting.

What we should turn to now is what a person ought to do. I will not even try to produce a theory about what a person ought to do. I will only make some suggestions about the structure that I think such a theory should have.

PART TWO: ADVICE

I.

The word "ought" is probably just about as commonly used as the words "good" and "bad" are. When we say such things as "Alfred ought to drink some hot lemonade" or "Alfred ought to pay Bertha five dollars," what does or would make what we say true? These assertions have a common form, which I will write

> *A* ought to *V*

—they are obtainable from that expression by replacing somebody's name for "*A*" and some verb or verb phrase for "*V.*" (I should point out that what replaces "*V*" may be the likes of "refrain from paying Bertha" as well as the likes of "pay Bertha.") So what we are asking is: what does or would make an assertion of that form true?

It is certainly plausible to think that what a person ought to do is intimately connected with what would be good or bad. But assuming that I was right to say, as I did in Part I, that there are no such things as goodness and badness, or betterness or worseness, we cannot say

> *A* ought to *V* if and only if *A*'s *V*-ing would be good

or

> *A* ought to *V* if and only if *A*'s *V*-ing would be better than *A*'s doing any of the other things it is open to him to do.

A's *V*-ing can't be *just* good: it is at best good in this or that way or ways. And *A*'s *V*-ing can't be *just* better than *A*'s *X*-ing, or *A*'s *Y*-ing, or *A*'s *Z*-ing: it can at best be better than those in this or that way or ways.

These considerations might tempt one to agree with those who say that the word "ought" is at least three ways ambiguous.

On any view, the word "ought" is at least two ways ambiguous. We say "The train ought to arrive by 3:00," and when we do, we are not saying about the train what we say about Alfred when we say he ought to drink some hot lemonade. What we say about the train is roughly that the train may be expected to arrive by 3:00; what we say about Alfred is roughly that it is advisable that he drink some hot lemonade. I will throughout be using the word "ought" in the latter sense, which might be called the advice sense.

Now some people say that there is no such thing as *the* advice sense of the word "ought": they say that "ought" has at least two advice senses. Suppose I ask whether Alfred ought to pay Bertha five dollars. They would reply: "What do you mean? Do you mean 'would it be good for Alfred to pay Bertha five dollars?' If that's what you mean, then maybe the answer is no. Or do you mean 'would it be morally good for Alfred to pay Bertha five dollars?' If that's what you mean, then maybe the answer is yes." And if I say "Look, what I asked was just, simply, whether Alfred ought to pay Bertha five dollars," they reply that there is no such question—no such thing as its *just* being or not being the case that a person ought to do a thing.

This idea might seem to square well with what I have been saying about goodness and badness. Thus it might be said that "ought" is multiply ambiguous: that it has a different meaning for each way in which an act can be good. In particular, it might be said that what we need is the following:

> A ought$_W$ to V if and only if A's V-ing would be better in way W than A's doing any of the other things it is open to him to do instead.

So, for example, that we should say about Alfred:

> Alfred ought$_{\text{good for Alfred}}$ to pay Bertha if and only if Alfred's paying Bertha would be better for Alfred than Alfred's doing any of the other things it is open to him to do instead,
>
> Alfred ought$_{\text{morally good}}$ to pay Bertha if and only if Alfred's paying Bertha would be morally better than Alfred's doing any of the other things it is open to him to do instead,

and no doubt also

> Alfred ought$_{\text{enjoyable}}$ to pay Bertha if and only if Alfred's paying Bertha would be more enjoyable than Alfred's doing any of the other things it is open to him to do instead,

and so on for each of the ways of being good. A proponent of this idea says that if anyone asks whether Alfred ought to pay Bertha, we cannot answer the question; indeed, no question has even been asked, unless what the speaker means to be asking is, for some particular way of being good W, whether Alfred ought$_W$ to pay Bertha. We can call this the Multiple Ambiguity Idea.

It is in one way an attractive idea: as I said, it is plausible to think that what a person ought to do is intimately connected with what would be good or bad, and this idea expresses that connection in a very simple way—while accommodating the fact that all goodness is goodness in a way.

On the other hand, it is a very bad idea, and that for two reasons. First, it is wildly implausible to think that the word "ought" is multiply ambiguous in that way. Second, it gives moral goodness and badness the wrong role in assessments of what a person ought to do. I will return to moral goodness and badness later. Let us first look at the proposed ambiguity.

Suppose that Alfred is ill, and that only a dose of a certain medicine will cure him. It tastes truly awful, however. Alfred asks us "Ought I really take it?" It is a wildly implausible idea that we can reply only: "Well, your taking it would be very unpleasant, so in one sense of 'ought,' it's not the case that you ought to take it, namely the 'ought$_{enjoyable}$' sense of 'ought.' But your taking it would be good for you, so in another sense of 'ought,' you ought to take it, namely the 'ought$_{goodness\ for\ Alfred}$' sense of 'ought.'" It is likely that Alfred will repeat his question: "But ought I take it?" It surely won't do to reply: "Are you deaf? I just told you that in one sense you ought to and in another sense it is not the case that you ought to, and that's all the advice that anyone can give you." We *can* give more advice: we can say what the case presumably warrants saying, namely that he ought to take the medicine.

Similarly for cases in which what is good for one is bad for another. Suppose that Alfred's paying Bertha five dollars would be good for Bertha but bad for Alfred. Alfred asks whether he ought to pay Bertha five dollars. A proponent of the Multiple Ambiguity Idea says that the only advice we are in a position to give him is that in the 'ought$_{goodness\ for\ Bertha}$' sense of "ought" Alfred ought to pay Bertha, whereas in the 'ought$_{goodness\ for\ Alfred}$' sense of "ought," it is not the case that Alfred ought to pay Bertha. Surely there remains a further question, namely whether Alfred just plain ought to pay Bertha.

In asking the question whether Alfred ought to take the medicine or ought to pay Bertha, we are using the word "ought" in *the* advice sense. That sense is what is sometimes called the 'all things considered' sense of the word. I think that "ought" has no non-all-things-considered sense.[1] But I will not argue for that here; I will merely use it in its all-things-considered sense throughout what follows.

I am going to make four suggestions that bear on it. As I said at the end of Part I, I will not offer a theory about what people ought to do. What I will do is just to draw a sketch of the structure of the theory I think we need to replace Consequentialism with. Alas, a theory with this structure would lack the simplicity of Consequentialism. But then we really shouldn't have expected a theory of what we ought to do to be simple as Consequentialists take it to be.

2.

I said it is plausible to think that what a person ought to do is intimately connected with what would be good or bad. It is very plausible to think that it is certain particular ways of being good and bad that we should be attending to.

Let us begin with the easiest cases, namely those in which what I will call (Isolation)—

(Isolation) A's V-ing would neither be bad for anything other than A, nor infringe anything's rights—

is true. They include cases in which A's V-ing would be bad in one or more ways. Indeed, they include cases in which A's V-ing would be bad for him. They exclude cases in which, while A's V-ing would be bad for nothing other than A, it would infringe a right of B's. (This is surely possible: it might be the case that B has a right that A not V, though it would not be bad for B or anything else if A V-ed.)

The first of my four suggestions, then, is the following:

(I) If (Isolation) is true, and if also A's V-ing would be better for him than his doing any of the other things it is open to him to do instead, then it follows that A ought to V.

I stress: I am suggesting that it *follows* that A ought to V. In particular,

---

[1] Some philosophers think that "ought" does have a non-all-things-considered sense; I describe their view very briefly in section 8 below—see note 10.

there is no need to add a further premise to the effect that *A* wants to do what it would be best for him to do. A person's wants do have a bearing on what he ought to do, but their bearing is indirect; we will return to the bearing of wants in the following section.

Another way to put that point is this. On some views, we should distinguish between categorical and hypothetical 'imperatives.' I put scare-quotes around the word "imperatives" since friends of those views would have us distinguish not merely between imperatives, such as "Drink that medicine" and "Pay Bertha five dollars," but also between sentences of the form that interests us, namely the likes of "Alfred ought to drink that medicine" and "Alfred ought to pay Bertha five dollars." On one interpretation of those views, then, some sentences of our form are categorical: one who asserts them asserts that the person named is to do the thing (drink the medicine, pay Bertha five dollars) whatever his wants may be. Others are hypothetical: one who asserts them asserts only that if the person wants most strongly what he would get in or by doing the thing, then he is to do it.[2] Then the point I made in the preceding paragraph can now be re-put as follows: what follows from the fact (supposing it a fact) that Alfred's drinking the medicine would be best for him, and bad for nothing other than Alfred, and would infringe no one's rights, is not a hypothetical but a categorical imperative—not that he ought too drink it if he wants most strongly to do what's best for him, but, simply, that he ought to drink it.

If Alfred does not at all want to do what is best for him, then it may well be, of course, that he will not drink the medicine. So also if, while he wants to do what is best for him, he wants more strongly to avoid the medicine's nasty taste. Either way, more's the pity for him—he is behaving imprudently.

Several considerations need to be mentioned before we move on. My first suggestion was that if (Isolation) is true, and also *A*'s *V*-ing would

[2] This is only one interpretation of the distinction between categorical and hypothetical 'imperatives.' On the interpretation I supply in the text above, the distinction is between two kinds of sentences. On another interpretation, the distinction is between two kinds of propositions a person might be asserting in asserting any given sentence of our form. Presumably there are other ways of interpreting the distinction. For our purposes, these differences do not matter.

My own view on this matter is that no such distinction can plausibly be made: that is, there is no use of the English word "ought" according to which one who asserts "*A* ought to *V*" asserts what is called a hypothetical imperative on any interpretation of that term. If I say "You ought to put antifreeze in your car in the winter," and it then turns out that you don't want to protect your car, and indeed, that it would be bad for you to protect your car, I don't say "Still, you ought to put antifreeze in your car in the winter, though of course I mean only to be asserting a hypothetical imperative." What I say is rather: "Sorry, I was mistaken in thinking you ought to put antifreeze in, etc. etc."

be better for him than his doing any of the other things it is open to him to do instead, then it follows that A ought to V. What if there is a tie?—that is, what if A's V-ing and A's X-ing would be equally good for him, and both better for him than his doing any of the other things it is open to him to do instead? I think that we should say here what, in Part I, I said the Consequentialist would say by way of reply to the same question. Thus we should say that in case of such a tie, it is not the case that A ought to V and not the case that A ought to X; rather, he may do either, and ought not do anything other than either.

A second consideration that needs to be mentioned is this: my first suggestion does not imply only that whether A wants to do what it would be best for him to do is irrelevant to the question whether he ought to V: it implies that A's knowing, or even believing, that his V-ing would be best for him is also irrelevant to the question whether he ought to V. But that, I think, is exactly as it should be. Suppose, for example, that Alfred will be cured if and only if he drinks a certain medicine, and that his doing so would be bad for nothing other than himself, and infringe no one's rights. But suppose that while we know this, Alfred does not—suppose he not only does not know it but does not even believe it. Is it true, all the same, that he ought to drink the medicine? I recommend that we say that it is true. For suppose he asks us whether he ought to drink it. It would be weird to reply that we can't tell whether he ought to drink the medicine until he first tells us what he believes about it and about himself. We don't need to find out what he believes: whatever his beliefs may be, he ought to drink it. He has asked us for advice, and that is the advice we should give him.

Similarly, my first suggestion implies that what A would be intending in V-ing (if he V-ed) is also irrelevant to the question whether he ought to V. That too is as it should be. If Alfred asks us whether he ought to drink the medicine, it would be equally weird to reply that we can't tell until he first tells us what he would be intending in drinking it. Whatever he intends, he ought to drink that medicine.

I think it clear quite generally that what fixes whether a person ought to do a thing is not the person's subjective state of mind, but instead the objective facts of the situation he is in. I will summarize this point by saying that the question what a person ought to do is (not subjective, but rather) objective.[3]

[3] For more on this point, see Jonathan Bennett's distinction between first-order and second-order morality in his *The Act Itself* (Oxford: Oxford University Press, 1995).

There is a third consideration that needs to be mentioned. I said that we were to be considering cases in which

(Isolation) *A*'s *V*-ing would neither be bad for anything other than *A*, nor infringe anything's rights

is true. Why "not be bad for anything other than *A*" rather than "not be bad for any person other than *A*"? I meant to be setting aside cases in which *A*'s *V*-ing would be bad for anything. An animal, for example. Or for a living thing of some other kind, such as a plant. Or for some non-living thing, such as an artifact or a river. There obviously is such a thing as an act's being bad for an animal or a plant; if less obvious, it is also true that an act may be bad for an artifact or a river. Wherever *A*'s *V*-ing would be bad for something other than *A*, then that is in one or another way relevant to whether he ought, or even may, *V*: the question whether *A* ought to *V* is not settled by the mere fact that it would be best for him to do the thing and bad for no other person.

Again, why "not infringe anything's rights" rather than "not infringe any person's rights"? I meant to leave open that things other than people have rights. Organizations. Animals, perhaps. Wherever *A*'s *V*-ing would infringe anything's rights, then that is in one or another way relevant to whether he ought, or even may, *V*: the question whether *A* ought to *V* is not settled by the mere fact that it would be best for him to do the thing and infringe no person's rights.

We will turn to cases in which (Isolation) is not true in section 5.

3.

It is intuitively clear that the concepts 'good for' and 'bad for' play an important role in fixing whether a person ought to do a thing. We should therefore have a look at them.

There is a large literature on what it is for something to be good for a person, but I think that any plausible theory will serve our purposes well enough.

I assume three constraints on the plausibility of a theory about what it is for something to be good for a person. First, the theory must allow for the possibility that a person's doing a thing would be good for him, even best for him of all his alternatives, and yet bad for another person. Similarly, it must allow for the possibility that a person's doing a thing would be bad for him, even worst of all his alternatives, and yet good for another person. That this is a constraint on the plausibility of a theory is probably obvious enough.

A second constraint is stronger: the theory must allow for the possibility that a person's doing a thing would be good for him, even best for him of all his alternatives, though he ought not do it; and that his doing a thing would be bad for him, even worst for him of all his alternatives, though he ought to do it. Perhaps this second constraint is also obvious.

But even if it is obvious, it does have a certain bite, for there are views according to which it is mistaken: on those views, it can't be, can't *really* be, can't really be *in the long run* or *all things considered* good for a person to do what he ought not, or bad for him to do what he ought to do. Friends of these ideas think that moral requirement in particular has this feature. On their view, the nature of a person, and the content of moral requirement, are such that necessarily, a person's obedience to the requirement conduces to the good of the person. This strikes me as an excessively high-minded conception of the nature of a person, and therefore of what is good for a person; I will not argue against it, but merely set it aside.

The third constraint is this: the theory must allow for the possibility that a person's doing a thing would not be good for him, even though it is what he most wants to do—and indeed, even if his wants are appropriately restricted.

What I have in mind here is this. There is something right about the idea that what is good for a person is importantly connected with satisfaction of his wants. If a man most wants to become a veterinarian, what could possibly make it fail to be good for him to do so? No doubt he'd make more money as a lawyer, but that hardly matters. If a woman most wants to spend her free time knitting scarves for her friends, what could possibly make it fail to be good for her to do so? On some views, then, what is good for a person is not just importantly connected with satisfaction of his wants, but analyzable into satisfaction of wants—thus: what is good for a person is what conduces to satisfaction of his wants.

But no one thinks this idea even remotely plausible unless the wants that matter to goodness for a person are appropriately restricted. The relevant wants are not passing wants, as where a person has a momentary desire to kick somebody in the shin. Nor wants due to ignorance, as where a person wants to drink a certain liquid, not knowing that it contains cyanide. Nor wants due to improper preference-bending, as where a person has been hypnotized. The relevant wants are, rather, relatively stable, resting on correct information, and autonomously arrived at. Another way to put the point is this: the relevant wants are those a person would have "in a cool hour," in possession of full relevant information, and under no improper pressure to conform his will to that of others. These are vague conditions, but it is an intuitively attractive idea that assessing what would be good for a person does require assessing exactly these things, hard though it may be to arrive at a correct judgment about them.

Analogously for badness for a person: what is bad for a person is what interferes with satisfaction of his relevant wants.[4]

Now the third constraint I impose on a theory of goodness for people rules this attractive idea out, so it has even more bite than the second constraint. My reason for thinking the idea should be ruled out is this. Consider a doctor who leaves her comfortable practice to go across country to help deal with an epidemic at risk of her own health, perhaps even of her life. Going across country to do this is what she most wants to do, and we can suppose that her wants meet the restrictions I mentioned; are we to say that her doing so is good for her? Or again, consider a man who gives a kidney to his friend, who needs it for life, despite the risk to his health of doing so. Giving the kidney is what he most wants to do, and we can suppose that his wants too meet the restrictions I mentioned; are we to say here that his doing so is good for him? Surely it is intuitively wrong to say that these acts are good for their agents. And we make too little of the moral impressiveness of what they do if we say that what they do is good for them. Their acts are morally impressive precisely because, though good for others, they are not good for them.

---

[4] This account of goodness and badness for a person is complicated. I think it pays to draw attention to the fact that there is no future in the idea that goodness for a person is analyzable, more simply, in terms of needs. A person needs food and drink, and it is good for the person to get these things. But your doing a thing might be good for you without its being the case that you *need* it done. For example, it might well be good for you to learn Russian without its being the case that you need to learn Russian. What a person needs is not just anything that it would be good for him to get, but rather what it would be bad for him to not get. And I see no more reason to think (indeed, less reason to think) that badness for a person is analyzable in terms of needs than there is to think that needs are analyzable in terms of badness-for.

So also for animals, plants, and artifacts. Animals and plants also need food and drink, and it is good for them to get these things. A lawn mower may need oiling; if so, it would be good for it to get oiled. But the fact that animals, plants, and artifacts need these things is a product of its being bad for them to not get them.

The possibility I point to here is not restricted to cases in which an act is morally impressive. Consider a master chess player who spends his time studying chess, gets no exercise, and smokes heavily because he finds that smoking helps him to concentrate. These are things he wants to do because he wants to become world champion. But I think we cannot at all plausibly say that doing them is good for him.[5]

What works against the idea that what is good for a person is what conduces to satisfaction of his wants is the idea that what is good for a person is what conduces to his health. Many people do sometimes want most to do what interferes with their health, and this even though their wants do meet the restrictions I mentioned above.

So perhaps we should instead opt for a theory according to which goodness for people is analyzable into conduciveness to health? There are at least two objections to this idea. First, the idea is far too narrow. It might be good for your daughter to be accepted by a good law school; I find it hard to believe that this would conduce to her health. Second, and more interesting, if we ask why it is good for a person to be healthy, there seems to be an answer: health does of course have its special pleasures, but what seems fundamental to its value to us is that it is a prerequisite for our being able to do much of what most people most deeply want to do. These two objections head us back toward the idea that goodness for people consists in satisfaction of wants.

My own impression is that the best theory of what is good for a person lies somewhere in between these two ideas. If this is right, then it is clear that, if not exactly how, a person's wants are relevant to what he ought to do: they are so by being relevant to what it would be good for him to do.

Fortunately for our purposes, it does not really matter exactly where, between those two ideas, the best theory of what is good for a person lies. Our main concern will be what is to be said of cases in which a person's doing a thing would be good (or bad) for him, but bad (or good) for another person. So long as the criteria for goodness for and badness for a person are general, in the sense that they bear on both parties—and so

---

[5] This is obvious enough if his efforts do not succeed, so that he does not become champion. But what if they do and he therefore does? Should we say (i) that his becoming champion is good for him, though his taking the necessary means to that end was not? Or (ii) that, given those were the necessary means to that end, and that they were not good for him, it follows that his becoming champion is not itself good for him? or (iii) that, given his becoming champion is good for him, it follows that his taking those means was, after all, good for him? I leave this open.

long as the three constraints I listed are met—that will suit us well
enough.

4.

Less has been written about what is good or bad for an animal or plant,
and hardly anything about what is good or bad for an artifact or a river.
I will have to be brief about these matters.[6]

What is good for a plant is obviously what conduces to its health. I
said there were two objections to the idea that goodness for people is analyzable into conduciveness to health; neither arises in the case of plants.
First, everything that is good for a plant, whatever it may be, conduces
to its health: more strongly, if something is good for a plant, then that is
because and only because it conduces to the plant's health. Second, if we
ask why it is good for a plant to be healthy, there is no answer. Plants
have no wants, and a fortiori, their being healthy is not good for them
because it is a prerequisite for their being able to do what they want.

This difference between what is good for people and what is good for
plants is pretty plainly due to the very fact that people have wants and
plants do not.

Even the higher animals are more like plants in this respect than
they are like people. Unlike plants, they do have wants; unlike people,
their range of wants is narrow. (No doubt that is due to the fact that
their range of experiences is narrow. They have a more or less wide variety of sensory experiences, and they feel pleasure and pain; but they feel
no resentment, indignation, ambition, pride, envy, admiration, and so
on.) In light of the fact that they are conscious beings, a plausible account of what is good for them should presumably lie somewhere between that for people and that for plants.

What is it for a person, animal, or plant to be healthy? Curiously
enough, I think we are helped if we have a look at artifacts first.

Your doing a thing might be good for your lawn mower—for example, oiling it might be good for it. How so? Oiling it would conduce
to its being in good condition. What does that come to? Oiling it would

---

[6] My own views about these matters appear, in greater detail, in "The Right and the
Good," *Journal of Philosophy* 94, no. 6. Though I still think that my remarks there about
goodness for other things are true, my remarks there about goodness for people now strike
me as false—they are argued against in section 3 above.

conduce to its being able to do what it was designed by its manufacturer to do, namely enable a person who uses it properly to mow lawns easily, safely, and well. We don't call an artifact that is in good condition a healthy artifact, but the idea is surely similar.

Similar in that a living creature is healthy just in case it is able to do what it was 'designed by nature' to do—among other things, grow in ways suitable to members of its species, and propagate itself. Animals are designed by nature to do more than plants are, and human beings to do more things still. But feeding any living creature the food suitable to members of its species, and in a suitable amount, would be good for it in that doing so would conduce to its being in a condition in which it is able to do those things.

It is important to recognize that what is good for an animal or plant is not reducible to what is good for people. It might be good for a cat's owner to have it declawed; it is nevertheless not good for the cat to do so. It might be good for a lawn's owner to kill the dandelions that grow in it; it is not good for the dandelions to do so. What is good for human beings plays a more subtle role in the case of artifacts. There are such things as artifacts because of human wants. But whether or not doing a thing is good for an artifact is not a function of human wants. I might want my lawn mower to become unusable to mow lawns with; that is compatible with its being bad for the lawn mower to do so. So also, I should think, for animals and plants that are not in fact designed by nature but instead by human beings—that is, animals and plants that are bred by humans for special purposes: once bred, what is good for them is a function of their design and not our purposes.

Rivers, lakes, mountains, and ravines are quite another matter. In their case, it is what is good for human beings that fixes what is good for them. The Charles River in Massachusetts had become polluted; it was good for the river that measures be taken to decrease the pollution. But that was not because doing so conduced to the river's being able to do what rivers are designed by nature to do: there is no such thing. Rather it was because human beings wished to be able to sail, fish, and swim in the river, and to avoid the nasty look and smell that pollution brings with it.

These differences must surely have a bearing on whether a person ought or ought not or may do a thing where the person's doing it would be best for him but bad for a thing of one or another of these kinds. A theory about what a person ought to do should deal with them. I have no such theory, however, and will only be able to indicate the structure into which I suggest they should be fitted.

5.

What we have been looking at so far are the easy cases, namely those in which

> (Isolation) *A*'s *V*-ing would neither be bad for anything other than *A* nor infringe anything's rights

is true. The first of my four suggestions was about those easy cases, and it said:

> (I) If (Isolation) is true, and if also *A*'s *V*-ing would be better for him than his doing any of the other things it is open to him to do instead, then it follows that *A* ought to *V*.

We should turn now to the hard cases, namely those in which (Isolation) is false. They are the ones of most concern to moral philosophy.

The second of my four suggestions is this:

> (II) Justice and generosity are second-order ways of being good; injustice and (what I will call) miserliness are second-order ways of being bad.

For a reason that will emerge in section 7, it is injustice and miserliness that will primarily matter to us. So let us begin with injustice.

To act unjustly is to fail to do what is owed; that is, it is to fail to do what another person has a right to one's doing. More precisely, to act unjustly is to fail to do what another person has a *non-overridden* right to one's doing. Suppose that Alfred has a right that you meet him at the corner of High and Main at 3:00 P.M. today. How might Alfred have acquired that right? Perhaps you promised him that you would meet him there then. Here are two kinds of case in which Alfred's right is overridden. (i) Bertha has a more stringent right that you not meet Alfred there then. Perhaps you promised her that you would not do so, which is what gave her a right that you not do so. What would mark her right as more stringent? Well, perhaps while Alfred will merely be annoyed if you do not turn up on time, she will suffer greatly if you do. (ii) Alfred's right that you meet him there then is weak (that is, nonstringent), and no one has a right that you not be there then, but your being there then would be very bad for you, or for Bertha, or for Bertha and Charles. Perhaps while Alfred will (once again) merely be annoyed if you do not turn up on time, you or Bertha or both Bertha and Charles will suffer greatly if you do. In cases of kinds (i) and (ii), Alfred's right that you meet him at the corner of High and Main at 3:00 P.M. today is overridden; and if you fail to meet him there then, your doing so is not unjust.[7]

By hypothesis, Alfred has a right that you meet him at the corner of High and Main at 3:00 P.M. today. What if (iii) Bertha has an equally stringent right that you not meet him there then? (For simplicity, let us suppose that no one else would be affected, whichever you do.) Here we have a tie again. I think that nothing theoretically interesting turns on which choice we make; since I think it simpler, and somewhat more plausible, to conclude that neither of them has a non-overridden right in respect of your meeting or not meeting Alfred, I will assume so. (A good idea for you in such a situation would be to try to get them to agree to your flipping a coin. If they do, then presumably the winner, and only the winner, has a non-overridden right.)

In sum, then: to act unjustly is to fail to do what something has a non-overridden right to one's doing.

A feature of this account of acting unjustly calls for explicit mention. What I refer to is the fact that according to this account, the question whether a person's act is unjust does not turn on what the person's beliefs or intentions are. What fixes whether the person's act is unjust is not the person's subjective state of mind, but instead the objective fact that something else does or does not have a non-overridden right against him. That seems to me exactly as it should be. Suppose Alfred does not believe that anything has a non-overridden right that he send Bertha a check for fifty dollars. But suppose that is because he has sim-

---

[7] Some philosophers hold the view that there is no such thing as a right that is overridden; on their view, all rights are 'absolute.' Thus they would say that in cases of kinds (i) and (ii), Alfred has no right that you be there then, for the facts about Bertha in (i) and about you or Bertha or Bertha and Charles in (ii) make Alfred cease to have the right you gave him when you made your promise to him. Other philosophers—I include myself—hold the view that Alfred does have the right you gave him, though it is overridden, and justice therefore does not require your according it to him. My reason for preferring this second view is the fact that if you do not keep your promise to Alfred, you will at a minimum owe him an apology: this fact seems to me to show that the right you gave him did not simply go out of existence. I will throughout assume without argument that this second view is correct. For our purposes, it does not really matter which is correct, and what I say below could easily enough be revised in such a way as to square with the first view.

I supply more detail on these matters in *The Realm of Rights* (Cambridge: Harvard University Press, 1990).

ply forgotten that he had promised her that he would, and suppose also that her right that he do so is non-overridden. Then his failing to send her a check would be unjust. If it is not his fault that he forgot his promise, then we may well think he would not be to blame for failing to send her a check; but that his failure would be unjust seems quite clear. I will summarize this point by saying that the question whether a person's act is unjust is objective—just as, as I said earlier, the question whether a person ought to do a thing is objective. I think it clear that this is true of justice too.[8]

Let us turn now to miserliness. I will so use that word that it stands for the contrary of generosity. My use of the word is therefore broader than the ordinary use of it, for I think that we call an act miserly only where its agent is mean or grudging about money. Suppose that Bertha is drowning and Alfred alone can save her, as it might be, by throwing her his life preserver. If Alfred refuses to do this on the ground that he is feeling tired, and does not want to bother, then I will say that his refusal to throw it is miserly, despite the fact that his refusal is not due to meanness about money.

By way of preliminary characterization, I will describe as "miserly" any act that provides its agent with a small gain—whether financial or otherwise—or even no gain at all, despite the act's being very bad for another person. Thus an act of gratuitous cruelty, inconsiderateness, or discourtesy may also be miserly.

Why "another person"? Is it only where the 'victim' of the act is a person that an act is miserly? I will suppose not. If animals lack rights, then it is not possible for one's treatment of them to be unjust; I mean to allow that it is possible for one's treatment of an animal to be miserly whether or not animals have rights. This use of "miserly" is as it should be if miserliness is to be the contrary of generosity, for I should think it possible to be generous to an animal.

What about plants, artifacts, and rivers? Rivers we can set aside, since nothing is bad for them except by way of being bad for people. I am inclined to think, however, that we should allow for the possibility that one's treatment of a plant or artifact is miserly. If you gain nothing

---

[8] It might pay to make explicit that my point in the text has to do with *acts* only. The questions whether a *person* is unjust and whether a person is just are not, or anyway are not wholly, objective. I will shortly opt for a similar point about the questions whether an act is miserly, and whether an act is generous; opting for it is compatible with accepting that the questions whether a person is miserly, and whether a person is generous, are not, or anyway are not wholly, objective.

from destroying a tree or a painting, by which I mean to include that it would cost you nothing to refrain from destroying it, then I will say that your treatment of it is miserly—even if there is no person whose property rights you violate, or whom you affect for the worse.

So here is an interesting difference between injustice and miserliness: your treatment of a thing can be unjust only if the thing is a right-holder, whereas your treatment of a thing can be miserly even if it is not. I will draw attention to yet another difference between injustice and miserliness shortly.

In any case, let us emend the preliminary characterization of miserliness that I gave above. It is surely right to think that Alfred's V-ing is miserly only if

(i) Alfred's V-ing provides Alfred with at most a small gain, despite its being very bad for something else

is true.

Another condition is necessary, however. Suppose that (i) is true of Alfred's V-ing. Suppose, however, that someone has a non-overridden right to Alfred's V-ing. Then I will say that Alfred's V-ing is not miserly.

Here is an example. Suppose that Bertha is using Alfred's typewriter without his permission; she needs it to complete some work she is doing, the doing of which is important to her. Suppose that Alfred has no need of the typewriter himself, and indeed, that he would gain nothing at all by requesting its return. Suppose he nevertheless requests its return. Then his requesting its return gains him nothing, despite being very bad for Bertha. It sounds, therefore, as if Alfred's requesting the return of the typewriter is miserly. But suppose, last, that Cora has a non-overridden right that Alfred request the return of the typewriter. (Alfred has promised Cora that he will get it back from Bertha to give to Cora, who needs it more than Bertha does.) Now it is clear that Alfred's requesting the return of the typewriter is not miserly.

So we need to add a further condition on miserliness: Alfred's V-ing is miserly only if

(ii) Nobody has a non-overridden right that Alfred V

is also true.

Condition (ii) is not unique to miserliness, for it holds of generosity too. If somebody has a non-overridden right that Alfred V, then his V-ing is not miserly. So similarly: if somebody has a non-overridden right that Alfred *V*, then his *V*-ing is not generous. (It is not generous in a person to pay his grocer's bill on time, however good for his grocer his doing so would be.)

In sum, I take it that conditions (i) and (ii) are both necessary for an act to be miserly. Are they jointly sufficient? I should think not. That is because of a feature of miserliness—and generosity—that I will call context-dependence.

Suppose that I have never given to the needy, and it is proposed to me now that I make a small contribution to them. If I refuse, my refusing is miserly; indeed, it is very miserly. By contrast, suppose that you have very often given to the needy, and it is proposed to you now that you make yet another small contribution to them. If you refuse, your refusal is markedly less miserly, and perhaps is not miserly at all. (Why so? Presumably because your total contribution is already not small.) This feature of miserliness is what I am calling context-dependence.

Context-dependence is also a feature of generosity: your making a further small contribution now is the more generous given you have very often contributed in the past.

But context-dependence is not a feature of either injustice or justice, and therefore constitutes yet another difference between injustice and miserliness. My failing to pay my grocer's bill on time is not less unjust if I have very often paid my grocer's bill on time in the past. Nor is my paying my grocer's bill on time more just if I have paid it on time very often in the past.[9]

Expressing the context-dependence of miserliness in the form of a further condition on miserliness would be a complex business, and not, I think, an interesting one. So I leave open how this is to be done. I leave open also the possibility that further conditions should be placed on miserliness.

But what I do not leave open is the possibility of adding a condition concerning the agent's subjective state of mind. I will so use the word "miserly" that the answer to the question whether a person's act is or is not miserly does not turn on his beliefs or intentions: rather it turns on

---

[9] I will suggest in section 7 below that we ought to avoid miserliness and injustice. Taking liberties with Kant's terminology, we might say that we have perfect duties to avoid miserliness and injustice in the sense that we are on all occasions to avoid both—but that we also have an imperfect duty to avoid miserliness in the sense that miserliness (unlike injustice) is context-dependent.

what he (objectively) does, as condition (i) requires, and on whether nobody has a non-overridden right against him, as condition (ii) requires. I will summarize this point by saying that the question whether an act is miserly is objective. Miserliness, however, was to be the contrary of generosity; and isn't our ordinary use of "generous" subjective? I think it is, or that it at least mostly is. Suppose that muddled Alfred intends to be helping Bertha, and believes that he is succeeding in doing so, but he is mistaken: what he is doing in fact harms her. Do we say that his act was nevertheless generous? I think we do.

On the other hand, I am not sure that our use of "generous" is always subjective in this way. Consider the muddled miser, who intends not to help, and thinks he is not helping. Unbeknownst to him, however, he is in fact helping. Mightn't we say that unbeknownst to him, his act was generous? (If a person says "I didn't mean to be generous," do we always conclude that his act was not generous? Mightn't we sometimes reply "All the same, you were"?)

In any case, I will throughout use the word "generous" in such a way that it—like its intended contrary, "miserly"—is objective. The muddled miser, whose act was (as I will say) generous certainly deserves no praise for it; he may even deserve blame for it. By contrast, while muddled Alfred's act was (as I will say) not generous, and perhaps was even miserly, he may deserve no blame for it; he may even deserve praise for it.

6.

To return now to my suggestions. The second of my four suggestions was:

(II) Justice and generosity are second-order ways of being good; injustice and (what I will call) miserliness are second-order ways of being bad.

We now have in hand an account of injustice and anyway a good enough preliminary account of miserliness to be able to see, as follows, that (II) is true.

It is presumably clear enough that injustice and miserliness are ways of being bad, and justice and generosity are ways of being good.

My ground for saying that injustice is a second-order way of being bad has already emerged, for what I have in mind about it is this. The answer to the question whether an act is unjust turns in part on whether those affected by it have the relevant rights; but it also turns in part on whether those rights are overridden, and that turns in part on how good or bad the act would be for those affected by it. Goodness-for and badness-for are first-order ways of being good; whether an act is unjust cannot be settled unless it is first settled how good or bad it would be in the relevant first-order ways.

That miserliness is a second-order way of being bad is perhaps even clearer than that injustice is—for it is clear that whether an act is miserly is in part a function of how good refraining would have been for others, and how bad refraining would have been for the agent.

The analogue of this point also holds of justice and generosity.

A word or two should probably be said here about moral goodness and badness. I said that injustice and miserliness are ways of being bad, and justice and generosity are ways of being good. Couldn't we have said that the first pair are ways of being morally bad, and the second pair ways of being morally good?

I am inclined to think that the ordinary use of the terms "morally good" and "morally bad" is such that the questions whether they apply to an act are subjective, not objective. Thus consider again a person who means to be acting justly, and thinks he is succeeding in doing so. As I said, he may be mistaken: it may be that his act is in fact unjust. If the mistake is not his fault, then (as I said) we may well think he is not to blame for his unjust act. Indeed, he might even deserve praise for it. Suppose he does deserve praise for it. Then I think we would conclude that, although his act was unjust, it was morally good.

Similarly, consider again the muddled miser, who intends not to help, and thinks he is not helping. Unbeknownst to him, however, he is in fact helping. I said I would so use the word "generous" that his act is generous. He does not of course deserve praise for it; rather, he may deserve blame for it. Suppose he does deserve blame for it. Then I think we would conclude that, although his act was generous, it was morally bad.

In short, our ordinary use of those terms seems to me to be such that their applicability to an act turns on its agent's subjective state of mind, in particular, on his beliefs and intentions.

I see no good reason to reject that usage, and I therefore think we should agree that the questions whether an act is morally good or morally bad cut across the questions whether it is just or unjust, generous or miserly.

Moreover, we should agree that the questions whether an act is morally good or morally bad cuts across the questions whether its agent ought or ought not be doing what he is doing—for, as I argued earlier, the questions whether a person ought to do a thing, or ought not do it, are not subjective, but instead objective.

Our concern here is what a person ought or ought not do. I therefore bypass moral goodness and badness.

7.

The third of my four suggestions is about what a person ought to do:

> (III) *A* ought to *V* if his not *V*-ing would be either unjust or miserly, and *A* ought not *V* if his *V*-ing would be either unjust or miserly.

I think that, given the characterizations of injustice and miserliness I offered in section 5, this suggestion is intuitively very plausible.

We should notice that (III) says "if," and not "if and only if." That is because there may well be other grounds for saying that a person ought to do a thing or ought not do it than injustice and miserliness. For example, my first suggestion said:

> (I) If (Isolation) is true, and if also *A*'s *V*-ing would be better for him than his doing any of the other things it is open to him to do instead, then it follows that *A* ought to *V*—

where (Isolation) says:

> (Isolation) *A*'s *V*-ing would neither be bad for anything other than *A*, nor infringe anything's rights.

Wherever (Isolation) is true, *A*'s *V*-ing is neither unjust nor miserly; yet it may all the same be the case that *A* ought to *V*, or ought to refrain from *V*-ing. And we should not suppose that the word "ought" has different senses, according as injustice and miserliness are or are not in question. I have invited you to agree that there is such a thing as *the* advice sense of the word "ought," which is the sense that I am taking it to have throughout.

It is worth noticing that, given (III),

(II) Justice and generosity are second-order ways of being good; injustice and (what I will call) miserliness are second-order ways of being bad

is more important than it may initially have appeared. Suppose that Alfred's doing a thing would be good for him, but that his doing it would be unjust. If (III) is true, then Alfred ought not do the thing. That, I am sure, will seem plausible to most people. Perhaps not to others. But whether it seems plausible or not, many people ask for a justification. *Why* does the fact that Alfred's doing the thing would be unjust yield that he ought not do it?—when, by hypothesis, it would be good for him to do it?

Another way to put this question is this. I said in Part I that the fact that a person's doing a thing would be good in a way counts in favor of his doing it, and the fact that a person's doing a thing would be bad in a way counts against his doing it. For (III) to be true, it is required that the fact that Alfred's doing a thing would be unjust (hence bad in a way) counts more strongly against his doing it than the fact that his doing it would be good for him counts in favor of his doing it. Why (it is asked) should we think this true?

If (II) is true, this question has not the interest it has been thought to have. According to (II), we are not to weigh the fact that Alfred's doing the thing would be good for him against the fact that his doing it would be unjust, leaving open the possibility that the fact that his doing it would be good for him counts more strongly in favor of his doing it. For given that injustice is a second-order way of being bad, the fact that his doing the thing would be good for him has *already* been taken into consideration in arriving at the conclusion that his doing it would be unjust. To allow the fact that his doing the thing would be good for him to have a further, independent, bearing on what he ought to do would be to double-count it.

There is a more general point in the offing. Suppose that Alfred's doing a thing would be unjust or miserly. According to (III), it follows that Alfred ought not do it. In saying that Alfred ought not do it, I am saying that Alfred ought not do it, whatever the consequences of his doing it—that is, however good the consequences of his doing it may be in whatever ways they may be good. That his act would possess the second-order features of being unjust or miserly is a conclusion arrivable at only after consideration of the first-order ways in which Alfred's doing the thing would be good.

Suggestions (I), (II), and (III) can be connected in the following way: we can say that they jointly yield that what a person ought to do is what gives adequate weight to the interests of all who would be affected. Suppose that (Isolation) is true of Alfred's drinking some hot lemonade. It follows that only Alfred's own interests are relevant to the question whether he ought to drink some. According to (I), he ought to drink some if his doing so is best for him. And we can say: his doing so would give adequate weight to his own interests. His choosing any option less good for him would give inadequate weight to his own interests—it would be imprudent.

Suppose, however, that (Isolation) is not true of Alfred's drinking some hot lemonade. (Perhaps he has promised Bertha that he would not.) Then the interests of others are relevant to the question whether he ought to drink some. According to (III), he ought not drink some if his doing so would be unjust or miserly; according to (II), the question whether it would be turns in part on how good or bad his doing so would be for him and for those others. If his doing so would be unjust or miserly, so that he ought not, then we can say: his doing so would be his failing to give adequate weight to the interests of all who would be affected—those of the others as well as his own.

8.

But is

> (III) *A* ought to *V* if his not *V*-ing would be either unjust or miserly, and *A* ought not *V* if his *V*-ing would be either unjust or miserly

true? There is a possible objection to it that I think worth taking note of.

Suppose that *A*'s *V*-ing would be unjust. According to (III), it follows that *A* ought not *V*. Can we consistently also suppose that his not *V*-ing would be miserly? Suppose we can. Let us do so, then: we now suppose also that *A*'s not *V*-ing would be miserly. According to (III), it follows that he ought to *V*. So it follows both that *A* ought not *V*, and also that *A* ought to *V*.

Some philosophers are quite content to make room for the possibility that

(1) *A ought not V*

and

(2) *A ought to V*

are both true.[10]

Other philosophers—I include myself—think it is not possible that (1) and (2) are both true. We must therefore either reject (III) or rebut the objection to it that I have just drawn attention to.

The rebuttal is easy, however, given my characterizations of injustice and miserliness. I said just above: suppose that *A*'s *V*-ing would be unjust. I then asked: can we consistently also suppose that his not *V*-ing would be miserly? The answer is that we can't. Given my characterization of injustice, *A*'s *V*-ing is unjust only if

(3) Somebody has a non-overridden right that *A* not *V*

is true. But given my characterization of miserliness, *A*'s not *V*-ing is miserly only if

(4) Nobody has a non-overridden right that *A* not *V*

is true. It is plain that (3) and (4) are incompatible. So it cannot be the case both that Alfred's *V*-ing is unjust and that his not *V*-ing is miserly.

9.

My fourth suggestion emerges on consideration of the question why I have focused on injustice and miserliness, which are ways of being bad, rather than on justice and generosity, which are ways of being good.

To begin with justice. According to (III), the fact that *A*'s *V*-ing

[10] It is obviously not possible that (2) and

(*) It is not the case that *A* ought to *V*

are both true, so that if (1) entails (*), then those philosophers are mistaken—that is, it is not possible that (1) and (2) are both true. But those philosophers simply deny that (1) entails (*).

The philosophers I refer to here are those who accept that there are what they call "moral dilemmas." I indicated earlier that my own use of "ought" would be all-things-considered, and it is surely clear that if "ought" is construed as I construe it, then (1) does entail (*), and (1) is therefore incompatible with (2).

would be unjust entails that A ought not V. But the fact that A's V-ing would be just does not entail that A ought to V. That, I should think, is obvious. There might well be cases in which you have several options for action—as it might be, several ways of distributing a benefit you owe—each entirely just, there being no one of them that you ought to choose.

A similar point holds of generosity. It might well be that while you cannot give aid to both Alfred and Bertha, giving aid to Alfred and giving aid to Bertha would each be generous, neither option being such that you ought to choose it.

In short, we cannot say that a person ought to do a thing if his doing of it would be either just or generous.

A further, and more interesting, reason why we cannot say that a person ought to do a thing if his doing of it would be either just or generous issues from a fact about generosity. An act can be more or less generous, and a very generous act may be, as it is sometimes put, supererogatory, that is, as we say, 'above and beyond the call of duty.' The person who saved a life at risk of his own acted very generously. It does not follow that he did what he ought. Indeed, it would not have been true to say of him that he ought to save that life. What he did for the other person was beyond what he ought.

This point does not also hold of justice. While some generous acts are beyond what one ought, no just act is. No matter, for our purposes. The fact remains that we cannot say that a person ought to do a thing if his doing of it would be either just *or* generous.

I said earlier that what a person ought to do is what gives adequate weight to the interests of all affected—not lavish weight. What "You ought" requires of us is the adequate minimum. That is my fourth suggestion:

(IV) Doing what one ought only requires giving the adequate minimum weight to the interests of all who are affected.

It pays to stress, however, that accepting (IV) does not commit us to a conclusion about praise. Certainly the person who saved a life at risk of his own deserves much praise for doing so: and I should think, by contrast, that one rarely deserves praise for doing what one ought. But it may on occasion be the case that a person does deserve praise for doing what he ought—as, for example, where his avoiding injustice requires more courage and a stronger will than are normally required in our dealings with others.

Suggestion (IV) says *all* who are affected, which of course includes *A* himself. On the one hand, whether someone's right against *A* is non-overridden turns on what is good or bad for *A* as well as on what is good or bad for others. On the other hand, there are limits to what avoiding miserliness requires of us. I said that the person who saved a life at risk of his own acted very generously, and deserves much praise for doing so. Would it be very generous, deserving of much praise, to cure someone's sore throat at risk of one's life? I hardly think so. The beneficiary's gain is too small in comparison with the loss the agent risks. There is nothing praiseworthy in making a major sacrifice in order to forestall another person's small loss. Surely such an act is not merely not praiseworthy, its agent ought not perform it. Why so? Presumably the answer lies in the fact that a person who makes a major sacrifice in order to forestall another person's small loss does not give adequate weight to his own interests—and a fortiori does not give adequate weight to the interests of all who are affected.

10.

It is time now to make contact with the proposals I made in Part I about reasons for action. I said there that the concept 'reason for a person to do such and such' has been thought to have an intimate connection with the concept 'ought'. Some philosophers hold that *A* ought to *V* only if there is a reason for *A* to *V*. Or even more strongly: *A* ought to *V* if and only if *V*-ing is precisely what there is most reason for *A* to do.

I then proposed that a fact is a reason for *A* to *V* if and only if it is a fact to the effect that

> *A*'s *V*-ing would be good in a way, or
> *A*'s not *V*-ing would be bad in a way, or
> *A*'s *V*-ing would be better in a way than *A*'s doing anything else, or
> Someone has a right that *A V*, or . . . ,

leaving open that other evaluative facts should be added to this list.

What has emerged in the preceding sections is the idea that some of these kinds of fact are good reason to believe that *A* ought to *V*. Indeed, some are themselves conclusive reasons to believe that *A* ought to *V*. Thus the fact that *A*'s not *V*-ing would be unjust, or would be miserly, is conclusive reason to believe that *A* ought to *V*. And some are—not themselves, but in conjunction with other facts—conclusive reasons to believe that A ought to V. Thus the fact that A's V-ing would be better for him than his doing anything else is not itself conclusive reason to believe A ought to V, but the conjunction of it with (Isolation) is.

Suppose we say that wherever there is a fact that is—or is, in conjunction with (Isolation)—conclusive reason to believe that A ought to V, then there is "most reason" for A to V. Then we can say: A ought to V *if* V-ing is what there is most reason for A to do.

Can we also say: A ought to V *only if* V-ing is what there is most reason for A to do? I should think it very plausible that we can. That a person ought to do a thing is not a fact that floats free of anything that might be thought to make it a fact; and what would make it a fact is surely facts of the kinds we have been looking at. Have we have looked at all the relevant kinds? An agent's advantage, where (Isolation) is true, covers a good bit of territory. So does injustice. So does miserliness, understood in the way I have been taking it. (As I said, an act of gratuitous cruelty, inconsiderateness, or discourtesy may be miserly.) But I will not try to argue that there are no others.

In any case, if the stronger claim—namely that A ought to V *if and only if* V-ing is what there is most reason for A to do—is true, then so also is the weaker claim that A ought to V only if there is reason for A to V.

However, the availability of these conclusions turns on our opting for the broad construal of reasons for action. According to the narrow construal, a fact to the effect that A's V-ing would be good in a way is a reason for A to V only if A wants to do something good in that way. Similarly, a fact to the effect that A's not-V-ing would be bad in a way is a reason for A to V only if A wants to avoid doing something bad in that way. For example, the fact that A's not-V-ing would be unjust or miserly is a reason for A to V only if A wants to avoid injustice or miserliness. As I said in Part I, section 13, this narrow construal of reasons for action strikes me as out of accord with our ideas about reasons for action.

But as I also said, I see no theoretically important reason for rejecting this narrow construal. Or for opting for it. Whatever we wish to accomplish in moral theory had better be accomplishable whether we opt for this narrow construal of reasons for action or for the broad one. There is something interesting that motivates opting for the narrow one, and I will discuss it in the following section. It is enough for our purposes to notice here that whether we call the kinds of facts I pointed to above "reasons for A to V" does not really matter. Some of them are—or together with (Isolation) are—conclusive reasons for believing that *A* ought to *V*. *That* is the point important to moral theory.

11.

Why is it that many contemporary moral philosophers have focused on the concept 'reason for action'? Why do many of them think, in particular, that *A* ought to *V* if and only if *V*-ing is what there is most reason for *A* to do? I suggest that that is because they wish to have it turn out that it is always *rational* for a person to do what he ought. Indeed, that rationality requires doing what one ought.

They swim upstream, however. That is because there is a familiar, because attractive, theory of rationality in action according to which *A*'s *V*-ing would be rational if and only if it would satisfy *A*'s wants. More precisely: if and only if it would satisfy *A*'s appropriately restricted wants. As I said in section 3, the restriction excludes merely passing wants, wants due to ignorance, and wants due to improper preference-bending. As I also said in section 3, the fact that *A*'s *V*-ing would satisfy *A*'s appropriately restricted wants cannot be thought sufficient to mark *A*'s *V*-ing as good for him. But it is no surprise that many people suppose that fact is sufficient to mark *A*'s *V*-ing as rational.

If one accepts this familiar theory of rationality in action, then one cannot plausibly also accept that it is always rational for a person to do what he ought. For it is wildly implausible to suppose that wherever a person ought to do a thing, it will also be the case that his doing it would satisfy his wants—even if we appropriately restrict his wants.

So those many contemporary moral philosophers who think that *A* ought to *V* if and only if *V*-ing is what there is most reason for *A* to do— and think this because they wish to have it turn out that it is always rational for a person to do what he ought—have a hard job ahead of them. They need to find an alternative to that familiar theory of rationality in action.

Its very attractiveness is in fact what motivates opting for the narrow construal of reasons for action, according to which a fact is not a reason for action unless the agent has the appropriate wants—thus, for example, that the fact that *A*'s *V*-ing would be good in a certain way is a reason for *A* to *V* only if *A* wants to do something good in that way. If one accepts that familiar theory of rationality in action, then one is very likely to think that a fact is a reason for A to V only if A's acting on it would conduce to the satisfying of A's wants. Moral philosophers who think that A ought to V if and only if V-ing is what there is most reason for A to do need to be able to reject the narrow construal of reasons for action; so (to repeat) they need to find an alternative to that familiar theory of rationality in action.

There surely is some pressure on us, whatever our views about reasons for action, to find an alternative. After all, it would be at a minimum unfortunate to have to agree that Alfred's paying his grocer's bill is irrational if his wants would be better satisfied if he did not. Moreover, we give advice when we say "You ought"; how can it be thought coherent to advise Alfred to pay his grocer's bill in the words "You ought to pay it, though I grant that your paying it would be irrational"?

But what alternative is available? One possibility begins by fixing on the fact that we are taking "ought" to have only one advice sense. We are supposing that its one advice sense is 'all things considered,' where among the things considered is what would be good or bad for the agent. And it might be asked: "How could it be rational to believe that you ought (in that sense) to do a thing, and yet not do it?"[11] One obvious objection to the idea that this couldn't be rational is rebuttable. Thus suppose someone objects that a person might perfectly well believe he ought to do a thing and yet not want to do it, and therefore not do it. A friend of this idea replies: "I don't deny that this is possible, I say only that it is irrational."

Curiously enough, support for the idea can be found in a phenomenon observable in many of those who accept the familiar theory of rationality in action. What I refer to is the fact that they are inclined to resist the idea that a person ought to do a thing when, as it turns out, it would be (on the familiar theory) irrational for him to do it. They are inclined to say that if it would be irrational for the person to do the thing, then it is at a minimum doubtful that he ought to do it. *Nobody* is happy to allow that it might be true to say to Alfred: "You ought to pay your grocer's bill, though your paying it would be irrational."

My own impression, however, is that it just is not clear enough what the dispute between those who accept the familiar theory of rationality in action and those who are in search of an alternative is a dispute *about*. One way in which this unclarity emerges is the following.

Let us look again at reasons for belief. A fact F is a reason for believ-

[11] I am grateful to Robert Streiffer for drawing my attention to this idea.

ing a hypothesis H just in case F counts in favor of H. For F to count in favor of H is for F to lend weight to H. And there is such a thing as a fact's being a conclusive reason for believing a hypothesis: F is a conclusive reason for believing H just in case F entails H. Suppose that F is a conclusive reason for believing H, and thus that F entails H. Then there is a quite clear sense in which it is 'against reason' for a person to believe that there is such a fact as F, while believing that H is false: it is self-contradictory to believe these things.

A fact F is a reason for A to V just in case F counts in favor of A's V-ing. I suggested in Part I that for F to count in favor of A's V-ing is for F to be a fact to the effect that A's V-ing would be good in a way, or that A's not V-ing would be bad in a way, or . . . Is there such a thing as a fact's being a conclusive reason for A to V? Suppose (i) we say that the fact that A ought to V is a conclusive reason for A to V. What could we mean by that? In what sense could it be thought to be 'against reason' for A to fail to V while believing that he ought to? Certainly no fact entails an action; what other sense is available?

I hasten to add that life is no easier for friends of the familiar theory of rationality in action. Suppose (ii) we say that the fact that A's appropriately restricted wants would be satisfied if he Ved is a conclusive reason for A to V. What could we mean by that? In what sense could it be thought to be 'against reason' for A to fail to V while believing that his appropriately restricted wants would be satisfied if he V-ed?[12]

I think that it would pay to notice something further about the familiar theory of rationality in action. Suppose we accept the equally familiar Humean account of explanation of action. (I drew attention to it in Part I, section 11.) Thus suppose we accept that what a person will in fact do is what he believes will most efficiently satisfy his wants. Suppose, last, that Alfred's wants are all appropriately restricted, and that he believes that refraining from paying his grocer's bill will most efficiently satisfy them. The friend of the familiar theory of rationality says that for Alfred to pay his grocer's bill would be irrational. But that can't be right if Hume is right. For if Hume is right, then Alfred's paying his grocer's bill would not be irrational. It would be unintelligible. It would be inexplicable.

Moreover, if we say to Alfred "You ought to pay your grocer's bill,"

---

[12] The questions I am raising in the text here are also raised by the (in my view at best suspect) idea that there is such a thing as practical reasoning which contrasts with theoretical reasoning in the following way: while the conclusion of a bit of theoretical reasoning is a proposition, the conclusion of a bit of practical reasoning is an act.

we are not advising him to do something it would be irrational for him to do. If Hume is right, we are instead advising him to do something his doing of which would be inexplicable. So be it. No doubt we do not give a person advice unless we think, or at least hope, that our doing so will affect his wants and thereby his actions. But alas it is not in the least uncommon for efforts of this kind to fail.

Yet isn't the familiar Humean account of explanation of action at least as attractive as the familiar theory of rationality in action?

There is much more to be said on this topic, but I suggest that we bypass it. For my own part, it seems to me good enough for the central purposes of a moral theorist if it should turn out—as I hope it has turned out—that some of the kinds of facts I pointed to earlier are conclusive reasons for *believing* that A ought to V. Whether they are therefore in some appropriate sense conclusive reasons for A to V is a question we can leave aside.

                              12.

The suggestions I have made obviously do not constitute a theory about what a person ought to do. What I have wanted to do is only to set out some features of the structure that I think such a theory should have. It should take account of the multiplicity of the ways of being good and bad, and it should tell us how the ways of being good and bad bear on what a person ought to do. The resulting theory would of course be more complex than Consequentialism, but that is only to be expected.

Filling the structure in requires supplying an account of what rights people have, and what makes it the case that they have them. I have said almost nothing about that here; I have simply helped myself to the notion of a right, in my characterization of justice and injustice in particular.[13]

More generally, it requires supplying an account of what marks an act as giving or failing to give adequate weight to the interests of all affected by it. I have no such account.

On the other hand, I think it unclear what such an account would have to look like—that is, how much precision should be expected of it. Comparisons between gains by one person and losses by another are no-

---

[13] My own account of these matters appears in *The Realm of Rights*.

toriously difficult. Extreme examples are easy enough to construct: if Alfred gains relief from a sore throat, he gains something, but if Bertha loses her life, she loses markedly more. How much more can be said than that that difference is *sufficiently great* to mark as miserly an act by Alfred by which he relieves his sore throat with a drug he could easily have given to Bertha, who needs it for life? Again, injustice is breach of a non-overridden right, and the question whether a right is non-overridden turns on how stringent the right is, and how good for others infringing the right would be. Extreme examples are easy enough to construct: Bertha's right to not be killed by another is very stringent, and the fact that Alfred would gain relief from a sore throat by an act by which he would kill Bertha does not override Bertha's right.

There plainly is much room for differences in opinion about what counts as giving adequate weight to the interests of all who would be affected. The kind of theory I see the need of cannot be expected to contain an algorithm for settling such disputes. It has to be allowed to contrast much and little, and to invite us to attend to, and to argue by analogy from, particular cases in which it is clear on any view that a gain by one would be large and a loss to another would be small.

Moreover, it seems to me that such a theory should leave open the possibility that some such differences in opinion are not settleable at all. Not just that there may be nothing that will bring the parties to a dispute to come to agreement with each other; rather, more strongly, that there may be no correct answer to the question under dispute. The fact that there are such disputes on moral matters (if there are) should trouble us no less than does the fact that there are unsettleable disputes on nonmoral matters. No less, but also no more.

If we take practical reasoning to be reasoning about what to do, then conducting it well requires making exactly those more-or-less delicate contrasts between much and little and arguing by analogy from them. Allowing for the possibility of unsettleability is allowing for the possibility that in some cases, no conclusion can be shown to be correct. But that leaves plenty of room for cases in which conclusions are reachable— and I see no good reason to think that we are incapable of reaching them when they are.

Spirit Visions

MARINA WARNER

THE TANNER LECTURES ON HUMAN VALUES

Delivered at

Yale University
October 20 and 21, 1999

MARINA WARNER is a historian, novelist, and critic who lives in London. She has been a Getty Scholar at the Getty Research Institute and is the recipient of honorary doctorates from the University of St. Andrews, Scotland, and the University of York, among others. She is currently a visiting professor at Birkbeck College, London, and at Stanford University. Her scholarly and critical works include *Alone of All Her Sex: The Myth and Cult of the Virgin Mary* (1976); *Joan of Arc: The Image of Female Heroism* (1981); *Monuments and Maidens: The Allegory of the Female Form* (1985), which was awarded the Fawcett Prize; *From the Beast to the Blonde: On Fairy Tales and Their Tellers* (1994); and *No Go the Bogeyman: On Scaring, Lulling, and Making Mock* (1998). Her Reith Lectures on BBC radio were published as *Six Myths of Our Time: Little Angels, Little Monsters, Beautiful Beasts, and More* (1995). She also writes fiction, including short stories and two opera libretti. Her novels include *The Lost Father* (1988), which was short-listed for the Booker Prize and which won the Commonwealth Writers' Prize; *Indigo* (1992); and *The Leto Bundle* (forthcoming).

I. THE INNER EYE: FIGURING THE INVISIBLE

Socrates: Didst thou never espy a Cloud in the sky,
            which a centaur or leopard might be?
        Or a wolf or a cow?

Strepsiades: Very often, I vow:
        And show me the cause, I entreat.

Socrates: Why, I tell you that these become just what they please...

Aristophanes, *The Clouds*[1] ca. 420 B.C.

1. FATA MORGANA

Over the straits of Messina between Sicily and Calabria, the enchantress Morgan Le Fay, or, in Italian, Fata Morgana (figure 1), occasionally conjures castles in the air. When the Normans became rulers of southern Italy, they carried with them their cycle of Celtic legends in which Morgan Le Fay figures as a seawitch who ensnares mortals into her palace under the sea.[2] In a later, Italian, legend, she falls in love with a mortal youth and gives him the gift of eternal life in return for her love; when he becomes restless and bored with captivity, she summons up fairy spectacles for his entertainment.[3]

Professor Peter Brooks of the Humanities Research Institute at Yale was a most considerate host for the Tanner Lectures, and I would like to thank him and his staff very much indeed for their support and cheerfulness throughout. I would also like to express my gratitude to Professor Terry Castle, of Stanford University, who responded to this lecture, for her inspired reflections on the topic.

[1] Trans. Benjamin Bickley Rogers (Cambridge, Mass., and London, 1960), lines 345–47.

[2] Thomas Keightley, *The Fairy Mythology* (London, 1910), p. 433; see "Mor-Rioghain," in Daithi O'Hogain, *Myth, Legend, and Romance* (New York, 1991), pp. 307–10; Barbara Walker, *Women's Encyclopaedia of Myths and Secrets* (London, 1983), pp. 674–75.

[3] See Domenico Giardina, "'Discorso sopra la Fata Morgana di Messina,' con alcune note dell'eruditissimo Sig. Andrea Gallo," in *Opuscoli di autori siciliani* (Catania, 1758); Antonio Minasi, "Dissertazione sopra un Fenomeno volgarmente detto Fata Morgana...," in Antonio Minasi, *Dissertazioni* (Rome, 1773); Ippolito Pindemonte, "La Fata Morgana," in *Poemetti Italiani* (Turin, 1797), pp. 144–67.

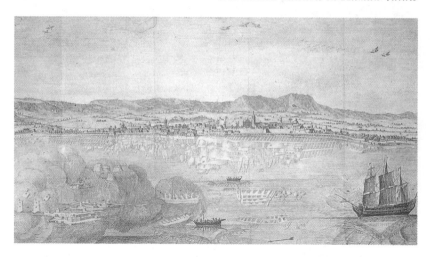

Figure 1. Fata Morgana, Sicily, engraved by Guglielmo Fortuyn, 1773.
(British Library, London)

The Jesuit polymath Athanasius Kircher reports a vision of Fata
Morgana in the second part of his magnum opus, *The Great Art of Light
and Shadow,* published in 1646, where he reprints a letter from a fellow
Jesuit in Sicily, raptly describing a manifestation, on August 15, 1643,
of the spectacular enchantments of Fata Morgana:

> On the morning of the feast of the Assumption of the Most Blessed
> Virgin, standing alone at my window, I saw so many things, and so
> many novelties that I shall never be sated or tired to think on them
> again. It seems to me that the most holy Madonna made appear . . . a
> trace of Paradise that day . . . . The sea that bathes Sicily swelled up
> and became ten miles in length all round, like the crests of a black
> mountain, and the [sea] of Calabria flattened out and appeared in a
> moment the clearest crystal, transparent as a mirror . . . and in this
> mirror there suddenly appeared, in chiaroscuro, a line of more than
> 10,000 columns of equal width and height, all equidistant from one
> another . . . then a moment later, the columns halved their height
> and arched over like certain aqueducts in Rome, or the somersaults
> of Salome.[4]

Kircher was above all a scientist; he turned his back deliberately on
Fata Morgana as magic or miracle and sternly reminded his colleague

[4] Athanasius Kircher, *The Great Art of Light and Shadow* (Rome, 1646), book X, pars II,
p. 704.

that, feast of the Assumption or not, the glimpse of paradise he had seen was a trick of the light. Kircher went on to denounce "necromancers" who are quick to seize "such marvels, produced without any work, as the mockery of demons." Following in the steps of the Italian humanists, he would have no other miracle outside scripture, except the natural, created world. Leon Battista Alberti had personified Nature as the supreme artist ("Natura pictrix") who takes pleasure in making pictures in her own works: on a large scale—faces in rocks, in clouds—and, on a small scale, the skull in the death's head hawkmoth was a favorite example.

Kircher himself collected, for his private museum in Rome, stones and fossils that bore the marks of letters until he had completed the alphabet, as well as adventitious images of the Madonna and child, the crucifixion, and so forth[5]—when the name of Allah is found inscribed in the heart of an aubergine, as happened in Bradford, England, recently, or a tomato, as has also been found, we find ourselves back on highly respectable, hermetic territory.

More than a hundred years later, in 1758, yet another member of the Society of Jesus in Sicily was investigating the illusion of Fata Morgana, and he was still exercised by popular superstition:

> Until now, in a century of so little culture, the spectacle was a matter of great horror to the common people . . . . [6]

Father Domenico Giardina's evocation of the Fata Morgana is both more analytical than his predecessor's and far more extravagantly rococo: "Nature unveils these 'grandi e maravigliosi treatri [*sic*]' [great and marvellous entertainments] without the enormous defects with which art is filled," he writes.[7] Nature here is not only a supreme artist, but knows how to combine Albertian laws of architectural harmony and proportion with a Raphaelesque playfulness in capricious decoration.

[5] Kircher's eclectic accumulation of God's wonders in his private museum was recorded in a magnificent illustrated catalogue: Francisco Mariae Ruspolo, *Musaeum Kircheranium* (Rome, 1709).

[6] "Fin quì lo spettacolo fu alla bassa gente, ed in un secolo sì poco colto, una gran materia d'orrore . . .": Giardina, *Discorso,* p. 122.

[7] The vision includes "a city all floating in the air, and so measureless and so splendid, so adorned with magnificent buildings, all of which was found on a base of a luminous crystal, never beheld before . . ."; this then transformed itself into a forest, and a garden, where the "most capricious figures in the world" were arranged, followed by enormous armies in full battle array, mounted men, prospects of flocks, mountains, half-ruined towns, all disposed "according to the canons of a perfect perspective": Giardina, *Discorso,* pp. 118–34.

Some ascribe the wonder to enchantments, others to a divine miracle, he goes on, but he himself offers a chemical analysis of the minerals and salts in the region—talc, selenite, antimony, glass—which rise up in hot weather in vapors from the sea to form clouds, which then condense in the cooler upper air to become a *mobile specchio,* a moving, polyhedrical mirror.[8] He emphasizes the effects of fire and brimstone, which create the illusion of columns, arches, pyramids, and pinnacles in infinite recession and distinguishes these from what he calls *l'iride fregiata,* the festooned rainbow. Giardina relates the spectacle to the aurora borealis, or Northern Lights. But the rainbow also offers an orthodox metaphor for insubstantial presence that inspires, for example, Dante's ingenious invocation of the aethereal nature of ghosts. In Purgatorio 25, Virgil carefully expounds the Thomist view of the immortal soul, and to describe the condition of the shades of the departed, he draws on metaphors of elements in play, of rays refracted through vapors and imbuing them with color, and then of flames forming shapes as they move:

> e come l'aere, quand'è ben pïorno,
>   per l'altrui raggio che 'n se si reflette,
>   di diversi color diventa adorno;
>   così l'aere vicin quivi si mette
>   in quella forma che in lui suggella
>   virtualmente l'alma che ristette;
>   e simigliante poi alla fiammella
>   che segue il foco la 'vunque si muta,
>   segue lo spirto sua forma novella.
>   Però che quindi ha poscia sua paruta
>   è chiamata ombra. . . .[9]

Ingeniously conjured from effects of light, insubstantial and incorporeal, yet endowed with presence and sense, Dante's prismatic wraiths approximate to the enchantments of the Fata Morgana. And this condition of the soul that Dante describes eerily foreshadows the insubstantial state of a photograph, or, more particularly, of a slide projection as in the magic lantern show: light and color hanging in the air, flames dancing, without body, but visible—Fata Morgana.

[8] Ibid., pp. 133–34.

[9] Purgatorio 25, lines 94–101. Translated by John D. Sinclair, *The Divine Comedy of Dante Alighieri* (London, 1958), p. 329: "and as the air, when it is full of rain, becomes adorned with various colors through another's beams that are reflected in it, so the neighboring air sets itself into that form which the soul that stopped there stamps upon it by its power, and then like the flame that follows the fire wherever it shifts, its new form follows the spirit. Since it has by this its semblance henceforth, it is called a shade . . . ."

2. SIGNS AND WONDERS

The visionary tendency of Judaeo-Christianity probes the heavens to discern therein the workings of divine providence, and Fata Morgana can be connected to other signs and wonders of a meteorological nature in the Bible—the rainbow after the flood, the pillar of cloud through the desert, the shekinah hovering over the Ark of the Covenant, the writing on the wall at Balshazzar's Feast, the darkness at noon, the cloud enveloping Christ's body at his ascension.

More particularly, in the Second Book of Maccabees, for example, in the midst of the heroic resistance of the Jews to Roman oppression, during the battle that took place in 164 B.C.:

> As the fighting grew hot, the enemy saw in the sky five magnificent figures riding horses with golden bridles, who placed themselves at the head of the Jews, formed a circle around Maccabaeus, and kept him invulnerable under the protection of their armour. They launched arrows and thunderbolts at the enemy, who, confused and blinded, broke up in complete disorder.[10]

The field where Judas Maccabaeus triumphed against the odds was famously echoed in crusader history, when visions of Saints George, Demetrios, and Mercury appeared to the besieged at Antioch during the First Crusade. Many later episodes include a phantom army seen fighting in the sky above Verviers in Belgium in June 1815, a little before the Battle of Waterloo took place nearby, and, most famously of all, "The Angels of Mons," who mustered in the clouds overhead to support the Tommies in the trenches in World War I, wrapped them in cloud to give them shelter, and even inflicted inexplicable *arrow* wounds on the Germans. The stories spread rapidly, by word of mouth, and thereafter through press reports, psychic journals, purported eyewitness memoirs, and films, including Cecil B. de Mille's *Joan the Woman,* which opens with a scene set in the fields of Flanders, with angelic warriors, including Joan of Arc, overhead.[11] Legends of celestial apparitions persist to this day: in one of the most recent instances, the Virgin Mary was found

---

[10] II Maccabees 10: 29–31. Later in the campaign, during the subsequent bitter siege, another divine horseman appears in the sky, "arrayed in white, brandishing his golden weapons," and again, this heavenly ally leads the Jews to victory, against the host of the enemy with his thousands of warriors, some of them mounted on elephants: II Maccabees 11: 8–12.

[11] The legends were sparked by a short story written by the popular occultist Arthur Machen in the *London Evening News* in August 1914. He followed this, the same year, with a

in a "spontaneous photograph" taken circa 1985 of the sky above the Monte Gargano, the shrine of Padre Pio.

The term "Fata Morgana" came to be applied to spectral illusions more generally, to hallucinations and eidetic images, fantasies formed in and by the mind's eye. Thomas Carlyle said of the poet Samuel Taylor Coleridge that he "preferred to create lyrical fatamorganes for himself on his hither side."[12] Later, the word is used again with the explicit sense of ominous portent in the original, faery metaphor, the artist and writer Alfred Kubin, for example, even using it for the horror of the Nazi era.[13]

In this first lecture, I explore how a mirage (Fata Morgana) casts clouds as veils or gauzes—as "airy films"[14]—on which phantom wonders appear, and how the pursuit of fantasy, in meditating on fluid, evanescent, arbitrary forms, presents an important strand in the story of the Imagination. The interaction between the signs and wonders of scripture and mythology and technical processes and contrivances, from the magic lantern to the phantasmagorias of late-eighteenth- and nineteenth-century entertainment, to today's cinematic special effects and virtual reality, is highly dynamic, and certainly cannot be assumed to be altogether fortuitous. But the very word "film" builds on the physical similarities of vapor and the medium of the movies.

Clouds are interfused with anagogic ideas of the highest heaven, the aether; they mark out the space of the world above, creating pontoons and bridges between the two spheres, human and divine; they are vectors of otherworldly beings from heavenly realms; they pun, with dream wordplay, on the nature of spirits. Clouds, vapor, smoke, foam, steam, and their spirituous, sublimed counterparts among airy, misty, gaseous substances have served to make manifest the invisible, supernatural, imponderable, and ineffable according to the promptings of belief and fantasy. Clouds and cloudiness offer a magical passkey to the labyrinth of unknowable mysteries, outer and inner. And they operate all unconsciously, sometimes at the most patent levels, as a perennial visual and verbal expression for inner space.

---

volume called *The Bowmen and Other Legends of the War* (London, 1915): see his introduction, followed by the story itself, ibid., pp. 1–38.

[12] Thomas Carlyle, *Sterling* 1.viii.78; *Oxford English Dictionary.*

[13] Alfred Kubin, *The Other Side,* trans. Denver Lindley (London, 1969).

[14] [Attrib. C. Taylor] *Landscape Magazine* (1793): 84–87; I am grateful to Anne Lyles of the Tate Gallery, London, for bringing this description to my attention.

For example, even in a popular form, the comic strip, the British cartoonist Posy (Simmonds) uses various frames to indicate different inner visions of her heroine Gemma Bovery: internal cursing ("uuh... Patrick... bastard!...") and insomniac phantoms; fantasies of domestic bliss (hiding with a baby in a rural idyll); or dreams of romantic ravishings by her lost love. Significantly, these last are contained within a thought bubble, a fleecy cloud shape with scattered flakes. This cartoonist's device remains the most direct, conventional way of conveying to the reader that these are the products of the heroine's inner eye.

Whiteness, vaporousness, filminess, insubstantiality: spirits are literally a *cloudy* matter. The imagery of the "animula vagula blandula... pallidula...nudula [Dear little fleeting pleasing little soul...pale little...naked little thing]," in the Emperor Hadrian's image, endures with variations, through Thomist theology to fairy legends.[15] *Corpus sed non caro* (body but not flesh): so did Saint Augustine define the substance of angels, and this impossible conjunction can be extended to convey departed souls and spirits. In representations, light, as both radiance and weightlessness, buoys the spiritual or aetheric body, incorporated but not enfleshed, and renders it at once palpable and insubstantial.

Nebulousness has served to meet a need for expressing the bourne beyond which matter still materializes, but not as body, or, if within its bourne, the forms and shapes it takes. In his last, despairing entreaty, Christopher Marlowe's Doctor Faustus turns from one power to another to escape the fires of hell. When he begs his birth stars to come to his aid, he stirs a strange brew of cloudy vapors to describe how his soul might be hidden and saved:

> Now draw up Faustus, like *a foggy mist,*
> Into the entrails of yon lab'ring clouds,
> That, when you vomit forth into the air,
> My limbs may issue from your smoky mouths,
> So that my soul may but ascend to heaven![16]

This compacted meteorological vision casts dying Faustus as a vapor, drawn up by the heat of the stars to be swallowed up by clouds figured as women's wombs. These stars are also endowed with mouths that can

[15] *The Penguin Book of Latin Verse,* trans. Frederick Brittain (Harmondsworth, 1962), p. 61.

[16] Christopher Marlowe, *Dr. Faustus,* ed. A. H. Sleight (Cambridge, 1961), Sc. 14, lines 92–96 (emphasis added).

both breathe and spew; Faustus seems to be begging to be turned into a fine rain that might issue from the clouds, but be too misty, too light, to fall to earth so might rather rise, like high cirrus to the upper heaven. The contortions of the image sequence reflect dramatically the agonizing of the doomed magus only half an hour before his death.

In a lighter vein, John Dryden and William Davenant's intriguing and much performed revision of *The Tempest, The Enchanted Island,* written in 1669, also evokes the soul through metaphors of breath and condensation, as in this exchange between two of its beguiling *ingénus:*

Dorinda:	But I much wonder what it is to dye.
Hippolito:	Sure 'tis to dream, a kind of breathless sleep.
	When once the Soul's gone out.
Dorinda:	What is the Soul?
Hippolito:	A small blew thing that runs about within us.
Dorinda:	Then I have seen it in a frosty morning run
	Smoaking from my mouth.
Hippolito:	But if my soul had gone, it should have walk'd upon
	A Cloud just over you, and peep'd . . . [17]

It is not only Christian souls or the angels of orthodoxy whose nature lends itself to nebulous metaphor. The Reverend Robert Kirk, a Scottish antiquarian and divine, described the nature of Fairies, in his intimate guide to the supernatural, *The Secret Common-Wealth of Elves, Fauns and Fairies,* of around 1692. They were

> intelligent Studious Spirits, and light changable bodies (lyke those called Astrall) somewhat of the nature of a condens'd cloud, and best seen in twilight. These bodies be so plyable thorough the subtilty of the spirits, that agitate them, that they can make them appear and disappear at pleasure. Some have bodies or vehicles so spungious, thin . . . that they are fed by only sucking into some fine spirituous liquors . . . . [18]

In the seventeenth century, clouds are widely accepted, in both visual and poetic works, as the departed soul's appropriate vehicle.

---

[17] John Dryden with William Davenant, *The Enchanted Island,* in *The Works of John Dryden* (Berkeley and London, 1970), vol. 10, Act V, Sc. ii, lines 16–25.

[18] R. Kirk, *The Secret Common-Wealth & A Short Treatise of Charms & Spells,* ed. Stewart Sanderson (London, 1976), pp. 49–50. Kirk was stolen by the fairies, or so it was widely reported and later recorded by Sir Walter Scott.

The story I am going to tell in these two lectures will proceed along two complementary paths: first, oracular cloud effects such as Fata Morgana are dynamically related to the development of optical instruments, from the magic lantern, called camera obscura, to the movie camera, and they have influenced the scope and character of visual media. As I hope to show, the wonders of the rainbow, mirages, and other cosmic effects of weather and climate provide the vehicles for communicating spectral nature and presence and have interacted with innovatory, technical means of expression and influenced their development.

Joel Snyder has argued, in an important essay,[19] that optical devices were invented and modified in order to deliver images that fitted Albertian and Vitruvian ideals; this quest culminated in the photographic camera, which did not and does not function as a trusty replicator of human visual experience or beheld, experiential reality. Extending Snyder's view into the realm of fantasy, I am going to propose here that optical and other technical means were also developed to reproduce mental or eidetic images, that these came arrayed in metaphorical vesture that served to communicate the conditions of supernatural other worlds and their creatures. They succeeded by obeying axioms embedded in religious iconography, in mythological visual narratives, and in speculation about the function and character of the Imagination and of the senses, especially the visualizing faculties. Models of mind, as proposed in the sixteenth and seventeenth centuries by a range of philosophers and mystics, drew the terrain for picturing visions that did not present themselves to the eyes of the body.

My second principal line of argument focuses on the historical character of signs: even something as cloudy as a cloud has a changing story to tell within the history of signs and of the language of value, so I will be trying to convey how wonder and the sublime themselves have shape-shifted. Clouds have acted as a predominant metaphoric vehicle for spirit, but, like all figures in a semiotic vocabulary, they are intertwined with temporal context, with epistemologic, scientific, and social developments, which can extend, or narrow, their meaning. Thus a Coleridgean commitment to the powers of Imagination will lead, along one line of psychological development, to the Rorschach test,[20] while

---

[19] Joel Snyder, "Picturing Vision," *Critical Quarterly* 6 (1980): 499–526.

[20] In the mid-nineteenth century, Justinus Kerner proposed that ink blots could be used to prompt psychological revelations; Herman Rorschach then developed the theme with a series of ten test cards to serve as stimuli: the Rorschach test entails precisely finding mean-

analysis of the aether will precipitate, in turn of the century seances, the phenomenon of ectoplasm.

3. "VERY LIKE A WHALE..."

The game of descrying shapes in the skies, faces in the clouds, and images in stones, according to the complementary vagaries of individual reverie, should be distinguished from the effects of weather, the causes of rainbows, the so-called Brocken spectre, St. Elmo's fire, will-o'-the-wisps, foxfire, ignis fatuus, and other Fata Morganas. But their very names, endowing phenomena with supernatural origins, reveal how it is in practice difficult to keep the experiences distinct, how subjective dreaming alters the experience of the natural event. As Nature abhors a vacuum, so does the mind resist meaninglessness, accord stories to haphazard incident, invent reasons and origins, mythical etiologies; the amorphous, the inchoate, the formless have beckoned irresistibly to the shaping powers of thought and fantasy.

Reflecting on "the image made by chance," H. W. Janson distinguished between two ways of seeing: the first, as famously invoked by Alberti, describes the artist discovering, within the stone or other material, the body inscribed there by nature—a procedure Michelangelo's *Slaves* most powerfully and eloquently embody.[21] Janson associates this approach with mimesis, because the sculptor is trying to deliver something believed to be already there: the figure in the marble, the faces in the rock. Gutzon Borglum, the sculptor of Mount Rushmore, would study rocks for days and nights, sleeping in the mountains until the image formed; he also borrowed Native American interpretations of landmarks, peaks, and other features. It could be said that his mammoth monuments represent the terminus and the nadir of this method.[22] But

---

ings where there is nothing except random marks, and it applied the results for medical diagnosis of character. See Bruno Klopfer and Douglas McGlashan Kelley, *The Rorschach Technique: A Manual for a Projective Method of Personality Diagnosis* (Yonkers-on-Hudson, 1942).

[21] "The 'Image Made by Chance' in Renaissance Thought," in *De Artibus Opuscula,* vol. 40, *Essays in Honor of Erwin Panofsky,* ed. Millard Meiss (New York, 1961), pp. 254–68.

[22] Cf. Robert J. Dean, *Living Granite: The Story of Borglum and the Mount Rushmore Memorial* (New York, 1949), p. 32: Borglum's abortive sculpture of General Lee was inspired by "studying the formation of the rocks, watching the effects of light and shadow on the face of the cliff at various times of day. And on the third day, toward evening, when there was a pale young moon in the sky, he seemed to see the shades of a gray Confederate host, with Robert E. Lee, Stonewall Jackson, and Jefferson Davis, stealing across the great expanse of rock in gigantic proportions...." This memorial was never finished, but Borglum carried the idea on with him to Mount Rushmore.

a book of photographs, recently published in England, continues this primitivist and esoteric tradition, discerning secret faces in the ancient megalithic circles and avenues of stones at Avebury in Wiltshire.[23] The author and photographer Terence Meaden does not rule out the possibility that these might be among the very earliest intentional figurative carvings.

The second way of making images organizes them through the power of *fantasia:* seeing shapes in clouds, on rocks, that Nature has not put there. The most patent and most ancient evidence of this arbitrary and mythopoeic faculty lies far beyond the province of art, in the enduring and wonderful ancient fantasies of starmaps, which link up the random scattering of the skies into pictures and stories—the constellations, the Zodiac.

Janson concludes that today "we have [thus] at last resolved the ancient Greek dichotomy of *mimesis* and *fantasia* by assigning each of them to its own separate domain." I would like to modulate this stark contrast, by exploring how mimetic picturing itself depends on a language of signs that is rooted in the work of the imagination with analogy, metaphor, and associations. In the struggle to represent the unseen, to figure spirit, men and women considered they were mimetists, turning the lens of empiricism on hidden forms, deciphering existing and inherent secrets and codes; however, as I hope to show, their *fantasia* led them, and it in turn was shaped by diverse, buried codes as well.

Reading what the contemporary American poet Charles Edward Eaton has called the sky's "secret album of nephographs"[24] has a very ancient history indeed: on the one hand, Aristophanes mocks it gleefully and mercilessly in *The Clouds,* a satire on philosophy's arbitrariness and vagueness. But on the other, taking a cue from Lucretius, Leonardo da Vinci finds in the contemplation of formlessness a crucial stimulus. In two entries in his Notebooks (later appearing in the edited *Treatise on Painting* in around 1550) Leonardo advocated the scrying of stains on walls, or the ashes of a fire, or mottled and grainy stones, or mud, or clouds—the list drifts through "like things" that are formless and, he writes later, "*confused,*" inscrutable in themselves for they are intrinsically meaningless. They will, however, offer the subjective fantasy "una nuova invenzione di speculazione [a new invention of speculation]" by

---

[23] Terence Meaden, *The Secrets of the Avebury Stones, Britain's Greatest Megalithic Temple* (London, 1999).

[24] Charles Edward Eaton, "Cloud Pictures," *Sewanee Review* 92, no. 4 (1984): 534.

which "if you consider them well, you will find really marvellous ideas."[25] Elsewhere, Leonardo cites Sandro Botticelli as an advocate of following the prompts and biddings of *fantasia:* "Our Botticelli said, that such study [of landscape] was vain, because by merely throwing a sponge full of diverse colors at a wall, it left a stain on that wall, where a fine landscape was seen."[26] The Paduan philosopher Pietro Pomponazzi (1462–1524) openly yoked the power of dreaming with meteorological and optical illusions: "If one admits that apparitions can be produced in dreams, one must give credence to the possibility that they can also be produced in the atmosphere."[27]

Shakespeare invokes this type of daydreaming both in *Anthony and Cleopatra* ("Sometime we see a cloud that's dragonish . . .") and in *Hamlet* when Hamlet ribs Polonius, exposing the old courtier's slipperiness and duplicity:

Hamlet:	Do you see yonder cloud that's almost in shape of a camel?
Polonius:	By th'mass, and 'tis like a camel indeed.
Hamlet:	Methinks it is like a weasel.
Polonius:	It is back'd like a weasel.
Hamlet:	Or like a whale?
Polonius:	Very like a whale.[28]

In *The Tempest,* Prospero's art—his "insubstantial pageant"—not only harks back to Faustus's conjurings, but also hints at Fata Morganatic effects that may reflect contemporary stagecraft.[29] It is worth noting that Shakespeare, who was sparing with stage directions, twice specifies the pixilating paradox that Ariel, that airy spirit, "enters, invisible."

Ideas of conjuration and magical illusion were intertwined with conceptions of mental or eidetic images, produced in the mind's eye by fantasy.

[25] Leonardo da Vinci, *Treatise on Painting,* ed. and trans. Philip McMahon (Princeton, 1956), vol. 1, pp. 50–51.

[26] Ibid., p. 59.

[27] Pietro Pomponazzi, "Des causes des merveilles de la Nature ou des Enchantements," quoted in Jurgis Baltrusaitis, *Le Miroir, essai sur une légende scientifique; révélations, science-fiction et fallacies* (Paris, 1978), p. 63.

[28] *Hamlet,* Act III, Sc. 2.

[29]   and, like the baseless fabric of this vision,
The cloud-capped towers, the gorgeous palaces,
The solemn temples, the great globe itself . . .

4. THE EYE OF THE IMAGINATION

Robert Fludd was an Oxford esoteric philosopher and one of the leading Rosicrucians; he published his thoughts about human consciousness and its relationship to the macrocosm of divine creation in his spell-binding book *Utriusque Cosmi* (Of the Other World) in 1617–21, a decade after *The Tempest*. The magnificent illustrations (figure 2) were probably devised by the author in collaboration with the great engraver-printer Theodore de Bry.

In the beautiful plate entitled "Vision of the Triple Soul in the Body," Fludd has disposed the faculties in haloes around the profile of a man with suitably enlarged and sensitive external organs: a luminous single eye, a prominent ear, a hand raised to display the fingertips, swollen sensual lips. The senses radiate into a series of concentric circles, and these are hyphenated to a constellation of *animae*, or souls, inside the cranium: on the left is the sensitive soul, of which the circumference is interlaced with the imaginative soul. Another bridge or hyphen leads upward from this to another planetary system, the world of the Imagination (*Mundus imaginabilis*), where, in good Neoplatonist fashion, all is shadow—the rings of this system, the *Umbra Terrae*, or shadow of the World, are all shadows of the elements. Fludd writes, "[This] soul [is] called the imaginative soul, or fantasy or imagination itself; since it beholds not the true pictures of corporeal or sensory things, but their likenesses and as it were, their shadows."[30]

One of the most remarkable illustrations places an eye over the exact position of the imaginative soul in the earlier diagram. The *oculus imaginationis,* or eye of the Imagination (figure 3), radiates a tableau of images: a tower (of Babel?), a guardian angel showing the way, an obelisk, a two-masted ship on a high sea, and the Last Judgment with Christ in glory on a rainbow among trumpeting angels while the dead rise with supplicating hands.

These images belong to various orders of representation, based on memory or Imagination, but it is clear that the inner eye in Fludd's Neoplatonist conception does not receive images: it projects them onto

---

Shall dissolve,
And like this insubstantial pageant faded,
Leave not a rack behind.
(*The Tempest*, Act IV, Sc. 1)

[30] Robert Fludd, *Utriusque Cosmi,* 2 vols. (Oppenheim, 1617–21), vol. 2, p. 218.

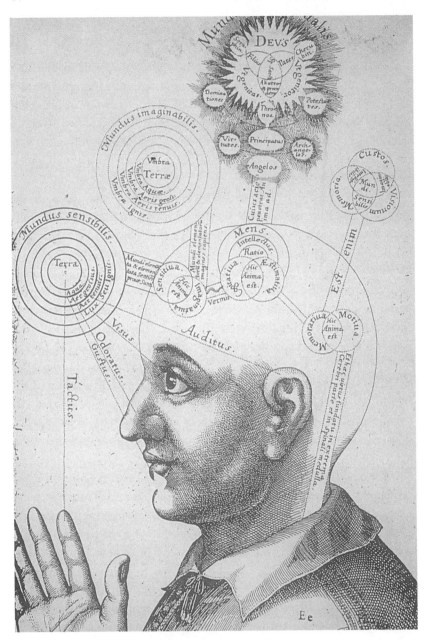

Figure 2. "Vision of the Triple Soul in the Body," from Robert Fludd, *Utriusque Cosmi,* 1617–21. (London Library, London)

Figure 3. "The Eye of the Imagination," from Robert Fludd, *Utriusque Cosmi.*
(London Library, London)

Figure 4. A magic lantern, called camera obscura, from Athanasius Kircher, *Ars Magna Lucis et Umbrae* (Rome, 1646). (Bill Douglas Centre, University of Exeter)

a screen that lies beyond the back of the head, floating in a space that does not exist except in fantasy.

Athanasius Kircher, a generation younger than Fludd, knew his work, and its direct influence can be felt in *The Great Art of Light and Shadow* (Rome, 1646). The illustrations of the magic lantern are the earliest extant of this device, and for a long time Kircher was credited with inventing it. He does not claim to have done so, but he describes his pioneering experiments, when he prepared glass slides with salts and chemicals for the shows he gave in the Jesuit College in Rome.[31] The engraving in *Ars Magna* (figure 4) contains certain elementary errors that make it certain that Kircher himself did not oversee the artist at work: for example, the painted slides would need to be upside down in the projector in order to appear right side up on the wall, as illustrated clearly elsewhere in the book, in one of the first edition's many optical diagrams.

---

[31] The initial invention of the instrument is now attributed to a contemporary of his, the brilliant Dutch horologist and astronomer Christian Huygens.

But illustrations of the magic lantern's prototypes have a significant feature in common: the subjects in the images projected cannot be seen with the eye of the body, except in representations by artists. The subjects in these examples of visual phenomena are fantastic, and they give that certain frisson of the grotesque, designed to excite fear as well as pleasure. These are images that *ipso facto* connote the visions of the mind's eye, and in order to do so they draw on a supernatural lexicon. They depict hallucinations. It is hardly an accident that a naked soul in the flames of hell or purgatory appeared burning on the slide projected onto the wall or that Death was shown as an animated skeleton with the scythe of the reaper and the hourglass of Father Time. An engraving published in Leiden in 1720–21 also included an illustration of an early slide projector, and, despite the learned and scientific title of the mathematical treatise in which it appears, it showed a huge, magnificent devil leering on the wall. The device was thought to reproduce the mind's capacity to fabricate what the eyes of the body cannot see.

Athanasius Kircher's seances were attended, in the Jesuit College in Rome, by cardinals and grandees who gathered to witness "what was known, in jest," writes his fellow Jesuit Giardina later, "as the enchantments of the reverend father . . . ."[32] But the later Jesuit's uneasiness is well grounded, for Kircher significantly chose to project supernatural images, and in this he comes perilously close to the goety, or black magic, denounced by the Inquisition in his own day. One Inquisitor, writing in 1641 (i.e., during Kircher's heyday), gives a full inventory of the disruption and mayhem that the rebel angels create. In the midst of a terrifying and overheated litany of evil and catastrophe, the Inquisitor instances metamorphoses of animal and human bodies. But these are not changed in their substance, "sed aliam ex vaporibus extrinsecus circumponendo . . . [but only by *investing them in another aspect, composed of extrinsic vapors . . .*]."[33]

Cloudy vapors figure strongly in his account of the phantasmic powers of Imagination. Kircher explores the dominant metaphor of a screen and then two dependent metaphors: first, the blackened surface of a mirror, and, second, the smoky and boiling vapors in the brain of a person afflicted with melancholy. He borrowed the image of the mirror

[32] Giardina, *Discorso,* p. 140.

[33] Cesare Carena, *Tractatus De Officio Sanctissimae Inquisitionis* (Cremona, 1641), pp. 217–18, quoted in Maurice Slawinski, "Marino, le streghe, il cardinale," kindly lent by the author, forthcoming in *Italian Studies.*

from optics and the image of the inchoate and turbulent spirits from explanations of cosmic origin in hermetic physics, as represented in Fludd's work; it is not clear how metaphorically he intends their application to the mind.

These means of the imaginative soul (the play of shadows, the opaque surface of a mirror, and vaporous swirling clouds—for producing and rendering fantasy) return as palpable, physical instruments of projection in the first cinematic public entertainment, the phantasmagoria. Its subject matter was spectral illusion, morbid, frequently macabre, supernatural, fit to inspire terror and dread, those qualities of the sublime, and it enjoyed terrific popularity from the end of the eighteenth century, in Paris just after the Terror, until the invention of true moving cinema displaced it. The association between diabolical phantoms and spectral phenomena influenced the content and material of optical illusions and shaped the characteristic uses and development of those varied and wonderful technological devices that have been used to represent the supernatural, to make present what eludes the senses and to make visible the invisible.

Etienne-Gaspard Robertson was the brilliant innovator in this proto-cinema: he thought of blacking out the background, and coating the gauze with wax to give it greater translucency, and putting the projector on rollers (figure 5). Audiences accepted an unspoken, unexamined equivalence between the ghosts, skeletons, bleeding nuns, and ghouls that a burning lamp, flickering smoke, a series of mirrors and lenses, and a painted transparency can project and the invisible screen on which the mind casts its own envisionings, be they fantasized or recalled through memory. This equivalence recurs in the development of optical languages that culminate in the conventions of contemporary media from cinematic voice-overs, flashbacks, and dream sequences.[34] Robertson also projected onto smoke. In one slide, for example, the eerie head of Danton, recently guillotined, rose flickeringly, like his shade.

As Terry Castle points out so inspiringly in *The Female Thermometer,* the uncanny took a turn away from external, supernatural, and mysteri-

[34] Early cinema drifted, as if naturally, to depicting the inner world of Imagination. Think of the pioneer Georges Méliès, who filmed a journey to the moon as well as the frolics of fairies, or great silent movies such as Robert Wiene's *The Cabinet of Dr. Caligari* (1919) and F. W. Murnau's vampire film *Nosferatu* (1921).

Figure 5. The phantasmagoria of Etienne-Gaspard Robertson, Paris, 1790s, in a contemporary engraving. From John Barnes, "The History of the Magic Lantern," *New Magic Lantern Journal* 1/1, no. 3/2 (1984): 29. It also appears in Laurent Mannoni's *Le Grand Art de la lumière et de l'ombre* (Paris, 1994). (Bill Douglas Centre, University of Exeter)

ous causes of dread and terror, earthed to a common religious faith, and began to inhabit instead unstable, internal hallucinations, seething with personal, idiosyncratic monsters extruded from the overheated brain by the force of vehement Imagination, or, as Goya would write on the opening *Capricho,* with monsters generated by the dream of reason. Even supposedly natural wonders, which became a favorite theme with magic lanternists, take on a fantastic appearance. Icy vistas, with heaped snowbanks and aurora borealis (figure 6), as painted by a London firm in the second half of the nineteenth century, partake, I think, of the character of Fata Morgana.[35]

The sublime spectral cinema of meteorology, evoked in different works of early Romanticism, disquietingly and even thrillingly disturbs the grounds on which the question of a phenomenon's internal or external nature can be decided. The undecided, debatable relationship of the visionary to the vision, of witness to portent, of the scryer to the encrypted message or the scrying mirror, still vexes arguments about

[35] "Icebergs," ca. 1860, and "Aurora Borealis," ca. 1900, Carpenter and Wesley, London, in the Whipple Museum, University of Cambridge.

Figure 6. Icebergs, from magic lantern slides, made by Carpenter & Wesley, London, mid-nineteenth century. (Whipple Museum, University of Cambridge)

memory and fantasy, with regard to phantasmagoric revelations of childhood ordeals, for example. This unsettled problem is grounded in the anxiety about diabolical origins and gained extension, depths, and strength from images of doubles, shadow selves, spirit enchantments, summonings, and hallucinations in early Romantic writings of the celebrated, heroic, and haunted poets, Coleridge, Percy Bysshe Shelley, Victor Hugo, and Alfred de Musset, but also, very markedly, in the work of lesser-known writers like Thomas Lovell Beddoes and James Hogg. The book I am going to concentrate on here is James Hogg's *The Private Memoirs and Confessions of a Justified Sinner,* written in 1824.

5. HALOES OF GLORY

James Hogg communicates a metaphysical thriller of a plot in a language wrought from the stinging rhythms and rhetoric of Low Church
liturgy, compounded by the ghastly, eerie fairy lore of the Highlands
and a Coleridgean intensity of fantasy. His hectic and macabre novel
splits and doubles itself, its themes, and its characters. Two texts, one
following the other, are written from two different points of view;
narrating the same terrible story, they contradict each other here and
there, forming an asymmetrical diptych, all the more compelling for its
discordancy and conflicts. These two versions stage the fatal enmity of
two brothers, George, who is fair of face and sanguine of temper, and
Robert, saturnine, fanatical, and malignant, brought up in a blazing,
antinomian extreme conviction that the "justified sinner" who has been
saved can do no wrong. In his pride, Robert acquires—attracts? gener-
ates?—a mysterious mentor and benefactor who encourages him to
believe in his irrecusable salvation and goads him and cajoles him into
an ever deeper and more violent hatred of his brother. Hogg bores deep
into the theme of paired opposites, who, while distinct as well as repellent to each other, may be at the same time symbiotically interdependent (like north and south, black and white). George finds himself
continually accompanied by his brother:

> Yet he had never sat or stood many minutes till there was the self-
> same being, always in the same position with regard to himself, as
> regularly as the shadow is cast from the substance, or the ray of light
> from the opposing denser medium.[36]

The optics in these similes will recur. Meanwhile Robert, too, is being
shadowed, by his Mephistophelean mentor.

Hogg stages one of the novel's climactic struggles between the two
brothers in the open, elevated ground of Arthur's Seat, near Edinburgh,
on a radiant morning. The scene, with its phantasmagoric epiphanies,
its violent, near fatal encounter, and its hallucinatory multiplication of
the *doppelgänger* figure, fuses modern dilemmas about the stability of
the self with visual metaphors of meteorological wonders and optical

---

[36] James Hogg, *The Private Memoirs and Confessions of a Justified Sinner,* ed. John Carey
(Oxford, 1999), p. 36.

illusion. An analogous wonder to the Fata Morgana here unfolds as natural prodigy and spectral fantasy at once, an objective epiphany of the
sublime and an interior nightmare wrought by personal devils.

George has ascended onto the brilliant illuminated summit partly to
evade the constant unwelcome attendance of his brother:

> As he approached the swire at the head of the dell, —...he beheld,
> to his astonishment, a bright halo in the cloud of haze, that rose in a
> semi-circle over his head like a pale rainbow. He was struck motion-
> less at the view of the lovely vision; for it so chanced that he had
> never seen the same appearance before, though common at early
> morn. But he soon perceived the cause of the phenomenon, and that
> it proceeded from the rays of the sun from a pure unclouded morning
> sky striking upon this dense vapour which refracted them.[37]

He continues to draw nearer, and the delicious morning vision changes:

> Gracious Heaven! What an apparition was there presented to his
> view! He saw, delineated in the cloud, the shoulders, arms, and fea-
> tures of a human being of the most dreadful aspect. The face was the
> face of his brother, but dilated to twenty times the natural size. Its
> dark eyes gleamed on him through the mist....
>
> George conceived it to be a spirit. He could conceive it to be noth-
> ing else; and he took it for some horrid demon by which he was
> haunted, that had assumed the features of his brother in every linea-
> ment, but in taking on itself human form, had miscalculated dread-
> fully on the size, and presented itself thus to him in a blown-up,
> dilated frame of embodied air, exhaled from the caverns of death or
> the regions of devouring fire.[38]

When it comes nearer, George flings himself upon it, only to find
that it is "a *real* body of flesh and blood," his fearsome brother Robert,
who cries "Murder." Then, "...being confounded between the shadow
and the substance, [George] knew not what he was doing or what he had
done...." He assaults the demon shape—an act that will land him
with a charge of attempted murder and precipitate the tortuous and terrible sequence of events that leads to his death.[39]

[37] Ibid., pp. 39–40.

[38] Ibid., pp. 41–42.

[39] In the second half of the novel, Robert's first-person account of his misdeeds, he also
describes the violent encounter in the clouds: he goes there, at the urging of his evil genius,
to kill his brother. He too there suffers visions: a woman in white appears to him out of the
mist and upbraids him for his evil intentions, but Robert's "prince" and "counselor" rema-
terializes on the instant and, in archaic, lofty tones, orders his minion not to be so faint-
hearted, but to throw his wretch of a brother from the pinnacle into "the foldings of the
cloud."

James Hogg footnotes his protagonist's vision on the mountain, saying that "this terrestrial phenomenon of the early morn cannot be better
delineated than by the name given of it by the shepherd boys, 'The little
wee ghost of the rainbow.'" But Hogg was very likely familiar with
magic lantern spectacles that were popularly touring the country then:
Phillip de Philipstahl, known as Philidor, staged his phantasmagorias
in Edinburgh in 1802, raising many ghosts, spectres, bleeding nuns,
and the like to the terror of his audiences.[40] He had also sought out a so-
called Brocken spectre, as a certain mountain phenomenon was known:
it "appeared to my affrighted imagination as the enemy of mankind."[41]
But *The Confessions* does not share the rationalist stance of the galanty
men, who liked to claim that they spooked the public merely to show
how vain such fears were. Hogg's vision occurs early in the novel and
embodies the character of the book, for it is not possible to know what
George experienced exactly, what he sees, who is possessed, who is
haunted.

Hogg knew Coleridge's work well, and his halo of glory interestingly reclaims the phenomenon for a more profound psychological uncanny than the older poet's use of it. Coleridge, on a walking tour of
Germany with some friends in 1799, made a pilgrimage to the Harz
Mountains to catch a glimpse of this famed conjunction between
clouds, sky, and shadow that casts a huge phantom figure across the
cloudfloor. Coleridge and his friends were twice disappointed in their
quest to see the spectre, though at the second attempt they were "re-
payed by the sight of a Wild Boar with an immense Cluster of Glow-
worms round his Tail & Rump."[42]

Robert goes, but at the crucial moment fails to push George over the edge; we have his
word for it that his soul rebelled. Throughout his account, he portrays himself as the puppet
of his princely counselor, his understanding clouded, his nature distorted by the unceasing
shadowing and possession of his "adviser." It is a fervid, intemperate, memorable rendition
of the idea of an inner voice at odds with the self, speaking the unutterable.

His evil genius has the necromantic capacity to change his shape: either he takes on the
semblance of his victims, impersonating Robert in the execution of numerous further
crimes, or he propels Robert to commit evil in a somnambulist state:

Either I had a second self, who transacted business in my likeness, or else my body was
at times possessed by a spirit over which it had no controul [*sic*], and of whose actions
my own soul was wholly unconscious. This was an anomaly not to be accounted for by
any philosophy of mine.... To be in a state of consciousness and unconsciousness, at
the same time, in the same body and same spirit, was impossible. (ibid., p. 182)

[40] Valentina Bold, *The Magic Lantern: Hogg and Science,* in *Studies in Hogg and His World,*
no. 7 (Stirling, 1996), pp. 5–17.

[41] *Chambers' Edinburgh Journal,* September 28, 1833, pp. 273–74 (quoted by John
Carey, "Introduction," in Hogg, *Confessions,* p. xviii).

[42] Richard Holmes, *Early Visions* (London, 1989), pp. 229–31, 236.

In spite of this disappointment, Coleridge later explored the phenomenon in a love poem, "Constancy to an Ideal Object." The diabolical phantom of medieval German legend reappears here completely transformed into an image for the split consciousness of the yearning lover, who transfigures the "image with a glory round its head," into an extended metaphor for a lover's vivid fantasy, in his mind's eye, of his beloved's presence.

The poet addresses his own thought, which is all so taken up with his love object in her absence and questions its status: *can a mental image have material presence?* "And art thou nothing?" he asks. And then answers himself:

>   Such thou art, as when
> The woodman winding westward up the glen
> At wintry dawn, where o'er the sheep-track's maze
> The viewless snow-mist weaves a glist'ning haze,
> Sees full before him, gliding without tread,
> *An image with a glory round its head;*
> The enamoured rustic worships its fair hues,
> Nor knows he makes the shadow, he pursues![43]

In this Orphic key, Coleridge summons a phantom Eurydice from the Fata Morgana illusion. "Constancy to an Ideal Object" ironizes, in its very title, the contrast between the persistent obsessive attachment of the mind to its fantasies and the insubstantial character of their objects, and dramatizes, with rapt poignancy, the split consciousness of the lover who knows he himself creates the presence of the love object he pursues. Unlike Hogg, who leaves in doubt the source of his two protagonists' supernatural visions, Coleridge explicitly invokes the explicable, meteorological wonder in order to communicate the happier state of the rustic who does not know that the vision has no substance, except as the shadow side of his own state; the *doppelgänger* seals the loneliness of the Romantic lovelorn poet, then pining for his beloved Sara Hutchinson, too self-aware not to acknowledge that the boons her image summoned for him—security and home, warmth and love—exist only as longings projected in air, as rainbows that have indeed been unwoven.

---

[43] Samuel Taylor Coleridge, *Poems,* ed. John Beer (London, 1993), pp. 311–12 (emphasis added); footnoted "This Phenomenon which the Author has himself experienced, and of which the reader may find a description on one of the earlier volumes of the Manchester Philosophical Transactions, is applied figuratively in . . . . *Aids to Reflection* (1825)."

The conflict between a meaningful uncanny portent, as in James Hogg's great novel, and desolate Coleridgean subjective perception expands and takes in a new direction the earlier quarrel between Biblical divine design and natural artistry and chance; the oscillating nuances of the difference continue to vibrate in the nineteenth century, in the spiritualists' efforts, and stir uncomfortably in the struggles of Victorians over the question of the paranormal.[44]

It is a commonplace to point out that inquiry paradoxically took a positivist bent in the era of high Romanticism; that Nature was then being laid out on the operating table and the dissecting block and parceled up into the specimen case. What is pertinent here is the desire to make the sky legible as well, to interpret the iconotexts of the clouds, to marshal even the vaporous, inchoate chaos of cloudscapes into reasonable order. This desire burgeons into two principal endeavors in the Romantic period: first, the early scientific and analytical voyages into the upper air, through the clouds and beyond, were accompanied by ground-breaking inquiries into the nature of clouds; second, these explorings were themselves accompanied by different, subjective trials to uncover meaning within inchoate and indeterminate mutability through the faculty of Imagination. This last attempt is nevertheless braided with the first, characteristic Enlightenment quest, and does not proceed in opposition to it.

6. CLOUD STUDIES

The variety and structure of clouds first came under scientific scrutiny almost at the same time as Coleridge was seeking the Brocken spectre. While Benjamin Franklin was probing the powers of lightning and electricity, other scientists—biologists, astronomers, physicists—sailed up up up into the new territories of the upper air in Montgolfier balloons and wondered at the sublime view of cloudscapes. Luke Howard named the varieties of cloud, for the very first time, in an article in 1802–3; Goethe was inspired by this work to hymn the heavens in scientific mode.

---

[44] Henry Sidgwick extended the argument's reach into theology, particularly in relation to a theory of miracles. "As for spirit-rapping," wrote Sidgwick in 1873, "I am in exactly the same mind towards it as towards religion. I believe there is something in it, don't know what, have tried hard to discover, and find that I always paralyse the phenomena. My taste is strongly affected by the obvious humbug mixed with it, which at the same time my reason does not overestimate." Quoted in C. D. Broad, "Henry Sidgwick and Psychical Research," *Proceedings of the Society for Psychical Research,* part 156: 136.

Of an earlier generation, and in a quieter mood, the Russian-born English watercolor artist and draughtsman Alexander Cozens, born in 1717, painted from observation, *en plein air,* the particularities of cumulus and stormclouds and of moonlight and the sun's rays on their volumes.

Clouds were significant elements in the fluid incoherence of natural forms and Cozens, in the mid-1770s and 1780s, was struggling to trap them into a system, numbered, annotated, and set out in a grid for the benefit of his pupils.[45] But Cozens took his study of mutability and formlessness in a remarkable direction: he adapted the ancient scrutiny of clouds and other random patternings, as in Leonardo's precept, to form what he called *A New Method for Assisting the Invention of Drawing Original Compositions of Landscape* (1784–85).[46]

Very meticulously, Cozens outlined the use of "blots" (figure 7) as a way of enhancing Imagination and memory, and he made an instinctive identification of this practice with finding shapes in clouds, quoting on the title page Shakespeare's passage from *Anthony and Cleopatra.* He advised: "Possess your mind strongly with a subject," and then "with the swiftest hand make all possible variety of shapes & strokes upon your paper," letting the hand move unpremeditated and unguided and unconscious. He furthermore suggested crumpling the paper, in order to create more accidental marks.

Cozens writes that he stumbled across this odd, Zen-like practice when he pulled an old, "soiled" scrap of paper from a pile to demonstrate something for a student and found that the marks it bore helped to crystalize his ideas. When reminded of Leonardo, Cozens said he had not known of his comments but was delighted with this corroboration, for his ideas aroused a great deal of ridicule, Aristophanes-style.[47] "This theory is in fact," he wrote, *"the art of seeing properly . . . ."*[48]

Alexander Cozens advocated combining objective reproduction of the observed natural randomness, aethereal flux, and the adventitious

[45] Cozens had private pupils, including William Beckford, and was drawing master at Eton College.

[46] See A. P. Oppé, *Alexander and John Robert Cozens inc. A. Cozens, A New Method for Assisting the Invention of Drawing Original Compositions of Landscape* (1784–85) (London, 1952); Hubert Damisch, *La Théorie du nuage* (Paris, 1972), pp. 255–56.

[47] It does not seem possible that Cozens had somehow come across Chinese watercolor theory of cloud paintings and dream stones, though his new Method resembles it in many respects; see Damisch, *Théorie,* pp. 277–311; Roger Caillois, *Roger Caillois, The Writing of Stones,* trans. Barbara Bray, introduction by Marguerite Yourcenar [L'Ecriture des pierres, 1970] (Charlottesville, 1985).

[48] Oppé, *Cozens,* p. 173.

Figure 7. Alexander Cozens, blot painting, from *A New Method* (London, 1784–85). (Tate Gallery, London)

camouflage mottling of light and shade with an extraordinary attempt to probe such forms' potential for personal expression. The Platonic predicament of mortals in the cave, receiving experience in partial, fragmentary, and deceptive form of flickering shadows was already resisted by both Botticelli and Leonardo when they placed heroic humanist confidence in the powers of Imagination to winkle meaning from the most inauspicious hiding places. Cozens, with his quasi-scientific tables—William Beckford, who was his friend, patron, and pupil, commented that Cozens was "almost as full of Systems as the Universe"[49]— attempts to flatten this work of *fantasia* into a simple tool, a kind of spinning jenny or Davy lamp of landscape painting.

The opening page of an album of his sketches shows two pages of proposed schemata for "Principles of Landskip" that make no concession to the picturesque;[50] they are diagrammatic, understated, spontaneous, and spare. Yet these abstract squiggles, tending ever more intensely to condensation and simplicity, have a simple provisional esthetic that is startlingly gripping for a contemporary viewer, uncannily proleptic of

[49] Ibid., p. 44.

[50] "Sundry Studies of Landscape Composition by Cozens the Elder," British Museum 198.a.2.

modern composition. In Cozens's tiny drawings—each one about half an inch square—we can feel the urgency of "seeing properly": he was observing empirically, training fantasy not to be deluded, using the scrying faculty for scientifically and esthetically harmonious purposes, so that rather than perceive castles in the air and phantom armies in the clouds as heavenly portents, fairy enchantments, or mental delusions, the artist becomes a master of vision and the disposer of its incoherent offerings, like drifts and assemblies of the clouds. Cozens, while traveling further than any of his contemporaries into methods of mental picturing, was also set against—even defending himself against—the unruly procession of images in phantasmagorias and other optical effects, such as the Hogg halo of glory.

7. "The Domain of Arnheim"

The human eye's dilemma, in front of nature's incoherence, provoked Edgar Allan Poe to one of his most lingeringly peculiar fancies: his tale of 1847, "The Domain of Arnheim,"[51] features a certain Mr. Ellison, a vastly wealthy esthete who then inherits an even more fabulous fortune. This American progenitor of Charles Baudelaire's dandy and J.-K. Huysmans's Des Esseintes deplores the flaws that spoil every view from whatever vantage point the spectator takes before Nature's pictures. But as he and the narrator expand on the errors and infelicities of "Natura pictrix," Ellison reverses the point of view, and with a breathtaking, Borgesian leap suggests that the world might be disposed, composed, and pleasingly beheld by others beside humans; that Nature itself, as we experience it, might itself be a Fata Morgana of hidden patterns and harmonious order for some other, higher gaze. He suggests:

> "There *may* be a class of beings, human once, but now invisible to humanity, to whom, from afar, our disorder may seem order—our unpicturesqueness picturesque; in a word, the earth-angels, for whose scrutiny more especially than our own, and for whose death-refined appreciation of the beautiful, may have been set in array by God the wide landscape-gardens of the hemispheres."[52]

Ellison's idea of earth-angels who have been refined by death projects

---

[51] Edgar Allan Poe, "The Domain of Arnheim," in *The Complete EAP Tales,* ed. Alix Perry (New York, 1981), pp. 546–56.

[52] Ibid., p. 550.

the signifying faculty beyond the human altogether and in so doing proposes a relationship between Art and Nature that differs entirely from Albertian mimesis or Leonardoesque *fantasia.*

Poe's omnipotent hero will not accept human limitations, however, and he dedicates himself to reorganizing Nature's scenery in order to adapt it for the human gaze, to please "the eyes which were to behold it on earth,"[53] and so he embarks on a Faustian performance of the picturesque.

The eerily still, enthralling tale sets out the possibility of gaining happiness through estheticism and willpower—it is not surprising that Baudelaire, who brilliantly translated Poe into French, exclaimed when he came across him that here was his very own *semblable,* his own double casting a mimick shadow across his writing from an America twenty years before. For "The Domain of Arnheim" ends with a dream voyage to an artificial paradise of Ellison's devising: a canoe takes the voyager gliding down a river and through a gorge, and the tale then climaxes in a truly entrancing finale:

> Meantime the whole Paradise of Arnheim bursts upon the view. There is a gush of entrancing melody; there is an oppressive sense of strange sweet odor; —here is a dream-like intermingling to the eye of tall slender Eastern trees—bosky shrubberies—flocks of golden and crimson birds—lily-fringed lakes—meadows of violets, tulips, poppies, hyacinths and tuberoses—long intertangled lines of silver streamlets—and, upspringing confusedly from amid all, a mass of semi-Gothic, semi-Saracenic architecture, sustaining itself as if by a miracle in mid-air, glittering in the red sunlight with a hundred oriels, minarets, and pinnacles; and seeming the phantom handiwork, conjointly, of the Sylphs, of the Fairies, of the Genii, and of the Gnomes.[54]

This is a Fata Morgana of a city, a castle in the air, for, significantly, Poe's poetry carries him beyond Mr. Ellison, the supreme landscape gardener, on to more aethereal makers—those genii and gnomes. The "Domain" was inspired, it is thought, by reports of Fonthill, Beckford's summer retreat, where Alexander Cozens had studied the shapes of clouds and reconfigured blots in more harmonious arrangements than he found in observation.

Edgar Allan Poe was the favorite writer of René Magritte, who knew

---

[53] Ibid., p. 549.
[54] Ibid., p. 556.

him in the intense, jeweled translation by Baudelaire.[55] One of Poe's "histoires sérieuses," "The Domain of Arnheim" inspired, a hundred years after it was written, the title of three of the Belgian Surrealist's many paintings that densely conjugate clouds, mirrors, reflections, and optical illusions: Magritte refused explication, and it is beside the point to make sense of his puzzles, though not entirely redundant to unpick the many knots he ties in the eyestrings of ordinary perception. His clusters of images will not parse or come out with a solution, however, and I will come back to this intrinsic condition of enigma, for it represents the last condition of cloudiness I want to put to you.

What is it that we, the earthling spectators, see in Magritte's 1949 version of this picture, *The Domain of Arnheim* (figure 8)? Beyond the shattered windowpane, appears—perhaps—one of the *anges terrestres* or earth-angels, from Poe's class of invisible beings who hold the unseen pattern of Nature in their gaze. Here it takes the form of a metamorphic eagle-mountain, and its non-reversed image appears in the shattered pieces of the windowpane as if the pane were a two-way mirror. "The outside is brought inside in a devastating way," writes David Sylvester, the painting giving the impression of that claustrophobic moment of terror when a bird hurtles into a window.[56] But this impact cannot quite have happened in this manner, as the artist contrives his favorite confusion between reality and image, and the stone bird remains in and of the mountain. So it is Magritte who configures the mountain as a bird, in the same way as plains- or valley-dwellers give anthropomorphic or zoomorphic names to landmarks and peaks. Looking at the picture, we follow his lead. Adding to the puzzlement, these broken shards of mirror, as in other pictures by Magritte, retain the image that had appeared through the window to be an insubstantial reflection and give it painted materiality, a kind of actuality that establishes its illusory condition as belonging to a different perceptual universe, one that could exist from another, unseen category of perceptive beings. The brainteaser itself belongs to the *Domain of Arnheim* because it is not possible for us to know, or even to imagine, what might be the harmonious arrangements devised by Nature to please the earth-angels. Magritte responds to the Paris

[55] Edgar Allan Poe, *Histoires grotesques et sérieuses,* trans. Charles Baudelaire (Paris, 1966), pp. 151–71.

[56] David Sylvester, *Magritte,* exhibition catalogue, Tate Gallery (London, 1969), pp. 52–53, 87, 100; and idem, *Magritte* (London, 1992), p. 302.

Figure 8. René Magritte, *The Domain of Arnheim* (1949). (Private Collection)

Surrealists' doctrinal trust in the unconscious's powers to pattern vision, writing, life, and destiny, by offering a dead end to interpretation.[57]

Typical Magritte clouds float above this vision; fleecy white trooping cushions, against an uninflected azure sky, such conventionally idyllic aetheric heavens, bland and placid vehicles bringing *calme* and *volupté,* provide the signature motif in the music of the Magrittean uncanny. These "intrusive skies," in David Sylvester's phrase, appear nearly twenty years before the *Domain of Arnheim,* in an early picture (ca. 1929), which is tellingly entitled *The False Mirror,* showing a huge Cyclopean eye with the iris swimming with clouds around the disturbingly blind spot of the pupil. The clouds sail into view in such pictures as ciphers that encipher nothing: no phantom images lurk in their fluffy pillows, no Fata Morganas or haloes of glory fill their vacuity.

8. Conclusion

A seer who recomposes the languages of sign and vision that obtain at the human level postulates another form of subjectivity, a subject who is indeed outside our frame of reference. This seer or earth-angel is a cyborg *avant la lettre*—occupying an instrumental space analogous to that of the proliferating processes and instruments that were invented to probe the mysteries of the invisible, hidden worlds, both inner and outer.[58]

Many devices of intricate ingenuity were developed in order to see further, to see more, to see into and through. The eighteenth and nineteenth centuries were the prodigious era of inventions, when media were developed that could magnify, eavesdrop, register, and record all kinds of signals that are imperceptible to ordinary faculties of human sense. The catalogue of sensory prostheses, including the earlier telescope and the microscope, finds its first recording angels in photography and phonography, and it includes methods still very much in use—

[57] Magritte painted other versions with the same title in 1938 and 1962, and a variation on the image, *L'Appel des cimes* (1943), with a painting of the bird-mountain on an easel in front of the window. See Sylvester, *Magritte* (1992), p. 298.

[58] As Carol Mavor has written, "We [also] try to imagine that we can see ourselves seeing (that we can see *inside*), in order to defeat the fact that vision is always outside of us and that we could never know how the other perceives us . . . . This unproblematized (and mythical) approach to looking is sustained in order to carry the all-seeingness of the vision we desire—so that we can see what we want to see." Carol Mavor, *Pleasures Taken, Performances of Sexuality and Loss in Victorian Photography* (Durham and London, 1995), p. 82.

X-rays, ultrasound, computer-aided tomography (CAT scans), magnetic resonance imaging. Unseen forces that are not anchored in any individual human consciousness or applied idiosyncratically by any Leonardoesque master or author, but belong as it were to the objective stratosphere, became the means of detecting the hitherto incomprehensible and hidden order and meaning of the invisible in the universe. Some of these forces have stood the scientific test: radio waves, gamma rays. But others that were ardently advocated and exploited—and wholly believed—have disappeared to the echoes of embarrassed titters: animal spirits, Odic (magnetic) light, "radiant matter," and the Aether itself, with its emanation, ectoplasm.

The process is complex, two-way, and tightly raveled. First, the new methods of detection are intertwined with models of mind, including ideas of the subject and the subject's agency, and the newly understood limits of individual vision and fantasy. The camera obscura, or magic lantern, mirrored the melancholic mind, and early magic lanternists projected through their novel media a refraction of imagined interior processes and their characteristic products. The technical means introduced to create mental pictures were not determined by them, nor did they shape them; their interaction depends rather on the necessary limits of Imagination itself, which cannot imagine itself outside its own boundaries. The Rorschach test, for example, invented in the late nineteenth century and introduced in 1921, adapted Leonardo's ideas of Imagination and even Cozens's blots to psychological purposes. Numerous techniques of unraveling Nature's riddles and reconstituting its secret patterns to become intelligible show a riotous Imagination in play with curiosity, desire, and the longing for consolation. They are intertwined with a freshly imagined, Other subjectivity or Other consciousness, not divine, not perhaps omnipotent, but endowed with the aethereal intelligence of earth-angels and capable of discovering coherence and cogency where they appear to be missing.

Second, just as Kircher and later phantasmagorists evoked the invisible and hidden worlds of the supernatural and ghostly within fantasy—"invented the uncanny"—so Victorian scientists, followed by some eminent moderns, endeavored to apply their innovatory techniques to probing interior mysteries, to making legible the invisible. They wanted to bring out the unseen in an effort at rationality, and their efforts could be seen as a struggle to subdue the uncanny. If instrumentalized, the beyond-the-human faculties postulated in the stratosphere would make available to our limited, fallible human senses those hitherto tough, recalcitrant mysteries of inner landscape, of soul and spirit; if understood and properly applied, they would at last descry the figure in the rock, the face in the cloud; they would decipher the aether, and materialize the impalpable. The enterprise, which would culminate in spiritualism's bizarre ectoplasmic phenomena, reveals the irreducible primacy of *fantasia* over *mimesis,* of Imagination over Empiricism.

II. ECTOPLASM: MATERIALIZING THE IMPALPABLE

1. CAPTURED ECTOPLASM

Under "Duncan Helen, Mrs." in the catalogue of the archives of the Society for Psychical Research, now kept in the Manuscript Reading Room of the University Library, Cambridge, there is this entry:

> Sample of Ectoplasm. Material alleged to have been captured from Mrs Helen Duncan, materialising medium, at a seance in 1939.

I asked to see the "sample of ectoplasm." The librarian looked at me strangely; he said, "Are you sure? It's very nasty." My response was, "Would you prefer me to look at it somewhere else?" I thought there might be a desk of shame, where I could be supervised and other readers would not be disturbed. He said, "No, but be discreet."

There was nothing corporeal about the sample when it arrived, in the strict sense of human or animal tissue. Instead, inside the box, there was a folded heap of dressmakers' lining satin, the cheapest cloth, a synthetic fibre, and a yellowing white in hue. About four yards had been cut straight from the bolt, with no hems at either end and the selvedge left plain. It had been washed and ironed, but the creases where it had been crumpled were still marked; the pattern of these showed it had

I would like to thank the Master and Fellows of Trinity College, Cambridge, and especially the staff of the Wren Library for their help and support during the research for this lecture. I am also grateful to the Society for Psychical Research for permission to use their archive in the University Library, Cambridge.

I would also like to thank Esther da Costa Meyer, of Princeton University, for her rich and thoughtful response to these lectures. I hope to be able to develop some of the ideas that emerged the following day in the seminar with her and Terry Castle in my future book on this theme.

been tightly wadded. There were traces of old blood that the laundry had not erased. The volume of it was astonishing to me: I went over to the librarian and asked him if he had any scales.

Pliny experimented to discover whether bodies weighed more dead than alive and claimed to have found that corpses were heavier, once the light part—the spirit—had fled. Thomas Browne, continuing the long inquiry into the weight of the body after death, could not agree. He found that lesser animals rather became lighter when dead:

> for exactly weighing and strangling a chicken in the Scales, upon an immediate ponderation, we could discover no sensible difference in weight, but suffering it to lye eight or ten howres, untill it grew perfectly cold, it weighed most sensibly lighter; the like we attempted, and verified in mice . . . .[1]

But Browne's curiosity was not satisfied:

> Now whereas some alledge that spirits are lighter substances, and naturally ascending do elevate and waft the body upward, whereof dead bodies being destitute contract a greater gravity; although we concede that spirits are light, comparatively unto the body, yet that they are absolutely so, or have no weight at all, wee cannot readily allow . . . .[2]

He then makes a distinction between spirit and soul that is important in the context of spiritualism and other nineteenth-century quests for invisible forces: "for since Philosophy affirmeth that spirits are middle substances between the soule and body, they must admit of some corporeity which supposeth weight or gravity."[3]

The librarian agreed that it would be a good idea to weigh the sample; he suggested the postroom, where there would be scales. We put it on the tray; Mrs. Duncan's material weighed 236 grams (about 8 ounces)—less than I thought it would, for the satin felt slumpy and heavy to the touch. I had expected lighter, diaphanous stuff—muslin and cheesecloth were said to be mediums' preferred fabrics.

Helen Duncan was a Scottish medium (born in 1898, died in 1956) who specialized in materialization, the word used in Spiritualist circles

---

[1] "Of the Popular and received tenets concerning Man, which examined, prove true or false," in Thomas Browne, *Pseudoxia Epidemica,* ed. Robin Robbins (Oxford, 1981), p. 315.

[2] Ibid., p. 316.

[3] Ibid.

to describe a phenomenon that became common in seances from the
1870s onward: the appearance of objects and of bodies, or traces of objects—touches to the cheek or hands of the sitters, slaps or caresses or
breezes as of something passing, sometimes fingerprints or other traces,
sounds of bells ringing or aethereal music, apported flowers and other
gifts from the spirits, and, above all, ectoplasmic manifestations. These
took two predominant forms: luminous, veiled, phantom-like beings,
or nameless, amorphous parts of such beings, called pseudo-pods—
which issued from the mouth or the head or other entrance and exit
points of the medium's body.[4]

Helen Duncan was often photographed with her spirit control,
known as "Peggy," an ectoplasmic manifestation who regularly appeared during this medium's seances (figure 1).

The move from a visual illusion, as in Fata Morgana or in spectral
apparitions, from dematerialized bodies into a haptic experience of palpable matter, as in Helen Duncan's sheet, will be sought and endlessly
repeated in the Spiritualist seance. How the imponderable and aethereal
could be made palpable, weighed and verified, by touch above all, but
also by smell and hearing, occupied some of the best minds of the last
century, as they postulated the possibility of paranormal phenomena.

Aristotle singled out the sense of touch in *De Anima* as the supreme
mark of human intelligence:

> in the other senses he [man] is behind many kinds of animal, but in
> touch he is much more discriminating than the other animals. This
> is why he is of all living creatures the most intelligent. Proof of this
> lies in the fact that among the human race men are well or poorly en-
> dowed with intelligence in proportion to their sense of touch, and no
> other sense . . . .[5]

This is a startling endorsement from a philosopher more usually associated with the sovereignty of vision, and it throws light on the primacy
of touch in the verifying methods of the nineteenth century. Numerous
scientific experimenters, including Spiritualists, were not to be satisfied

[4] Franek Kluski, one of the rare male materializing mediums, specialized in ectoplasmic
gloves and socks. See Gustave Geley, *L'Ectoplasmie et la clairvoyance: observations et expériences
personelles* (Paris, 1924), pp. 240–41, plates XXI, XXX.

[5] Aristotle, *De Anima* II, ix, 20–25, trans. W. S. Hett (Cambridge, Mass., and London,
1995; first published 1936), pp. 120–21.

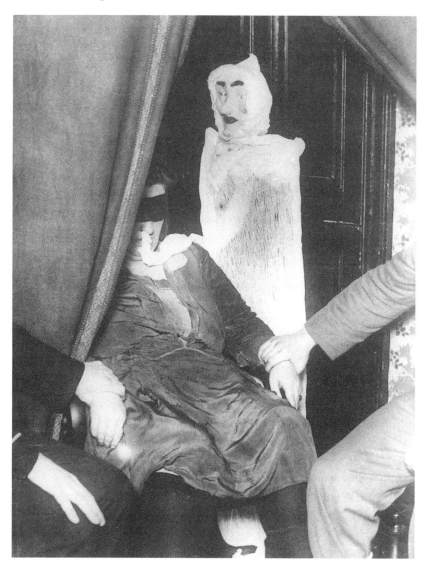

Figure 1. Helen Duncan and "Peggy," her spirit control, England, ca. 1935.
(Harry Price Library, University of London)

with the risen Christ's injunction to Mary Magdalene, "Noli me tan-
gere"; they were Doubting Thomases one and all, and wanted to push
their fingers into the wounds in the spirit body's side, to palpate the
stuff of the other side, to feel its temperature and texture. Touch becomes the guarantor of the paradoxical presence of spirit, as we shall see.

2. Divinity in a Cloud

When Correggio painted Io around 1532 in his sequence of *The Loves of Jupiter,* he showed her clasped close by the god in the form of a cloud (figure 2). The artist took his cue from Ovid's *Metamorphoses,* in which the poet writes that Jupiter wrapped the earth in darkness in order to conceal his actions, but that the ever vigilant Juno's suspicions were aroused, for she "wondered that floating clouds should give the appearance of night mists," and so glided down to earth and chased them away. But by then Jupiter had changed Io into a white heifer, the nymph's far more common appearance in paintings.[6]

Correggio's divine ravisher emerges from the soft indigo-grey massed mist as if he is consubstantial with cloud. His pointed, almost elfin face shimmers out of the miasma to kiss the nymph, and his right hand appears through a semi-transparent cocoon of cloud to embrace her; this Io does not flee a rapist, as she does in terror in Ovid's poem, but surrenders raptly to the enveloping fog, embracing its soft solidity with her left arm and curling toes. Correggio wonderfully communicates the haptic sense of Io's flesh brushed all over with some feather-light, shivery, close caresses.[7]

Jupiter was a god of all severe weathers: in the *Io,* he is clearly wrapped in a kind of storm cloud, and it is suggestive that Ovid associates rain, in the same first book of the *Metamorphoses,* with human genesis itself. At the time of creation, the sky is divided from the earth, with "the fiery aether" in the highest heaven, and the air where storms blow below it. When Prometheus creates the first human being, he takes earth, which

> being such a new precipitate
> Of the etheric heaven
> Cradled in its dust unearthly crystals[8]

and mixes it with rainwater. In the light of these preceding verses in Ovid, Correggio's picture clearly casts the cloud's embrace as a dynamic fecundating principle; in this it rhymes with the painter's *Danae,* from the same sequence of mythological paintings of *The Loves of Jupiter,* which depicts the nymph receiving the god in her lap from another

---

[6] Ovid, *Metamorphoses,* book 1, lines 599–606.

[7] David Ekserdjian, *Correggio* (Norwich and London, 1997), p. 284.

[8] Ted Hughes, *Tales from Ovid* (London, 1997), p. 7.

Figure 2. Correggio, *The Loves of Jupiter: Io.*
(Kunsthistorischemuseum, Vienna)

cloud, in this case amber-gold, more solid and compact, an itinerant
rain cloud, just beginning to emit a few gold drops from the shower that
will inseminate her.

In Greek sources, the child of Jupiter and Io was called Epaphus, a
name related to the word for touch, because Io conceived at the *touch* of

the god.[9] But this association of Io with tactility, to which Correggio may have responded, suggests several further variations on clouds and their meaning that I am going to explore. For while Fata Morgana casts clouds as films or screens on which the invisible and the spectral are captured, and this provides a metaphor for eidetic dream images, a complementary but divergent tradition finds clouds to be a vehicle of spirit and a metaphor for the paradisical state, and deploys it, generously, extravagantly, and often unconsciously, as the most satisfying and convenient embodiment of an impossible conundrum: aethereal materiality. Billowing cumulus, fleecy altocumulus or louring thunderheads, and the more solid-seeming manifestations are presented through inadequate metaphors, visual and verbal, as apprehensible by other senses besides sight.

Ectoplasm's appearance borrows features from this tradition of making visible the invisible, of rendering material the immaterial. Ectoplasm also bodies forth the aetheric or astral body, an idea about the spiritual dimension of human personality that was expounded in Theosophical thought and twists and turns through the history of the occult.

The French art historian Henri Focillon, in his book *La Vie des formes,* first published in 1934, proposed a radical view: forms have a life of their own, and forms in art both derive from and generate other forms autonomously, according to their own internal principles, both organic and abstract. He argues that no amount of explanation of the historical, social, economic, or personal circumstances in which the Gothic develops will ever give you the *particular shape* of the Gothic arch. "The time that gives support to a work of art does not give definition either to its principle or to its specific form."[10] He also insists that forms exist independently of signification, so that while the Gothic arch might symbolize aspiration, divinity, aethereal lightness, it does not intrinsically do so, and could attract other meanings. Focillon's argument strikingly offers a path out of a certain impasse in the study of signs and symbols; it frees them from the fixity inflicted by ideas of the collective unconscious, on the one hand, and, on the other, from the relativism of historicism that denies any intrinsic properties to bodies of any form. "[Form] prolongs and diffuses itself," he writes, "throughout our dreams and fancies: we regard it, as it were, as a kind of fissure through which

---

[9] See P. M. L. Forbes-Irving, *Metamorphosis in Greek Myths* (Oxford, 1990), pp. 212–15.

[10] Henri Focillon, *The Life of Forms in Art,* trans. Charles B. Hogan and George Kubler (New York, 1989), p. 15.

crowds of images aspiring to birth may be introduced into some indefinite realm—a realm which is neither that of physical extent nor that of pure thought."[11] Expressions of the subtle body—the form of spirit—pour through this fissure. Mixed in with the cluster of amorphous forms—with blots and smudges, clouds and vapors—the larval ghost, who takes its place worldwide in the conventional language of the supernatural, carries the weight of transhistorical associations. But such a ghost also arrives at definition and differences according to temporal circumstances—individual quests, mass fads. I shall unfold some of the work performed by clouds in this sphere, both as an enduring metaphorical form of disembodiment and as a sign forged and altered by external circumstances.

Renaissance nebulae appear as solid bodies; pillows, cushions, divans of cloud fill paradise. Correggio created exuberant, candyfloss seraglios in the *Assumption of the Virgin* in the dome of Parma cathedral, where angels and saints swim, frolick, recline and perch on reefs and banks of cumulus as if they were as buoyant as surf, and as docile as featherbeds. Cloudiness has palpable substance here; it is tactile, ductile, plastic— Aristotelian attributes of matter—in a strict sense; a variety of voluminous foam with its own dependable organic structure, it persuades us of the character of aethereality. Heaven tumesces with froth turned solid. Embodied in sensuous paint strong enough to support its emanations, amoretti gambol in and out of the flossy fleece, and are, like the painter's Jupiter, apparently consubstantial with air and airiness.[12] In a study after Raphael, attributed to Parmigianino (figure 3), a knot of drapery is doing duty for cloud support for an angelic foot; it is possible to see the riddle of disembodied substance that artists were attempting to encompass. Experientially, the viewer is able to understand the angels' and saints' aethereal state precisely because they can recline so confidently on banks of mist; nor do they disappear into it, as humans do when fog envelops them.

[11] Ibid., pp. 34–35.

[12] I am aware here that I diverge from Hubert Damisch, who explicitly theorizes Correggio as a pioneer painter of optical subjectivity, on account of his use of perspective, which posits a viewer's vantage point below the tumultuous scene in the heavens. Damisch is taking his cue from Alois Riegl, who considered these frescoes by Correggio as a fulcrum in the movement effected by the baroque from the tactile or objective mode to the optical or subjective mode. But I feel that Riegl's argument entails associating the tactile with the close-up, with the painting of surfaces (e.g., Giotto), rather than empathizing with the imagined substances of the bodies as rendered in paint. See Hubert Damisch, *La Théorie du nuage: Pour une histoire de la peinture* (Paris, 1972), pp. 20–21.

Figure 3. *Study of a Left Foot,* after Raphael (attributed to Parmigianino). (The Governing Body, Christ Church, Oxford)

Although Correggio takes clouds to extremes of blissful presence that they had hardly enjoyed before, he is painting in a recognizable dialect of Christian iconography, not coining a new language.

Invisibility and cloudiness form a pun or perhaps a rhyme: they both convey the condition of ineffability that the unknown and the supernatural inhabit. In the Bible, God hides in a mist on the summit of Mount Sinai. In Christian iconography, his disembodied nature takes the form of synecdoche: as a hand in glory—the glory expressed by a little white puff of cloud such as sails sometimes into view on a perfect summer's day, as in a mosaic from a conch in the portal of St. Mark's, Venice (1545), or as a floating torso, legless, with trunkless heads of putti surrounding him, in the stratosphere, as depicted by Giovanni Bellini in the *Baptism of Christ* in S. Corona, Vicenza.

Figure 4. Bartolomeo Schedoni, *Coronation of the Virgin*. (Denis Mahon Collection, Fitzwilliam Museum, Cambridge)

In Bartolomeo Schedoni's delicious *Coronation of the Virgin* (figure 4), the amoretti hug the giant whipped cream clouds and appear to bob and swim through their incandescent puffs, but do their bodies begin and end as bodies, or as this froth, this foam? Cherubim also emerge from and dissolve back into the glowing nimbus around Bartolomé Murillo's

Virgin and the Child in Glory, as if consubstantial—or perhaps one should say conaethereal—with light, air, and holy fire.

In such pneumatic extravaganzas—which point forward to the *Silver Clouds* of Andy Warhol as well as to the wobbly castles of children's playgrounds—clouds pun on the association of spirit and breath, *pneuma;* they also mark ascensions, providing saints with uplift. When Pier Francesco Mola painted St. Bruno in ecstasy, he communicated the saint's state by raising him off the ground on a small cloud; more lavishly, Nicolas Poussin caught up to a much higher stratum an enraptured Santa Rita of Cascia as she was swept by supernatural means to the convent her father had forbidden her to enter.

The Virgin Mary, when she appears to contemporary seers in Fatima, or in present day Croatia, still favors this mode of transport (figure 5). But it is worth noting that, as the twentieth century progressed, the nebulous spiritual sphere was washed whiter than white: for reasons I shall be coming to later, no religious image-maker today would paint the murky turmoil that buoys some ascending saints, or wraps inky Jupiter, or wreathes smoky haloes round the sphere of divinity in high Renaissance baroque art.

3. THE SMOKE OF SACRIFICE

Metonymic affinities between aether and clouds, between disembodied spirits and smoke, infuse the symbolism of sacrifice: in the Bible, and Judaic ritual, the offerings are accompanied by the burning of incense; the symbolic reenactment of Christ's death in the Catholic mass also takes place in a smoky atmosphere. Mary Douglas, the anthropologist, commenting on the regulations of sacrifices in the Temple detailed in Leviticus, has demonstrated that the barrier of cloud screening God from Moses's view on Sinai returns by design in the smokescreen of incense that conceals the Holy of Holies from view in the temple.[13] However, incense itself only replicates symbolically the actual combustion of sacrifice: it was when God snuffed up the "sweet savour" of Noah's burnt offerings that he decided to leave off cursing and smiting humankind (Genesis 8:21). The holocaust of animals and cereals in the temple ritual

---

[13] Mary Douglas, *The Eucharist, Its Continuity with the Bread Sacrifice of Leviticus* (Durham, N.C., 1998). My thanks go to Professor Mary Douglas, of University College London, for lending me unpublished chapters from her book *Leviticus as Literature* (Oxford, 2000), pp. 66–86.

Figure 5. Our Lady of Fatima, shrine souvenir, purchased in Pittsburgh, ca. 1990. (Author's collection)

dematerializes their material bodies: they are turned to smoke, which then ascends to heaven, joining matter and aether through the medium of cloud. This language still underpins the iconography of Christian saints' translation to an unearthly state: the swelling clouds that carry up an Ignatius or Aloysius or Teresa, in paintings of apotheosis, annex the vocabulary of clouds to express a process of aetherealization. The clouds that wrap the holy and translated beings rise up like smoke from the altar, like incense from the thurible, communicating their ascension into heaven, their mutation from this element to another. They function as part of a sacred syntax, making visible within the limits of figuration a noncorporeal body that has become vaporized through salvation, sublimed from matter to air.

You can see this crucial and magical enterprise of linking this world to the world above, the corporeal to the incorporeal, in Poussin's *Assumption* (figure 6), a perfectly achieved expression of its theme even though the doctrine of the Virgin's incorruptible body, which was translated to heaven intact, contradicts the principles of purification and immolation by fire that sacrifice implies. The Virgin rises with dark smoke spiraling around her ascending body as if the sarcophagus were an altar and she were ascending wrapped in the smoke of sacrifice; putti support her airy flight in her swelling mantle, frolic in and out of the clouds, and direct her aloft through the gap opening up above her head.

In *Cinders,* an essay of 1984, Jacques Derrida develops eloquently the metaphorical division between ashes and smoke, those symbiotic doubles of sacrifice that are both emblematic of transitoriness, of the fugitive, and of mortality, but are also packed with oppositional distinctions from each other:

> I have the impression now that the best paradigm of the trace [for him] is not, as certain people have believed...[he himself too, perhaps], the hunter's tracks, the furrow, the line in the sand, the wake in the sea, the love of the footstep for the footprint, but ash (that which remains without remaining from the holocaust, from the burned offering [*brûle-tout*], the incense of the fire [*de l'incendie l'encens*]).[14]

Derrida's focus rests on the ash that stays behind—the terrestrial and material residue, and he sends his readers to a sonnet by Stéphane

---

[14] Jacques Derrida, *Cinders,* trans. Ned Lukacher (Lincoln, Neb., 1984), p. 43.

Figure 6. Nicolas Poussin, *The Assumption of the Virgin.* (Louvre, Paris)

Mallarmé, in which the poet plays on the ancient twinning of breath and soul in a thoroughly contemporary conceit—the smoking of a cigar (!). The poem opens with the lines

> Toute l'âme résumée
> Quand lente nous l'expirons
> Dans plusieurs ronds de fumée . . .

> [All the soul summed up,
> When slowly we breathe it out
> In several rings of smoke . . .]

Mallarmé elaborates: the soul leaves the body as the ash falls from the glowing end:

> La cendre se sépare
> De son clair baiser de feu.

> [The ash parts
> From its bright kiss of fire.][15]

These doubles—soul/body, smoke/ash—are not in tension, but part of a process that hyphenates body and soul through the metamorphosis of substances, as in smoking, or, one could add, as in sacrifice. Derrida later exclaims, "What a difference between ash and smoke: smoke seems to lose itself, and better, without leaving a sensory residue, rises, takes the air, becomes subtle and sublimates itself. Ash falls, weary, heavy . . . ."[16] At the end of the poem, Mallarmé takes sides with smoke against ash, which he identifies with "le réel" (the real), and furthermore, which is, he writes, simply *vil,* that is, base, and the poem closes with a symbolist affirmation of nebulousness:

> Le sens trop précis rature
> Ta vague littérature.

> [Too precise a meaning erases
> Your mysterious literature.][17]

---

[15] "Toute l'âme resumée," from "Hommages et tombeaux," in *Mallarmé,* ed. and trans. Anthony Hartley (Harmondsworth, 1965), p. 96.

[16] Derrida, *Cinders,* p. 73.

[17] Hartley, *Mallarmé,* p. 96.

4. THE AETHER

It is worth noticing that Mallarmé's smoke, as it aetherealizes its source, is necessarily heated, even fiery, chemically and physically distinct from breath. This difference was even more clearly marked in pre-modern physics than it is understood today in the age of passive smoking, and, counterintuitively perhaps, it informs the history of aether, with consequences that can help us to understand the imagery of spiritual spheres, its intrinsic limitations and its historical contingency.

In his *Ecstatic Journey* of 1656, for example, Athanasius Kircher describes his alter ego, one Theodidactus (Taught by God), being transported through the firmament by the angel Cosmiel. When they reach the upper air or aether, Theodidactus can no longer breathe, it is so rarefied—"subtle"—and when they reach Jupiter a powerful, fragrance wafts toward him, "sweeter than all amber and musk." It revives him wonderfully. The angel explains, "That is the healthy breath and outpouring of that sphere of Jove, a clear sign that we are now near its atmosphere."[18] It resembled, perhaps, the atmosphere in the Holy of Holies, or in the chancel of a Catholic church.

Ten years later, the Jesuit wizard published his most beautifully illustrated volume of all, the *Mundus Subterraneus* (1665), a fantastical work about volcanoes and underground water courses and caverns (figure 7). There, the all-encompassing airy space beyond the earth, where he and the angel were transported, is designated *Etherium Spatium*—aetheric space. Significantly, though the verbal accounts describe emptiness, the engraver working for Kircher filled the space with charcoal-grey puffballs of clouds, for otherwise, in visual terms it might have looked blank, inert, and meaningless.

The theory of the aether is far too complicated and multifarious to review or sum up here, so I shall follow one strand, present in Kircher's writings, which perceived the aether as light-bearing, fiery. This conjunction of elements departs from the vaporous and moist rainmaking nature more normally ascribed to the stratosphere and its demarcating clouds. The greys and indigos and purples of metaphysical space, assumed by artists, adumbrate this character, suggesting that the aethereal element is fire, not water, and shifting its vapors toward smoke, not

---

[18] Athanasius Kircher, *Itinerarium Exstaticum quo Mundo Opificium* (Rome, 1656), part 1, p. 205.

Figure 7. The hydraulic system of the earth, from Athanasius Kircher, *Mundus Subterraneus* (Amsterdam, 1665). (Wren Library, Trinity College, Cambridge)

mist. This will prove a step with potent consequences for the language of signs. The smoky affinities of the aether were inspired by a strand of classical physics, from Democritus, Heraclitus, Lucretius, through to the widely known Ovid: the last actually calls the upper air simply "ignis" or fire, a word that many translators expand to "fiery aether," since otherwise the lines from the *Metamorphoses* become almost incomprehensible to present-day readers.[19]

It seems contrary to us now that any part of the air should be interpreted as fire, however radiant, however bright; that volcanoes, the earthly image of hell, should belong somehow in this discussion of the aether at all seems even odder, but Kircher's cosmology, later in the century, links the principles in an intricate hydraulic and combustive cycle. His truly wonderful hypotheses were translated into English, in an

---

[19] "Over all these regions hangs the air, as much heavier than the fiery aether as it is lighter than earth or water." Ovid, *Metamorphoses,* book 1, lines 52–53, trans. Mary M. Innes (Harmondsworth, 1973; first published 1955), p. 30.

abridged version, in 1669. The author quotes Ovid to support Kircher's cosmological equivalence of air and fire:

> The Earth resolv'd is turned into streams;
> Water to Air; *the purer Air to flames.*
> From whence they back return; The fiery flakes
> Are turn'd to Air; The Air thickened takes
> The Liquid form of Water; that Earth makes.[20]

"The luminiferous aether" was thought to be formed of invisible, imponderable, flimsy, springy, fiery light vapors. As such, it inspired persistent theorizing, including differing views from both Isaac Newton and René Descartes; for Newton, the aether was composed of "aetherial spirits, or vapours," and he proposed that it constituted the original protoplasm of the physical world, shaped by Nature.[21] The legacy of exquisitely imaginative aetheric theories about subtle matter, the elements of the universe, and the nature of light and fire underlies the phenomena of the spiritualist experiments, as I hope to show when we come back to ectoplasm.

The fiery aether does not fade after the seventeenth century: Newton's reflection of 1675 was only published in 1744, with important reverberations.[22] The artist Cornelius Varley imagined, as did many of his scientific peers, that clouds were formed by "atmospheric electricity." After observing rain gather over Snowdon, he wrote, "Here I believe I

---

[20] Athanasius Kircher, *The Vulcano's or, Burning and Fire-Vomiting Mountains, Famous in the World: With their Remarkables, Collected for the most part out of Kircher's Subterraneous World* (London, 1669), p. 55 (emphasis added). The writer clearly has some difficulty with Kircher's plan, viz his tracking back and forth over the material:

> But how the said matters should conceive fire was above-said. As how indeed; scarcely from the Sun; not from the Thunder and Lightnings; not from any other efficient: but from the very subterraneous fire it self [*sic*], making its way unto them through hidden passages of the Rocks, which it burns. Or, if they be not immediately touched by actual Fire; then certainly from the Marine waves and billows, intruded by the force and impetuousness of the Winds, through the submarine gutters and chinks at the bottom of the Sea. For that it cannot be that from the vehement dashing of the billows in strait & narrow places, and the agitation of the spirits of combustible matter thereby, and the attrition & striking of the fat and Sulphureous Air, that they should not presently conceive Fire. (Ibid., p. 60)

[21] G. N. Cantor, "The Theological Significance of Ethers," in *Conceptions of Ether Studies in the History of Ether Theories, 1740–1900*, ed. G. N. Cantor and M. J. S. Hodge (Cambridge, 1981), pp. 135–55.

[22] As the historian Logie Barrow remarks, "Beginning in 1745 . . . all significant British electricians [i.e., physicists] postulated a special electrical matter identical with, or similar

saw and understood the gradual progress from a cloudless morning to universal rain here was a silent invisable [*sic*] flow of electricity to the mountains."[23] William Blake's *Song of Experience,* when the baby enters the world,

> Helpless, naked, piping loud;
> Like a fiend hid in a cloud[24]

echoes contemporary meteorology and natural sciences.[25]

Even the pioneering watcher of the skies, Luke Howard, the first meteorologist to devise a taxonomy for clouds, speculated that they were formed by electromagnetic attraction, as well as condensation, and that "rain is in almost every instance the result of the electrical action of clouds upon each other. . . ."[26] Howard first gave the names that still endure: cumulus, stratus, and cirrus (after the Latin for a curl of hair), and he scrutinized their mutations like a physiognomist, invoking "the countenance of the sky" and stating that "they are commonly as good visible indications of the operation of these causes [of the atmosphere] as is the countenance of the state of a person's mind or body."[27] The skies could be grasped; the formless itself could not elude the grasp of enlightenment science, itself the handmaiden to divine revelation.[28] Howard's work reached Goethe in Germany the following year, and the old poet was moved to write a sequence of cloud poems as well as a paean to Howard and his work.[29] Howard himself was a devout Christian (a Methodist) and Goethe, the scientist-poet, accordingly exults in his demonstration that God's handiwork and intelligibility can be woven

---

to, the springy, subtle, universal Newtonian aether." Logie Barrow, *Independent Spirits, Spiritualism and English Plebeians, 1850–1910* (London, 1986), p. 73.

[23] Quoted by Anne Lyles, "'That Immense Canopy': Studies of Sky and Cloud by British Artists c. 1770–1860," MS kindly lent by the author, to be published in *Constable's Clouds,* exhibition catalogue, Walker Art Gallery, Liverpool, April–July 2000.

[24] William Blake, "Infant Sorrow," in *Songs of Experience* (London, 1794), in *The Complete Poetry and Prose of William Blake,* ed. David V. Erdman (New York, 1988), p. 28.

[25] See Erasmus Darwin's personification of clouds, in "The Botanic Garden," *The Loves of the Plants* (Oxford and New York, 1991; first published 1789).

[26] Luke Howard, "On the Modifications of Clouds, and on the Principles of Their Production, Suspension, and Destruction . . ." *Philosophical Magazine* 16 (1802): 97–107; 17 (1803): 5–11.

[27] Ibid., 16 (1802), p. 97.

[28] "[A]s a rule, they [clouds] show the effects of these causes with the same truth and clarity with which the physiognomy and the whole being of a person betray the feelings of his soul and the state of his health": *Gilberts Annalen,* 1805, quoted by John Gage, "Clouds over Europe," in *Constable's Clouds.* I am most grateful to John Gage, University of Cambridge, for kindly lending me the article before publication.

[29] See Karl Badt, *John Constable's Clouds* (London, 1950), pp. 15–21.

together with Enlightenment system, scientific nomenclature, and analysis. In the poems, he plays the game of finding faces, animals, shapes in the clouds. "A ghost seems forming ghosts," he writes in "Stratus."[30]

The fiery aether crackles and flares in one of the most dazzling and distilled of Gerard Manley Hopkins's hymns to divine creation: "That Nature is a Heraclitean Fire and of the Comfort of the Resurrection," written in 1888. A letter of that year gives the poet's sources in "early Greek philosophical thought," but stresses how "the liquor of the distillation did not taste very Greek, did it?"; and, indeed, Hopkins's imagination conjures its own cosmology from nineteenth-century hypotheses as well as Pre-Socratic theories. Again, the spectacle of the cloud layer delimits the space of the aether and offers in the opening lines the most eloquent metaphor for the dynamics of Nature's vital force:

> Cloud-puffball, torn tufts, tossed pillows   flaunt forth, then chevy
>   on an air-
> built thoroughfare: heaven-roysterers, in gay-gangs   they throng;
> they glitter in marches.

The fantastic word picture of the glittering cloudwrack swept by gusts continues, and of its effects on the earth, parching it, and marking it, until a short, spondaic, finite sentence interrupts the fugue:

> Million-fuelèd,   nature's bonfire burns on.

Hopkins then laments how the aethereal spark in man has died, drowned, blacked out, blotted out, and so forth; he turns to God, and to salvation, and this reprieve is conveyed through an explicit contrast in metaphors of combustion: the "world's wildfire" consumes its objects and "leave[s] but ash," but the great conflagration at the end of world will precipitate the poet into a new form, in an alchemical process of transubstantiation:

> In a flash, at a trumpet crash,
> I am all at once what Christ is,   since he was what I am, and
> This Jack, joke, poor potsherd,   patch, matchwood, immortal
>   diamond,
>   Is immortal diamond.[31]

---

[30] Johann Wolfgang von Goethe, "Stratus," in ibid.

[31] See Gerard Manley Hopkins, *Poems and Prose,* ed. W. H. Gardner (Harmondsworth, 1985), pp. 65–66, 244–55.

At the end of the nineteenth century, when Mallarmé offers us his combustible soul as a smoke ring, and Hopkins his alchemical precipitate of dust, they were writing against a background of unprecedented ferment about exploring the invisible, and they reached, as it were naturally at that time, for metaphors taken from combustion, condensation, and other physical aetherealizing processes.

5. Plumbing the Heights

The air was growing ever more crowded, yielding up all manner of mysteries to new instruments devised to detect and inventory its components. But these findings continually interplayed with metaphysics and were brought to bear on psychic forces as well as physical forces. Mesmeric theories were woven into concepts of electricity; similarly, the discovery of X-rays in 1895, the identification of radio waves and the subsequent invention of the wireless, of telegraphy, of the telephone, produced a fevered—and delighted—search to penetrate the unseen: the channels of communication through the aether presented themselves *in potentia* as deliriously numberless; they became intertwined with the physical possibility of moving *objects* at a distance by finding some vehicle analogous to radio waves.[32] It is difficult from our inured vantage point today to imagine how exciting, fascinating, and extreme seemed the possibilities that the new instruments opened up for their first users. The new media left the trace of their passage: indeed their activity became legible only through such traces through contact. Radio waves could not be grasped by the human senses, only the effects of the new methods of transmission: i.e., the marks of a needle quivering on a drum as the taps came through, the translated and disincarnate voices from the radio set. Visible verification surrendered its hegemony to other warranties of presence—acoustic and haptic.[33] Material impressions of the new media's work were in high demand. In the absence of

[32] See Michael Roth, "Hysterical Remembering," *Modernism/Modernity* 3, no. 2 (1996): 1–30; Lawrence Rainey, "Taking Dictation: Collage Poetics, Pathology, and Politics," *Modernism/Modernity* 5, no. 2 (1998): 123–53; Roger Luckhurst, "(Touching on) Tele-Technology," in *Applying: To Derrida*, ed. John Brannigan, Ruth Robbins, and Julian Wolfreys (London, 1996), pp. 171–83; Steven Connor, "The Machine in the Ghost: Spiritualism, Technology, and the 'Direct Voice,'" in *Ghosts*, ed. Peter Buse and Andrew Stott (London, 1999), pp. 203–25.

[33] Steven Connor emphasizes the aural desires, arguing that "an observational, calculative scientific culture organized around these questering powers of the eye began in the last

natural sensory means to verify the principle at work, a dependence on second-order technological proof of hidden energy arose, translating touch into sight, as in the photograph or the X-ray plate. The extension of the word "medium" itself, in the early 1850s, to someone with paranormal powers reveals the parallelism perceived between the vehicle— the aether—and its products. The new technologies offered a model for understanding that was extended to phenomena as yet beyond the reach of scientific empiricism. William James put his finger on the similarity of the scientific and spiritualist experiments, as perceived at the time, when he wrote that phenomena like automatic writing were "instruments of research, reagents like litmus paper or the galvanometer for revealing what would otherwise be hidden."[34]

The unseen was teeming, and not only with waves. Several different gases were detected in this period of scientific excitement. Gas, a word related to "chaos" and to the group that gives "ghost," "ghastly," and "geist," or breath, as well, blows gustily through the metaphor of the sublime, with its passion for eruptions and turbulence. Hydrogen had been analyzed in 1700, oxygen in the mid-1800s; in 1810, Humphry Davy had isolated the deadly and suffocating gas chlorine and made his famous experiments with laughing gas. But in the 1890s, there came an astonishing flurry of new, invisible and virtually imperceptible inert gases: Sir William Ramsay and Lord Rayleigh discovered argon (1894), helium (1895)—lighter than air—and neon, xenon, and krypton in 1898.[35] Furthermore, these inert gases, termed "noble," were placed at the top of the Periodic Table of the Elements above the volatile or combustible gases. They were thus aligned with the perceived eternity and

---

quarter of the nineteenth century to produce new forms of technology, especially communicative technology, which themselves promoted a reconfiguring of the sensorium in terms of the ear rather than the eye." I am very grateful to Steven Connor for letting me see his unpublished paper "Voice, Technology and the Victorian Ear," from the conference "Science and Culture 1780–1900," Birkbeck College, London, September 1997, to be published in *A Cultural History of Ventriloquism* (forthcoming).

[34] William James, "Frederic Myers's Service to Psychology" (1911), in *Essays in Psychical Research* (Cambridge, Mass., 1986), p. 196; quoted by Rhodri Hayward, "Popular Mysticism and the Origins of the New Psychology, 1880–1910," Ph.D. thesis (University of Lancaster, 1995–96), p. 133.

[35] The names Ramsay gave these gases are themselves revealing of the symbolic value attached to properties of air; argon is named after Argos, the many-eyed custodian appointed by Jupiter to watch over Io after he has changed her into a heifer. Does Ramsay's train of thought suggest that this pervasive substance (1 percent of the atmosphere) wraps us in its unseen gaze? Helium, whose existence had been guessed at by Joseph Lockyer in 1868, is the lightest gas of all and was named after the Greek god of the sun, Helios. Xenon means strange, neon new, krypton secret.

unchangingness of divinity, as against base matter, with its propensity for transformation or decay (the Mallarméan combustion of tobacco and its ashy residue, "le réel . . . vil").

From the 1840s onward, the visual illusions of Fata Morgana did not meet the standards of the new positivists in Spiritualist circles: tangible proofs were needed—real objects, actual matter. In Manchester, for example, a medium who called herself Mlle. E. d'Espérance materialized "apports"—the most exquisite plants, ferns, and fruits: a golden lily lasted a week, then "dissolved and disappeared."[36]

The medium Mrs. Guppy ate her productions—which one of her Spiritualist colleagues considered a mistake ("a great weakness").[37] But it was photographs of course that became the most popular documentary proof of spirits' real presence. Psychic images, in which spiritual bodies manifested themselves as ectoplasmic smudges, haloes, and phantoms, appeared to guarantee the truth-telling of seances.

It is no mere coincidence then, but an effect of a dynamic convergence of ideas, that the Society for Psychical Research was founded in 1888, in England, mainly by men associated with Trinity College, Cambridge, and its American counterpart was established in Boston, Massachusetts, a few years later. One of the tasks the members set themselves, with all the assiduity of high-minded Victorians, was to investigate the truth of the myriad paranormal and psychical phenomena that were literally making an impression in the world of material reality. Frederic Myers, poet, classicist, and one of the founders of the Society for Psychical Research, coined the word "telepathy" in 1882; the prefix was being used to form any number of compounds, some now incontrovertibly physical and others challenged by doubt: telephone, telegraph, telekinesis, teleportation. Television followed in 1925.

This enterprise—to weigh the imponderable, to measure the immeasurable—caught imaginations all over the world in the last decades of the nineteenth century. Their theories proved as inviting, as contested, and as ambiguously persuasive in their time as alchemy before them, and they have become as haloed in doubt today (a lesson in a certain necessary heuristic humility for our time, too). One of Franz Mesmer's followers, Karl von Reichenbach in Germany, in 1844 proposed an analogous invisible and imponderable force to Mesmer's earlier animal magnetism. He called it the Od, and declared it to be a different

---

[36] E. d'Espérance, *Shadow Land or Light from the Other Side* (London, 1897).

[37] Georgiana Houghton, *Chronicles of the Photographs of Spiritual Beings . . . Invisible to the Material Eye* (London, 1882), quoted by Connor, "The Machine in the Ghost," p. 208.

form of light, one transmitted by magnetic force. By means of subjects he called "sensitives," Reichenbach saw—and took photographs of—Odic lights and Odic smoke in darkened rooms, as they radiated from magnets that his collaborators held and energized. Their touch provided the crucial contact between the empirical realm and the aethereal. Interestingly, from the point of view of the Fata Morgana, he theorized that the Od was the principle that produced the aurora borealis, and he built a model of the earth—a *terrelle*—which demonstrated that the colored lights grew far more intense at the poles while "Odic smoke rose in abundance from the globe above the polar flames."[38] Dancing balls of radiance and flaring haloes around gifted mediums became a feature of early spiritualism.[39]

In Geneva, another "sensitive," the somnambulist and trance medium known as Hélène Smith, was collaborating with the eminent psychiatric doctor Théodore Flournoy to summon several spirit controls, through whom she rediscovered manifold curious previous existences, one as Marie-Antoinette no less, and another as the daughter of an Arab sheik, who subsequently married a Hindu prince, who himself was reincarnated as a Martian overlord, Astané. His 1899 account of their seances and her prodigious feats went through edition after edition—it is a pioneer of New Age publishing—under the title *Des Indes à la planète Mars*....[40] Hélène Smith is probably the first amply recorded case of multiple personality; in trance, she was able to communicate in the Martian tongue, write Martian script, and sketch the scenery and the people she had known there. "Aucune verdure [no greenery]," commented Flournoy, as if relieved that there was no mistaking Mars. "Everything brick-red, purple and violet," he appended to the black-and-white reproduction of the Mars countryside. Astané, who had a yellow complexion to match his native planet, traveled by means of flying-machine, a handheld flame-thrower something like a combination between a loud hailer and a child's toy *girouette* or windmill; he merely held it in his right hand as he flew.[41]

[38] Baron Charles (Karl) von Reichenbach, *Physico-Physiological Researches on the Dynamics of Magnetism, Electricity, Heat, Light Crystallization, and Chemism* [sic] *in Their Relations to the Vital Force*, trans. John Ashburner, 2 vols. (London, 1850–), vol. 2, p. 573. Reichenbach also discovered paraffin and creosote.

[39] See Elizabeth Barrett Browning, *Aurora Leigh*, 7.565–68; also Browning, *A Lovers' Quarrel*, stanza 7. I am most grateful to Margaret Reynolds for pointing out these references.

[40] Théodore Flournoy, *Des Indes à la planète Mars: Etude sur un cas de Somnambulisme* (Geneva, 1899), ed. and trans. Sonu Shamdasani (Princeton, N.J., 1996); see Terry Castle, "Flournoy's Complaint," in *London Review of Books*, May 23, 1996, pp. 6–7.

[41] Flournoy, *Des Indes*, p. 155.

In Paris, in the 1890s, Reichenbach's investigation of the Od or vital force inspired another enraptured experimenter, the doctor Hippolyte Baraduc, to tap psychic energies and record them in an exquisite series of *Epreuves* or Proofs (in the double sense of trial and confirmation).

His first book, published in Paris in 1896, appeared in 1913 in an English version, *The Human Soul: Its Movements, Its Lights, and the Iconography of the Fluidic Invisible.* It included an album of his remarkable photographs, which were taken, he wrote, without apparatus, by direct application of the sensitized plate to the electrically emitting sensitive mediums. It was this special force, the intelligent mode of the aether, that caused the emanations that were recorded in his photographs. "The vital force is intelligence in movement," he wrote, "rendering matter concrete."[42] By infra-red light he made exposures of a young boy—in mourning for a dead pheasant (!)—and showed the Odic light of his sorrow lifting the curtain behind him; he laid the plate to the forehead or hand of his living patients to draw out, by electrical magnetism, the "nuée fluidique" (the fluidic mist); he also grasped the "Ame-Germe et son Corps fluidique" (The Seed-Soul and its fluidic body) of dead friends. He meticulously categorized the images under different rubrics, calling some "Psychicônes" (Physicons) and others "Nuées odiques" (Odic mists). He was certain he had captured, for the material world, the Somods, or Odic bodies of his subjects. The images are tiny, sometimes half an inch square, and several show only tiny streams of bubbles, like spray, or a pale wispy blur, or a starburst or cloud of light. It is interesting to compare these images with the astronomer Camille Flammarion's prints of astronomical nebulae, in his work *Astronomie populaire,* published in 1900.

In *L'Ame humaine,* Baraduc quotes from Zoroaster and Jacob Boehme, and he seems to have been in touch with Parisian occultists such as Eliphas-Lévi. By the time his second book appeared in 1904, Baraduc was openly interested in hermetic mysticism. But *Les Vibrations de la vitalité humaine* also focuses on images of states of mind, and includes an image of a meteor shower, the Odic impression of anger, as well as a magnificent mare's tail portraying "the aetheric vortex," which was taken, he tells us, by holding his right hand motionless over the photographic plate, in the dark one night "à la suite de tristesse [following (a time of) sorrow]" at 10 P.M., in February 1895. At a macro scale,

---

[42] Hippolyte Baraduc, *The Human Soul: Its Movements, Its Lights, and the Iconography of the Fluidic Invisible* (London, 1913).

and a micro scale, the imagery of the luminiferous effects exercises its tenacious influence.

I have not enumerated these Faustian spells of the past to mock them; nor simply to entertain you, but to try to show how widespread—Western worldwide—was the quest to materialize the unseen and capture a hitherto imperceptible supernatural stratum to existence.

The suggestive emptiness of the upper sky continued to beckon into this century. Oliver Lodge, a physicist who made a major contribution to the understanding of radiotelegraphy with his experiments in wavelengths in 1888–98, thereby paving the way to Albert Einstein's theory of relativity, published a book called *Ether & Reality* as late as 1925. One of the most staunch supporters of the Society for Psychical Research, Sir Oliver, as he became, gamely persevered in the Einsteinian world, with his theory of the Ether, a word that he always capitalizes. It was "the *tertium quid,* the essential intermediary" between mind and matter. Ether itself was not "what we ordinarily speak of as matter," but nevertheless it was "a very substantial substance, far more substantial than any form of matter.... [A] physical thing...the vehicle of both matter and spirit...it is manifestly the vehicle or substratum underlying electricity and magnetism and light and gravitation and cohesion...." He concluded, rapturously, "It is the primary instrument of Mind, the vehicle of Soul, the habitation of Spirit. Truly, it may be called the living garment of God."[43]

Oliver Lodge affirmed that one of the Ether's functions was "to transmit vibrations from one piece of matter to another," and he argued that because the Ether vibrated at a frequency different from that of matter it would reveal itself in certain, very carefully constructed experiments—fleetingly, aethereally—in the form of ectoplasm.

6. THE SOCIETY FOR PSYCHICAL RESEARCH

In 1891 Oliver Lodge joined Henry Sidgwick, the Cambridge philosopher, and his wife Eleanor at the house of Charles Richet, future winner of the Nobel Prize for Medicine (1913), to investigate the truth of Eusapia Paladino, a middle-aged, illiterate southern Italian materializing medium who had won the approval of no less a forensic champion

[43] Oliver Lodge, *Ether & Reality* (London, 1925), p. 179.

than Cesare Lombroso. Paladino was one of the most accomplished producers of ectoplasm at the turn of the century, but her specialities also included table-turning, guitars playing by themselves and floating through the air, and "the conveyance of a vase full of jonquils . . . the highly increased perfume of the flowers' bells ringing by themselves."[44] The company was assembled to witness her powers.

The word "ectoplasm," from the Greek *ektos* (outside) and *plasma* (something that can be formed or molded, as in "plastic"), enters the discourse of spiritualism in Germany and France in the 1880s.[45] Ectoplasm is shapeless, it is "informe," a kind of primordial paste—and to show itself as this it annexes semiotic markers that designate intermediate spirit worlds.

The *Critical Dictionary,* edited and written by Georges Bataille and others in the late 1920s, included an entry on ectoplasm with characteristically mischievous mock learning: it defined it as

> part of the human body, external to it, unstable, sometimes soft, occasionally hard, from time to time vaporous, variable in volume, visible only in semi-darkness, making an impression on photographic emulsion, presents to the sense of touch a humid and slippery sensation, leaving in the hand a residue which, when dry, has under microscopic examination the appearance of epithelial cells, without odour or definite taste, in other respects fleeting and transient, whether projected or otherwise, of uncertain temperature, fond of music.

It adds, knowingly, "Fish- and game-birds' intestines, even inflated with a bicycle-pump, are not ectoplasms."[46] It is cosmic goo: the joke shops of the New Age, picking up on the tradition, now sell "Space Mucus" in "Slime Eggs" that glow in the dark.

---

[44] "Hesperus," "Eusapia Paladino," in *Light,* May 23, 1896, pp. 243–44.

[45] It is worth noting that, in the late 1850s, when Robert Browning was composing his long dramatic monologue "'Mr Sludge,' the Medium," he may have wanted his fraud's name to hint at ectoplasmic sludge, but he does not introduce such phenomena specifically into his plausible villain's weaselly rigmarole of self-justification, grievance, and malice. D. D. Home, who, after the Brownings attended a seance in Ealing in 1855, inspired the character of Mr. Sludge, did not produce ectoplasmic structures, but focused his energies on other prodigies: his most celebrated being his ability to levitate. He once flew out of one window and came in feet first and horizontal from another; Harry Houdini, who made a habit of exposing supernatural claims by reproducing them as conjuring tricks, countered with a promise to repeat the feat, but called off the event—to the delight, of course, of D. D. Home's supporters. See Robert Browning, *The Complete Works,* ed. John C. Berkey, Allan C. Dooley, and Susan Dooley (Waco, Tex., and Athens, Ohio, 1996), vol. 6, pp. 285–351.

[46] Jacques Brunius, "Ectoplasm," in *Critical Dictionary,* ed. Georges Bataille, published as the *Encyclopaedia Da Costa* (1948), *Encyclopaedia Acephalica,* ed. Robert Lebel and Isabelle Waldberg (London, 1995), pp. 110–11.

Darkness was essential for the phenomena to appear: light, almost everyone agreed, was highly destructive to their organism. The great chemist William Crookes preferred moonlight, and reported excellent results by this pale illumination; the French doctor Gustave Geley hankered after the light emitted by certain animals, vegetables, and microbes, reporting wistfully that highly successful seances had been held in Brazil by the light of glow-worms, but that this was very difficult to realize in practice.[47] But, given a darkened room, and willing, supportive sitters, the "substance" might appear.

Paladino was not photographed in action as exhaustively as her contemporary, the medium Eva Carrière (figure 8). Eva C., as she was known, began extruding ectoplasms during seances conducted under the auspices of Juliette Bisson, a wealthy woman who promoted the seer's powers through her friendship with a Bavarian doctor and minor aristocrat, Baron von Schrenk-Notzing. In 1890, in Germany, he published exhaustive minutes of the seances and the phenomena in a bizarre, alarming volume filled with photographs of the medium in trance, sufferings spasms as she produced a wide range of materializations. The book was translated into English in 1920 under the title *Phenomena of Materialisation,* and it made the type of seances featured internationally famous.

The word "ectoplasm" was borrowed across from biological usage: the *Oxford English Dictionary* gives as its first citation a quotation from 1883 that discloses vividly the operating metaphor: "Its [amoeba's] jelly-like body becomes faintly parcelled out into an outer form (ectoplasm) and an inner soft (endoplasm) layer."[48] It is "the substance from which spirits make themselves visible forms . . . alive, sensitive to touch and light . . . cold to the touch, slightly luminous and having a characteristic smell . . . ."

In the 1920s, Dr. Gustave Geley asserts: "The colour white is the most frequent. . . . On touch . . . it can seem soft and a bit elastic when it spreads; hard, knotty or fibrous when it forms strings. The substance is mobile. At one moment it evolves slowly, rises, falls, wanders over the medium, her shoulders, her breast, her knees, with a creeping motion that recalls that of a reptile . . . ."[49] Sometimes faces and even bodies of the departed appeared, like Fata Morganas, in its webs.

After making its appearance, ectoplasm was reabsorbed into the

[47] Gustave Geley, *Ectoplasme,* p. 15.

[48] J. E. Ady, *Knowledge,* June 15, 1883, 355/2.

[49] Geley, *Ectoplasme,* p. 199.

Figure 8. Photo of Eva C.[arrière], from Baron von Schrenk-Notzing, *Phenomena of Materialisation* (London, 1920). (Wren Library, Trinity College, Cambridge)

medium's body—unless it was rudely captured, as in the case of Helen Duncan.

When looking at these unformed forms, it is worth recalling that the word "larva," used in English for the early stage of a caterpillar, meant "ghost" or "spectre" in Latin, but is also used by Horace to designate a mask, such as might frighten an observer, while the Latin verb *larvere* meant to bewitch or enchant. Ectoplasmic masks and limbs are indeed larval: they promise the emergence of forms, but do not deliver them. The term "pseudo-pods," used for some of the "structures," catches this relationship with the embryonic—and indeed with the abortion.

Henry Sidgwick was an unlikely subject for voyeurism or tomfoolery: with his wife Eleanor he was a pioneer campaigner for female higher education and co-founder of Newnham College, Cambridge. They were high-principled, liberal-minded, progressive, scrupulous and kindly Victorians. Yet Sidgwick, in the desolation after Darwin, left holy orders, and became the first president of the Society for Psychical Research in 1882.

Sidgwick and his close friend and former student F. W. H. Myers, from the 1850s onward, visited numerous mediums, with inconclusive results; rooted scepticism and unappeasable curiosity writhed in Sidgwick's energetic mind for four decades. Questers like Myers and the Sidgwicks were feeling out a scientific position toward some of the basic tenets of Christian theology, such as the existence of the individual soul and its immortality. In the course of his life's work, *The Survival of Human Personality after Bodily Death* (1915), Myers developed a secular, psychological theory of the subliminal self. This self enjoys continuity over time and place, unconsciously carrying memories that preserve its integrity over eternity; these can be awakened or recalled through mediums and other supernatural means. As Rhodri Hayward puts it: "Myers's subliminal self...operated as a kind of filter for the sacred, combining the extracarnate communication with the fragmentary memories and desires of the individual's own past.... The sacred was relocated within the field of memory."[50]

The two philosophers evinced no self-consciousness about their own motives. Astonishingly naive letters pass between them about whether the kisses they received in seances were given by materialized lips, for

[50] Hayward, "Popular Mysticism," pp. 157, 186.

example. Nor does any of the surviving correspondence in the archives illuminate the *interior* life and thinking of the mediums themselves—women such as Eva Carrière, Eusapia Paladino, or, later, the Bostonian Margery Crandon—from their point of view.

The women did not write memoirs—unlike the sitters. Paladino could not read or write; Margery left one exchange of letters (with E. J. Dingwall) in the archives, where she complains about pains in her nose—hardly surprising when she was expelling so much stuff from her nostrils during the seances. Yet again, nobody connects her physical distress, which caused her to cancel quite often, with her ectoplasmic production. Her spirit control Walter once commented, it is recalled, "Pay no attention to her. Let her groan. She hasn't any pain. Blow your nose, Kid. I'm like an octopus, I can attach myself anywhere and then put life into it. She must sit very tight. Don't ask her how she feels."[51]

The travelers into the unknown were precisely attracted by the mediums' near-death states, in which they lost their self-possession. The trances, fits, numbness, and transports that the mediums experienced opened them up as channels for others. This psycho-sexual story, about unconscious gratifications, can be explored more fully; this approach can be woven, as Alex Owen has done in her fine study *The Darkened Room* (1989), into a historicist analysis of the conflict of power, of class and gender, between men and women, the learned and the uneducated, and, often, the native and the foreigner.

After exciting but ambiguous seances at Richet's, the Sidgwicks invited Paladino to stay with them in Cambridge to continue the experiments.

Here are some examples of the minutes, now in the archives, written up the day after one of the seances by the scrupulous Alice Johnson, the secretary of the Society for Psychical Research.

Th. Aug 1/95

With Mr and Mrs M[yers] Prof. and Mrs. S.[idgwick] Mrs Verrall Dr. Rogers, Mr. E. T. Dixon. A. J.[ohnson].

. . . .

7.30 Mr Myers lay down on the floor again so that he could see her knees.

[51] *Proceedings of the Society for Psychical Research,* part 98, vol. 36 (November 1925): 44.

7.40 Eusapia begins to laugh; indicating the arrival of John King. [John King was her spirit guide] then moans & becomes quiet again. Dr Rogers remarks that her eyeballs are turned up.

8.14 Medium comes out of trance asks who is holding her legs & is told. Prof. Sidgwick comes out from under table.

8.20 trance returning: Prof Sidgwick goes in again.

. . . .

8.30 *Mrs Myers said she saw something white. Mrs. Verrall also saw it.* [This has been crossed out; emphasis added.]

. . . .

9.10 . . . Eusapia says she wishes her feet to be left alone, & Prof Sidgwick comes out from under the table. Mr Myers says 'my chair is being dragged from under me & I am being gently dug in the ribs' Here Prof. Sidgwick goes under the table again & holds Eusapia's feet . . . .

9.12 Mr Myers says 'her head is on my shoulder.' Mrs Verrall says 'I saw a great white thing appear behind Mr Myers, perhaps the cushion.' . . . Mr Dixon grabbed at it & touched it; then it drew back. He said it felt like a hand or at all events something more solid than a cushion.[52]

The Sidgwicks remained hopeful that Paladino was not a humbug, one of their favorite words, but unconvinced; Oliver Lodge stayed a believer—in Paladino, in life after death, in ectoplasmic apparitions, in psychic photographs—especially after losing a son and several friends' sons in World War I.

The craze for such experiences did not abate after numerous exposés of the mediums' claims. In the 1920s, Margery Crandon caused a furore in Boston, where she was married to a society gynecologist from Beacon Hill, Boston; he was more than twenty-five years her elder. Margery's brother Walter had died in a railway accident in 1911, and he became her "spirit control," the character who appeared at her seances, often whistling loudly, ribbing the participants and even taunting them. Among her most admired phenomena (figure 9) were Walter's thumbprints, which appeared in the course of a seance, imprinted onto dental wax: the spirit from the other side being substantial and heavy enough to leave his unique seal. But Margery/Psyche surpassed even this

---

[52] MSS, notes, Society for Psychical Research archives, University Library, Cambridge.

Figure 9. Margery Crandon producing ectoplasmic phenomena, London, ca. 1925. (Harry Price Library, University of London)

remarkable spirit signature, when Walter began to form teleplasmic hands and heads, and even, most significantly, promised to deliver an ectoplasmic fetus.

Lady (Florence) Barrett, who did the examination of Margery Crandon before the sitting, explained afterward that she considered that the ectoplasmic rods had been "formed by a kind of birth process."[53] It has to be said as well that the notes to these "birth processes" make sordid and dismaying reading.

The symbolic range of ectoplasm as spirit made matter stretches from aethereal, phantasmic whiteness, exemplified by Helen Duncan's

[53] Letter from Mowbray, to London Spiritualist Alliance, June 13, 1947. Society for Psychical Research archives, University Library, Cambridge.

yards of white satin, to a state of emergent being, typified by the cold, formless lumps of some sort of tissue, as produced by Eva Carrière and Margery Crandon. These two poles correspond to two classes of phenomena that were conflated under the term: Myers defined them as first projections of the double—namely the spirit of a person—and secondly, precipitations of the *akas*—*akas* being a Hindu term borrowed by the Theosophists and designating the invisible energy that flows through and unites creation. However, once these two forms are distinguished, it is clear that ectoplasm uneasily converts two contradictory concepts of person and spirit's relation to person: the phantom makes manifest an individual who has died, as does the ectoplasmic mask. But the ectoplasmic effluvia and pseudo-pods that Carrière and Crandon also spewed do not body forth the mediums' own vital spirits, or even the spirit of their spirit controls; they are phantasmic templates on which the conjured spirit—the IPA or "incorporeal personal agent"—makes his or her mark, using touch to guarantee presence.

The very subject of ectoplasm now tends to provoke involuntary laughter, shivers, and, on closer look, real horror; the documentary images strike us now as foolish, crazy, embarrassing, prurient, repellent. That anyone could have believed that such phantoms, vomitings, and excreta were manifestations of spirit fills the contemporary observer with revulsion. That anyone could have participated in good faith at their performance and production seems highly unlikely. It seems to us now a highly peculiar and shameful chapter in the history of intellectual and spiritual inquiry.

7. Profitable Waste

Making spirits present through this nebulous stuff reproduces some of the characteristic features of sacrificial ritual. Some are obvious: the sitters forming the ring are vital to the event, and to the success of the event; they gather as a solemn, ritual congregation, bonded together to follow prescribed steps in making contact with spiritual powers. But other similarities are more confusing. The medium's role is multi-layered—it might appear that Paladino, Carrière, and Crandon take the place of the sibyl, priestess, or priest, since they act as conductors of spirit. However, this position in the seance is complicated by the lack of identification between them and the spirit control or IPA who appears and then, sometimes, forms ectoplasmic phenomena that attest the coming of another being, a relation of one of the sitters or a famous figure from history. Mediums are habitually treated as mere instruments, through whom the participants access the supernatural: they themselves have the power to contact the uncanny, but this uncanny then is transmitted to the others. On account of this necessary, sibylline, but somehow disparaged, position of the medium, she seems to me to approach the place of the sacrificial victim, with the sitters as the hierophants, who, through a contact "high," become mediums themselves.

But the ordeal, the self-abnegation and exposure of a medium such as Margery Crandon when producing ectoplasm, reverses the process of ritual sacrifice in one respect: animal tissue is not oblated, offered to the powers above, destroyed by fire in order to be metamorphosed into the rising smoke of the holocaust on an altar, but is produced from insubstantial lights and breezes and wispy vapors to take form down below as living matter—temporarily. The medium is desecrated in an act of psychological abjection in order to recuperate from the other side lost flesh, consumed creatures, and offer proof of the existence of life after death: she turns smoke into live cinders, to borrow—and reverse—Mallarmé's startling metaphor. She transforms the lost dead into the living. It becomes less surprising that so many classicists were involved in the quest for spirit. This perspective can help us to understand, I suggest, why wise, philanthropic, dignified thinkers—men and women of the calibre of the Sidgwicks and F. W. H. Myers, Margaret Verrall (who was a classicist) and her daughter Helen Salter, and Lady Barrett—were prepared to take part, day after day, in experiments that transgressed their society's codes of social intercourse, gendered behavior, dignity and decorum.

The spiritualist seance does not replicate a blood offering to the gods—but it recasts sacrifice in the context of an industrial and scientific age, just as the medium, uttering messages from spirit controls, or marking gnomic phrases at the promptings of voices, harks back to the sibyl and Delphic oracles of which Myers had written, while also reproducing the action of modern, technical media. One can take this modernizing tendency further: a materializing medium like Eusapia Paladino or Margery Crandon acts as a producer; the forms she makes, sometimes nebulous, sometimes shapeless, convert the combustion of the sacrificial victim—the smoke from the altar—into a force of production, in mimicry of the steam engine and the steamhammer and the factory chimney and the gas-fired boiler, where vapors no longer signify clouds of divine glory, but the energy of industrial output.

Sacrifice entails surrender of something valued in order to gain something even more strongly desired. Abraham is prepared to kill his only son, Isaac. The medium's physical self-abandonment and psychological self-effacement could have fulfilled this necessary condition for the success of the ritual. But a sacrifice can also involve a mere chicken—or some other lowly, less valued thing; then it takes on the primary role of transformation, of sublimating the humble vehicle into heaven-climbing fragrance and vapor. The selection of victim hallows it, however low, according to the symbolic axiom that transfigures the profane, base, vile, and real, into the sacred, into "immortal diamond." The imagination operates in response to "the elementary subjective identity between types of excrement (sperm, menstrual blood, urine, fecal matter [and one might add here, ectoplasm]) and everything that can be seen as sacred, divine or marvellous."[54] The grim and sordid proceedings of a seance summoned unseen forces and made them materially present—if temporarily—in the nebulous wraiths and figures of ectoplasm. It converted the medium's energy into something palpable by combining figures, like clouds and smoke, from the traditional language of the divine, by applying new instruments, such as the camera, to their interpretation, and by inserting them into the schedule of an industrial economy, which served to make of ectoplasm the valued residue of the sitters' joint labor. The inexplicable emptiness of space was refused, the dead were not consigned to waste, a new, paranormal form of excreta was transfigured, and the epitome of nebulousness was attributed to intricate, objective meaning: the production of ectoplasm constituted a profitable struggle with conditions of labor, and a triumph of knowledge.

What connects this enterprise with visions or illusory images, as discussed in my first lecture, is three-fold: first, the visual lexicon of nephography is instrumentalized by innovatory media; second, order and pattern are imposed on non-sense in order to avoid the unbearable scandal—for Christian humanism—of meaninglessness; third, and crucially, the conception of subject or self to which the idea of mediumship contributed is shown to be apt for occupation by another. Subjectivity is

---

[54] Georges Bataille, *Visions of Excess: Selected Writings 1927–1939*, ed. and trans. Allan Stoekl (Minneapolis, 1985), p. 94, quoted in *Formless: A User's Guide*, ed. Yve-Alain Bois and Rosalind E. Krauss (New York, 1997), p. 51.

diffused, decentered, dislocated, and the long, Thomist, unbreakable pact between soul and body cracked—with immense consequences for psychology, for writing, and for visual modes of story telling. While Myers is almost forgotten and widely dismissed, his theory of the subliminal self has spread, appropriately, through other channels besides himself (including Sigmund Freud) to permeate popular ideas of the personality. The voice-over, stream of consciousness, collage, and cutups are only some of the methods practiced to capture this paranormal model of spirit, which imagines the individual dispersed in space, the unified viewpoint shattered, linear temporality confused, memories and fantasies intermingled, selves scattered through time and place, but united by an inextinguishable subliminal subjectivity.[55] Both cinematic and acoustic media convey and contribute to this new writing of the subject. As proclaimed in *The X-Files,* the truth is no longer within, but out there.

However, it is a profound paradox that, while Myers's metaphysics shadow forth the late psychological turn of this century, the astral language of spirit that he and his peers deployed has been denatured by the same decades' deepest experiences. Myers's and the Sidgwicks' yearnings for an immortal and metaphysical dimension to human life—not survival in others' memories, but survival itself, as a wraith, as a spirit—present us with the final, doomed twist in the religious wager that Darwin and Freud had closed down. As Adam Phillips writes in his book *Darwin's Worms,* "Darwin and Freud, in their quite different ways, are persuading us to become good losers.... It is as though, they suggest, we have added to the ordinary suffering of biological life the extraordinary suffering of our immortal longings, of our will to permanence."[56] These late Victorians and their faithful remnant among Edwardians were not prepared to be losers. One of the recurrent events in the lives of all the members of the Society for Psychical Research is prize-winning: these men were stars at school, in college, and expected to master a world that would not offer them the kind of contest they had anticipated. They did indeed suffer from immortal longings, from a will to permanence. It is almost too apt, though it shows the punning agility of dreams, that for a time they even tried to turn spirit solid, to grasp a cloud, to capture the aether as ectoplasm.

[55] See Connor, "The Machine in the Ghost," p. 208, where he quotes Walter Ong's *The Presence of the Word:* "Sound situates man in the middle of actuality and in simultaneity, whereas vision situates man in front of things and in sequentiality." "Sound" here could be expanded to include touching—especially in the dark.

[56] Adam Phillips, *Darwin's Worms* (London, 1999), p. 127.

8. ENVOI

Helen Duncan's sample of cheap satin embodies the bankruptcy of a long chapter of spiritual questing. But it also reveals how far signs, under pressure from history, can move. As white cloth, her ectoplasm discloses the anxiety that surrounds murkiness and smoke: visions of the Virgin Mary today invariably depict her in unadulterated cotton wool. Titian or Tintoretto's swirling and laden clouds have been banished from the supernatural lexicon. Combustion announces only the fires of hell, warns of danger, of pollution and poison.

It is industrial progress that would eventually abolish for us, in the present, the baroque meanings of the gamboling cloud-babies, the underlit vortices of the empyrean, the radiant nimbuses that sheathe angels in rainbow vapors.[57] For the Victorian artist, smoke and steam could represent a secular and glorious combustion, energy harnessed in the here and now for mercantile and colonial purposes of the greatest power of the times.

But again, photography—that medium of *contact,* sensible to impression—makes a crucial difference to the cloud family of symbols to which ectoplasm belongs. Whereas in psychic images the camera obeyed the traditional tropes of the supernatural, in this case its contribution canceled the old order. The Crimean War was the first to be documented by photography, but Roger Fenton's famous images show a hushed and still desolation, for the camera speeds then were simply too slow to capture action or explosions as they were happening.

The first images of shellbursts, bomb-blasts, and billowing gusts of smoke (figure 10) in warfare seem to have been taken in World War I. They are military records, made in a spirit of discovery of new weapons, presented in the archive of the Imperial War Museum as evidence, historical and scientific. Black-and-white photographs show the effect of mines exploding, of shells' impact, of gas canisters spewing out their

---

[57] There were earlier rumblings: at the end of an *Entertainment at Rutland House,* performed in 1656, Sir William Davenant wrote a Song:

London is smother'd with sulph'rous fires;
    Still she wears a black hood and cloak,
        Of sea-coal smoke,
As if she mourned for brewers and dyers.

Chorus:

But she is cool'd and cleans'd by streams
Of flowing and of ebbing Thames.

(*The Dramatic Works of Sir William D'Avenant* [Edinburgh and London, 1873], vol. 3, pp. 228–29.)

Figure 10. The bursting of a Livens bomb (containing poison gas), ca. 1917. (Imperial War Museum, London)

poisons, of rifle fire igniting: sometimes, roiling plumes of grey smog, or solid walls of smoke and debris, sometimes soft, miasmic bodies of cloud floating above the ground, apparently the purest shade of white, all innocence and aethereality.

Poison gas filled the landscape of the trenches with light, spiraling heads of cumulus; infantry smokescreens raised tall, impenetrable barriers of cloud. The new horrors of chemical warfare proved parts of the invisible air materially present and undeniably tangible. The contamination of industrial emissions added to the new experience of air, to the newly identified, malignant character of smoke of the fiery aether.

Once upon a time Raphael painted the Madonna of Foligno upwafted by curling surf of blue-grey angel-clouds, Correggio depicted the ravishing approach of a god as a mass of blue-grey smoke, Titian invited us to believe in the Assumption of the Virgin taking place within and upon a roiling mass of shadowy cumulus, and Poussin caught Mary up to heaven on a roll and blast of thundercloud. Now we live as successors to the splitting of the atom and the nuclear-powered ascension of the mushroom cloud at the end of World War II and during the hydrogen bomb tests in the South Pacific.

Photographs of artillery and nuclear explosions produce a twisted effect on me as a spectator: the undeniable power and terror of the event delivers a hit, a rush; the images impact viscerally, inspiring the wonder and awe that has been coupled with beauty in that psychological and esthetic zone diagnosed so eloquently by Edmund Burke. But morally it is hard—impossible—to admire this phantom of death, this foreshadowing of the megaweapons of our century. Yet this very complexity of response encapsulates a pervasive cultural dilemma, about the relations of pleasure and representation. These images open up another huge zone of questions, which must await another day. But assaying the pleasurable weights of different signs, such as clouds and cloudiness, learning their history and modifications over time, can at least help us to analyze the effect that such images of bombs and bombing have on us now. For as signs of possibility, clouds still float through our world: as the default setting of the computer screensaver, and in innumerable advertisements for future investments, insurances, fortunes. Clouds are still buoyed by ancient exhalations of aethereal paradises, divine power, immortal longings, futurity.

However, alongside the billowing plumes of cooling towers, the smog of car-choked cities, the oil-clogged plumage of seabirds, the growing asthmatic problems of children and older people, and the refusal to sign the test ban treaty, we need another constellation of metaphor to convey the unpolluted, uncontaminated zone of spirit. The language of the aether opened casements onto the realm of the unseen, but it depended on conditions and on aspirations that have since been stifled in a new kind of cloud: we breathe a different air now.

Poetry and the Mediation of Value:

Whitman on Lincoln

HELEN VENDLER

THE TANNER LECTURES ON HUMAN VALUES

Delivered at

University of Michigan
October 29 and 30, 1999

Helen Vendler is A. Kingsley Porter University Professor in English at Harvard University. She was educated at Emmanuel College, the University of Louvain, and Boston University, and received her Ph.D. from Harvard University. She is a member of the American Academy of Arts and Letters, the American Academy of Arts and Sciences, the American Philosophical Society, and the Norwegian Society of Sciences and Letters. She is the recipient of the Charles Stewart Parnell Fellowship, Magdalene College, Cambridge; she has also received fellowships from the Wilson Center and the Guggenheim Foundation. In addition to her academic duties, she is the poetry critic for the *New Yorker*. Her many published works include *Yeats's Vision and the Later Plays* (1963); *The Poetry of George Herbert* (1975); *Wallace Stevens: Words Chosen out of Desire* (1984); *The Music of What Happens: Essays on Poetry and Criticism* (1988); *Soul Says: On Recent Poetry* (1995); and *The Art of Shakespeare's Sonnets* (1997).

The Tanner Lectures consider questions of human value. I take as my texts today, as examples of how the art of poetry mediates value, Walt Whitman's four poems on the death of Abraham Lincoln. Lincoln was shot by John Wilkes Booth, in conspiracy with others, on April 14, 1865, while the Civil War was still ongoing. In the twenty days between the assassination and Lincoln's May 4 burial in Springfield, Illinois, many events occurred. There was first the shocked five-day interim following the assassination; then the thronged April 19 state funeral for Lincoln in Washington; then the seventeen-hundred-mile ceremonial journey of the funeral train bearing Lincoln's coffin through Baltimore, Harrisburg, Philadelphia, New York, Albany, Buffalo, Cleveland, Columbus, Indianapolis, Michigan City, and Chicago. On April 26 Booth had been apprehended and shot, and by April 27 eight conspirators were in jail (awaiting the trial that would end in the hanging of four of them on July 7). All of these events were available to Whitman as he wrote his four poems, as was the fact that the body of Lincoln's son Willie (who had died three years earlier) was exhumed from its grave in Washington and reburied in the Lincoln tomb at Springfield.

Whitman's poems on Lincoln were composed in the following order: the short occasional poem "Hush'd Be the Camps Today" (dated April 19, 1865, the day of Lincoln's funeral service in Washington, and printed in the May 1865 edition of *Drum-Taps*); the formally rhymed poem "O Captain, My Captain" and the free-verse elegy "When Lilacs Last in the Dooryard Bloom'd" (both added to the second edition of *Drum-Taps*, September 1865); and the later epitaph "This Dust Was Once the Man" (1871). The assassination of Lincoln of course provoked a flood of writing—journalistic, biographical, poetic. Of the many poems then written, Whitman's memorials have lasted the best; and in considering what values they select, enact, and perpetuate, I want to ask by what aesthetic means they make those values last beyond the momentary topical excitement of Lincoln's death.

Poetry mediates values differently from prose. In prose, values are usually directly stated, illustrated, clarified, and repeated. One has only to think of the classical form of the oration—and its descendants the sermon, the stump speech, and the university lecture—to see the importance placed, in an oral form, on reduplication of matter. Whitman's poetry retains many vestiges of the oration; and we can see such vestiges in "Lilacs." But most lyric poetry, being short, cannot avail itself of the ample terrain of oratory; it has consequently had to find extremely compressed ways by which to convey value. Readers of poetry not only become adept in unfolding the implications of a poetic language; they also learn to see—by exercising historical knowledge—what is being left out that might well have been present. In respect to the conveying of value, what is left out is always as important as what is put in. Let me give one quick example: Lincoln was assassinated on Good Friday, and commentary on his death quickly attached to him—probably for that reason—the word "martyr" with its overtones of Christ's sacrifice. Whitman offers no word placing Lincoln in the context of Christ's passion, Good Friday, or Easter Sunday. He does not put Lincoln in a Judeo-Christian frame at all—even though contemporary commentators such as Bishop Matthew Simpson at the Washington funeral compared Lincoln to Moses.

I will come back to what is left out by Whitman, but I want to return now to the main question—how we can examine poetry's mediation of value. To relate what is left out to what is put in is a task relatively easier with respect to narration than with respect to lyric. One can see that a novelist (say, Herman Melville in *Moby-Dick*) has included no female characters and suggest what effects and values are enabled by, and also prohibited by, this stratagem. But in lyric, there is no such obvious norm. A symphony score employing no violins would be visibly anomalous; but nobody noticed at first when Georges Perec wrote a novel (*The Void*) without the letter *e* because letters—and words—are less visible than women or violins.

It is imagination, then, that is our first recourse in thinking about poetry and value—the imagination of what is left out. This imagination operates not simply on the grosser level of images (such as the Judeo-Christian ones of Moses or Christ that I have mentioned) but also on the level of syntax—in what other manner could this sentence have been framed?—and of diction—what words might have occurred by contrast to the ones we have? The critical imagination must operate even in the realm of sound, especially at crucial poetic moments, asking what alternative phonetic effects might have been used instead of the given ones.

It is generally agreed that images and the semantic content of words mediate value, but syntax and sound are rarely conceded that potential. In prose, syntax and sound are generally less powerful than in poetry; in poetry they provide a crucial ground to the assertions of value carried by images and words. And, since a short poem is in fact a single complex word in which all individual components are bound together in an inalterable relational syntax, there is, strictly speaking, nothing that does not become a carrier of value in poetry (even such harmless-looking particles as the indefinite and the definite article).

Every lyric belongs to one or more anterior theoretical paradigms of genre. The paradigm may be a formal verse-whole, such as the sonnet, which brings with it certain values—those of courtly life—and general expectations (that it might concern, for instance, love or politics). Or the paradigm may be a formal stanza, such as *terza rima,* which brings with it overtones of Dante, the afterlife, and the value of spiritual self-scrutiny. Or the paradigm may be that of a genre that has no formal shape: the English elegy, for instance, can take any verse shape, but must reflect the death of one or more persons and must meditate on the value of a given sort of human life. Or the paradigm may be that of a genre which, while having no prescribed shape, does have a prescribed length and tone: an epitaph, for instance, must be short and impersonally phrased, and it must assert a final judgment. Or the anterior paradigm may prescribe only one part of the stanza: the presence of a refrain at the end of each stanza, for instance, suggests the value of folk-motifs and of incremental intensification of emotion. A poem can ally itself with the first-person singular paradigm (which is the most common lyric self-presentation, valuing individual experience), or it may depart from that norm by choosing a first-person plural paradigm, in order to claim collective utterance and, with it, collective value.

A poem is expected not only to inscribe itself within the subject-matter and values implied by its paradigms, but also to extend, reverse, or otherwise be original in respect to those very paradigms. It is in the use and critique of its own antecedent paradigms that a poem most fully reveals its own value-system. It is this that I hope to show in reflecting on Whitman's poems concerning Lincoln. The value-system of an original poet—and therefore of his or her poems—will be in part consonant with, in part in dispute with, the contemporary values of the society from which he, and they, issue. Were the poetry not intelligible with respect to those social values, it could not be read; were it not at a distance from them in some way, it would not be original. The most disturbing lyrics are those, such as Whitman's, in which so many shared social values appear that one is surprised when interior divergence manifests itself. Whitman's memorials of Lincoln are patriotic ones, devoted to the image of Lincoln, voiced in solidarity with the Union army, sharing the nation's grief at Lincoln's death and at the carnage of the Civil War, and (in "Lilacs") proud of the much-celebrated beauty of the American landscape. What is it, then, that makes them original? And what values does that originality consecrate? And why is "Lilacs"—the longest of Whitman's poems about Lincoln—also the best? What does it allow that the others do not?

"To have great poems, there must be great audiences, too," Whitman had declared in the 1855 preface to *Leaves of Grass*. His poetic depended on a close connection, even an erotic one, with his imagined listeners: he not only wished to be their spokesman, he wanted *them* to call out to *him* to *be* their spokesman, thereby legitimating his writing. It is not surprising, then, that Whitman's first literary response to Lincoln's death—after the wordless silence that followed the shocking news of the assassination—was to speak in the collective voice of the Union army, as soldiers call on the poet to "sing . . . in our name . . . one verse." They ask that the subject-matter of this verse should be "the love we bore him." What the soldiers want is not a eulogy of Lincoln's personal life and actions, of the sort pronounced from the pulpit in Washington, but rather an articulation of their mourning. It is the soldiers themselves, as the poem opens, who devise the liturgy appropriate to the death of their commander-in-chief: "Let the camps be hushed, let the weapons be draped, and let us each retire"—to do what? to mourn, to muse, yes, but above all to "celebrate"—in the liturgical, not the festive sense—"our dear commander's death." Any human being can perform these personal acts of silence, weapon-draping, and musing, just as any human being can voice the consolation of the second stanza, as the soldiers say that Lincoln has escaped "time's dark events, / Charging like ceaseless clouds across the sky."

Only after they have invented a collective ritual, and offered a collective consolation, do the soldiers feel the absence of something necessary to their ceremony—an elevated, that is, sung form of utterance offered in their name. It is significant to them that it should be sung by one who, because he has been a "dweller in camps," knows the particular heaviness of soldiers' hearts. This short poem values collectivity—in the voice it adopts, in the rituals it devises. It not only values—more than all pomp-filled state memorials—the love borne by the common soldiers, but it also views poetry as merely one ingredient in an indigenous ritual, devised by the people for the people. Why, then, do the soldiers need a verse at all? The poem answers by showing the omnimobility of words. The soldiers remain bound in their camps, but the poet's invisible verse, as the syntax shows, can insert itself into the very circumstance and moment of far-off burial: "As they invault the coffin there, / Sing—as they close the doors of earth upon him—one verse." Lincoln is valued in this collectively voiced poem less as president of a country than as beloved commander of a brave army, themselves accustomed to "time's dark events, / Charging" at them. Yet the view of Lincoln is still a hierarchical one—not in a feudal, but in a military, sense. He is not king or president, but he is the commander. It is not surprising that the democratic Whitman will eventually turn to valuing Lincoln outside a military hierarchy.

Now that he has written the collective call beckoning him to sing, Whitman can compose the verse that will show, from the inside, the army's love and their heavy hearts. "O Captain, My Captain" is sung in the voice of a Union recruit. He is a young boy; he has sailed on the ship of state with his captain, whom he calls, Oedipally, "dear father"; the tide of war has now turned and victory is in sight, as cheering crowds welcome the victorious ship. At this very moment the captain is shot, and dies. The moving turn of the poem comes two-thirds of the way through the poem. In the first two stanzas the boy addresses the captain as someone still living, a "you" who, cradled in the boy's arm, can hear the words directed to him. But in the third stanza the young sailor unwillingly resorts to third-person reference, marking his captain as dead: "My Captain does not answer, his lips are pale and still." The hierarchy of commander—remote from his troops—has been lessened to the hierarchy of captain—sharing a ship with his men—and then lessened to the familial hierarchy of father and son, as Lincoln's relation to others becomes ever more democratic, even intimate.

Two stylistic features—its meter and its use of refrain—mark "O Captain" as a designedly democratic and populist poem. In each stanza, four seven-beat lines (each the equivalent of two standard ballad lines of tetrameter and trimeter) are followed by a slightly changing ballad refrain. The refrain—after two trimeters—returns to the tetrameter/ trimeter ballad beat. The poem, by its form, implies that soldiers and sailors have a right to verse written for them in the sort of regularly rhyming stanzas that they like best. And because Whitman has chosen to speak now as a sailor-boy, the diction of the poem offers the clichés of victory that such a boy might use: "Our fearful trip is done, / The ship has weather'd every rack, the prize we sought is won, / The port is near." Everything on shore adheres to the expected conventions of popular celebration—"For you the flag is flung—for you the bugle trills, / For you bouquets and ribbon'd wreaths." Even "the bleeding drops of red," the "mournful tread" of the sailor, and the captain "fallen cold and dead" come from the clichés of war-journalism.

Whitman was not, I think, hypocritical in writing such a poem; he was answering his first poem with the second poem that he thought the first had called for. But in adopting the voice of the young boy mourning his "father," Whitman had sacrificed his own voice entirely. Because he valued, and validated, the claim of his audience that he represent their heavy hearts, Whitman thought to do so by becoming one of them. Wanting to value democracy, he thought he had to exemplify it by submitting to the rhythms and rhymes and clichés of the popular verse prized by the soldiers, rather than inventing a democratic form of his own. Because he was bent on registering individual response as well as the collective wish expressed in "Hush'd Be the Camps," he took on the voice of a single representative sailor, silencing his own idiosyncratic voice. And wanting to show the sailor and his father-captain as participants in a national endeavor, he adopted the allegorical cliché of the Ship of State as the ruling metaphor of his poem.

Though we do not know, factually, that "O Captain" was composed before "Lilacs," it seems to me that the sailor-boy's dirge must have been the direct response to the call in "Hush'd Be the Camps." "Lilacs" is, by contrast, the outburst of individual voice following on Whitman's attempt to honor collectivity by writing in the voice of the heavy-hearted soldiers and to defend representativeness in verse by writing in the voice of the mourning sailor. He was valuing Lincoln as commander in the one and captain-father in the other; he was valuing poetry as a contributor to collective ritual in the one and as a form of populist expression in the other. When we come to "Lilacs," all the values change.

"Lilacs" is written not collectively, and not representatively, but in Whitman's own original lyric voice. In it, Lincoln is not placed in a vertical social hierarchy as president, commander-in-chief, captain, or even father, but is rather placed horizontally, as a fellow-man, even if one distinguished by superlative wisdom and sweetness. There is ritual in the poem—even received ritual, carried out by other mourners but even by the poet, as he lays conventional bouquets of lilies and roses on the coffins of the dead; but there are also strange new rituals, to which I will come, outnumbering the conventional ones. And—most striking of all—there is a suppression of the coincidence of the day of the assassination with Good Friday, as well as a refusal to echo the Christian rituals of services and sermons and hymns that pervaded the twenty days preceding Lincoln's burial.

In "Lilacs," the coffin-train indeed makes its long and mournful journey—in a funereal ritual unprecedented in American history, and therefore attractive to Whitman as an original event—but aside from the mentions of the mourning ceremonies attending the train at each of its stops, nothing in the poem depends on historical fact. The poem never mentions the assassination, the assassin, or the jailed and executed conspirators; the Emancipation Proclamation and other acts of Lincoln's presidency are passed over in silence. Even the startling fact of the re-burial of Lincoln's son is omitted. We are given, instead of facts, three symbols—the lilac of this earth, the star of the evening sky, and the hermit-thrush of the dark swamp. By apportioning his poem among the classic three realms of upper-world, middle-world, and underworld, Whitman gives cosmic importance—rather than the political importance ascribed to it by historians—to Lincoln's death. The poem does not value facts: it does not value politics; it does not value Christianity; it does not value speaking in a voice other than one's own. It is written in free verse of the most original sort; it does not value debased popular taste in poetry. Has Whitman repudiated "Hush'd Be the Camps" and "O Captain"? Or does something of them linger in "Lilacs"?

What does "Lilacs" value? And how are its valuings enacted? And what aesthetic value do they exhibit? These questions have answers too complex to be fully enunciated here, but let me give some brief observations. "Lilacs" is a sequence constructed of sixteen cantos ranging in length from five to fifty-three lines. It builds up to its longest and most lyrical moment in canto 14, achieves its moral climax in canto 15, and ends with a coda of "retrievements out of the night" in canto 16. The nonreligious "trinity" that opens the poem (perennial lilac, Lincoln-star, and the "thought of him I love") will become, by the end, the trinity of "lilac and star and bird": that is, the bird and its carol become the equivalent of the opening "thought" of the poet. It is unusual for Whitman to establish such a firm symbolic constellation; his secular trinity is set as a memorable elegiac emblem of the formality that is one of the poem's values. This is not an intimate elegy: Lincoln is named a "friend," but he is also the "powerful western fallen star" who is due formal honor as a symbol of the ideal. That honor is given character in the symbolic trinity dedicated to his memory.

The first act of the speaker—after he has initially lamented his helplessness in the grasp of the "harsh surrounding cloud that will not free my soul"—is to break off (in line 17) a sprig of lilac from the lilac-bush growing in the dooryard. No explanation is given for this act; it is not until line 45 that we learn why he took the sprig. It is to have a flower to lay on Lincoln's coffin: "Here, coffin that slowly passes, / I give you my sprig of lilac." This is not the conventional sort of floral offering; it has passed through no florist's hands. The speaker knows the conventions of arranged "bouquets" made of the rarer "roses and early lilies" and indeed later observes these conventions, as his mourning becomes generalized to "the coffins all of you." Still, he prefers his roughly torn and unarranged lilacs:

> All over bouquets of roses,
> O death, I cover you over with roses and early lilies,
> But mostly and now the lilac that blooms the first,
> Copious I break, I break the sprigs from the bushes,
> With loaded arms I come, pouring for you,
> For you and the coffins all of you O death.

The poem dismisses the idea of personal immortality; when the star sinks, it is gone forever:

> . . . I watch'd where you pass'd and was lost in the netherward black
>   of the night,
> As my soul in its trouble dissatisfied sank, as where you sad orb,
> Concluded, dropt in the night, and was gone.

What the poet can confirm, as a principle of hope, is the natural vegetative resurrection from which Christ took the metaphor of the risen wheat: the funeral train, he says, passes "the yellow-spear'd wheat, every grain from its shroud in the dark-brown fields uprisen." And in the old woods, "lately violets peep'd from the ground, spotting the gray debris."

The chief stylistic trait of this first part of the poem is the long-withheld subject of its sentences. The run of sentences with postponed subjects begins in the one-sentence, six-lined canto 3: "In the dooryard . . . / Stands the lilac-bush . . . / With many a pointed blossom . . . / With

every leaf a miracle—and from this bush in the dooryard . . . / With del-
icate-color'd blossoms . . . / A sprig with its flower I break." In canto 5,
with its seven-line sentence, the continuo is carried by a series of adverbs
and participial adjectives—"Over . . . / Amid . . . / Amid . . . / Passing
. . . / Passing . . . / Carrying . . . / Night and day journeys a coffin." We
can see that this sentence-form imitates the long passage of the train
across the eastern third of the North American continent. It is important to Whitman to ally his single tributary sprig of lilac with all the
preceding civil and religious ceremonies honoring the dead man; and
canto 6 is the poem's chief concession to factual reporting; but this canto
is staged so that the public observances lead up to the poet's anomalous,
solitary, and unarranged sprig:

> Coffin that passes through lanes and streets,
> Through day and night with the great cloud darkening the land,
> With the pomp of the inloop'd flags with the cities draped in black,
> With the show of the States themselves as of crape-veil'd women
>   standing,
> With processions long and winding and the flambeaus of the night,
> With the countless torches lit, with the silent sea of faces and the
>   unbared heads,
> With the waiting depot, the arriving coffin, and the sombre faces,
> With dirges through the night, with the thousand voices rising
>   strong and solemn,
> With all the mournful voices of the dirges pour'd around the coffin,
> The dim-lit churches and the shuddering organs—where amid
>   these you journey,
> With the tolling tolling bells' perpetual clang,
> Here, coffin that slowly passes,
> I give you my sprig of lilac.

The poem here gives what all the contemporary photographs of the
journey cannot: movement, silence, sound, tonality, atmosphere. While
other poems about Lincoln's death mostly contented themselves with
abstractions of praise and grief, Whitman renders the very scenes of
mourning in present-participial form, making them unroll before our
eyes in what seems real time. The journey comes to a telling climax—after all the elaborate tributes of the cities—in the single lilac-sprig. The
poem, it is evident, values showing over telling, and the senses over
abstraction; it emphasizes the contribution of each individual act to the
tally of mourning gestures. It also values drama—not only in the changing chiaroscuro tableaux of homage presented here, but also in the

narrative syntactic drama of the sentence that presses toward the gift of the dooryard lilac.

One could think that the poem could end here. The poet has contributed his flower: is that not enough? We soon learn that it is not: he puts aside the summons of the bird heard in canto 9 to ask the three questions of canto 10: "How shall I warble? . . . / how shall I deck my song? . . . / what shall my perfume be for the grave?" The last problem is easily solved: the perfume will be the sea-winds and the breath of the poet's chant. But the first two are less rapidly answered. In fact, the first—"How shall I warble?"—is not at this point replied to at all, while "How shall I deck my song?" mutates into the specific question, "What shall the pictures be that I hang on the walls, / To adorn the burial-house of him I love?" This question originates from Whitman's knowledge of Egyptian tombs, decorated on the interior with idyllic pictures of daily life. He will renew this convention in canto 11, making resonant pictures of American landscapes and action: "Pictures of growing spring and farms and homes . . . / And all the scenes of life and the workshops, and the workmen homeward returning." He includes no religious iconography on the walls of the tomb; he employs only the iconography of the land, catalogued in terms redolent of aesthetic bliss: "With floods of the yellow gold of the gorgeous, indolent, sinking sun, burning, expanding the air . . . / In the distance the flowing glaze, the breast of the river, with a wind-dapple here and there." The praise of the beauty of America and its "gentle soft-born measureless light" almost distracts the poet from the still-unanswered question "How shall I warble?"; and though he once again turns toward the chant of the bird, "limitless out of the dusk," and calls it, unexpectedly, a "Loud human song, with voice of uttermost woe," he represents himself as still held back from "the swamps, the recesses," by the star above, and the lilac beside him.

He is really held back by his prolonged cataloguing of beauty, which spills over into the beginning of canto 14, as the poet glosses "the large unconscious scenery of my land." Whitman values very highly, as a poetic structure, the accumulation of sentences of inventory. Beyond the formal triad of his symbols, beyond the conferring of cosmic significance on Lincoln's death by showing its consequence to upper and lower and middle worlds, beyond the drama of the periodic sentence pressing toward its climax, beyond the rendition of theatrically lit atmospheres, he valued the multiplicity and beauty of the world's objects, landscapes, and inhabitants, even in the moment of mourning. Inventories fill most of the poems of *Leaves of Grass* (and all parodies of Whitman begin with a swell of egotism followed by unbridled lists of categories).

But the beautiful categories of canto 13, though they overflow into canto 14, continue under a shadow. While the poet, ravished by the "heavenly aerial beauty . . . / and the summer approaching with richness," watches the ample scene, "—lo, then and there, Falling upon them all and among them all, enveloping me with the rest, / Appear'd the cloud." The poet finds "the knowledge of death" walking on one side of him and "the thought of death" walking on the other side, "and I in the middle as with companions, and holding the hands of companions." He finally flees to the swamp, which is then revealed as an underworld of "shores of . . . water" and "solemn shadowy cedars and ghostly pines so still." This is not the Christian afterlife, but the underworld of shades and ghosts in the midst of the waters of Lethe and the Styx that we know from Greek myth. By annexing the afterworld of classical Greece to the tomb-decorations of Egypt, Whitman tells us that he prefers these ways of knowing and encountering death to those offered by the Christianity in which he had been raised. In 1891, the last year of his life, after he had suffered strokes and other disabling illnesses, he wrote: "The philosophy of Greece taught normality and the beauty of life. Christianity teaches how to endure illness and death. I have wonder'd whether a third philosophy fusing both, and doing full justice to both, might not be outlined" (*Collected Writings II, Collect and Other Prose,* ed. Floyd Stovall [New York: NYU Press, 1964], p. 708). But when he was writing "Lilacs," it was the "normality" of Egypt and Greece, rather than Christian patience, that Whitman valued.

We have reached, in the second half of canto 14, the lyric center of "Lilacs," the song of the hermit-thrush, where one supreme aesthetic value of the poem—the value of free musical language—resides. Though this is the poetic center of the elegy, it is not its moral climax, which will come in canto 15, when the poet fully accedes to vision. However, we must ask ourselves first about this lyric center. "And the charm of the carol rapt me," says the poet: what is that charm? The "carol" is a hymn to a female deity, Death, and is therefore allied to the earliest lyrics we have, the Orphic hymns to abstractions such as Death and the Homeric hymns to the gods and goddesses such as the maternal goddess Demeter, mother of the lost Persephone in Hades. The song of the thrush, beginning in invocation ("Come lovely and soothing death"), and becoming a song of praise ("praise! praise! praise! / For the sure-enwinding arms of cool-enfolding death"), invents a celebratory ritual ("Dances for thee I propose saluting thee, adornments and feast- ings for thee") to replace the mourning ritual of somber dirges and tolling bells and shuddering organs invented by Christianity. Yet the re- pudiation of Christian melancholy, forceful as it is, is less memorable than the seductive oceanic rhythms of lyric loosed to be itself. Whitman "overwrites," with this rhythm, the dragging journey of the train. As the train moved across the land, we heard it go "Over the breast of the spring, the land, amid cities": now we hear the carol float above the train, over the same landscape:

> Over the rising and sinking waves, over the myriad fields and the
>   prairies wide,
> Over the dense-pack'd cities all and the teeming wharves and ways,
> I float this carol with joy, with joy to thee O death.

As the song of blissful death "overwrites" the journey of melancholy death, lyric claims its right to the joy that resides in art, even in art of tragic import.

As the bird sings the acceptance of death, the poet, tallying the song in his soul, finds that as he lets go of his former fear and denial, his vision awakes: "My sight that was bound in my eyes unclosed, / As to long panoramas of visions." The painful silent moral visions, gifts of memory, replace, with a wrench, the aesthetic sights of the earth seen earlier by the eye of sense. Whitman first admits to a "screen vision" of mutilated battle-flags ("pierc'd with missiles / . . . and torn and bloody, . . . And the staffs all splinter'd and broken"). As he persists in his resolve to remem- ber all, the splintered flags of the "screen vision" give way to the greater mutilations of flesh they were hiding:

> I saw battle-corpses, myriads of them,
> And the white skeletons of young men, I saw them,
> I saw the debris and debris of all the slain soldiers of the war.

At this point the elegy for Lincoln resumes in an explicit way its earlier guarded gesture ("For you and the coffins all of you O death") toward all those ordinary soldiers who have died in the war. This is the moment of highest moral value in the poem, as the poet allows himself to see all that the war has cost. At the same time, by resurrecting a word used ear- lier, apparently casually, in the mention of the violets that peeped from the ground, "spotting the gray debris," Whitman reminds us that debris is the compost of new growth. It was the Union that was to grow strong from the battle-corpses.

The drama of canto 15 is enacted in the style of a chronicler of apocalypse:

> And I saw in the right hand of him that sat on the throne a book . . . .
> And I saw a strong angel proclaiming . . . . And I beheld, and lo . . . .
> And I saw when the Lamb opened one of the seals . . . . And I saw, and behold a white horse. (Revelation 5, 6)

> And I saw askant the armies,
> I saw as in noiseless dreams hundreds of battle-flags . . . .
> I saw battle-corpses, myriads of them,
> And the white skeletons of young men, I saw them,
> I saw the debris and debris of all the slain soldiers of the war.

This style boldly claims, if implicitly, that Whitman expects his vision to be granted the same credence as that granted the book of Revelation; the passage is his most blasphemous transvaluation of Christian value.

In the coda of canto 16, the poet resumes his earlier themes, and finds his trinity complete—"Lilac and star and bird twined with the chant of my soul"—but unexpectedly is not permitted to leave, in memory, the underworld. Though in real life the lilac is "there in the door-yard, blooming, returning with spring," the poet finds "Lilac and star and bird twined with the chant of my soul, / There in the fragrant pines and the cedars dusk and dim." Because the underworld is "there," the poet is by implication "here" in the normal world—but the poem cannot enact the "here" in which he finds himself. The living part of his soul is still there in the dusk and the dimness of Hades, twined with his trinity.

If we seek out the originality of "Lilacs"—beginning with its refusal to name Lincoln and its suppression of his civic and military roles—we can see that though it indeed obeys many paradigms of its genre, the English elegy, it wears its rue with a difference, subduing Christian symbols to those of Egypt and Greece, celebrating the natural beauty of life rather than the prospective beauties of heaven, finding its consolation in new joyous rituals of death, and asserting that its revelation of corpses and skeletons is as prophetically binding as St. John's revelation of heaven. Its style asserts the value of showing rather than telling, the value of the idiosyncratic voice over the collective or representative voice, and—in its journeying sentences that climax in a definite halt—

the value of acceptance, rather than denial, of the full stop of death. Its other striking sentences, phrased not in the progressive pressure to end, but rather in arias ebbing and flowing without resolution, assert the fluctuating harmonies and contrasts of the expansive but inconclusive rhythms of experience:

> Victorious song, death's outlet song, yet varying ever-altering song,
> As low and wailing, yet clear the notes, rising and falling, flooding
>   the night,
> Sadly sinking and fainting, as warning and warning, and yet again
>   bursting with joy,
> Covering the earth and filling the spread of the heaven.

After "Lilacs," Whitman wrote one other poem concerning Lincoln—the only one left to write, Lincoln's epitaph. It was published in 1871, six years after Lincoln's death. Lincoln is no longer friend or wise and sweet soul; he is reduced to dust. The poet grasps the dust to himself: "This dust," he says. He does not point to the grave, saying "That dust." This is not a poem gesturing outward toward the "there" of the lilac or the "there" of the underworld. The poem is massively imbalanced: the four words "This dust was once" make up the left half of the copula, while the right half requires thirty words. The proportion is therefore appropriate to the light dust versus the complex description of the consequential man. Lincoln, in becoming dust, becomes historical, "the man who guided the preservation of the Union." The initial adjectives are themselves complex, as the initial personal "gentle" is played off against the final official "resolute," while in between we see the "plain" of Lincoln's upbringing set against the "just" character of his legal profession. I hear the line with the emphasis on "and": "Gentle, plain, just—*and*—[when the hour came] resolute." The next adjective, applied not to Lincoln but to his guiding hand, is "cautious"—this speaks to his wisdom. What is most surprising about the epitaph is that it, unlike most such honorific inscriptions, gives no active verb to its subject. Lincoln is not said to be "the man . . . Who saved the Union of these states." That would give him the power of a monarch. It was the thousands of soldiers, alive and dead, who saved the Union; the president, *primus inter pares,* was merely their supervising fellow-participant. But the soldiers are left unmentioned as such: they exist only subsumed within the passive verb. Yet they are the saviors, and as such they are the ultimate repository of individual value, even in an epitaph praising their leader. The very peculiar syntax of this epitaph reserves the main subject and verb of the subsidiary adjective clause—"The Union of these States was saved"—to the very end and inverts the normal word order to "Was saved the Union of these States," thereby putting the Union in the climactic syntactic position of national value, placed even above the actions taken to save it. Tucked in between the presiding cautious hand and its salvific agents is the averted horror: the continuation of slavery. Slavery is here named by euphemism, as though its proper name should never again be uttered in human hearing. It becomes, superlatively, "the foulest crime," and it is placed in a cosmic spatiotemporal field: it is "the foulest crime known in any land or age."

What makes this epitaph a poem? Above all, its tortured syntax, which tries to tuck into thirty words the personal, professional, ethical, and prudential qualities of a single historical personage; his relation to the Union Army; the soldiers' relation to the winning of the war; the chief result of that victory; and a description of the ancient, widespread, and evil crime against which both president and soldiers opposed their lives. Syntax, when tortured, becomes a sign of a complexity too great to be naturally contained within a single sentence and yet bent on being thus contained because all the elements of that given complexity are inextricable one from another and must therefore be named in the same breath. Whitman's last word on Lincoln emphasizes his historical greatness, based on greatness of character, while reserving to him merely a guiding role in the ultimate value, the salvation of the Union. This is a poem of Roman succinctness and taciturnity, betraying its depth of feeling chiefly in the implicit figure of the scales—in which a handful of dust is equal in weight to the salvation of the Union, with the copula serving as the needle of equilibrium. In it the poet speaks not collectively, not representatively, and not idiosyncratically and lyrically; he speaks impersonally, as the recording angel. This poem places value on the voice of history in final judgment. Walt Whitman, the man, is sublimed away; this poem is—to use Elizabeth Bishop's words—one of those "admirable scriptures of stone on stone." One can see its words chased on a tablet: it is itself a tombstone. But did any tombstone ever carry such an epitaph?

There is more to say about the values imaged and implied by these four poems. In attempting the subject of Lincoln from four different perspectives, Whitman (who had often seen Lincoln and had described him in prose of a journalistic and mimetic nature) turns away from personal and historic mimesis of the man and president to symbolic mimesis, framed for the conveying of value. In each case the aesthetic vehicle—the collective voice of the soldiers in the camps, the single voice of the grieving novice-sailor, the idiosyncratic voice of the poet coming to know death, and the impersonal voice of historic judgment—offers a different possibility of expression. The shorter poems show us, by contrast, how and why "Lilacs" reaches its heights and its amplitudes. All of the poems show us Whitman debating what stance the American poet should adopt when speaking of important national events. If each stance—collective, representative, idiosyncratic, impersonal—has something to be said for it, then we are shown that value can be mediated by poetry in any number of ways and that both the poet and his audience are modeled differently in each. We are warned, by the greater success of the most original of the four poems, of the dangers to the poet in attempting to speak collectively or within the bounds of popular taste—or even with the impersonal voice of historiography. It is chiefly when a public crisis evokes some crisis in the soul of the poet—here, Whitman's crisis in judging what could be truly said of human mortality—that a public poem takes on lasting aesthetic value.

The End of "German Culture"

WOLF LEPENIES

The Tanner Lectures on Human Values

Delivered at

Harvard University
November 3–5, 1999

WOLF LEPENIES is professor of sociology at the Free University, Berlin. He received his Ph.D. at the University of Münster. He has been a fellow of the Center for Advanced Studies, Vienna, and the Institute for Advanced Study, Berlin. He has also been a member of the School of Social Science, Institute for Advanced Study, Princeton; the German Academy for Language and Literature; the Academia Europaea; the Berlin-Brandenburgische Akademie der Wissenschaften; and International P.E.N., among others; and was a founding member of the Academy of Sciences and Technology, Berlin. He is the author of numerous books, including *Between Literature and Science: The Rise of Sociology* (1988) and *Melancholy and Society* (1992). He is a recipient of the French *Légion d'Honneur*.

I. EXILE AND EMIGRATION:
THE SURVIVAL OF "GERMAN CULTURE"

INTRODUCTION

In 1941, the Hungarian ambassador in Washington paid a courtesy call to the State Department, since Nazi Germany had forced his country to declare war against the United States. It turned out to be a very civilized meeting indeed and after the ambassador, following the rules of diplomacy, had fulfilled his somewhat delicate mission, the secretary of state politely asked him to sit down so that the two of them might take the rare opportunity for a good talk over crackers and a glass of brandy. The following conversation ensued.

"I cannot hide from you, Mr. Ambassador, how much I regret that the Hungarian Republic has decided to wage war against my country, the United States of America!"

"Sir," the ambassador replied, "please believe me when I say how much I personally resent this decision. I must, however, correct a minor point: I do not have the honor to serve the Hungarian Republic, but the Kingdom of Hungary!"

"*Gosh,* why didn't anyone tell me! Would you be kind enough, Your Excellency, to elaborate on the reasons that led the Hungarian king to make this decision, which, after all, could have serious consequences for both of our countries?"

"Excuse me once more, sir, but our head of state isn't a king, he's an admiral."

"Isn't that interesting! Then, excuse me if it's top secret, but can you please tell me how big your fleet is and how many aircraft carriers and submarines are stationed on the Danube?"

"Mr. Secretary, now I'll tell you a secret indeed: we don't have any warships at all!"

"I'm sorry. So how many war planes do you have?"

"None."

"Very well, this obviously means that you will have to attack with

I want to thank Mitch Cohen, Britta N. Cusack, and Dirk Zorn for their invaluable help in preparing these lectures.

your land forces. Which of our allies will you attack first? Poland, I suppose?"

"No, by no means, sir, the Poles are our best friends!"

"Well, do you want to attack anyone at all then, in this most peculiar of wars?"

"Yes, indeed, Mr. Secretary, we would love to attack the Romanians as quickly as possible."

"So why don't you do it?"

"Because the Romanians are our allies!"

"For heaven's sake, then why don't you declare war against the Russians instead of taking on the United States of America?"

"Because we are already thinking of the time after the war."

"What do you mean?"

"We would rather be occupied by the Americans than by the Red Army!"

A Hungarian diplomat told me this story when I first came to Budapest in the fall of 1989 to explore the possibility of founding an Institute for Advanced Study there on the model of the Wissenschaftskolleg in Berlin. The Hungarians know how to charm you while criticizing you: hidden behind the self-irony of my interlocutor was the advice to learn more about the history of Hungary and its neighbors before embarking on the adventure of institution-building there. I had other meetings in Budapest in which humor and irony played a much smaller part. When talking to the minister of culture about my ambitious project, I mentioned the names of the Hungarian colleagues I was asking for help and advice. He somewhat nervously began to note them down while muttering: "There are just too many of them, there are just too many." When I asked him what seemed to disturb him so profoundly, he answered that there were too many Jews among those with whom I hoped to build the institute. The minister was not an anti-Semite at all; he just wanted to be helpful by drawing my attention to the deplorable fact that, in Hungary, anti-Semitism was not restricted to the past but was very much a current concern, and that I should be aware of it if I wanted to succeed. He accepted the outrage with which I reacted to his remarks—but not without intimating that he felt somewhat ambivalent about a German's outrage over his alleged anti-Semitism.

I began to feel more and more insecure. How should I ever be able to understand the political and cultural context in which I wanted to operate? My feeling of insecurity reached its peak when a professor of history, who, like many of his colleagues, had turned into a politician, solemnly declared that now, after the fall of communism, the time had come to revise the Paris treaties. Above all, he said, it was time to correct the "infamous agreements" of Trianon in 1920, in which Hungary ceded large parts of its territory to Austria, Yugoslavia, and Romania. By now, I was accustomed to expressing my outrage, and I told the historian-turned-politician how absurd his words sounded to me. But when the new war in the Balkans broke out, I remembered these incidents and suddenly became aware that my Hungarian colleagues' remarks might have been much less surprising than I had thought ten years ago. Whether you call it "short" or "long," the twentieth century was not over yet. All of a sudden it seemed as if, at our own fin de siècle, we were returning to its beginning. "Versailles" once again became a term in our political vocabulary.

Though it may seem so, given the themes of my Tanner Lectures, I do not want to follow the shrewd advice an American colleague once gave me when I was about to embark upon my very first lecture in this country: he said to begin by telling a story that your audience isn't sure is relevant to your topic at all. To find out, they will listen through to the end of your presentation. Instead, I will try to indicate the kind of work I have been doing over the past ten years and thus to describe the background against which my lectures should be understood. Since 1989, I have become engaged in various experiments of institution-building that have established or enlarged four institutions of higher learning and scholarship in countries of the former Communist bloc: the Collegium Budapest, the first Institute for Advanced Study in Central and Eastern Europe; the New Europe College in Bucharest; the Graduate School for Social Research in Warsaw; and the Bibliotheca Classica in Saint Petersburg, which is associated with a classical secondary school, a "Gymnasium." In addressing problems of cultural policy today and tomorrow, and that is how I would roughly describe the theme of my Tanner Lectures, I am speaking from recent experience. Trying to improve local contexts of knowledge in Central and Eastern Europe, I have begun to understand the degree to which the division of Europe was not only a problem for the East, but also a problem for us in the West. This has provided me with a fresh view of the past and present of German culture.

To give the Tanner Lectures on Human Values is a task as honorable as it is awesome. I, for my part, cannot pretend that I shall be able to "contribute to the intellectual and moral life of mankind," as Obert Clark

Tanner hoped when he endowed these lectureships. I can only aim at doing something modest in scope and in ambition. The subject of my lectures is "German Culture," i.e., the overrating of culture at the expense of politics. I thereby address a past and present threat to the intellectual and moral life of a country and of a continent, of Germany and of Europe.

LESSONS IN DIMINISHED PARTICULARITY

If there is anything like a German ideology, it consists in playing off Romanticism against the Enlightenment, the Middle Ages against the modern world, culture against civilization, the subjective against the objective, and community against society—in the end glorifying German particularity. This "exceptionalism" was always a point of pride—not least because it was based to a considerable degree on cultural aspirations and achievements. The subjective, inward realm established by German idealism, the classic literature of Weimar, and the classical and romantic styles in music not only preceded the founding of the political nation by more than a hundred years: they were hailed as being a political act that henceforth legitimated any withdrawal from society into the sphere of culture and private life.

Having given a similar résumé in a book some years ago, I was pleased when Hans Magnus Enzensberger quoted it at length in one of his essays. Pleasure turned into perplexity, though, when I realized that he had used my words to characterize the modern history of—Spain. Thus, I was taught an ironic lesson: German history is not nearly as exceptional as the Germans are inclined to believe. In recent decades, this lesson in diminished particularity has been convincingly taught in attempts to show the persistence of the *ancien régime* in all of modern Europe; in the examination of the interconnectedness of Europe's societies and their politics in the decade after the First World War; in the reconstruction of a cycle of German national doctrines whose ideological transitions, rather than ideological persistence, are seen as characteristic; and in the assurance that cultural pessimism was not a German specialty, but rather a feature of bourgeois societies in general.[1]

---

[1] I am alluding to publications by Arno Mayer, Charles Maier, Harold James, Jim Sheehan, David Blackbourn, and Geoff Eley.

These attempts, persuasive in different ways, and yet convergent in counteracting "the chronic overstatement of the unfolding and ultimate triumph of modernity,"[2] did much to reinsert Germany's peculiar past into a broader context of European history. They reflect rather than having created a climate of opinion that enticed revisionist historians to insist on the imitative character of National Socialism, whose ideology, they alleged, was modeled on the earlier fascisms of Latin Europe, and whose atrocities mirrored the earlier crimes of Stalinism. Using chronology not only as an explanation but, equally falsely, also as an excuse, German particularity was thus seen as almost a European normality. The Holocaust was reduced to not much else than a dreadful accident on a road where careless and ideology-intoxicated driving was not the exception but the rule. The search for embeddedness led to understanding and understanding eventually led to forgiveness and to oblivion: *Tout comprendre c'est tout pardonner.*

To understand German history and its peculiarities has been a challenge not only for professional historians, but for philosophers as well. Even more: it seemed as if only philosophy could come up with an explanation for historical developments that, at first glance, eluded historical understanding. That was the argument in John Dewey's *German Philosophy and Politics* as well as in George Santayana's *Egotism in German Philosophy,* which were published in 1915 and 1916, respectively. Dewey singled out Kant's doctrine of the two realms—"one outer, physical and necessary, the other inner, ideal and free . . . primacy always [lying] with the inner"[3]—as the most important element for understanding German national life; and George Santayana did the same when he described transcendental philosophy as its preferred "method of looking in one's own breast"—adding, somewhat caustically, that "the German breast was no longer that anatomical region which Locke had intended to probe, but a purely metaphysical point of departure . . . ."[4] For Santayana, the perversity of German thought consisted in glorifying an egotism that other nations regarded as an impediment to be gotten rid of as quickly as possible. But Dewey, who was not less critical, also admired

---

[2] Arno J. Mayer, *The Persistence of the Old Regime: Europe to the Great War* (New York: Pantheon, 1981), p. 5.

[3] John Dewey, *German Philosophy and Politics* (Freeport, N.Y.: Books for Libraries Press, 1942), p. 69.

[4] George Santayana, *Egotism in German Philosophy* (New York: Charles Scribner's Sons, 1940), p. 21.

the pervasiveness of the transcendental method, which had made Germany the only country in the world where even cavalry generals employed philosophy to bring home practical lessons. The most striking parallel between Dewey and Santayana, however, is that, at the beginning of and during the Second World War, both republished books they had written in the middle of the First World War and now felt entitled to reprint without any alteration. In the same vein, Thorstein Veblen's study on *Imperial Germany and the Industrial Revolution,* which was originally published in 1915, was reprinted in 1939. Apparently, Germany and German culture had not changed at all.

THE TYPICAL GERMAN

Thus, not only Germans themselves saw inwardness as Germany's political predicament and cultural ideal; in a mixture of adversity and admiration, foreign authors asserted this as well—and possibly more than the Germans did. When, in 1942 and 1943, the London Institute of Sociology took the suggestion of Morris Ginsberg and organized a series of lectures and discussions on *The German Mind and Outlook,* the result was quite flattering for the nation with which England found itself at war for the second time in a generation. The debates were chaired by G. P. Gooch, who proudly identified himself as the president not only of the Institute of Sociology, but also of the English Goethe Society. The institute's secretary summed them up: "Whatever may be the coming shape of German society, it is impossible to envisage a condition that shall be stable, pacific and humane, unless it embodies the master ideas of Goethe: faith in individual development, sympathy and unity with nature, vision and imagination unceasingly transforming the mundane and commonplace into symbol, drama, and poetry."[5] This meant that the failure of German politics must be repaired at home—and that, in fact, it could be repaired by drama and by poetry. The better Germany, the cultural nation, would survive the war unharmed.

Although by now I have already moved up to the year 1945, there might still be too much history around for those concerned that the Tanner Lectures should not deteriorate into antiquarian deliberations. So let me give you an example of how much debates like those of the

[5] Alexander Farquharson, "Summary," in *The German Mind and Outlook,* ed. G. P. Gooch et al. (London: Chapman and Hall, 1945), p. 218.

London Sociological Society. which ended in a kind of Goethe epiphany, still matter today in the land of poets and thinkers. In 1949, the Allensbach Institut, the German equivalent of the Gallup Institute, asked a representative sample of Germans about their knowledge of and relationship to Johann Wolfgang von Goethe. This was the year when the Federal Republic was founded, as the institute proudly recalls. Generously funded by the largest German TV station, the Goethe poll was repeated this year, when the poet's 250th anniversary was celebrated with much pomp and circumstance.[6] Mentioned abroad, these polls sound rather funny—at home they were and are still taken seriously indeed. In 1949, for instance, Germans were asked whether, after 1945, they had had "a major spiritual experience." Only a disappointing 46% answered "Yes"—a result the pollsters judged so dismal that it had to be compensated by the answer of a publisher, who claimed he had a major spiritual experience each day. Somewhat mischievously, he added: "This is a stupid question indeed. I would go so far as to say that any German who had not had a major spiritual experience since 1945 had better hang himself."

The Goethe polls make it possible to compare the Germans of 1949 with those of today and to compare East and West almost ten years after reunification. Asked, for instance, whether they considered Goethe a typical German, 47% in the East, but only 31% in the West answered in the affirmative—16% less than in 1949. Do Goethe's novels still matter today?: 37% in the West, 49% in the East say yes. Do you know at least one Goethe poem by heart? Only 10% in the West, but 25% in the East do. In every respect, East Germans seem to feel closer to Goethe and his legacy than West Germans do. The German press found much food for thought in the fact that, in 1949, the majority of Germans considered Faust the most important character in Goethe's drama, whereas fifty years later Mephisto had sneaked into first place—if only in the West. In the East, Faust still played the leading role.

The most intriguing aspect of the Goethe polls, however, does not lie in the answers they yielded, but in the importance both the interviewers and the public attributed to these surveys. The people's image of Goethe was seen as a litmus test for the state of the nation. Two results were especially reassuring. First, Goethe's popularity had not dramatically diminished since 1949. Second, Goethe was even more popular in

[6] Institut für Demoskopie Allensbach, *Demoskopie und Kulturgeschichte,* eine Goethe-Umfrage für das Nachtprogramm des NWDR 1949 (rpt. Allensbach/Bodensee: ZDF-Nachtstudio, 1999).

the East than in the West. This meant that the cultural nation was alive and well. It also meant that German unification had turned out to be an asset, not a liability, in the attempt to preserve the best that Germany has to offer to itself and to the world: culture. The polls also showed some disturbing results: for instance, why do only 27% of those Germans who regard themselves as moderately leftist see in Goethe the typical German, whereas 48% of the political right do? This question has remained unanswered, because unasked.

A Strange Indifference to Politics

Whenever George Santayana taught German metaphysics at Harvard College, he felt "under its obscure and fluctuating tenets . . . something sinister at work, something at once hollow and aggressive"[7]—a statement of inspired vagueness sharpened, twenty-five years later, by John Dewey, who spoke of the "underlying strains of continuity connecting the creed of Hitler with the classic philosophic tradition of Germany."[8] Such claims of continuity—which often were stretched to claims of causality—were reinforced by the Holocaust, the singular collective crime that doomed German culture and seemed to seal its separation from the mainstream of Western civilization once and for all. Yet attempts to construe causal links between the sphere of politics and the spiritual realm have not been very convincing—regardless of whether individuals like Luther, Kant, Schelling, and Nietzsche or intellectual movements like Idealism or Romanticism were seen as the beginning of a road that inevitably, with Hitler, turned out to be a dead end. Whether one calls it introspection or inwardness, emotional individualism or philosophical egotism—none of these traits belongs exclusively to the German national character.

The question how Germany could become a modern economy without fostering modern social values and political institutions is generally answered by referring to the preponderance of the state, which gave from above what, in other countries, the bourgeoisie had to fight for and acquire through its own efforts. Modern Germany, it has been argued, "thought primarily in terms of the might and majesty of the state, modern England primarily in terms of the rights and liberties of the citi-

[7] Santayana, *Egotism in German Philosophy,* p. viii.
[8] Dewey, *German Philosophy and Politics,* p. 15.

zen."[9] This view, which contrasts Germany, land of obedience, with England, the land of the free, has come under heavy attack. Still, one can hardly deny that idolization of the state has shaped the contours of German society and the course of German history to a large extent. This has involved a considerable weakening of politics and of the public sphere. At times, it could seem as if Germany was a state without politics. Yet it never aimed at being a state without culture.

Fritz Stern has convincingly argued that the strange indifference to politics that characterized German private and public life can be largely explained by the high premium placed on cultural preeminence and on the illiberal elitism that has prevailed in Germany since the time of Weimar classicism. Culture was the arena of the absolute, a realm without compromise. Its exaltation led to the illusion that culture could be a substitute for power and therefore a substitute for politics.[10] From here on, when I speak of "German Culture," I use the term in exactly this sense. Unlike "civilization," "culture" has remained a term that, in the German language, is almost naturally distant from, if not contrary to, politics. The connotation of "culture" is as positive, warm, and promising as that of "politics" is ambivalent, cold, and suspicious. Even today, the term "Weimar Republic" suffers from linguistic bruises, whereas "Weimar Culture" is nostalgically remembered as a great promise that has remained largely unfulfilled. The elevation of culture and the degrading of politics contributed to the downfall of the first German Republic. This ambivalence survived well into the Federal Republic, whose battle cry was "Bonn is not Weimar," and it survives in the reunited Germany.

The Holocaust, the great divide of Western civilization, should have marked the point of no return, after which the exaltation of culture over politics was no longer possible in Germany. That is, I believe, what Theodor Adorno wanted to say when he called barbarous any attempt to write a poem after Auschwitz. The poems Paul Celan wrote after Auschwitz were anything but barbarous—not because Celan had survived, but because his poetry reflected the helplessness, not the power, of culture. Yet the Holocaust did not become a point of no return, at least not for a long time. It did not mark the end of "German Culture."

---

[9] Gooch et al., *The German Mind and Outlook,* p. viii.

[10] Cf. Fritz Stern's books *The Politics of Cultural Despair: A Study in the Rise of the Germanic Ideology* (1961; Berkeley: University of California Press, 1974) and *The Failure of Illiberalism* (New York: Alfred A. Knopf, 1972).

One reason for this, as preposterous as it may seem, is the aesthetic appeal of fascism and later National Socialism, which shaped the mental makeup of much of the intelligentsia and the cultural elite in Germany beyond the end of the Second World War.

THE AESTHETIC APPEAL OF FASCISM

Today we are inclined to think of National Socialism and culture as a contradiction in terms. A look at Hitler and his companions at the Munich exhibition of "degenerate art" in 1937, poking fun at some of the greatest expressionist paintings of our century, is enough to strengthen our belief that the Nazis could not but destroy the *Kulturstaat* that had, for centuries, been the idol of German self-understanding and national pride. True, many Nazi figures—Hitler the painter, Joseph Goebbels the novelist, and Albert Speer the architect—still carried the artistic ambitions of their youth around with them after they seized power, sometimes turning meetings of the inner circle of the National Socialist Party's leadership into a quixotic *salon des refusés.* Yet today we can only laugh or shake our head in disbelief when we read about Hitler telling Sir Nevile Henderson, the British ambassador, that he was tired of politics and longed to return to oil painting, "as soon as I have carried out my program for Germany.... I feel that I have it in my soul to become one of the great artists of the age and that future historians will remember me, not for what I have done for Germany, but for my art."[11]

In her famous article in *Foreign Affairs* in April 1940, Dorothy Thompson described Germany as the problem child of Europe, pointing out that many of Hitler's character traits resembled those of a sick society that eventually brought a sick person to power: "What frustrations must be in this man, one thought—so sensitive, so cruel, so weak, and so aggressive! And those characters around him—perverts and adventurers, frustrated intellectuals who could not hold a job in any good newspaper or get their plays produced or their books published." In Hitler she saw a man who, after the common adventure of the First World War, took refuge the rest of his time in a dream-world, "a man whom nobody 'understood,' full of envy, furtive hatred, frustrated cre-

---

[11] As reported in an article in *Time* on September 11, 1939, p. 29. The caption of the article was "Painters' War," alluding thereby to the fact that the Polish commander-in-chief, Marshall Edward Smigly-Rydz, was "an able if academic landscapist."

ative power."[12] One should not read into Thompson's article a futile attempt to reduce to psycho-babble the political and moral catastrophe that National Socialism meant for Germany. Rather, I see in it a useful hint that here—in exact contrast to the German ideology as described above—we are confronted with attempts to compensate cultural failure or unfulfilled artistic aspirations by political means. In Germany, that was a revolutionary move indeed, which may also help us understand why the totalitarian character of the National Socialist state also expressed itself through aesthetics.[13]

Through ritual, not through belief, National Socialism was able to cast an aesthetic spell even outside Germany and even on those who had no great sympathy for Hitler or who had lost it as the criminal aspects of his politics became increasingly apparent. Wyndham Lewis was not the only one who—in his book on the Hitler cult published after the outbreak of the Second World War—originally regarded Hitler as a politician with a muse, though he added immediately, as if shocked by his own words, that if Hitler were a poet, he would be "one of the most boring poets."[14] In France, members of the political far right envied Germany because National Socialism was seen as the legitimate heir to the fascist movements that had their origin in the Latin countries of Europe. But while fascism had become sclerotic and unsure of itself in both Italy

---

[12] Dorothy Thompson, "The Problem Child of Europe," *Foreign Affairs* 18 (1940): 391.

[13] I do not know whether Goebbels read Dorothy Thompson's article or whether its content was brought to his attention by his staff. If so, he must have been especially appalled by it, since he saw the German war against the United States in large part as a culture war—unlike the war against France and England, whose culture was criticized but basically accepted, or the war against Communist Russia, which was denied any cultural achievement whatsoever. On April 23, 1942, Goebbels wrote in his diary: "I have the impression . . . that the Americans participate in a European war every quarter century in order to be able to take for themselves as cheaply and easily as possible whatever cultural work has been done in Europe. The American continent is hardly in a position to bring forth anything of its own in the cultural realm. It is dependent upon imports from Europe, and since the Americans are so crazy about money, they naturally like to take possession of the results of our creative and inventive labors as far as possible without paying for them." Goebbels ridicules an incident that he takes as the final verdict on the inferiority of American culture: "The Metropolitan Opera has been closed. And that in a country that has only a single opera and whose leadership is insolent enough to wage war on behalf of a European culture allegedly threatened by us!" Joseph Goebbels, *Diaries 1942–1943,* ed. Louis P. Lochner (Garden City, N.Y.: Doubleday and Co., 1948), pp. 180–81. To set the record straight: the Met was never closed at any time during World War II. The only occasions for which the Met ever closed were Kennedy's assassination, the death of a singer during the opening night of *The Makropulos Case,* and a blackout in the city caused by a snowstorm. In 1942, there were opera houses in Cincinnati, San Francisco, Chicago, Denver, Milwaukee, Pittsburgh, Hartford, Miami, Charleston, and other cities. I would like to express my thanks to John Church, information service director at OPERA America, who was kind enough to provide this information.

[14] Wyndham Lewis, *The Hitler Cult* (1939; New York: Gordon Press, 1972), p. 47.

and France, it had been vigorously transformed and thus survived in Germany. National Socialism had preserved the anarchistic and artistic attitudes characteristic of early fascism: a youthful disrespect for established authority and the general will to *épater le bourgeois,* especially since the bourgeoisie was, to a large extent, identified with Jewish culture.[15]

Rilke had once seen in Mussolini above all a man of poetic qualities. Fascism was seen by many as the equivalent of *l'art pour l'art* in politics.[16] For authors like Brasillach, Drieu, and Alphonse de Chateaubriant, it seemed only natural that any politician who dreamed of being a poet must become a fascist—as Degrelle, Mussolini, Hitler, and Codreanu did. This was a curious statement in a country where socialists like Léon Blum also dreamed of being Flaubert. And yet, admiration for what Brasillach would call "the aesthetic sensibilities" of Hitler as an individual and National Socialism as a movement also had a political effect.[17] Many *hommes de lettres* who were skeptics when they set out to attend the rallies of the National Socialist Party in Nuremberg returned as fanatics: "Oui, Hitler est bon" was Alphonse de Chateaubriant's résumé in 1937, whereby a strange aesthetic fascination was turned into a dangerous moral judgment.[18] These writers and intellectuals, without necessarily becoming unmitigated admirers of the Nazis or, certainly, of Germany at large, helped to create a context of empathy and understanding that made collaboration not only possible but honorable and even necessary. This helps to explain why the SS division "Charlemagne," which consisted of French and francophone volunteers, was among the last troops defending Hitler's Chancellery in Berlin against the Red Army. Fired by anti-Communist feelings and the deeply engrained anti-Americanism of the French Right of the thirties, they be-

[15] Here I cannot pay due attention to the difference between "collaboration with Germany" and "collaborationism with the Nazis" that has been stressed by Stanley Hoffmann. Cf. his article "Self-Ensnared: Collaboration with Nazi Germany," in *Decline or Renewal? France since the 1930s* (New York: Viking Press, 1974), pp. 26–44.

[16] Cf. Erwin von Beckerath, *Wesen und Werden des faschistischen Staates* (Berlin: Julius Springer, 1927).

[17] William R. Tucker, "Politics and Aesthetics: The Fascism of Robert Brasillach," *Western Political Quarterly* 15 (1962): 608.

[18] Alphonse de Chateaubriant, *La gerbe des forces (Nouvelle Allemagne)* (Paris: Bernard Grasset, 1937), p. 69. But not only the French fascists were impressed by the Nuremberg party rallies. In 1937, Nevile Henderson went there for the first time: "The effect, which was both solemn and beautiful, was like being inside a cathedral of ice.... I had spent six years in St. Petersburg before the war in the best days of the old Russian ballet, but in grandiose beauty I have never seen a ballet to compare with it." Nevile Henderson, *Failure of a Mission* (New York: G. P. Putnam's Sons, 1940), pp. 66–67.

lieved they were fighting a culture war in which European values had to be defended against Asiatic bolshevism and American materialism. It is this far-reaching aesthetic underpinning of National Socialist politics that makes it so wrong to make light of the films of Leni Riefenstahl or an author like Paul de Man's predilections for German "aesthetic nationalism,"[19] to see them as expressions of a merely peripheral and hence morally defensible sympathy for Nazism. They point to the heart of the matter.

ART AND MORALITY

In 1939, an extraordinary and shocking portrait of Hitler was published in *Esquire*. The portrait was shocking not least because of its title: "That Man Is My Brother." The author was Thomas Mann. Not only was Hitler more representative of his country than the world had originally thought. Not only did even a likable observer come to detect, in the dreadful Nazi physiognomy, familiar German features. With Thomas Mann, a great artist seemed to take Hitler's artistic claims seriously. The disappointed bohemian painter who passed unopposed from one political triumph to the other was a catastrophe, a miserable phenomenon, and yet one could not help viewing him with a certain shuddering admiration: "Must I now, however much it hurts, regard the man as an artist-phenomenon? Mortifyingly enough, it is all there: the difficulty, the laziness, the pathetic formlessness in youth.... The lazy, vegetating existence in the depths of a moral and mental Bohemia; the fundamental arrogance that thinks itself too good for any sensible and honorable activity, on the grounds of its vague intuition that it is reserved for something else.... A brother—a rather unpleasant and mortifying brother. He makes me nervous, the relationship is painful to a degree. But I will not disclaim it."[20]

Thomas Mann's confession was convincing not least because here an artist made things difficult for himself by admitting, painful though it was, a certain aesthetic appeal in Hitler and in National Socialism. Given his admiration for Richard Wagner, in whom we saw one of the

[19] Cf. Lindsay Waters, "Paul de Man: A Sketch of Two Generations," in *Responses: On Paul de Man's Wartime Journalism,* ed. Werner Hamacher et al. (Lincoln: University of Nebraska Press, 1989), pp. 397–403.

[20] Thomas Mann, "That Man Is My Brother," *Esquire* 11, no. 3 (1939): 3, 132.

great German "Masters," Mann must indeed have hesitated to bring Hitler and Wagner together at all. Yet he qualified Hitler's ideas as "a distorted phase of Wagnerism" and called Hitler's reverence for the musician-artist well founded, if rather illegitimate. The hours when he hated Hitler the miserable, Mann said, were not his best hours. Mann said he was able to cope with Hitler only in those other hours when he overcame his hatred and used the device he recognized as the prerogative and prerequisite of all creative writing: irony. "That Man Is My Brother" is a literary masterpiece—and thereby points to the limits of art and literature. Caught in irony, Thomas Mann the artist was unable to come to terms with a phenomenon like Hitler, since "the moral sphere . . . is really not altogether the artist's concern." It was the moral distance inherent in the arts and in literature that, in European history, had led many to regard the great man, the genius, as usually an aesthetic, not an ethical phenomenon. So, whether one liked it or not, Hitler—in part an aesthetic phenomenon in which madness was tempered with discretion—must also be called a genius.

In portraying Hitler, Thomas Mann anticipated that, with National Socialism, "German Culture," strictly speaking, must come to an end. He also pointed to the moral limits of artistic aspiration and aesthetic judgment. He did not fall prey to the illusion and hope that there is an elective affinity between artistic Modernism and democratic beliefs. Almost the opposite seems to be true. Among the great painters whom Hitler and his comrades publicly despised, quite a few would have been only too glad to be accepted by this third-rate painter, because they felt close to his ideas. In calling Hitler his brother, Mann also helped an uncomfortable truth come to light. At its core, artistic Modernism was by no means genuinely democratic; rather, it overtly displayed a propensity for authoritarian if not totalitarian views. As an aesthetic program, Modernism could not be condemned on moral grounds. To avoid censorship, it had to be contained, as it were, in a social context in which moral considerations permeated politics and public life.

That's why the illusory overrating of culture played such a dangerous role in German history. When culture was accepted as a compensation for politics, the absence of morality in the public sphere was accepted as well. The aesthetic appeal first of fascism and later of National Socialism was not a superficial phenomenon. It must be a core element in any attempt to explain the attractiveness of Nazi ideology for a large segment of the German bourgeoisie and many German artists and intellectuals. When members of the London Institute of Sociology predicted that Germany would be able to survive Nazism only if its core cultural values, represented by Goethe, were restored, it fell prey to the grand German illusion: culture always came first, politics followed. The contrary was true. To survive the civilizational break it had inflicted upon Europe, Germany would have to give up the most German of all ideologies: the illusion that culture can compensate for politics. But this process took a long time. "German Culture" survived the Second World War well into the second German republic. One of the reasons for this was a blurring of exile and emigration.

THE BLURRING OF EXILE AND EMIGRATION

In the summer of 1948, the German writer Gottfried Benn, whose poems and prose had tested the German language to the extreme, wrote a letter from Berlin to *Merkur,* the magazine that was to become the leading intellectual publication in postwar Germany. Benn had been blacklisted by the Allies for his alleged adherence to the Nazi regime. In his letter, he offered a sweeping explanation for the past and future catastrophes of his times: "In my view, the West is doomed not at all by the totalitarian systems or the crimes of the SS, not even by its material impoverishment or the Gottwalds and Molotovs, but by the abject surrender of its intelligentsia to political concepts. The *zoon politicon,* that Greek blunder, that Balkan notion—that is the germ of our impending doom."[21] Benn, a master of surprising prose, thus turned the classical problem of Germany's intelligentsia upside-down. He did not deplore the aloofness of German intelligentsia from the public realm that had made them easy prey for the Nazis—he pretended that the intellectual had failed to remain unpolitical and had thereby contributed to a political catastrophe. Benn was an admirer of Plato's *Republic,* which he called the most impressive vision of humankind ever conceived. In Book X of the *Republic,* the philosopher explains why poetry must be exiled from the city.[22] Benn also wanted to separate poetry from politics. But whereas Plato had banned poetry from the city because it was concerned neither with truth nor with virtue, Benn turned things around and took

[21] Gottfried Benn, "Letter from Berlin, July 1948," in *Prose, Essays, Poems,* ed. Volkmar Sander (New York: Continuum, 1987), p. 80

[22] Cf. Leo Strauss, *The City and Man* (Chicago: Rand McNally and Co., 1964), pp. 133ff.

Plato's proscription as a warrant for cultural escapism. At the same time, he acted like a seer who claims a privileged point of view—thus sounding a strange echo of the preposterous ambitions that a free-floating intelligentsia had hatched during the Weimar Republic.

Benn closed his letter in bitter irony:

> And so farewell, and greetings from this blockaded city without electric power, from the very part of the city which, in consequence of that Greek blunder and the resulting historical world, is on the brink of famine. Written in a room of many shadows, where there is light for two hours out of twenty-four: for a dark, rainy summer, incidentally, robs the city of its last chance of brief happiness, and the spring lays autumn over these ruins. But it is the city whose brilliance I loved, whose misery I now endure as that of the place where I belong, the city in which I lived to see the Second, the Third, and now the Fourth Reich, and from which nothing will ever make me emigrate. Indeed, one might prophesy a future for it now: tensions are developing in its matter-of-factness, changes of pace and interferences are developing in its lucidity, something ambiguous is starting up, an ambivalence such as centaurs or amphibia are born from. Finally, let us thank General Clay, whose Skymasters will, I hope, convey this letter to you.

Written in his nervous and original prose, Benn's letter displays in a nutshell the German mindset immediately after the end of the Second World War: the lack of any feeling of responsibility or regret; boundless self-pity; and unwillingness to learn from past experience. If one had to explain why reeducation in Germany was bound to fail, this letter could provide the key. Yet neither the open disdain for democracy nor the tacit acceptance of the Nazi regime as a legitimate period in German history is the most important passage in this disturbing document. Let me quote Benn's words once more: This is "the city whose brilliance I loved, whose misery I now endure as that of the place where I belong, the city in which I lived to see the Second, the Third, and now the Fourth Reich, and from which nothing will ever make me emigrate." The poet could not even emigrate—because he perceived himself as already living in exile. Berlin, the blockaded city, is the metaphor for an existence in exile; and Benn—who had been expelled from the National Chamber of Writers (*Reichsschrifttumskammer*) in 1937, who had been no anti-Semite and had never even thought of joining the Nazi Party—believed himself to have lived in exile for most of his life, artistically as well as politically.

When the war ended, emigration and exile had become, in Germany, blurred genres of existence.[23] For much of the German intelligentsia—scientists, artists, and writers alike—confusing past moral options became the prerequisite for mastering the present and planning the future. It was accompanied by an attempt to obliterate the boundaries between the public and the private sphere. Undeniable individual suffering was enlisted in the cause of shedding collective responsibility. "I mention my family," Benn wrote after the war; "three of my brothers died in battle; a fourth was wounded twice; the remainder, totally bombed out, lost everything. A first cousin died at the Somme, his only son in the recent war; nothing is left of that branch of the family. I myself went to war as a doctor, 1914–18 and 1939–44. My wife died in 1945 in direct consequence of military operations. This brief summary should be about average for a fairly large German family's lot in the first half of the twentieth century."[24] In this tale, sad and true, suffering alone counted. There was no quest for the cause or search for responsibility.

Not 1945, the year in which the Second World War ended, but 1948, the year of the monetary reform, must be seen as the turning point in the history of postwar Germany. Not bad conscience but a new currency propelled the change that brought with it a new society. German history in the twentieth century is a disclaimer of discontinuities. Neither the year 1945 nor the year 1933 marked a break—at least not for large segments of the scientific intelligentsia and the cultural elite. When intellectual temperaments, similar in their antidemocratic *ressentiment* and yet as different from each other as the philosopher Martin Heidegger, the jurist Carl Schmitt, the poet Gottfried Benn, and the officer and anarchist Ernst Jünger, expressed their sympathy for the Nazis' seizure of power, one must see this not as a conversion, but as a sign of continuity. The year 1933 was a turning point in German history, all right, but it meant the return to a Germany that had not lost its sense of self-worth after Versailles; 1933 was not a break, it was the fulfillment of German history. As Gottfried Benn put it, the new state had to be commended not least because it promised to give culture its due: the separation between politics and culture was about to end. In the state of the Nazis, the cultural nation would be reborn.

Walter Benjamin made the distinction between the politicization of culture, which was characteristic of Communist regimes, and the

---

[23] The allusion is, of course, to Clifford Geertz's "Blurred Genres: The Refiguration of Social Thought," *American Scholar* 49, no. 2 (1980):165–79.

[24] Quoted from E. B. Ashton, "Foreword," in Benn, *Prose, Essays, Poems,* p. xiii.

aestheticization of politics, which was part of fascist ideology. Hard as it is for us to understand today, it was the aesthetic appeal that turned large segments of the German intelligentsia into followers of the Nazi regime—at least for a while. The sympathies of many fellow travelers dwindled only when, on June 30, 1934, dissidents within the National Socialist Party and suspected enemies of the state were executed without trial. Members of the intelligentsia who had sympathized with the Nazis reacted in disgust. However, it was more the absence of taste than the lawlessness that they found intolerable in the behavior of the Nazi death squads. They were not morally appalled, but aesthetically disappointed. Rather unwillingly, I believe, Gottfried Benn made this clear when he wrote to his friend, the writer Ina Seidel, on August 27, 1934: "I live with my lips pressed tightly together, inwardly and outwardly. I can't go along with this anymore. Certain events have pushed me over the brink. What a horrible tragedy. The whole thing begins to look to me like a third-rate theater that constantly announces a performance of *Faust* when the cast hardly qualifies for a potboiler like [the operetta] *Hussar Fever.* How great seemed the beginning, and how dirty it all looks today."[25] How dazzled must he and others have been to believe that the Nazis would ever be able to play *Faust,* i.e., to take culture seriously. This was the dream of much of the cultural elite: that Germany would become a state in which politics and culture would no longer be separated. It was the fascist dream of a theatrical state.[26] When the dream turned out to be an illusion, it was disappointment, not distance or opposition, that followed. After 1934, many German intellectuals would have gladly remained fascists—if the Nazis had only tolerated it.

The lips pressed tightly together—this was to become a prominent feature of Germany's intellectual physiognomy during the Nazi period. One could still think but hardly speak and certainly not speak up. After 1934, many intellectuals who stayed on went into what they called "inner exile." "On January 1," Gottfried Benn wrote, "I am going to leave my apartment, my practice, my whole life here in Berlin and I am going back into the army . . . . I don't know what place they will send me to.

---

[25] Quoted from Reinhard Paul Becker, "Introduction," in Benn, *Prose, Essays, Poems,* p. xxviii.

[26] I have not used the term "theatre state" because Clifford Geertz wrote that "the expressive nature of the Balinese state . . . was always pointed not toward tyranny" and that in Bali "power served pomp, not pomp served power." This qualification almost precludes the borrowing of even a term, not to mention a concept. Cf. Clifford Geertz, *Negara: The Theatre State in Nineteenth-Century Bali,* (Princeton: Princeton University Press, 1980), p. 13.

My future is uncertain.... But morally and economically I cannot go on living like this, I have to cut myself loose from all my ties here. It is an aristocratic form of emigration."[27] "German Culture" thus survived: the belief that while politics took its murderous turns, the better part of Germany, the *Kulturstaat,* would remain unharmed. After 1945, these intellectuals did not for a moment think of themselves as fellow travelers who had, though indirectly and with a certain degree of reluctance, added legitimacy to the Nazi regime and prolonged its criminal life span. Having felt aesthetically averse to the Nazis was enough to foster their conviction that, in the recesses of their heart, they had also been contemptuous of Nazi politics. They had lived in exile. They had been resistance fighters.

This strange yet powerful self-delusion was enhanced by a curious fact. There was one institution in Germany that withstood the Nazi seduction without compromise: the German language. Unlike France, where the literary quality of the *Nouvelle Revue Française,* for instance, hardly declined when Pierre Drieu la Rochelle took over from Jean Paulhan and where the *collabos* wrote as well as members of the *Résistance,* the German language put up decided resistance—admittedly, against the majority of its speakers and writers.[28] There is no National Socialist literature of any rank. As a consequence, those who had been writing in "inner exile" with no chance of publication later thought that they had also lived in opposition.

RETICENCE TO EMIGRATE

When Gottfried Benn was asked why he had remained in Germany even after 1934, he replied that the idea of emigrating had never occurred to him. First of all, there was no pressure to leave the country. More important still: to go into exile was no viable intellectual option, because it had no tradition in Germany. True, Marx and Engels had fled to London to wait for times to change and in recent years Spanish intellectuals had fled their country to escape persecution there. However, the notion of "emigration," which would only later acquire its entire ethical weight,

[27] Gottfried Benn, letter to Ina Seidel, quoted from R. P. Becker, "Introduction," in Benn, *Prose, Essays, Poems,* p. xxix.

[28] Cf. Pierre Hébey, *La NRF des années sombres, juin 1940–juin 1941* (Paris: Gallimard, 1992).

did not yet exist. When members of his generation left Germany, Benn
said, they were not taking the political action of emigration, they were
just trying to escape personal hardships and unpleasant circumstances
by traveling elsewhere. That was a curious statement and a cynical one
indeed. It seemed as if Benn, for instance, had never heard of Heinrich
Heine's Parisian exile—though, by the way, he quoted Heine only a few
sentences later. There was an anti-Semitic tone in the rejection of emigration and exile: a German could not possibly adopt what had been the
fate of the Jewish people for centuries.[29]

One may be inclined not to take Benn's argument too seriously. After all, it did not explain anything; it was just an excuse. The case of
Thomas Mann, however, shows how difficult it was for a non-Jewish
German intellectual to accept the idea of emigration and of exile. In
February 1933, Thomas Mann had left Germany for Amsterdam, Brus-
sels, and Paris, where, after a triumphant beginning in Munich, he was
scheduled to talk about Richard Wagner, whose art, as Mann was eager
to remind his audiences at home and abroad, was the epitome of "German Culture" insofar as it displayed "a complete anarchistic indifference
to the state, as long as the spiritually German, the "Deutsche Kunst'
survives."[30] A vacation in Switzerland was to follow. There, his children
convinced him not to return to Germany. In the beginning, Thomas
Mann tried to see the necessity of exile as spiritually beneficial and as a
welcome opportunity "to throw off those obligations I had assumed in
the course of the years out of social considerations [and] to concentrate
hereafter on my own life."[31] A more German reaction to the exile forced
upon him is hardly imaginable: no political outburst, just a quiet retreat into inwardness.

The thought of returning remained with Mann. His wish, hardly
understandable in hindsight, was to go back to Germany and live there
in a kind of inner emigration whose aristocratic character might have
resembled that of Gottfried Benn: "One would not have to behave like
[Gerhart] Hauptmann or [Richard] Strauss, but one could try to pre-

[29] In July 1934, Thomas Mann speculated about the fate of the German people after the
end of the Nazi regime: "Perhaps history has in fact intended for them the role of the Jews,
one which even Goethe thought befitted them: to be one day scattered throughout the
world and to view their existence with an intellectually proud self-irony." Thomas Mann,
Past Masters, trans. H. T. Lowe-Porter, (New York: Alfred A. Knopf, 1933), p. 220.

[30] Thomas Mann, "The Sufferings and Greatness of Richard Wagner," in *Past Masters,*
pp. 90, 86.

[31] Thomas Mann, March 15, 1933, in *Diaries 1918–1939* (London: André Deutsch,
1983), p. 127.

serve a noble attitude and refrain from any public appearance."[32] For him as well, the point of no return is reached with the Röhm massacres. Until then, Mann had withstood pressure from his children and his friends to react publicly to what was happening in Germany. Eventually, he yielded. The decision to act politically came with an artistic farewell. On August 9, 1934, Mann wrote in his diary: "The whole day nothing but rain and thunderstorms, so that one cannot go out. I made excerpts for my political statement.... In the evening I browsed through my diaries and noted passages of political importance.... Katia and the children were listening to the radio, which was broadcasting the 'Twilight of the Gods' from Bayreuth, which was constantly disturbed by the thunderstorm. I resisted listening to it, I do not want to hear anything from Germany anymore.... It's nothing but cultural propaganda. My toothache is coming back."[33]

Was that the end of "German Culture"? Not quite. Thomas Mann had taken the interest the Nazis expressed in cultural matters quite seriously, even though he found it appalling. On September 8, 1933, he read a Franconian newspaper

> that was sent to me for some mysterious reason, containing a speech by the "Fuehrer" about culture. Astounding. This man, a typical product of the lower middle class, with a limited education and an acquired taste for philosophizing, is truly a curious phenomenon. No doubt at all that for him, in contrast to types like Göring and Röhm, the main concern is not war but "German culture".... Never before have the men of power, the men of action in world affairs, set themselves up in this way as the preceptors of their people, even of mankind. Neither Napoleon nor Bismarck did so.... They took political measures to promote what aspects of...cultural life seemed useful to them, rigorously suppressing what went against them. But never would they have spoken *ex cathedra* to proclaim a cultural theory for the nation or to outline a cultural program.... To be sure, they had as yet no notion of the "totalitarian state," which provides not only a power base for everything and even dominates culture—culture above all.[34]

Mann despised the cultural ambitions of the Nazis, and yet there was a seductive power in their totalitarian attempt to give politics a cultural

---

[32] Thomas Mann, November 20, 1933; in *Tagebücher 1933–1934*, ed. Peter de Mendelssohn (Frankfurt am Main: S. Fischer, 1977), p. 14 (my translation).

[33] Ibid., p. 502 (my translation).

[34] Mann, *Diaries*, p. 170–71 (September 8, 1933).

base. That is why, even in exile, he had to say to himself: "Germany, even a Germany wracked by confusion, is a tremendous country [indeed]."[35]

The primacy accorded to culture so uniquely in Germany did not cease casting its spell on Thomas Mann—even when this idea was shrouded in something as dreadful and despicable as the Nazi ideology. Even though Mann had once declared himself to be above all suspicion of wanting to become a new Fichte, a *praeceptor patriae*,[36] he often toyed with the idea and almost burst into tears when he came to realize that the decision to remain in exile had made it impossible for him ever to play this role. On March 14, 1934, a visitor from Germany quoted a remark by Gottfried Benn: "'Do you know Thomas Mann's house in Munich? There is truly something Goethean about it.'" Mann felt tormented to the depths of his heart: "The fact that I was driven away from that existence is a serious flaw in the destined pattern of my life, one I am attempting—in vain, it appears—to come to terms with, and the impossibility of setting it right and reestablishing that existence impresses itself upon me again and again, no matter how I look at it, and it gnaws at my heart."[37] As these words make clear, the firm conviction was that, even in exile, "German Culture" would survive and could not only compensate for politics, but actually teach politics a lesson, as Goethe had been able to do, having once, almost without irony, exclaimed: "What do the Germans want? Have they not me?"[38] That was the poet's dream: not just to be readmitted to the city, but to become a teacher to its citizens. Only Goethe, so it seemed, had been able to fulfill this role, more than a hundred years earlier, in Weimar, far from exile.

WEIMAR AND ST. HELENA

Last year, I was asked to give a speech at the convention of the Goethe Institute in Weimar, where the Goethe medals are bestowed upon foreign scholars for their outstanding service to German culture abroad. My speech had the title "Goethe's Presence of Mind." Immediately after

---

[35] Ibid., p. 155 (May 3, 1933).

[36] Thomas Mann, "An Appeal to Reason" [1930], in *Order of the Day: Political Essays and Speeches of Two Decades* (New York: Alfred A. Knopf, 1942), pp. 46–68. Gottfried Benn especially liked this essay. He praised Thomas Mann for having almost played a singular role in trying to save the Weimar Republic while it was still alive.

[37] Mann, *Diaries,* p. 200 (March 14, 1934).

[38] Mann quotes Goethe, "that greatest unpatriot of them all," in "The Sufferings and Greatness of Richard Wagner," p. 86.

my talk, the prime minister of Thuringia, the German state in which Weimar is located, came to me and reproached me for having done Weimar and German culture a disservice by quoting a passage from another speech on Goethe.

I had quoted from the address in honor of Goethe that Paul Valéry had given in the Grand Amphithéâtre of the Sorbonne on April 30, 1932, one hundred years after the poet's death. Valéry had great difficulties in preparing his speech, as he wrote in a letter to André Gide. He did not know German and did not know much of Goethe, having read only few of his works, among them *Faust* in French translation and some biological stuff, *crâne et plante,* which he called, somewhat condescendingly, "not bad at all." It had taken him five whole days to type his speech on his old Remington typewriter, and when it was written he no longer wanted to read it. There was something in Goethe that disturbed him: "Il y a quelque chose qui me gêne chez Goethe." And yet I do not know of a greater tribute to Goethe, "the most complex figure in the world," than this speech. Valéry used the opportunity of his talk in the Sorbonne to dwell on a theme that had been the *idée directrice* of many of his own works: how might the world, and especially Europe, have developed if political and intellectual power "had been able to join forces, or at least if the relations between them had been less precarious."[39] Valéry never stopped dreaming of what he called a *politique de l'esprit,* but he knew that he was only dreaming: "The two forms of power may well be incommensurable quantities; and it is no doubt necessary that they should be so."

Among the handful of men in which Valéry's dream seemed to have come true were Napoleon and Goethe, "one of them no doubt . . . the wisest, the other perhaps the maddest of mortals . . . both of them . . . the most exciting characters in the world."[40] That's why 1808, when Goethe and Napoleon met in Erfurt, was such a priceless moment in world history: "Coquetry was essential at such a meeting. Each wanted to appear at his ease, and carefully arranged his smile. They were two magicians attempting to charm one another. Napoleon assumed the role of emperor of the mind and even of literature. Goethe appeared as the embodiment of mind itself. Did the emperor perhaps have a clearer sense of the true nature of his power than Goethe imagined? Napoleon knew better than anyone that his power, more than any other power in

[39] Paul Valéry, "Address in Honor of Goethe," in *The Collected Works of Paul Valéry,* ed. Jackson Mathews (Princeton: Princeton University Press, 1968), vol. 9, p. 147.

[40] Ibid., p. 173.

the world, was in the strictest sense magic—the power of minds over minds—a spell!"[41] Valéry's description of the Erfurt meeting is extraordinary, a drama in itself, full of a tension that, even today, has lost nothing of its vibrant power. It is not just a meeting of two men of genius that Valéry describes, it is the meeting of the French and the German minds in their highest forms; never before and never again has the culture war characteristic of Franco-German history found a more delightful and yet ironic description. Valéry does not hesitate to admire Goethe, but into his glowing admiration he stirs a pinch of disturbing and in the end devastating critique—not so much of Goethe as of the German understanding of him.

Goethe is nothing less than the incorporation of inwardness, he is "courtier, confidant, minister, a diligent official, a poet, collector, and naturalist" at the same time; the great, in Germany perhaps the greatest, "apologist of the world of Appearances.... In the evening of his days, in the heart of Europe, himself the center of attraction and admiration of all intelligent people, the center of the greatest curiosity, the subtlest and noblest master of the art of living and of deepening the taste for living," Valéry writes, Goethe probably thought of Napoleon, "perhaps his greatest memory, whose look still lingered in his eyes."[42] Valéry's words show nothing but admiration, so it seems, for the greatest German poet, though they were tempered by Goethe's admiration for a great French mind. In truth, this admiration served to prepare a deadly blow, not to Goethe but to "German Culture": "Wolfgang von Goethe was to die a little more than ten years after the death of the Emperor, in that little Weimar which was a sort of delicious St. Helena for him...."[43]

Weimar a delicious St. Helena—that meant that the happy coexistence of political and intellectual power had been nothing but an episode in German history, a remote island, an exile from which no Goethe would return. In Germany, there was a political promise in culture then that had not been fulfilled. Valéry gave his speech in 1932.

[41] Ibid., p. 171.

[42] Ibid., pp. 156, 161. In this context, it is interesting to note that Maurice Barrès called Goethe's drama *Iphigenie* "a civilizing work which 'defends the rights of society against the arrogance of the spirit'"—a rejection of "German Culture" if there ever was one. I am quoting Barrès from Thomas Mann's speech "Goethe and Democracy," which he delivered in the Library of Congress on May 2, 1949. It seems to me that this speech, in which Mann mentions the Sorbonne address from 1932, is an implicit answer to Paul Valéry—and full of complicity.

[43] Ibid., pp. 174, 175.

Nine months later, the Nazis came to power. One of the first concentration camps was built in the immediate vicinity of Weimar, at Buchenwald.

Tomorrow I shall speak on "The End of 'German Culture.'"

II. UNIFICATION AND EUROPEAN INTEGRATION: THE END OF "GERMAN CULTURE"

INTRODUCTION

Friedrich Nietzsche once remarked that the German spirit is an indigestion: it does not finish with anything. I have difficulties in finishing with "German Culture." Whenever it seems to be over with, it creeps back. As I have tried to argue in my first lecture yesterday, "German Culture"—by which I understand the traditional overrating of culture at the expense of politics—did not end with the Nazi regime and with the Second World War. It survived well into the Federal Republic, not least due to a blurring of exile and emigration. That is where I want to pick up today. First, I will discuss the argument that "German Culture" survived abroad. Notably in the United States, it was victorious in defeat. The "Westernization" of the Federal Republic almost sealed its fate. The division of Germany, however, kept it alive. The process of European integration has made it obsolete. But now "German Culture" has become a European problem.

"GERMAN CULTURE" ABROAD: VICTORIOUS IN DEFEAT

To prepare for these lectures, I read books at the Institute for Advanced Study in Princeton that once had been checked out by Ernst Kantorowicz and Erwin Panofsky or that were bequeathed to the institute by the late Felix Gilbert. I was very fortunate in having the chance to talk with friends like Albert Hirschman and Fritz Stern. I understand why Abraham Flexner, when asked who had done most for the institute, dryly replied: "Adolf Hitler." The names I have mentioned do not represent the tradition of "German Culture" as I have defined it here. Rather, they share with another émigré, Thomas Mann, the view that politics cannot be reduced to culture and that, for the intellectual, democracy is the readiness to be political. The best of Germany's cultural tradition that survived in exile, and notably in the United States, was not "German Culture."

A side-effect of emigration, however, was that "German Culture" survived as well. While the Allies fought Hitler, German thought conquered the West. "The new American life-style [became] a Disneyland version of the Weimar Republic for the whole family."[1] This is a quotation from what the *New York Times* called "that rarest of documents, a genuinely profound book."[2] I do not regard Allan Bloom's *The Closing of the American Mind* as a particularly good diagnosis. But it is a striking symptom of the uneasiness that the survival of "German Culture" caused in the United States. Bloom deplores an invasion that led to a dramatic change in American philosophical thought and to the formation of a new language, one the Americans from now on felt compelled to use in analyzing their own culture. Cabdrivers used worlds like *Gestalt* and Max Weber's terminology invaded everyday life, like the Charisma Cleaners, which Bloom, to his horror, found in Chicago.

In the nineteenth century, when authors like John Stuart Mill and Matthew Arnold tried to soften utilitarian thought by propagating what they called the "culture of the feelings," they turned to German philosophy and poetry—as did the French whenever they tired of Cartesianism. The same happened in the United States. Nietzsche's rejection of rationalism on rational grounds, Freud's discovery of the unconscious, Max Weber's attempt at disenchanting the world, Heidegger's Hellenism, Thomas Mann's mysteries and sufferings as described in *Death in Venice*—they all joined in an attack on the rational project of American culture. Americans thus forgot that their own intellectual legacy had been one of philosophical and political cosmopolitanism. They were no longer able to talk with any conviction about good and evil anymore and had become utterly dependent on German missionaries for their knowledge of Greece and Rome, Judaism and Christianity. Admiringly, Bloom tells the story of Alexandre Koyré, who was excited when, in 1940 in Chicago, i.e., in exile, one of his students, unaware that the philosopher was not his contemporary, always spoke in his paper of "Mr. Aristotle." That was his American dream: to send Professor Weber back

---

[1] Allan Bloom, *The Closing of the American Mind* (New York: Simon and Schuster, 1987), p. 147.

[2] Roger Kimball, "The Groves of Ignorance," *New York Times Book Review,* April 5, 1987, p. 7.

to Heidelberg and Dr. Freud back to Vienna, while not only Mr. Aristotle but also Mr. Plato and Mr. Locke and even Monsieur Rousseau would be granted permanent residency in the United States. The German émigrés and their legacy prevented this dream from coming true.

One must not forget, and certainly not at this point, that Allan Bloom's teacher at Chicago was an émigré—Leo Strauss. One could argue that *The Closing of the American Mind* is nothing but an updated sequel to *Natural Right and History,* the Walgreen Lectures that Leo Strauss gave in 1949, the year two separate German states were founded. He asked whether the American nation still cherished its original faith, i.e., the self-evidence of the natural and divine foundations of the rights of man. He came to the conclusion that the difference between German thought on the one hand and that of Western Europe and the United States on the other had completely vanished. There was no longer any difference between the abandonment of the idea of natural right and adherence to it. With bitter irony, Leo Strauss concluded: "It would not be the first time that a nation, defeated on the battlefield and, as it were, annihilated as a political being, has deprived its conquerors of the most sublime fruit of victory by imposing on them the yoke of its own thought."[3] Victorious in defeat, "German Culture" had proven its fundamental assumption: it could not only compensate, it could even take its revenge on politics.

"GERMAN CULTURE" AT HOME:
A MORAL FAILURE TURNED TO INTELLECTUAL ADVANTAGE

Leo Strauss complained that German thought had become indistinguishable from Western thought in general. In retrospect, one must see this complaint of a German émigré as the prophecy of one of the great political success stories of the twentieth century. First the Federal Republic and then all of Germany became part of the West. The "Sonderweg," German exceptionalism, has finally flowed into the mainstream of parliamentary democracy, the market, and the rule of law. The revolt of culture against civilization is over. It no longer makes sense to think of culture as a compensation for politics. Today, we are witnessing the end of "German Culture." Fifty years ago, however, things looked different.

[3] Leo Strauss, *Natural Right and History* (Chicago/London: University of Chicago Press, 1971), p. 2.

In the West, "German Culture" did not merely survive the war. It fared well after defeat and capitulation. Politics seemed to be discredited forever; a remilitarization of the country was unthinkable; only culture—due not least to the "inner exile" where it had taken refuge— was left with a legitimate past and hopes for the future. At the same time, it was shaped by emigration, exile, and reimmigration. It thereby became more and more difficult to identify purely German traditions of thought and scholarship; as a rule, a mixture of domestic and especially Anglo-Saxon traditions prevailed. The Federal Republic's political and military loyalty to the West was thus enhanced by its cultural "Westernization."

In 1964, when German sociologists recalled that an economist named Max Weber had written some interesting stuff around the turn of the century, the scholars they invited to talk about him were an émigré philosopher, Herbert Marcuse, who was now teaching in California; a French political scientist who had studied in Berlin, Raymond Aron; and an American sociologist who had graduated from Heidelberg, Talcott Parsons. It is almost beyond belief that in France an author like Emile Durkheim could have become a French classic only after a detour abroad. Ideas and ideologies of German origin, thoughts and thinkers, were not simply stored in exile; they survived in another cultural milieu by actively adapting to it. It was still easy for Georg Simmel to unmask pragmatism as nothing more than Nietzsche's thought in American disguise. After the Second World War, it had become much more difficult to identify the thoughts and traditions that first emigrated and then returned to Germany. Empirical social research, for instance, was widely regarded as an instrument of Anglo-Saxon reeducation; not many knew that it was already flourishing in Vienna when Columbia University was just taking shape.

The situation in East Germany was different. Forced political loyalty to the Communist régime in the Soviet Union was not conducive to restructuring scientific thought or cultural belief-systems in innovative ways. Yet, while the Federal Republic was Westernized, the German Democratic Republic did not undergo a similar process of Russification. While broken English became the *lingua franca* for West German tourists, many East Germans simply refused to speak Russian. The West was internationalized, while the East remained a province where the *Internationale* had to be sung daily. In the first German Republic of workers and peasants, no professor of German could read or teach Franz

Kafka, no philosopher could read or teach Ludwig Wittgenstein, no sociologist could read or teach Max Weber, no economist could read or teach John Maynard Keynes, no psychologist could read or teach Sigmund Freud in an unbiased way—if they could read and teach the works of these authors at all. Censorship took its toll. In the East, the years from 1933 to 1989 belong to a single epoch conspicuously lacking in cultural modernity.

In West Germany, a moral failure turned into intellectual advantage. Denazification foundered. The old élites were reactivated rather soon. The confrontation between émigrés and fellow travelers, between opponents of the régime and its collaborators, between Jews who had been driven out of their fatherland and anti-Semites who had been responsible for their flight, led to the production of works of art and scholarly books both provocative and full of innovative energy. In philosophy, the intellectual tension created by a constellation of thinkers like Martin Heidegger, Karl Jaspers, Karl Löwith, and Hannah Arendt was awesome. In sociology, the confrontation of the Frankfurt School with the émigré Karl Popper, on the one hand, and scholars like Arnold Gehlen and Helmut Schelsky, both members of the National Socialist party, on the other, shaped the development of the discipline. To this day, German historians are caught in bitter feuds over their professional legacy, haunted by past masters who were both moral cowards and intellectual bravados during the time of the Third Reich.

In East Germany, good moral intentions turned out to be an intellectual disaster. Communists who had survived Nazi persecution and Russian exile tried to make denazification work. Culture became politically correct, but also boring and repetitive. Debates among the intelligentsia dealt with minor corrections of the established cultural canon, but they never questioned the canon itself. Once seen as stimulating within the intellectual micro-climate of the GDR, these debates have today rightly been forgotten. Bertolt Brecht was something of an exception, but even he turned more and more into a principal who was, above all, interested in the survival of his company. The Communist émigrés first helped the GDR to win moral recognition, but this recognition withered away with the fall of communism. When the archives of the Communist Party in Moscow were opened, it became evident what an ignominious role the leading heroes of German emigration to the East had played during the purges and political trials of the thirties. They had left one totalitarian régime—only to succumb to another.

THE FAILURE OF THE INTERPRETING CLASS

What the cultural elite of the GDR had learned better than anything was the art of being ruled (Wyndham Lewis). Unlike Poland or Czechoslovakia, East Germany never had a sizable samizdat or a catacomb culture; and unlike Hungary, it did not—and could not—produce groups of engaged émigrés. Czech writers who fled to Paris or to London thereby became alienated speakers. Writers from Leipzig who went to Munich or to Berlin were still living in Germany. More important still: they remained native speakers. Those who stayed in the GDR found, as a rule, ways and means to come to an understanding with the *nomenklatura.* Not all intellectuals became fellow travelers, to be sure, but a great many of them enjoyed the security and subsidies accorded to the cultural elite by a Communist regime that leveled, but never equalized. When Carlyle spoke of the man of letters as a modern priest and of the "Priesthood of the Writers of Books" that had become so influential in modern times, he was not speaking merely metaphorically. He believed that literary men who wanted to fulfill their mission ought to be poor. They had to form a monastic order. Communist regimes in Central and Eastern Europe probably committed their worst mistake in forcing members of the cultural elite to either collaborate or join the lower classes. Many of them had to work as furnace stokers and road sweepers, as cabdrivers and handymen. Thus they became members of mendicant orders indeed. The Communist regimes in the East were dealt a deadly blow by an intellectual proletariat they themselves had created. The situation in the GDR was different. Its cultural elite suffered from a lack of discriminative strain: its members lived in a culture with blurred moral alternatives. When the cultural elite was put to the test with the breakdown of the regime, the elite's failure became obvious. It was the failure of the interpreting class.

The first successful German revolution was a true and spontaneous *levée en masse*—aided by the very visible hand of Mikhail Gorbachev. It was neither the result of a long and open struggle against Communist rule, like the fight of Solidarnosč in Poland, nor the final triumph of twenty years of resistance in the underground of Prague, nor the culmination of shrewd piecemeal reform in Budapest. The German November revolution was neither led by a workers' union nor designed by the cultural and intellectual elite. Its heroes were hundreds and thousands of ordinary people who grasped the chance to leave a dictatorship by fleeing to the West German embassies in Prague and Budapest. Its heroes were thousands and hundreds of thousands who took to the streets of Leipzig and of Dresden. Their exit and their voice created the revolution.[4] In this revolution, the intellectuals were with the crowd, but not of it. The heroes of this revolution were, with a few exceptions, no intellectuals. In contrast to the upheaval in Prague, for instance, artists and students were not spearheading the revolt. "Wir sind das Volk" (We are the people) was a most appropriate slogan indeed. Intellectuals admired the slogan—and misunderstood it completely. In the framework of their own mentality, this slogan had to be read as the wish for the immediate realization of a socialist dream, while in reality it expressed the farewell to any socialist utopia. When the Berlin Wall was breached on the eve of November 9 more than ten years ago, the slogan was only slightly changed. Now the masses no longer chanted: We are the people, but: We are one people. This minor exchange of just one single word, however, revealed their true intentions: to join the capitalist West. At that time it became obvious that the cultural elite—in the East as well as in the West—had been unable to read the public mood. Intellectuals had failed on their own ground. They had not only misjudged a political power structure and overrated the strength of the Eastern economy. They had misunderstood the meaning of words. Culture is about interpretation and making sense. In Germany, the cultural elite has had great difficulties in making sense of unification. The failure of the cultural elite was neither misjudgment of amateur-politicians nor the miscalculation of would-be economists: it was the failure of the interpreting class.

THE DEVIL AND THE ECONOMY

In decades of mutual denial, conflict, coexistence, and eventually cooperation between the two German states, "German Culture" survived in the center of political rhetoric and on the margins of reality. However deep the divide between a capitalist German state and a socialist German state seemed to be, allegedly they remained indivisible as a cultural nation. When the real wall collapsed more than ten years ago, it became

[4] Cf. Albert O. Hirschman's brilliant interpretation of the collapse of the German Democratic Republic: "Exit, Voice, and the Fate of the German Democratic Republic," in *A Propensity to Self-Subversion* (Cambridge, Mass.: Harvard University Press, 1995), pp. 9–44.

obvious that unification had not been seen as a realistic scenario either by the political leadership in the West or by the *nomenklatura* in the East. It also seemed as if the cultural elite in both Germanies had thought of unification as Béranger had thought of the Republic: "I want to dream it, but not have it." At least, it had not wanted unification to happen the way it did. In the East, the unwillingness of the masses to realize the socialist dream was as much deplored by the intelligentsia as the so-called Deutschmark-Nationalism was disdained by intellectuals in the West. The belief in a common culture had been a much weaker motive, the longing for democracy had been a much lesser goal in the German revolution than the cultural elite had hoped for. Asking what the real driving force of the revolution had been, the cultural elite was given a clear answer: "It's the economy, stupid!"

It's time now to come back to the devil. In my first lecture I mentioned the two Goethe polls that were conducted in Germany in 1949 and fifty years later.[5] One of the more interesting results of these polls is the brilliant career that Mephisto has made for himself in the West. In 1949, when the Germans were asked which character in Goethe's drama *Faust* fascinated them most, 18% voted for Faust, 12% for Gretchen, and only 7% for Mephisto. In 1999, however, the preferences have turned around: in West Germany, 12% are now fascinated most by Mephisto and a mere 10% by Faust. In the East, not much has changed, at least not at first glance: 24% vote for Faust, 18% for Mephisto. The differences between East and West become even greater when only those are asked who have actually read *Faust:* now 34% in the West prefer Mephisto, 20% Faust. In the East, the result is exactly the reverse: 33% vote for Faust, 24% for Mephisto. These results have been interpreted as an indicator of a deep change of value-orientation and mentality observable in Germany over the past thirty years. "Be practical, my dear good sir!" Mephisto urges Faust. The Germans seem to have followed his advice—more so than Faust ever did. The times are over when John Dewey could call Germany a country where even cavalry generals relied on philosophy to bring home practical lessons. There are no cavalry generals anymore, and philosophy has come down from its high horse.

For a long time, the majority of the German population could not embrace the idea that enjoying one's life could be a legitimate way of

[5] Institut für Demoskopie Allensbach, *Demoskopie und Kulturgeschichte,* eine Goethe-Umfrage für das Nachtprogramm des NWDR 1949 (rpt. Allensbach/Bodensee: ZDF-Nachtstudio, 1999).

giving meaning to it. When asked whether having fun could give meaning to one's life, only 26% answered yes in 1974, but 56% did so twenty-five years later. Hedonism and the pleasure principle, as embodied by Mephisto, reign supreme. The East-West divide still exists, but it points more to problems of the past then to troubles for the future. The younger people are, the more they prefer Mephisto to Faust, in the West as well as in the East. There is no longer, as Faust whimpered, "A curse upon vain property, / On wife and child and husbandry! / A curse on mammon, when his gold / Lures us to rash heroic deeds, / Or when his easeful arms enfold / Us softly, pampering all our needs!" Rather, Germans in East and West are eager to follow Mephisto's advice: "Strike out, be free, / And learn what the good life can be."[6] Mephisto symbolizes a society for whose members private well-being counts, not public ideology.[7]

In the German conception of democracy, social welfare plays a central role. More than anywhere else in the West, the legitimacy of democracy is inextricably bound to a good performance of the economy and the functioning of an all-embracing system of social security. The abbreviation SWR, Ernst Fränkel once mockingly said, stands for German democracy, which must be defined as a Society without Risk.[8] In 1930, when Thomas Mann tried to defend the declining Weimar Republic, he was aware of the intricate linkage between the legitimacy of the existing political system and the performance of the economy. His courageous public speech was called "Appeal to Reason." In the September elections, reason had been dealt a terrible blow: the National Socialist Party had increased its share of the vote from 2.6% to 18.3% thereby making it the second largest party after the Social Democrats. Yet even on this occasion where he vigorously defended the Republic, Thomas Mann still doubted "whether the parliamentary system of western Europe, which Germany took over as being somehow available and convenient after the collapse of the feudal system, is really quite suited to her case; whether it does not in some sense and to some extent warp and do

---

[6] Johann Wolfgang von Goethe, *Faust: Part One,* trans. with an introduction by David Luke (Oxford: Oxford University Press, 1987), pp. 48, 49 (v. 1597–1603, 1542–43).

[7] During the Second World War, when Thomas Mann wrote a novel whose subject might also be described as the legacy of "German Culture," he could not but name it *Doctor Faustus.* When his son Klaus, in 1936, wrote a novel whose subject was the adaptability of the German mind to any political circumstance, he called it *Mephisto.*

[8] Cf. Ernst Fränkel, *Deutschland und die westlichen Demokratien* (Stuttgart: Kohlhammer, 1968). Fränkel spoke of the GojR, the "Gesellschaft ohne jedes Risiko."

violence to her political ethic." The lack of authenticity prevented the Weimar Republic from winning political legitimacy; the lack of economic security deprived it of massive moral support. A combination of cultural and economic shortcomings doomed the Weimar Republic. It was too much, Mann said, to demand sound political thought from an economically ailing people—a very German sentence indeed. Having said this, Thomas Mann, a nonpolitical man no more but a committed Republican for quite some time, took refuge in "German Culture" again. When he affirmed that he did not want to become a *praeceptor patriae,* what he really wanted to say was almost the opposite: this was a time when—after politics had failed—the poet, the writer, the artist had to act. He proclaimed that form, "be it ever so playful, is akin to the spirit, to what leads one on to social betterment; and art is the sphere in which the conflict between the social and the ideal is resolved."[9] Culture had to come to the rescue of the Republic. But it was helpless, as it turned out before long. Four years after Mann had spoken of art as the sphere in which the great conflicts of the times could be solve, his books were burnt in Berlin.

THEOLOGY AND "REALPOLITIK"

The stability of the second German Republic was based on the exceptional success of its economy and on its integration into Europe. For its citizens, accepting the constitution and reaping the benefits of the economic miracle were two sides of the same coin. Germany thus became a "normal" Western democracy. To tell the fate of "German Culture" in the four decades of the Federal Republic would be rather repetitive—despite 1968 and the years of terror, when intellectuals tried to achieve a cultural revolution at all costs. "German Culture," however, became an issue again with unification and with a renewed intrusion of theology into politics. On the one hand, we came to realize, to paraphrase the son of a German pastor, the stillbirth of politics from the spirit of theology. On the other hand, we are probably witnessing today the end of a secular consensus that shaped the political culture of the Federal Republic.

In his attack on German philosophical egotism that I discussed in

---

[9] Thomas Mann, "An Appeal to Reason," in *Order of the Day,* pp. 46–52.

my first lecture, George Santayana had written that "just as in panthe-ism God is naturalized into a cosmic force, so in German philosophy the Biblical piety of the earlier Protestants is secularized into social and pa-triotic zeal."[10] Political opposition in the GDR was, to a considerable extent, propelled by Protestant zeal. The Lutheran church knew how to get along with the socialist state, but at the same time it was able to re-sist and to contradict, often at great personal sacrifice for individual members of the church. Their moral convictions, however, never devel-oped into a political strategy. The moralization of politics in the tradi-tion of "German Culture" led to a mentality of "all or nothing" that, in the end, desecrated for all time the concept of politics, at least of party politics, which is nothing else than politics in a democracy. I vividly re-member a meeting of a small group of former East German dissidents with Senator Edward Kennedy and Willy Brandt shortly after the fall of the Berlin Wall. The dissidents, sticking to principles, and the senator, trying to promote pragmatism, had nothing to say to each other. It was especially sad that Willy Brandt, the émigré, was not able to translate and remained almost speechless throughout the meeting.

So, unlike the aftermath of the Second World War, when the con-frontation of moral alternatives, the coexistence of fellow travelers and refugees, of victims and perpetrators, of internal and external exile, had created a cultural milieu full of tension and thus creativity, nothing comparable happened after 1989. The moral alternatives confronting each other were murky. There were no real émigrés and only a few dissi-dents. Most important perhaps was another difference: though many of them nostalgically represented the best of Germany's cultural past, the émigrés who returned after 1945 were also carriers of new ideas, whereas the East German dissidents were molded by a milieu conspicuously lacking cultural modernity. After 1945, pragmatism and a culture of compromise entered Germany; after 1989, idealism and inwardness were coming back. Even when the dissidents had won their freedom of political expression, their fundamental contempt for politics and the procedural elements of democracy remained. "We had hoped for justice, and all we got was the rule of the law," one of them quipped. Most of the dissidents rejected the idea of forming a party, and when parties were formed, it happened with great inner resistance indeed. The antipolitics of the East German protest movement thus created a political vacuum

[10] George Santayana, *Egotism in German Philosophy* (New York: Charles Scribner's Sons, 1940), p. 12.

that furthered the resurgence of the Communist Party in the East and remained without any influence in the West. Cultural protest in Germany continued to be inefficient because compromise was not accepted as a political value. On the level of party politics, the miracle of unification had no effect.

On the level of political philosophy, however, one might speculate whether the miracle of unification may have contributed to the abandonment of a secular moral consensus that had been a cornerstone of West German democracy. The partition of Germany was the enormous price exacted for the unpardonable crimes of the Nazi era. The theological undertones of this argument could not be ignored. German unity was no longer simply an idea condemned by history and reason, as Donoso Cortés maintained in the nineteenth century. After the Holocaust, even considering unity a viable political option had to be regarded as nothing less than a revolt against divine justice. The notion of German partition as penance was part of the political consensus in the Federal Republic. It was forged by a Rhenish Catholic, Konrad Adenauer, who insisted on penance, i.e., *Wiedergutmachung,* instead of mere repentance.[11] Deeds mattered more than thought. This pragmatic reasoning was something like a doctrine of predestination in reverse: Germany paid, ergo the Germans felt sorry.

In the frame of this "political theology," crime and punishment, penance and predestination, all had a role to play—only the notion of miracle was conspicuously absent. When the "miracle" of German unity actually happened, the unbelievable revision of German partition came to be regarded as an instance of divine grace. It was a German author, Martin Walser, who, in his speech in the Paulskirche last year, asked that the remembrance of the Holocaust be reduced if not outright terminated. Walser had been among the few who had always believed in the desirability of German unification. Once more, so it seemed, it was the poet who had surpassed political wisdom. Once more "German Culture," with "a voice as tender and as powerful as religion itself,"[12] claimed to be the better politics. We may deplore this new religious nationalism but we need not fear it. It is and it will be contained by Germany's adherence to the European Union.

---

[11] I am grateful to Arno Mayer for a conversation with him on this subject.

[12] Fritz Stern, *The Failure of Illiberalism* (New York: Alfred A. Knopf, 1972), p. 5.

THE END AND THE REKINDLING OF THE CULTURE WARS

The growing together of Europe made it possible for the two Germanies to become one nation again without falling back into the traps of nationalism. In the process of European integration the cooperation between France and Germany played a crucial role. Unthinkable for our grandparents, unbelievable for our parents, French-German friendship had become the cornerstone in building a unified Europe. For centuries, the armed conflicts between the two countries were always prepared, accompanied, and followed by "culture wars." These wars seemed to have ended with the process of European integration. The moment of German unification, however, did rekindle the culture war, if ever so gently. As a consequence, we could witness a further cooling of French-German relations, which has continued ever since. In order to understand what is happening here, I want to describe, however briefly, some stages of the culture wars between France and Germany.

Whenever one country lost a war, cultural policy had to serve the need for revenge until it regained enough spiritual strength to seek retaliation on the battlefield. This holds true for Germany after the defeat at Jena and Auerstedt, when the Prussian king's cry that the state must replace by spiritual forces what it had lost in material strength eventually led to the founding of Humboldt's university; it holds true for France after the Franco-Prussian war of 1870–71, when the desire to regain Alsace-Lorraine could best be fulfilled by learning from the enemy; it holds true for Germany during the First World War, when the "Ideas of 1789" were confronted with the "Ideas of 1914" and a great author like Thomas Mann poked fun at a civilization where country inns were named A l'Idée du Monde and even fishing trawlers were called Pensée or Honneur et Dévouement Moderne. Cultural revenge worked less well for France after the "strange defeat" of 1940. By then, the French had obviously forgotten how to use culture as a means for revenge.[13]

The culture wars between France and Germany were also fights about which country had proven more revolutionary in the past or possessed the greater revolutionary potential for the future. Friedrich Schlegel knew how to offend a neighbor by saying that the French

---

[13] "Nous lisons, quand nous lisons, pour nous cultiver: ce qui est fort bien. Mais nous ne penson pas assez qu'on peut, et doit, quand on agit, s'aider de sa culture." Marc Bloch, *L'Etrange défaite: Témoignage écrit en 1940* (Paris: Albin Michel, 1957), pp. 194–95.

Revolution, Fichte's philosophy, and Goethe's *Wilhelm Meister* were the highest achievements of the modern epoch, thus daring to set a German novel equal to a revolution in France. It was a German writer in Paris, Henri Heine, who gave the most vivid and prophetic description of this revolutionary contest and where it might lead:

> It seems to me that a methodical people, such as we are, must begin with the Reformation, must then occupy itself with systems of philosophy, and that only after their completion could it pass to the political revolution. I find this sequence quite rational.... Give yourselves no anxiety however, ye German Republicans; the German revolution will not prove any milder or gentler because it was preceded by the "Critique" of Kant, by the "Transcendental Idealism" of Fichte, or even by the Philosophy of Nature. These doctrines served to develop revolutionary forces that only await their time to break forth and to fill the world with terror and with admiration.... The thought precedes the deed as the lightning the thunder. German thunder is of true German character: it is not very nimble, but rumbles along somewhat slowly. But come it will, and when ye hear a crashing such as has never before been heard in the world's history, then know at last that the German thunderbolt has fallen. At this commotion the eagles will drop dead from the skies and the lions in the farthest wastes of Africa will bite their tails and creep into their royal lairs. There will be played in Germany a drama compared to which the French Revolution will seem but an innocent idyl.[14]

Dewey quoted this passage in 1915 and 1942. Alfred Rosenberg might as well have used it in his sarcastic farewell to the French Revolution— if a Nazi propaganda minister could have allowed himself to agree with a Jewish émigré.

On Sunday, July 14, 1940, the *Völkischer Beobachter,* the aggressive mouthpiece of the National Socialist movement, carried on its front page news of German victories and British war cruelties. But most important was the lead article by Alfred Rosenberg with the title: "The End of the French Revolution."[15] Rosenberg proclaimed that the era of the French Revolution was over. Its legacy had been used by the French

---

[14] Heinrich Heine, *Religion and Philosophy in Germany: A Fragment* [1833/34] (Albany: State University of New York Press, 1986 [1882]), pp. 158–60.

[15] Alfred Rosenberg, "Das Ende der Französischen Revolution: Zum Jahrestag am 14. July," *Völkischer Beobachter: Kampfblatt der national-sozialistischen Bewegung Grossdeutschlands* 53, no. 196 (1940): 1–2.

government for its cultural policies at home and for its cultural propaganda abroad. Germany, on behalf of a Europe that had grown tired of democratic politics and Jewish business, had ended these claims to cultural supremacy. Now, a so-called positive revolution would shape Europe's future, in which Germanic culture would play the leading role.

To justify their alliance with the Nazis, the French fascists not only had to admit that the Roman idea of Empire had been restored to vigor in the Third Reich. They also had to see in the German revolution the survival of their own Jacobin tradition or had to foresee soviets and *fasci* in the militant groups found in villages all over France in 1792.[16] In his hatred for the French Revolution—"1789, c'est Luther, Kant, Rousseau"—Charles Maurras went as far as to call any *fait révolutionnaire* a *fait boche,*[17] but even Marc Bloch, who would later be killed by the Nazis, had to admit, to his shame as he confessed, that it made sense to establish a link between the National Socialist movement and the French Revolution.[18]

Strange as these affinities between France and Germany may sometimes appear, they must be seen as part of a larger strategy in which a coalition of Latin and Germanic cultures would serve to strengthen political ties, notably the Rome-Berlin Axis. The "Sacred Mediterranean" had always greatly attracted the German mind. A love for all things Latin is a constant in Germany's cultural history, and with it comes a pro-Western shift, a willingness to accept liberty, legalism, and Christianity as core values of private and public life. Quite often the result of a conversion, this Latin love then becomes a violent passion—as in the case of Nietzsche, who eventually sacrificed Wagner for Bizet and begged the Roman pope to save Western civilization from Germany. When Germany joined the Western alliance, "Mediterranean Fever" was no longer a cultural passion—it had become part of political

---

[16] "En 1792, il y avait dans toute la France des soviets ou des faisceaux de combat, c'est-à-dire que dans chaque village, dans chaque quartier il y avait un groupe de militant autour d'un meneur." Pierre Drieu la Rochelle, *Chronique politique, 1934–1942,* (Paris: Gallimard, 1943), p. 63.

[17] Charles Maurras, *Réflexions sur la révolution de 1789* (Paris: Les Iles d'Or, 1948), pp. 157, 158.

[18] Marc Bloch, *L'Etrange défaite,* p. 204: "J'abhorre le nazisme. Mais, comme la Révolution française, à laquelle on rougit de la comparer, la révolution nazie a mis au commande, que ce soit à tête des troupes ou à la tête de l'Etat, des hommes qui, parce qu'ils avaient un cerveau frais et n'avaient pas été formés aux routines scolaires, étaient capables de comprendre 'le surprenant et le nouveau.' Nous ne leur opposions guère que des messieurs chenus ou des jeune vieillards."

normality. "German Culture" had lost a crucial *raison d'être*—until 1989, Europe's wonder year in this dreadful twentieth century and the 200th anniversary of the French Revolution.

On November 4, 1989, more than ten years ago, a huge demonstration in East Berlin organized by artists and writers announced the fall of the *ancien régime.* Intellectuals suddenly felt they were *philosophes* who had worked all their lives for the revolution; the French Enlightenment thinkers' dream of a *politique de l'esprit* seemed in the offing in a renewed socialist Germany. When the masses took to the streets in the autumn of 1989 and finally made the Berlin Wall collapse, they evoked the image of the Bastille, whose storming had started the French Revolution. The French Revolution, however, had no territorial limits. Robespierre was convinced that the revolution was nothing less than an anthropological mutation and that the French, a new species, were forging ahead on the path all of humankind would take. The French Revolution was not French or European; it was universal. In 1989, Germany's cultural revolutionaries desired merely to conserve socialism in one country. The revolution had opened, once more, a German "Sonderweg."

German exceptionalism took a new turn. Soon the nonviolent character of the German revolution was used as a political asset. Unlike the Czechs, who, after all, had also been able to stage a "velvet revolution," German politicians and intellectuals could not hide the triumphant feeling that the belated nation finally had not only caught up with France's revolutionary head start, but had surpassed it. After two hundred years, differently than Heine foresaw and much differently than Hitler wanted, a revolution without *terreur,* therefore morally far superior to the French Revolution, had succeeded in East Germany.[19]

"GERMAN CULTURE"—A EUROPEAN PROBLEM

In the last speech he gave in Germany before he went, unknowingly, into exile, Thomas Mann insisted on the modernity of Richard Wagner's Germanness, which was "broken down and disintegrating,... decorative, analytical, intellectual; and hence its fascination, its inborn

[19] In view of the enormous difficulties that the German courts have in sentencing those who were responsible for the crimes under East German dictatorship, one is reminded of Max Weber's remark that the tragedy of German history was that, unlike the Stuarts or the Bourbons, a Hohenzollern had never lost his head.

capacity for cosmopolitan, for worldwide effectiveness."[20] Wagner's nationalism was so soaked in the currents of European art that Germanness and Europeanism no longer excluded one another. As so often, Thomas Mann was also speaking about himself. He had always wanted to be a great German and hence a great European writer. This ambition could no longer be fulfilled in his homeland, where the Nazis had replaced the intellectual's dream of a European Germany with the dreadful reality of a German Europe.[21] During the First World War, Mann had somewhat coquettishly painted himself as an unpolitical man; now, in the ominous year 1933, he quoted Richard Wagner's sentence: "Whoever tries to get away from the political deceives himself" and called it a very un-German opinion indeed. In 1918, Mann had attacked his brother for his cosmopolitanism and for the outrageous ambition to be a German *homme de lettres;* thirteen years later, he called Heinrich Mann "a classical representative of the Germanic-Mediterranean artistic genius" and bid farewell to "German Culture": "If he ever did exist, the German master without the world, without Europe in his blood—today he cannot possibly exist,... in a Europe that is growing together intellectually and, in all likelihood in the near future, economically and politically as well; a mastery devoted to narrowness, to obduracy and the provincial nest would be a sorrowful phenomenon."[22] This prophecy has been fulfilled. The process of European integration—fueled much more, at the beginning, by coal and steel than by culture and science—has made the idea of "German Culture" obsolete.

And now, at the end of my second lecture, I want to come back to the beginning of my first lecture and to my recent experiences in Central and Eastern Europe. In a curious way, the problem of "German Culture"—the exaltation of culture and its use as a compensation for politics—has not disappeared. It is, however, no longer a German but a European problem.

Intellectuals in Central and Eastern Europe created a culture of quarrel and complaint that eventually helped to overthrow the old Communist regimes. Amos Elon has described how the revolutions in

[20] Thomas Mann, "The Sufferings and Greatness of Richard Wagner," in *Past Masters,* trans. II. T. Lowe-Porter (New York: Alfred Knopf; 1933), p. 92.

[21] Thomas Mann, *Doctor Faustus* (1947; New York: Everyman's Library/Alfred A. Knopf, 1992), p. 175 (chapter 21).

[22] Thomas Mann, "On the Profession of the German Writer in Our Time: Address in Honor of a Brother" (March 27, 1931), in *Letters of Heinrich and Thomas Mann, 1900–1949,* ed. Hans Wysling (Berkeley: University of California Press, 1998), p. 284.

the East, above all the Prague Autumn, led to a victory of culture over power: "In Czechoslovakia, where the struggle between reformation and counter-reformation had prevented the emergence of a national church, the world of culture had often been a breeding ground for liberal revolt—from the time of Magister Jan Hus down to the days of Professor Tomáš Masaryk in this century. A great book could be written on how, in our time, [culture was] able to survive the age of darkness. . . . When all other points of moral reference were failing, culture alone—the novelists, playwrights, actors, philosophers, poets, filmmakers, artists, musicians—retained a measure of moral credibility, dignity, and ability to inspire the young. To think that it all started right under Kafka's windows [on the old Town Square]! The Prague Autumn of 1989 was a victory of culture over power."[23]

The rapid transformation of cultural reputation into political influence became a common feature of the revolutions in Central and Eastern Europe. Artists and writers, scientists and scholars, were promoted to high political office. They became the heroes of the Eastern world. Artistic sincerity and moral probity were assets for a political career. It was a unique moment in postwar European history when it seemed as if, in the future, two political cultures would clash whose personnel consisted, on one side, of intellectuals with high moral credit but almost without expertise and, on the other, of professionals with much expertise but without too much moral concern. This constellation has remained an episode—with notable exceptions like that of Václav Havel in the Czech Republic or Andrei Pleşu in Romania. The routinization of charisma took its toll and many heroes, to adopt Werner Sombart's distinction, realized that they were in danger of disappearing from the political stage if they did not transform themselves into shopkeepers fast. While the cultural legacy of these early "heroes" of political change has largely been forgotten or belittled in the East, it enjoys, paradoxically enough, an ominous presence in the West. "German Culture" has become a European problem.

Today, Europe is facing the dilemma between a rhetoric that must invite all countries of the continent to join the Union and the harsh economic reality that leads the haves who would like to become the have-even-mores to protect themselves against the have-nots. I am not saying that the enlargement of the European Union would be easy and could be

---

[23] Amos Elon, "Prague Autumn," *New Yorker*, January 22, 1990, p. 132.

achieved with just a bit of economic sacrifice. I am only pointing to the
recurrence of the compensation scheme that I have described, throughout my lectures, as the core element of "German Culture." While the
countries of Eastern Europe are denied entrance into the common market, they are invited to join NATO and, above all, are praised for their
cultural achievements. The military and culture are expected to make
up for economic discrimination.

Western cultural policy, such is my experience, has acquired a rather
bad name in the East. It's seen as an escape and as a cheap excuse—as is
the case with a curious linguistic incident, the survival of the notion of
"Central Europe" in Western discourse. As part of their strategy, the
East European dissidents rejected the term "Eastern Europe" as a common political and geographical label. Using the term "Mitteleuropa" or
"Central Europe" instead, by which they also wanted to dissociate
themselves from Russia as the political East, they were able to turn a semantic opposition into a political issue. The vagueness of the term
"Mitteleuropa," which sounded like the name of a very distant utopia
indeed, offered a considerable advantage. It was an idea in constant need
of interpretation. It was much less the description of a geographical territory than a design for a cultural model. It was a political idea behind a
cultural mask. Pursuing this ideal was of great political significance—
until 1989. After the fall of communism, however, it lost its function
and its appeal. Politics no longer needed cultural camouflage. Today, the
rhetoric of "Central Europe" is coming back—in the West.[24] Once again,
it is used as camouflage: this time, cultural benevolence provides cover
for political indolence.

In various attempts at institution-building in the countries of the
former Communist bloc—in Hungary and in Romania, in Poland and in
Russia—we have tried to learn from this experience and pursue an alternative cultural policy. Any bilateral arrangement was avoided thereby.
Not for a moment, for instance, did we think of creating a German-
Hungarian institute in Budapest or of founding a German-Romanian
college in Bucharest. Six European countries, to give but one example,

---

[24] Friedrich Naumann knew that "economic considerations, however serious they may
be, will not of themselves suffice to arouse the necessary enthusiasm" for the idea of Central
Europe, which also needed, for its realization, "thinkers and poets." Yet his basic aim was "to
make of 'Central Europe' a largely self-sufficing and an effectively united economic idea."
Since this economic utopia can no longer be pursued, the reduction of "Central Europe" to a
cultural label is pointless and politically dangers. Friedrich Naumann, *Central Europe* (London: King and Son, 1917), pp. 34, x, 41.

are cooperating in Budapest. Extending the possibilities and chances for fund-raising was one reason, though not the decisive one, for this policy. More important was the insight that cultural cooperation on a bilateral level very often leads to attempts at cultural domination and that multilateral arrangements are in effective check against such attempts. I will not enumerate all the countries that are engaged in these institutions. But I want to stress that the cooperation with France has been of primary importance to us.

We donors have worked in multinational groups to make sure that, on the receiving end, not national but European institutions were created. Very deliberately, for instance, we created not a Collegium Hungaricum but a Collegium Budapest. The institutions that we have founded on the model of the Wissenschaftskolleg in Berlin have something in common with the Olympic games: they do not take place in a country but in a city. They are embedded in an urban, not in a national context. In the charter of these institutions were included, though to a different degree, what one might call European provisions, i.e., stipulations that require the institutes to appoint members from a number of countries, to attract students from various parts of Europe, and to teach and to learn in various European languages. The multilateral coalitions I have mentioned consist, as a rule, of private foundations and of governmental agencies. This public-private mix has had a considerable political impact because it showed, in an exemplary fashion, that the functioning of democracy consists not least in cooperation between the state and agencies of civil society.

To work in the field of cultural policy can be enormously rewarding—if one behaves less like an economist who generously gives advice and more like an anthropologist who humbly tries to understand. It is high time for us in the West to admit to ourselves that the long-lasting division of Europe has not just been a problem for *them,* but for *us* as well. Being cut off from intellectual traditions that made cities like Budapest and Warsaw, Bucharest and St. Petersburg, centers of great intellectual attraction in the European past has also impoverished us.

I want to conclude by quoting a parable by a great European author, Franz Kafka, a short, fragmentary text that bears no title:

> We are a group of five friends who once happened to leave the same house in sequence. The first to leave came out and stood near the gate. The second left or rather sailed out, smooth as a drop of mer-

cury, and moved quite close to the first. The third emerged soon after, followed by the fourth and fifth. We finally ended up standing in
a row. People soon began to notice us and started to point at us saying "those five there just came out of that house." We have been living together ever since. It would be quite peaceable if it weren't for a
sixth who insists on trying to edge his way in. He doesn't actually do
anything to bother us, but he's a nuisance and that's bad enough.
Why does he keep on trying to intrude if nobody wants him? We
don't know him and have no desire to take him on board. The five of
us didn't know each other beforehand either and, if you like, still
don't, but what we can accept and put up with among the five would
be ruined by the advent of a sixth. In any case, there are five of us and
we don't want a sixth. What is the point of constantly living in each
other's pocket anyway; it doesn't make sense for the five of us; however, now that we're together we'll remain so, but we see no reason to
fashion new alliances, especially judging from our own experience.
But how do you explain all that to the sixth party? Lengthy explanations could almost give the impression of acceptance into the circle.
Better say nothing at all and simply turn him away. No matter how
much he pouts, we continue to fend him off, but despite all our efforts, he keeps on coming back.[25]

Cultural policy has its limits. The political and economic division of
Europe persists. We must do everything we can to overcome it if we do
not want to risk the end of European culture.

---

[25] Franz Kafka, *Nachgelassene Schriften und Fragmente II*, ed. Jost Schillemeit (Frankfurt
am Main: S. Fischer, 1992), pp. 313–14.

Happiness

JONATHAN LEAR

THE TANNER LECTURES ON HUMAN VALUES

Delivered at

Clare Hall, Cambridge
November 29 and 30, 1999

JONATHAN LEAR is the John U. Nef Distinguished Service Professor at the University of Chicago, where he is a member of the Committee on Social Thought and the Department of Philosophy. He was educated at Yale, Cambridge, and the Rockefeller University. Before coming to Chicago, Professor Lear taught at Cambridge, where he was fellow and director of studies in philosophy at Clare College, and at Yale where he was the Kingman Brewster Professor of the Humanities. During the time he was teaching at Yale, Lear trained as a psychoanalyst at the Western New England Institute for Psychoanalysis. He is now on the teaching faculty at the Chicago Institute for Psychoanalysis. His books include *Aristotle and Logical Theory* (1980); *Aristotle: The Desire to Understand* (1988); *Love and Its Place in Nature: A Philosophical Interpretation of Freudian Psychoanalysis* (1990); *Open Minded: Working Out the Logic of the Soul* (1998); and most recently, *Happiness, Death, and the Remainder of Life* (2000).

I.

What difference does psychoanalysis make to our understanding of human existence? I have been living with this question for years, and in this lecture I want to begin to give an answer. These are the Tanner Lectures on Human Values, so I should on this occasion like to focus on the question of what difference psychoanalysis makes to our understanding of our life with values, in particular, of our life with ethical values.

Psychoanalysis teaches us that wish, if not hope, springs eternal. Here is a wishful thought that comes quickly to mind when we begin to think about psychoanalysis and ethics. Might it not be possible to expand our understanding of ethical life to take account of the fact that human beings live with unconscious motivations? The idea would be to use psychoanalysis to devise a more humane ethics—one that considered humans more fully and realistically before saying how they should live. The prospect might then open for some kind of reconciliation of individual human desire with the needs of society and civilization.

The tradition I am concerned with grounds ethical life in the development and expression of character. Perhaps the greatest achievement in this tradition lies at its origin—in Aristotle's ethics. For Aristotle, character is a developmental and psychological achievement. We are habituated into certain character formations by our parents, family, and teachers, who get us to act in certain ways repeatedly, before we can understand the reasons for doing so. We thereby develop certain stable psychic dispositions—to see and think about the social environment in certain ways and to act accordingly. This is our "second nature." Now, for Aristotle, certain character-formations are better than others. Those that facilitate the living of a full, rich, meaningful life—a *happy* life—are the human excellences, or virtues.

The attraction of this character-based approach is that it purports to account for ethical life in terms of the lived realities of human motivation and judgment. Consider, for example, human kindness.[1] This character-trait is not on Aristotle's own list of the virtues, but we do not have to stick to that list to preserve the overall ethical spirit. A kind person

[1] See John McDowell, "Virtue and Reason," in *Mind, Value and Reality* (Cambridge, Mass.: Harvard University Press, 1998).

[209]

will have a distinctive sensitivity to the world—and a special sort of motivation to act. To be truly kind, one needs to be able to distinguish a situation in which one ought to step *in* and help someone who is struggling, from a superficially similar situation in which one should step *back* and allow the struggling person to develop the requisite skills and sense of autonomy. A kind person will be sensitive to that difference—and in noticing that difference will thereby be motivated to act in the appropriate ways. On this character-based approach, there is no way to specify, in a particular set of circumstances, what is the kind thing to do independently of the judgment of a kind person.

Already the hope of an expanded Aristotelianism is coming into view. After all, if ethical life is an expression of character, and character itself can be shaped by the psychologically enlightened training of parents and teachers, why can we not include our understanding of the unconscious in that training? We might then differ with Aristotle over what the best character-formations are—a happy life might come to take a different shape from the one he imagined—but the overall approach would be Aristotelian in spirit.

It is a thesis of this lecture that such a project cannot work—and, in coming to see why not, we shall learn about the psychoanalytic unconscious and about the attempt to ground ethical life in character. In brief, I want to argue that the unconscious is too disruptive to be contained in any straightforward account of character-formation.

Ironically, this project of including the unconscious in ethical character-formation would be unassailable if psychoanalysis were one more science among others. On this normalized understanding, psychoanalysis would be distinctive because of its hitherto unexplored subject matter, the unconscious. In opening up a new realm of inquiry, psychoanalysis would be adding to our knowledge. On this conception, psychoanalysis is an extension of what philosophers tend to call "folk psychology." Folk psychology is the attempt to explain human action on the basis of beliefs, desires, and intentions to act. Indeed, its first systematic exposition is in Aristotle's *Ethics*. Of course, the term "folk psychology" is somewhat unfortunate insofar as it suggests that these are the mental states people ordinarily ascribe to each other before they are in the grip of some particular psychological theory. In fact, the situation is almost the reverse. People regularly ascribe all sorts of complicated motivations and emotional states—including unconscious ones—to each other. And they only talk about "folk psychology" after they are in the grip of a philosophical theory about the elementary explanation of action. Nevertheless, one can see the idea that is at play: folk psychology would have to be expanded to include unconscious wishes and fantasies along with beliefs and desires, but then we could formulate a character-based ethics designed to take account of the whole kit and caboodle.

But psychoanalysis is not another science in any normal sense: about this, the critics are right. Indeed, it seems to me not just mistaken, but ultimately complacent to treat it as such. For what psychoanalysis uncovers is not a new area of knowledge so much as something disturbing about ourselves. Could there be a nondisturbing way of doing this? By now it is, perhaps, a too-familiar idea that in life we somehow keep the unconscious at a distance. The process that Freud called "making the unconscious conscious" could not, he thought, be a straightforward discovery, but necessarily involved transformation of the soul. It always involved uncovering something disturbing—and the uncovering always occurred under conditions of resistance and repression. Should the uncovering be so fraught in ordinary life, but theorizing about it be straightforward? Or might the apparent straightforwardness of psychoanalytic theory itself be part of the covering over?[2]

But if in theory and in practice the unconscious is always being covered over, it is also always already present and manifest in the coverings over. It is this intuition I want to take back to the first systematic attempt to work out a psychologically minded ethics. The question of this lecture then becomes not "What do we have to *add* to Aristotle?" but, rather, "What is already there in Aristotle's ethics, disturbing the self-presentation, yet not quite conscious of itself?"

This question is of more than historical interest. For we live at a time when the promising approaches to ethics are broadly Aristotelian in spirit. Philosophical culture has grown weary of rule-based approaches to ethics. By now, the critiques of Kant's attempt to ground morality on the moral law are well known.[3] In briefest outline, from the moral law it is impossible to derive any specific conclusions about how to act in a specific set of circumstances. It is, in part, because this critique has become widely shared that there is a renewed interest in Aristotle. For

---

[2] We owe to Jacques Lacan and Jean Laplanche the idea that the history of psychoanalysis can be read as a history of the resistance to its own insight. See Jean Laplanche, *Life and Death in Psychoanalysis* (Baltimore and London: Johns Hopkins University Press, 1985); "The Unfinished Copernican Revolution," in *Essays on Otherness* (London and New York: Routledge, 1999); and Jacques Lacan, *The Ego in Freud's Theory and in the Technique of Psychoanalysis, 1954–1955* (New York: W. W. Norton, 1988); *Freud's Papers on Technique, 1953–1954* (New York: W. W. Norton, 1988).

[3] See, for example, Bernard Williams, *Ethics and the Limits of Philosophy* (Cambridge, Mass.: Harvard University Press, 1985).

Aristotle, it is precisely because it is impossible to specify a set of rules on how to act well that one must turn to a psychologically informed account of how to build good character.

Interestingly, this is an approach that Freud himself ignored. Freud's critique of ethical value is itself addressed to a certain law-based interpretation of the Judeo-Christian tradition. This interpretation focuses on the Ten Commandments, the Mosaic Law, the injunction to "Love thy neighbor as thyself," and so on. Freud was concerned with a certain inexorability of unconscious guilt that life within this ethical tradition tended to facilitate. Being brought up in the Law tended to produce in individuals cruel superegos, set up over against the ego, judging it harshly and inflicting ever-greater punishments and inhibitions. This was Freud's diagnosis of life within civilization. But Freud more or less equated life within the Law and life within the ethical, and he thereby overlooked this alternative, Aristotelian approach.[4] For Aristotle seems to hold out the prospect of an ethics based on an integrated psyche in which values are harmoniously expressed in a genuinely happy life. Is this, then, a real possibility that Freud simply ignored? It is striking that Freud turned to ancient Greece for its myths, but not for its ethics or philosophy. Returning to Aristotle, thus, opens up the possibility of a different type of psychoanalytical reflection on the ethical.

Of course, psychoanalysis is itself concerned with the returns we feel inclined to make. And there seems little doubt that in contemporary philosophical culture, the *Nicomachean Ethics,* whatever else it might represent for us, has become a fantasy of origins. It is where we return when we want to work our way back to the origins of an alternative to law-based approaches to ethics. And psychoanalysis teaches us to suspect that if there is a disturbance within the ethical, one ought to find at least hints of it at the origin. Certainly, the disturbance ought to be gaining some expression in the fantasy of origin. So this ought to be a return with a difference. The hope is to find out more, not just about Aristotle, but about ourselves in our previous goings-back. What have we had to overlook in order to treat Aristotle as an origin? What doesn't get seen in order to preserve the fantasy? In answering those questions, we may start to gain insight into the distinctive difference psychoanalysis makes.[5]

[4] Interestingly, Freud seems blind to the ways the Aristotelian approach to the virtues was itself taken up in the Christian tradition.

[5] I also have a personal reason for going back to Aristotle. My life in Cambridge—which stretched out over fifteen years—was one of the great personal and intellectual experiences

2.

There is, I believe, reason to question the foundations of the Greek ethical experience. One can glimpse the problem at the first moment in
which Aristotle invites us to participate in ethical reflection. For the very
first sentence of *The Nicomachean Ethics* induces a reflective breakdown:

> Every art and every inquiry, and similarly every action and choice, is
> thought to aim at some good; and for this reason *the* good has rightly
> been declared to be that at which all things aim. (*Nicomachean Ethics*
> [*E.N.*] I.1, 1094a1–3)[6]

As generations of commentators have noted, the inference is invalid.
From the fact that every art, inquiry, action, or choice aims at some
good, it simply does not follow that there is one good at which all things
aim. There has been no shortage of articles criticizing Aristotle—here
the oedipal struggle and the desire to get tenure converge—but are we
really to think that the founder of formal logic committed such a blatant fallacy? More insightful commentators assume that Aristotle could
not be making such a blunder, and so there have also been ingenious
attempts to make this sentence come out right. I am not going to go
through them all, but will take one example that I take to be among the
best attempts to make sense of this sentence: Aristotle is here trying to
state what the supreme good *would be* (if there were such).[7] The problem
for this interpretation is that there is no textual indication that Aristotle
is speaking hypothetically; indeed, he seems to emphasize that the good

---

of my life. It has certainly influenced everything that has gone since. Much of that time
studying and teaching was spent absorbed in a philosophical engagement with Aristotle.
When I left Cambridge, I wrote a book summing up my intellectual experience—and I
stopped reading Aristotle. I trained as a psychoanalyst, and when I wanted to read or teach a
Greek philosopher, I turned to Plato. Now, as I return to Cambridge fourteen years later, I
am fascinated by the question of what it would be, for me, to return to Aristotle. For me to
see how my reading of him would now differ from my earlier readings would be to take a
measure of how I have changed—of what difference psychoanalysis has made to me. Perhaps
I should note in passing that when I first came to Cambridge there was no Philosophy Tri-
pos. One read the Moral Sciences. What's in a name? As we shall see this lecture: a lot and
nothing. A lesson that emerges from these lectures is that psychoanalysis could never be included in the Moral Sciences—except as a limiting case, as that which disrupts the moral
sciences—whereas it could be included as peculiar kind of mental activity that was properly
called philosophical.

   [6] Aristotle, *Ethica Nicomachea* (*E.N.*) (Oxford: Clarendon Press, 1975). English transla-
tions, unless otherwise noted, are from *The Complete Works of Aristotle: The Revised Oxford*
(Princeton, N.J.: Princeton University Press, 1984).

   [7] See Sarah Broadie, *Ethics with Aristotle* (Oxford and New York: Oxford University
Press, 1991), p. 9.

has *"rightly been declared"* (καλως απεφηναντο; my emphasis) to be that at which all things aim. I suppose one can add "if there were such a thing," but it seems an interpretive stretch.

This looks like a dilemma: Either one accepts that Aristotle made a logical error in the opening sentence of his fundamental ethical work or one must make coherent sense of what he is saying. Rather than choose, however, I should like to shift the question away from what Aristotle is saying and ask instead what he is doing. I would like to suggest that Aristotle is here participating in a peculiar kind of *inaugural instantiation.* He is attempting to inject the concept of "the good" into our lives—and he thereby changes our lives by changing our life with concepts.

Aristotle does not do this on his own. For an inauguration to be successful there must be a context in which it occurs. The relevant context in this case is the Greek philosophical effort—notably of Socrates and Plato—to found ethics as a form of practical-rational inquiry. For Socrates, the fundamental question is "How shall one live?" Ostensibly Socrates is asking a question, but ultimately it makes more sense to see him as attempting to introduce a concept—the concept of *a life*—into life. We are now challenged to consider *our lives* in deciding what to do.

Why think of this as the introduction of a concept rather than, say, an invitation to reflect with a concept we already possessed? It is now possible to glimpse the lineaments of the twentieth century's legacy to philosophy. One of the most significant contributions of this century to philosophy—manifest in the work of the later Wittgenstein and of Heidegger—is a working-through of the idea that there can be no viable distinction between the existence of concepts and the lives we live with them. There can be no fundamental divide between thought and life. If we consider the confusion, anxiety, and anger that Socrates generated, there is little doubt that the Athenian citizens had, in Socrates' time, no way to think about the question he was asking. Indeed, Socrates regularly confused himself. One has only to read the *Charmides* to see Socrates get himself into serious confusions as he tries to think about how to think about one's life. And in the *Apology* Socrates famously says that he discovered the oracle that he was the wisest of men was right because of his peculiar ignorance. Although he did not know, at least he knew that he did not know, and that lone made him wiser than anyone else. But if no one knows the answers to the questions Socrates is asking—if, indeed, no one really knows how to go about finding an answer—then there is reason to believe that Socrates is not asking well-defined questions but is rather trying to introduce new ways of thinking and living.

This is the context, as elaborated by Plato, in which Aristotle injects "*the good*" into our lives.

Aristotle takes himself to be merely extending the locus of our pre-existing concern with our lives. But remember the case in Wittgenstein of a person who takes himself to be going on in the same way with the instruction "Add 2," but who at some point in the series starts going on in what we take to be strange ways: 1004, 1008, 1012 . . .[8] We realize in his bizarre goings-on that he hasn't really grasped the concept—or that he is operating with a different concept that we do not yet understand. Now look what happens *to us* when Aristotle invites us in the first sentence to move from a concern for the various goods in our lives to a concern with *the* good: we are stumped, we need his lectures to teach us how to go on. From a Wittgensteinian perspective, this is evidence that, whatever he says he is doing, Aristotle is inducting us into a new way of life.

Jacques Lacan and the later Wittgenstein have, each in his own way, argued that a successful inauguration will tend to obscure its own oc-currence. Lacan takes as an example the introduction of the concept of irrational numbers.[9] Once we have the concept of irrational numbers, it will look as though they were always there, awaiting discovery. But if we take the later Wittgenstein and Heidegger seriously, this cannot be right, Life before the "discovery" of irrational numbers was not "miss-ing" anything. People lived with lengths; they lived with numbers. The decision to apply numbers to lengths changed our lives with numbers and lengths: it opened our lives to new possibilities, to new ways of liv-ing and thinking. For the later Wittgenstein it only looks as though the irrational numbers were already there, waiting to be discovered, because our lives with numbers have fundamentally changed. Retrospectively, it will look as though earlier life without the concept of the irrational was incomplete, missing something. But that is because we are now embed-ded in a life with the concept, and it has become difficult to see any ear-lier form of life as anything other than incomplete.

Now if we go back to the first sentence of the *Ethics,* we can see an at-tempt to cover over its inaugurating nature. Aristotle himself says al-most nothing about goods or the good: his assertion is basically about what others have thought and said. "Every art . . . *is thought* to aim at

[8] Ludwig Wittgenstein, *Philosophical Investigations* I.185–89 (Oxford: Basil Blackwell, 1978).

[9] Lacan, *The Ego in Freud's Theory and in the Technique of Psychoanalysis,* pp. 15–21, 256–57. See also S. G. Shanker, *Wittgenstein and the Turning-Point in the Philosophy of Mathe-matics* (Albany: State University of New York Press, 1987).

some good": strictly, Aristotle is passing on some high-class gossip. Rhetorically, the claim presents itself as a certain kind of received knowledge—common knowledge of the right sort of group. Indeed, part of what it is to be in this group is to take it as obvious that this is what "is thought." Notice the impersonality and passivity: "and for this reason the good has . . . been declared. . . . " No one in particular is doing the declaring: impersonally, it is thus. No doubt, Aristotle's audience would have thought of Plato—it is hardly a secret who has done the declaring—but the sentence-construction pushes one away from the activity of Plato's activity and steers one in the direction of accepting something as common knowledge. In particular, the sentence tends to keep from explicit awareness that Plato's own declaring might itself have been part of this inaugural instantiating activity. Aristotle enters explicitly in his own voice only with the word "rightly": "the good has *rightly* been declared." His own activity here is all but effaced. Notice too that the inference is constructed in such a way as to suggest that there is no real question whether there is any such thing as *the* good—it is presented as though it were always already there—the only question is what it might be like. In these ways the performative activity embeded in this first sentence is hidden from view.

If the performance had succeeded, the sentence would have looked obviously true to us. Conversely, inaugural attempts will tend to draw attention to themselves when they misfire. Instead of looking like it was always already there, waiting to be discovered, in a failed inaugural attempt something will look odd, as though it doesn't fit in. This is what is happening in Aristotle's first sentence: Aristotle does not quite succeed in inaugurating "*the* good." Perhaps it is a fact about us that we can no longer take this sentence as obvious; and if it is not obvious, it must inevitably provoke some discomfort. It is worth getting clear about what is disturbing us.

In effect, Aristotle is trying to introduce the concept by means of which it would make sense for humans to take a teleologically oriented interest in their lives. For him, the birth of ethics as a serious reflective inquiry simply is the introduction of the concept of *the* good as the concept in terms of which one should reflectively evaluate one's life. Aristotle insists that this is of immense practical importance:

> *Will not the knowledge of it, then, have a great influence on life? Should we not, like archers who have a mark to aim at, be more likely to hit upon what*

we should. If so, we must try, in outline at least, to determine what it is. (*E.N.* I.2, 1094a22–25; my emphasis)

It should now be clear that for Aristotle's act to succeed the audience must remain unaware of its inaugurating nature. For Aristotle is, in effect, injecting the teleological into life, and that act cannot itself be understood in teleological terms. It is too strong to say that this insight is repressed. Nevertheless, to grasp the inaugurating aspect of this act is to bust open the form of knowing and living that it attempts to create.

One can now see how Aristotle could make his way effortlessly to the end of his first sentence—and expect his intended audience to follow along. In the context of a teleological worldview, it makes sense to inquire about *the* good for us. It is *we* who cannot follow along who are in the less comfortable position of realizing that we can no longer live like that. We can no longer live like that, in part, because we are no longer living like that: thus our discomfort with the very first sentence. And thus our mild disquiet about what else might be opened up in that recognition. For once we become alive to the idea that Aristotle might be engaged in an inaugural act that, by its very nature, would tend to cover itself, the overall argument begins to look more suspicious.

Consider, for example, the ways Aristotle justifies his claim. He points out that the goods we already recognize often form hierarchies.[10] The design and making of a bridle, for example, is ultimately evaluated by the contribution it makes to military victory. The suggestion seems to be that we could keep on going. But once we become suspicious, it becomes evident that there are significant asymmetries. First, in the familiar hierarchies, we already know what the master good is. In this case, it is military victory. Second, in these cases the master good already functions in determining the shape of the lesser goods. So, to continue the example, the goal of military victory does filter down and influence the shape of the bridles that are made. That is, the familiar hierarchies tend to work *from the top down:* the overarching and known good influences the shape of the lesser goods. Now Aristotle has suggested that, in considering these familiar hierarchies, we could just keep going in order to form the conception of a larger, all-encompassing hierarchy. But this is moving *from the bottom up*—and Aristotle has given us no clue how to do this. It would seem we have been invited to move in the wrong direction.

[10] *E.N.* I.1, 1094a4–18.

Aristotle goes on to argue that if there were not this final goal, desire would be vain:

> If, then, there is some end of the things we do, which we desire for its own sake (everything else being desired for the sake of this), and if we do not choose everything for the sake of something else (for at that rate the process would go on to infinity, so that our desire would be empty and vain), clearly this must be the good and the chief good. (*E.N.* I.2, 1094a18–22)

It is surprising that this argument has not caused more anxiety among readers. There is, of course, a reason for a fairly complacent reading: We know that the intended audience for these lectures are people who are well brought up and mature.[11] And we assume the lectures are intended to produce some form of intellectual and practical comfort: "to those who desire and act in accordance with a rational principle knowledge about such matters will be of great benefit."[12] That is why we tend to read the second conditional—"and if we do not choose everything for the sake of something else (for at that rate the process would go on to infinity, so that our desire would be empty and vain [κενην και ματαιαν]"—as offering a *reductio ad absurdum.* But suppose we don't assume from the start that the absurd is impossible. That is, suppose through a certain form of reflection we become aware that desire is inherently slippery. Then this line of reasoning would open up the real possibility that our desire *is* empty and vain. That is, this reasoning would open us to anxiety.

Of course, the first of Freud's two major discoveries is that unconscious desire is inherently slippery. But even ordinary reflection gives us grounds for suspicion. We know that desire must settle to some extent for us to be able to act, but we also know that it is possible, indeed usual, for us to act on the basis of limited reflection. In general, people can tell us to some extent what they are doing and why. But, if called up short for a full accounting, it is typical for people's accounts of their own desires to trail off, perhaps pointing vaguely in some direction.

Aristotle's argument seems designed to intrigue his readers. He invites us to reflect on the absurdity of the idea that desire does not have an end, yet he also insists that it is mysterious what that end might be. Mysterious, yet of the greatest practical importance: "Will not the

[11]*E.N.* I.4, 1094b27–95a11; 1095b2–13.
[12]*E.N.* I.3, 1095a10–11.

knowledge of it have a great influence on life?" Indeed, it seems that Aristotle is tempting us when he invokes the image of the archers. The implication seems to be that his inquiry will provide us with that distant mark that up until now we have lacked. If so, it would seem that Aristotle wants to have it both ways. He wants to keep us at a safe, perhaps complacent, distance from anxiety; but he also wants to suggest that without this knowledge we are missing something of the greatest importance for our lives.

Suppose Aristotle had brought us precisely to this point of the argument—and then just left us here. Wouldn't he have brought us into a position that he just declared absurd? That is, we would be desiring everything for the sake of something else (a something else that we could not yet specify because it purportedly lay just at the horizon of our understanding, but we hadn't yet been given the mark).

Imagine a courageous person who had not yet engaged in much ethical reflection—that is, an ideal member of Aristotle's audience. Such a person, when asked why he did something, would say, "because it was the right thing to do." He may, of course, be able to say more about what bravery is, what are the pleasures and dangers involved, but he wouldn't be trying to justify or explain his bravery by referring to some desire outside of his bravery. In other words, he would be lacking that distant mark that Aristotle's ethical reflection purports to be about to introduce. But then it would seem that the effect of introducing this distant, important, but as-yet-unknown mark is to open the virtuous person to the possibility of anxiety. For he is now being invited to understand his action in terms of *the* good—the archer's mark that has thus far only been mentioned, not yet shown. Of course, being virtuous, he will not *feel* anxious: anxiety is not a possibility he will take up. But to see that the impact of the argument is to introduce anxiety as a possibility, imagine Woody Allen getting this far in the argument, and then being left by his teacher to his own devices: "Wait a minute, you're telling me there's some distant mark in terms of which all of my actions will or will not make sense—and now you want to leave?!" On the surface it looks as though Aristotle is about to provide us, the virtuous, with some ultimate reassurance for the lives we are already living. But if he is about to give us that, the fact that we don't yet have it must mean that, at the moment, we are lacking something important.

Aristotle thinks he can turn to politics to give us a glimpse of the archer's mark. To complete the passage begun above:

Will not the knowledge of it, then, have a great influence on life? Should we not, like archers who have a mark to aim at, be more likely to hit upon what we should? If so, we must try, in outline at least, to determine what it is and of which of the sciences or capacity it is the object. It would seem to belong to the most authoritative art and that which is most truly the master art. And politics appears to be of this nature; for it is this that ordains which of the sciences should be studied in a state, and which each class of citizens should learn and up to what point they should learn them; and we see even the most highly esteemed capacities to fall under this; e.g. strategy, economics, rhetoric; now politics uses the rest of the sciences, and since again, it legislates as to what we are to do and what we are to abstain from, for the end of this science must include those of the others, so that this end must be the good of man. For even if the end is the same for a single man and for a state, that of the state seems at all events something greater and more complete both to attain and to preserve; for though it is worth while to attain the end merely for one man, it is finer and more godlike to attain it for a nation or for city-states. These, then, are the ends at which our inquiry, being concerned with politics, aims. (*E.N.* I.2, 1094a22–b11)

This passage is more problematic than it appears. First, this is the only case in which Aristotle tries to cite the end via the art, science, or capacity that is directed toward it. In every other case, it is the other way around. Architecture, for example, is the craft directed toward building houses, buildings, monuments. In politics, by contrast, we do not know what the good is ahead of time. Rather, Aristotle points to the inclusiveness of politics to suggest that *the* good, whatever it is, must be in its purview. Is this reversal a symptom?

Second, Aristotle is trying to reassure us that we have some *actual* grounds that there really is such a good. After all, we do have politicians legislating; the polis is the arena in which meaningful human activity occurs, and legislation does help shape that activity.[13] But if we look to actual activity, politics gives us little grounds for hope, and strong grounds for pessimism. Isn't Aristotle writing in the wake of the Peloponnesian War? In the aftermath of Socrates' death? It seems hardly likely that Aristotle was unaware of Plato's claim, put in Socrates' mouth in the *Gorgias,* that if the good is the end of politics then Socrates is the only true politician.[14] But if that is so, the claim "we'll know what the good looks like when we watch the activities of real politicians"

---

[13] See Broadie, *Ethics with Aristotle,* pp. 15–16.

[14] See Plato, *Gorgias,* pp. 515–21.

turns into "we'll know what the good looks like when Socrates runs the state." We might as well wait for pigs to fly. The seeming appeal to the actual to justify the claim loses its force.

Third, the question of the political is deferred. I do not believe that any previous scholar has noticed that, if translated properly, the last line of the *Nicomachean Ethics* is identical with the last line of *Portnoy's Complaint:* "So [said the doctor]. Now vee may perhaps to begin. Yes?"[15] Here is the revised Oxford Translation:

> Now our predecessors have left the subject of legislation to us un-
> examined; it is perhaps best, therefore, that we should ourselves
> study it, and in general study the question of the constitution, in or-
> der to complete to the best of our ability the philosophy of human
> nature.... Let us make a beginning of our discussion. (*E.N.* X.9,
> 1181b12–23)

In other words, in the closing lines of the *Nicomachean Ethics,* Aristotle admits that any serious political study of the good has gone unexamined by his predecessors and it is only now time for him to begin. But at the beginning of the *Ethics* it was precisely political activity that was supposed to reassure us that there was a supreme good at which one might aim.

Even in the opening paragraphs of the *Ethics,* Aristotle seems implicitly to recognize that it is hard to tie his subject-matter down. "Let us resume our inquiry and state..." (I.4, 1095a14); "Let us, however, resume our discussion from the point at which we digressed" (I.5, 1095b14); "Let us again return to the good we are seeking, and ask what it can be" (I.7, 1097a15); "but we must try to state this even more clearly..." (1097a25). From a psychoanalytic point of view, there is always a question: why does a person keep coming *back* to something? What is it about the previous attempts that, for Aristotle, remains unsatisfying? Why does he feel the need to try again? Why can't he just say what he means, be done with it, and move on?[16]

---

[15] Philip Roth, *Portnoy's Complaint* (New York: Random House, 1967).

[16] I do not want to hang anything in the argument on this, but one might note in passing that it is precisely here that Aristotle launches an explicit attack on his philosophical father: "We had better consider the universal good and discuss thoroughly what is meant by it, although *such an inquiry is made an uphill one by the fact that the Forms have been introduced by friends of our own.* Yet it would perhaps be thought to be better, indeed to be our duty, for the sake of maintaining the truth *even to destroy what touches us closely,* especially as we are philosophers; for while both are dear, *piety requires us* to honor truth above our friends" (*E.N.* I.6, 1096a11–16; my emphasis). One might wonder: why the need to appeal to truth and piety to justify an aggressive attack?

3.

Aristotle seems confident that he can fill in the gap:

> Let us resume our inquiry and state, in view of the fact that all knowledge and choice aims at some good, what it is that we say political science aims at and what is the highest of goods achievable by action. *Verbally there is very general agreement;* for both the general run of men and people of superior refinement say that it is happiness, and identify living well and faring well with being happy; but *with regard to what happiness is they differ,* and the many do not give the same account as the wise. For the former think it is some plain and obvious thing, like pleasure, wealth, or honor; they differ, however, from one another—and often even the same man identifies it with different things, with health when he is ill, with wealth when he is poor; but, conscious of their ignorance, *they admire those who proclaim some great thing that is above their comprehension.* Now some thought that apart from these many goods there is another which is good in itself and causes the goodness of all these as well. To examine all the opinions that have been held would no doubt be somewhat fruitless: it is enough to examine those that are most prevalent or that seem to have some reason in their favor. (*E.N.* I.4, 1095a14–30; my emphasis)

Aristotle, following Socrates and Plato, wants to argue that the value of our values is that they lead to and constitute a happy life. Of course, there is much to be said about this conception of happiness, but rather than follow Aristotle down that interpretive path, I should like to ask a tangential question: what is he doing when he introduces happiness at this point? I shall explore this question at length. But let me say right away that I think that Aristotle is performing a seduction in the psychoanalytic sense of the term.

Obviously, this needs explanation. To understand this claim I need to distinguish, first, a vulgar from a sophisticated sense of seduction; and, second, within the sophisticated sense of seduction, I need to distinguish a manifest from a latent content. By a seduction in the vulgar sense I mean the blatant sexual intrusions that Freud, before 1897, thought neurotics had been subjected to in childhood and had repressed.[17] Although Freud abandoned the so-called seduction theory, a number of psychoanalytic thinkers have tried to refine that theory rather than abandon it, in the hope of holding on to a more sophisti-

---

[17] See, for example, the *Studies on Hysteria,* in *The Standard Edition of the Complete Psychological Works of Sigmund Freud (S.E.)* (London: Hogarth Press, 1981), vol. 2.

cated truth.[18] In this more properly psychoanalytic account of seduction, there is recognition that even in healthy relationships between parents and child there are transmissions of unconscious messages. These are experienced as messages, but they are necessarily enigmatic. Precisely because these messages escape our understanding, they captivate us: and this moment of captivation is, from a psychoanalytic point of view, inevitable. In this sophisticated sense, seduction is constitutive of our entry into language.

Basically, we have just seen the manifest content of seduction. We are by our natures susceptible to enigmatic signifiers—oracular utterances, if you will, which we can recognize as having a meaning—indeed, as having a special meaning *for us*—but whose content we do not understand. But the latent content of seduction is the idea that there is an explanatory end-of-the-line, an Archimedian point of explanation beyond which one does not need to go. Freud originally thought that he could stop his explanatory-analytic quest when he traced a neurotic's story back to a real-life seduction. It was as though the simple appeal to reality—*this* reality—could be the explanatory end-of-the-line. It was here, Freud thought, that the restless mind that searches for explanations can come to rest.

In abandoning the seduction hypothesis, Freud did not abandon the idea that children were often seduced or abused; nor did he abandon the hypothesis that such seduction caused serious psychological harm. What he abandoned—at least, according to his own conscious understanding—was the idea that this happened always and everywhere in the causation of neurosis. The deeper idea, though, is the recognition that the mind is always active. In particular, it is always active in the creation of fantasies. Thus even when there is a real-life, blatant seduction, there is still a further question: what did the mind do with it? The recognition that the mind is active in producing fantasies of seduction is tantamount to the admission that there is no Archimedian point, no explanatory end-of-the-line in a brute appeal to reality.[19]

We are now in a position to call Aristotle a seducer. He injects a special use of an enigmatic signifier into our lives and he puts it forward as something that ought to be an explanatory end-of-the-line. *Verbally,*

[18] Most notably Laplanche, *Life and Death in Psychoanalysis,* and "The Unfinished Copernican Revolution." Compare Hans Loewald, "Primary Process, Secondary Process and Language," in *Papers on Psychoanalysis* (New Haven: Yale University Press, 1980), pp. 184–91.

[19] I discuss this interpretation of the seduction hypothesis in *Open Minded: Working Out the Logic of the Soul* (Cambridge, Mass.: Harvard University Press, 1998), ch. 2.

Aristotle says, there is very general agreement that *the* good is "happiness," but there is widespread disagreement about what happiness is. The agreement, then, seems only about a word—and about the place such a concept would hold in our lives, if only we could give it content. There is thus also general agreement that this would be a justificatory end-of-the-line, but there is at the same time a recognition that no one can say with confidence what this valuable condition consists in.

This seems to be the point of ethical reflection. The injection of "happiness" here does capture our attention. We seem to be seeking "*the* good," and we are on a path of inquiry that we already recognize as attractive to us, but we do not yet have a clear idea of what this attraction is. Aristotle has already said that *if* we had knowledge of the good, that knowledge would have a great influence on our lives. We can recognize now, before we have it, that we would be much better off with this knowledge than without it. He now identifies this good with our happiness: something we can recognize as an ultimate good before we really know what it is. Doesn't this heighten anticipation, exert *some pressure* on us to know? If we are creatures who desire our own happiness, and if happiness is attainable only through rational action (that is why animals cannot be said to be happy), then the injection of the idea that we can consider the happiness of our lives *taken as a whole* must serve to make us discontent. Even the virtuous person will feel, as Aristotle would put it, the "right amount" of discontent. For once this idea of happiness has been introduced, it must, as Aristotle himself recognizes, instill a longing to find out what it is.

Aristotle distinguishes the judgment of the many from the judgment of the wise. Now if we again remember the gift of the twentieth century to philosophy—the insight that there can be no fundamental gap between the content of our concepts and the life we live with them—it becomes clear that the use of "the many" cannot simply be a mistake about happiness. It must reveal something about the content of the concept of happiness. The use of "the many" reveals, first, that "happiness" is systematically inconstant. People use it to designate what they don't yet have, what they are longing for, that which they have just lost and would like again. People tend to fantasize that if they just had this missing thing, it would make them happy. Thus, as Aristotle points out, the sick man longs for health and thinks that if only he can be healthy again he would be happy. In his sickness, he is oblivious to the thought that it would be a sign of his regaining health that he turns his attention to something else that is missing and begins to fantasize that it would give him happiness.

Now there is supposedly a perspective—the perspective of "the wise"—from which once can see the fantastic nature of this longing. Nevertheless, the use of "happiness" is irretrievably entangled in that fantasy. Happiness is that which we would attain if our deepest longings (of the moment) were satisfied.

Second, the use of "the many" reveals that they are to some extent aware of their ignorance. "They admire those who proclaim some great things above their comprehension." The many are ready to fall in love with a pronouncement they do not understand. It seems to be intrinsic to our use of the concept of happiness that we are especially vulnerable to seductions invoking it.

But these features of the use of "the many" suggest that "happiness" is a perfect transference concept. It is a blank that holds a place for "that which would satisfy our deepest longings" (whatever they happen to be). Thus, in retrospect, one can see how Aristotle could use the concept to carry out a seduction. Aristotle asks, what is *the* good of all our actions? It seems that we have somehow to take our lives as a whole into account, to do so while we are still in the midst of living and somehow to answer what to do next on the basis of that consideration. There is no obvious way to do this. In effect, Aristotle takes the concept of "happiness" from its unreflective home—where, for instance, we call the rich happy when we are poor, and in general fantasize that if only we could get . . . , we would be happy—and places it in a reflective context in which it is not yet clear how it is to be deployed.

This claim requires explanation. Obviously, there had long been speculation and comment on what made for a happy life.[20] What Aristotle is injecting is the idea that we can somehow be sensitive to *the* good—the happiness of our whole lives—in every decision, every action, every practical deliberation. The problem is that we don't yet know what this sensitivity is, nor what it is that we are supposed to be sensitive to. In effect, there is an enigmatic signifier already circulating in the population—our "happiness"—and Aristotle, following Socrates and Plato, tries to inject a new use. The idea that there is a special use of "the wise" promotes the fantasy that there is already content to the concept, but that it is only perceivable by those who are in the know.

[20] See, for example, the account of Solon's visit to Croesus in Herodotus, *The Histories,* book I (New York: Penguin Books, 1972).

The seductive suggestion is that a very special, esoteric knowledge is needed. This is just how it looks when an enigmatic signifier is introduced: it will look like there is something mysterious and enticing and, if only we could get behind the veil, our lives would be, well, . . . happy!

4.

Aristotle now purports to fill in the blank. The good of each activity, he says, is "that for whose sake everything else is done." So "if there is an end *for all that we do,* this will be the good achievable by action."[21] Aristotle says that he is going to state "even more clearly" what this good is—and he does go through the motions of giving its marks and features—but there is an important sense in which he says nothing. Consider, first, Aristotle's claim that the good is complete.

> Since there are evidently more than one end, and we choose some of these (e.g. wealth, flutes and in general instruments) for the sake of something else, clearly not all ends are complete ends; but *the chief good is evidently something complete.* Therefore if there is only one complete end, this will be what we are seeking, and if there are more than one, the most complete of these will be what we are seeking. Now we call that which is in itself worthy of pursuit more complete than that which is worthy of pursuit for the sake of something else, and that which is never desirable for the sake of something else more complete than the things that are desirable both in themselves and for the sake of that other thing, and therefore we call *complete without qualification {ἁπλῶς δη τελειον} that which is always desirable in itself and never for the sake of something else.* (E.N. I.7, 1097a25–34; my emphasis)

Aristotle does not here tell us anything about what happiness is actually like. To say that the chief good is complete is basically to utter a tautology. It secures a logical space of an enigmatic signifier: something that holds the place for "the end of desire as such." But this laying out of the logic of an enigmatic signifier tends to obscure the fact that this space is itself created. For there is some sense in which Aristotle's fundamental claim is false: we do "choose" happiness for the sake of being able to live a life in which we conceive of it as forming a coherent whole. This

[21] *E.N.* I.7, 1097a18–23; my emphasis.

"choice" isn't made, so to speak, inside life: it is, rather, the kind of in-augurating instantiation that gives life an inside. Once we have in-stalled the idea of there being an end of all the things we do, life will thereby be so transformed that it will appear that there is (and always has been) such thing as *a life* having its own possible coherence and end. It will then appear that all possible choices occur in this field: within the context of a life. This is an indication that we have already been seduced into a certain way of life, a way of life that has been structured by the in-troduction of an enigmatic signifier into it.

Aristotle makes a similar move with the idea that happiness is self-sufficient:

> From the point of view of self-sufficiency the same result seems to follow; for the complete good is thought to be self-sufficient . . . . *the self-sufficient we now define as that which when isolated makes life desirable and lacking in nothing;* and such we think happiness to be; and further we think it most desirable of all things, *without being counted as one good among others*— . . . . (*E.N.* 1.7, 1097b5–17; my emphasis)

One should read this, I think, as the utterance of a fantastic tautology: the imagining of the logical space that happiness would have to occupy. Happiness is that—whatever it is—which makes life desirable and lacking in nothing. That is, happiness is that, whatever it is, which makes us happy.[22] Now, why do I call this tautology fantastic? Because although it is possible to make perfectly good sense of this claim, one can also see, just below the surface, the stirrings of a wish. After all, why formulate the condition of self-sufficiency in terms of a life *lacking in nothing?* It is a condition of life that we live with desires—and the expe-rience of desire is the experience of a certain kind of lack. In a happy life, presumably, we have the right sorts of lacks and are able to satisfy them in the right sorts of way. But to characterize such a condition as a life lacking in nothing hints at the idea that the truly happy life is somehow beyond lacks—that is, beyond desire. The hint is of a life that is beyond the exigencies and pressures of life itself. The fantasy of a happy life be-comes tinged with the suggestion of a life beyond life—a certain kind of living death. I shall return to this.

Aristotle himself seems to recognize that he has not yet said any-thing substantial:

[22] I owe this happy turn of phrase to Gabriel Richardson.

Presumably, however, to say that happiness is the chief good seems a platitude and a clearer account of what it is still desired. This might perhaps be given if we could first ascertain the function of man. (*E.N.* I.7, 1097b22–25)

What the translator calls a "platitude" is ομολογουμενον τι: strictly, "a certain same-saying." I do not think it a stretch to translate Aristotle thus: "to say that happiness is the chief good seems a tautology." ("Tautology" literally means a same-saying.) Aristotle himself recognizes that he is not making substantial claims about either happiness or the good but is rather laying out the structure of a certain kind of concern. This isn't simply a platitude, nor is it simply something that is agreed upon (another possible translation): it is rather the delineation of the logical space that any candidate for the title "happiness" would have to occupy. But he has not yet said anything about the occupant.

Now when Aristotle at last comes to his famous argument about the function of man, it looks as though he might at last be adding some content to the idea of happiness. But appearances can be deceiving.

There remains, then, an active life of the element that has a rational principle.... Now if the function of man is an activity of soul in accordance with, or not without, rational principle...the human good turns out to be activity of soul in conformity with excellence, and if there are more than one excellence, in conformity with the best and most complete. (*E.N.* I.7, 1098a3–17)

Hasn't Aristotle at last given us the content of happiness? I don't think so. Nothing of substance is added by bringing in the idea of rational activity. "Happiness" is the placeholder for the object of our concern when we take our whole lives into account (whatever it might be to do that). The rational principle here is nothing other than the intelligent, mind-directed approach to happiness (whatever that might be). But that is only to stake out the conceptual field in which happiness is placed. Aristotle himself says that we do not consider any of the other animals happy.[23] This is not because they are psychologically incapable of it, but because the concept has been introduced as the goal of a thoughtful approach to living well, taken as a whole. Again, Aristotle is doing nothing more than locating the place in which the enigmatic signifier must operate.

[23] *E.N.* I.9, 1099b32–1100a1.

"But we must add," says Aristotle, *"'in a complete life.'* For one swallow does not make a summer, nor does one day; and so too one day, or a short time, does not make a man blessed and happy."[24] This is the real transformation: the injecting of a concept into life that purportedly stands to our whole life as the good stands to any activity within that life. It should not be surprising, therefore, that the introduction of this concept raises conceptual problems that Aristotle has difficulty in resolving.[25] Can we call no man happy while he is alive? This is not just a matter of clearing up confusions, or brushing away sophistries. The injection of an enigmatic signifier carries with it the possibilities of contradictions, unworked-out problems.

Is it only the dead we can call happy, Aristotle asks, as being beyond misfortunes and reversals? But, he goes on, that would be absurd because we consider happiness to be an activity. And yet, he continues, "it is odd that when he is happy the attribute that belongs to him is not to be truly predicated of him because we do not wish to call living men happy, on account of the changes that might befall them . . . ."[26] This is a serious problem for Aristotle—and he has no real answer. He does offer certain empirical consolations: that the virtues are the best way to keep one's balance when misfortune threatens and that, even in misfortune, one can never become base. But there is no conceptual clarification. And this would suggest that there is no answer: it would suggest, that is, that we are not here dealing with an articulated concept known only to "the wise" but with an enigmatic signifier.

Aristotle even manages to get himself puzzled about how far the "concept" of happiness extends: can a person's happiness be affected after he is dead? The familiar point made by commentators is that the Greek conception of happiness is not coincident with our own. The less familiar point is that this "concept" is not tied down. Notice how tentative Aristotle is:

> That the fortunes of descendants and of all a man's friends should not affect his happiness at all seems a very unfriendly doctrine, and one opposed to the opinions men hold...and it makes a difference whether the various sufferings befall the living or the dead...or rather, perhaps, the fact that doubt is felt whether the dead share in any good or evil. For it seems, from these considerations, that even if

[24] *E.N.* I.7, 1098a18–20.
[25] See *E.N.* I.10.
[26] *E.N.* I.10, 1100a34–b1.

anything whether good or evil penetrates to them, it must be something weak and negligible . . . at least it must be such in degree and
kind as not to make happy those who are not happy nor take away
their blessedness from those who are. The good and bad fortunes of
friends, then, seems to have some effects on the dead, but effects of
such a kind and degree as neither to make the happy unhappy nor to
produce any other change of kind. (*E.N.* I.11, 1101a22–b9)

Now it may seem "unfriendly" to hold that the misfortunes of loved
ones will in now way affect the recently dead, but who says death is
friendly to our wishes? Again, this may run counter to the opinions of
most people, but is there any topic about which one should have less
confidence in "the many" than in their beliefs about what happens after
death? Aristotle cannot here be trying to get to the truth about happiness. At best, he can be working out the content of common belief. Aristotle does in general think one should consult common opinion—for
about features in this world people do tend to grab onto some aspect of reality, even if they do so in a distorted form.[27] But it is obvious that about
life after death, "the many" know nothing. In consulting common opinion on this subject one learns about cultural myths and fantasies; one
learns nothing about the happiness of the dead. But this is all right if
Aristotle is not trying to find out the truth about happiness, but is facil-
itating a seduction. For he is taking powerful and widely held wishes
about happiness and claiming that these wishes can legitimately attach
to the enigmatic signifier he is introducing.

Aristotle goes through the motions of "testing" his argument
against common beliefs:

We must consider it, however, in the light not only of our conclusion
and our premises, but also of what is commonly said about it: for
with a true view all the facts harmonize, but with a false one they
soon clash. (*E.N.* I.8, 1098b9–12)

On the surface this look like a kind of empirical confirmation, testing
one's position in the light of hypotheses that others hold. However,
when it comes to popular beliefs, we have seen that Aristotle has already
cut his cloth to fit current fashion. For the rest, he does no more than lo-
cate the logical space in which this enigmatic signifier is placed. Aristotle admits as much himself: "we have *practically defined* happiness as a
sort of living and faring well."[28] Similarly with the claims that it is a

[27] See, e.g., *E.N.* I.8, 1098b9–12.
[28] *E.N.* I.8, 1098b20–22.

kind of excellence, that it is itself pleasant and among the most godlike things.[29] Thus far we know practically nothing about happiness. But, ironically, knowing practically nothing is essential to seduction.[30]

5.

Note that Aristotle's remarks thus far have all the hallmarks of an interpretation—at least, according to one understanding of that term. It looks as though Aristotle is saying to his audience, "Look, this is what your life was already about. You might not have consciously understood that you were aiming toward happiness, but now that I've given you this interpretation you can take better practical hold of your lives." Thus it looks as though Aristotle is just passing onto us a piece of knowledge— something that was already true but about which we were ignorant. That is precisely what an inaugurating instantiation will look like—*if* it is successful. Aristotle has already said that reflective understanding of *the* good will change our lives in important ways. But, from the perspective of the later Wittgenstein and Heidegger, there is no coherent way to understand the idea of changing our lives with a concept in fundamental ways while holding the content of that concept constant.

In fact, it is arguable that Aristotle is striving for nothing less than

---

[29] *E.N.* I.8–9, 1098b30–99b17.

[30] In this context, note the way that Plato chooses to end the *Symposium:*

> At that point, Aristodemus said, Eryximachus, Phaedrus, and some others among the original guests made their excuses and left. He himself fell asleep and slept for a long time (it was winter, and the nights were quite long). He woke up just as dawn was about to break; the roosters were crowing already. He saw that the others had either left or were asleep on their couches and that only Agathon, Aristophanes, and Socrates were still awake, drinking out of a large cup which they were passing around from left to right. Socrates was talking to them. Aristodemus couldn't remember exactly what they were saying—*he'd missed the first part of their discussion, and he was half-asleep anyway—but the main point was that Socrates was trying to prove to them that authors should be able to write both comedy and tragedy: the skillful tragic dramatist should also be a comic poet. He was about to clinch his argument,* though to tell the truth, sleepy as they were, they were hardly able to follow his reasoning. In fact, Aristophanes fell asleep in the middle of the discussion, and very soon thereafter, as day was breaking, Agathon also drifted off. (Plato, *Symposium* 223b–d, trans. Alexander Nehamas and Paul Woodruf [Indianapolis: Hackett, 1989])

In other words, Socrates dramatizes a scene in which there is nothing left but an enigmatic message. Everyone has left or fallen asleep, there is no one left who can reconstruct the argument—and yet we feel that the message is crucial and somehow matters *to us.* Is there any choice but to create an interpretation? To understand the torrent of writing, thinking, interpretation that this seduction brought forth is to understand much of the history of Western literary criticism.

an ontological transformation of human being. To see this, let us start with Heidegger's idea that we are ontologically constituted by care. To see that this is more than a deep psychological fact about us, consider the following counterfactual schema:

If we were to cease to care, then . . .

The point is not that all counterfactuals of such form are false, but that they are all nonsensical.[31] We see this when we recognize that the antecedent is not specifying any coherent condition. In the closest condition in which we cease to care, "we" cease to be. No doubt, one can find human beings in psychiatric institutions in severe catatonic states, in massive autistic enclosedness, where it does make sense to say that they have ceased to care. But precisely in looking at this allegedly limiting case we can see what is at stake: in ceasing to care, they have ceased to be one of us. This is not to draw a line between one tribe and another, one culture and another: it is to gesture in the direction of what it is to fall out of human being. The "fact" that we care, then, is not simply an important fact about what we are like, it is a structuring condition of the universe of our possibilities.

Now it seems that Aristotle is trying to get us to recognize that we are in a similar position with respect to:

If we were to cease to care-about-our-happiness, then . . .

First, Aristotle insists that humans are the only animals capable of happiness. Other creatures may flourish in their distinctive ways, but only humans can be concerned about their happiness—and this concern seems to be a constitutive condition of happiness itself.[32] It seems that Aristotle is here trying to make an ontological distinction: he is mapping out the realm of human being. Second, Aristotle explicitly sees *all* forms of human being as various types of carings-about-happiness. Indeed, for Aristotle, one differentiates among these forms of being not by whether there is a concern for happiness or not, but over what form that concern takes. The virtuous person, for example, is harmoniously motivated in ways that accurately express and promote his happiness. Among people who suffered conflicts, Aristotle recognizes two types.

---

[31] I discuss a related point about our mindedness in "Transcendental Anthropology," in *Open Minded: Working Out the Logic of the Soul.*

[32] *E.N.* I.9, 1099b33–1100a1; see also X.8, 1178b24–2.

First, there is the "continent" person who feels a conflict but in the end manages to do the right thing. Second, there is the "incontinent" (or *akratic*) who decides to do one thing, but then acts against his best judgment. This is Aristotle's model of an irrational act. But both the "continent" and "incontinent" persons have it in common that their conflicts are among things they take to be goods. Temptation is the paradigm occasion for conflict, but whether or not one gives in, both sides of the conflict are directed toward some image of happiness. The wicked or intemperate person is the mirror image of virtue: he is pursuing some bad end—but only because he (mistakenly) believes it will promote his happiness. In short, for Aristotle, all forms of human being are structured by this concern.

This apparent universality of this concern helps Aristotle remain unaware of his ontological sleight of hand. For by introducing the idea that we are ontologically constituted by a concern for our happiness, he in effect slips in the idea that we are ontologically constituted by a concern for our lives *as a whole.* This does seem an unconscious attempt at making-true. For it is precisely the concern for our lives as a whole that serves to make our lives whole. And it is by introducing "happiness" as a way we might evaluate our lives as a whole, as a purported evaluative frame for our current understanding of what we are doing here and now, that life gets to be constituted as a whole. And insofar as Aristotle takes concern-for-our-happiness to structure all the possibilities of human being, he has endeavored to change our ontological constitution without noticing that this is what he is doing.

That, it seems to me, is the unconscious aim of Greek ethical reflection: to change our ontology without our noticing it. Thus we see the power of a certain form of interpretation: not just to change life, but to change the structure of possibilities in which life can be lived.

6.

In analysis, we are always interested when the analysand makes a sudden shift. And there is no doubt but that there is an abrupt shift in the last few pages of the *Nicomachean Ethics*—a shift that changes the meaning of the book as a whole. Had those pages not been there, the obvious lesson of the book would be that the happy life is the active life of the traditional ethical virtues informed by practical wisdom. But Aristotle famously closes the *Ethics* by claiming that, in fact, such a life would only provide "second-rate happiness."[33] The truly happy life is contemplative.

Generations of scholars have reacted in one of two ways. First, they have tried to show that the appearance of a shift is only an appearance. They point to hints earlier in the text and argue that contemplation is the direction in which Aristotle has been moving all along.[34] Second, philosophers who are interested in the contemporary value of an Aristotelian approach to ethics will tend to split off the end of the book and discount it. It is treated as part of Aristotle's theology: of historical interest but not relevant to the central ethical approach of the book. These philosophers focus on Aristotle's account of how virtues are instilled by habit and how they bestow their own distinctive ways of seeing and reacting to situations.

I don't want to move in either direction, for both seem to me to be the work of philosophy's ego. Not that I have anything against the ego per se. It *is* of value to show an underlying unity to the *Nicomachean Ethics* taken as a whole. But it is precisely the ingenuity of displaying this underlying unity that covers over the strain in doing so. Similarly, it is of course of value to use Aristotle as inspiration for contemporary approaches to ethics, but the beauty and excitement of that activity covers over the violence involved in lopping off a significant section of the book.

I should therefore like to try a change of tack. Leaving aside the question of the ultimate coherence or incoherence, I want to stay closer to the surface of the text and ask: what is the effect of this *apparent* disruption? What is involved in this last-minute recognition that the truly happy life is the contemplative one? The answer seems to me surprising. Just below the surface of the familiar arguments, the text serves to promote discontent and to valorize death.

7.

If the *Nicomachean Ethics* had ended at book X, chapter 6, the opening lines of the text would, in retrospect, have looked like a come-on. Why, after all, would we need an image of archers given a distant mark to aim at if the upshot of ethical reflection is that the life that we are already living is the happy one? The metaphor would be wildly off. A more appro-

---

[33] "Δευτέρως," *E.N.* X.8, 1178a9.
[34] See, e.g., *E.N.* I.5, 1095b14–96a5; I.9, I099b11–18; I.12, 1101b21–31.

priate metaphor would be the adding of a bit of mortar between the al-
ready-secure bricks of the solid edifice. But the introduction of the ideal
of a contemplative life does at last give us a mark to aim at, for it does involve a shifting of sights onto that mark. At the last minute, we are encouraged to think differently about the lives we are already leading. We
are now encouraged to see them as pointing elsewhere.

The shift is in our conception of what it is about our life that really
gives it value. And this will lead to a restructuring of our lives. Not that
the contemplative life is altogether different from the practical life, but
now that large part of life that is engaged in practical activity will be
understood from inside that life as aiming toward the contemplative
life.[35] That is, such a practical life, *when it succeeds in its project,* will be a
contemplative life. For a contemplative life is not one in which we are
always contemplating. Rather, what makes the life contemplative is,
first, that practical life itself is understood as organized for the sake of
providing time and space for contemplative activity; second, the practical activity of life is actually successful in securing room for contemplation; third, it is understood that it is this contemplative activity that
gives this life its deepest value. The move from a practical to a contemplative life will involve a rethinking of the value and organization of
practical life.

It is crucial to Aristotle's restructuring of ethical life that "happiness" has been functioning for him as an enigmatic signifier. He begins:

> If happiness is activity in accordance with excellence, it is reasonable
> that it should be in accordance with the highest excellence; and this
> will be that of the best thing in us. Whether it be intellect or some-
> thing else that is this element which is thought to be our natural
> ruler and guide and to take thought of things noble and divine,
> whether it be itself also divine or only the most divine element in us,
> the activity of this in accordance with its proper excellence will be
> complete happiness. That this activity is contemplative we have al-
> ready said. (*E.N.* X.7, 1177a12–18)

Aristotle seems to be pursuing a thought to its logical conclusion, but
note that this is possible because we do not yet know what happiness is.
It has been introduced as a standard, yet because it is enigmatic we are
susceptible to a last-minute shift in understanding what the point of our
lives might be. It is the ethical equivalent of receiving an oracle and only
at the last minute coming to understand its meaning *for us.* Aristotle, of
course, relies here on an overall teleological framework, and he appeals

[35] See Broadie, *Ethics with Aristotle,* on the central good; pp. 26–27.

to "the best thing in us." The effect, though, must be to set us at a distance from happiness. For let us just suppose that we are the intended audience for these lectures: we are already well brought up, mature, more or less leading an ethically virtuous life and are now following Aristotle in a reflection on that life. Until this moment we ought to have been thinking that we are already living happy lives; but now comes the moment of separation. We begin to realize that the lives we have been living are not *completely* happy. So, although we are at this moment the furthest away from "the many's" conception of happiness, this highest conception of happiness does have something in common with the lowest: we are again conceiving happiness as what we don't at the moment have. Aristotle will achieve this distance by retrospectively giving new content to what is meant by "complete happiness." And because we have already been seduced by the enigmatic nature of this signifier, there is pressure to go along.

Aristotle now argues that whatever the hallmarks of happiness are, one gets more of them in a contemplative life. Contemplative activity is, he says, more "continuous" and "self-sufficient" than ordinary practical activity.

> And the self-sufficiency spoken of must belong most to the contemplative activity. For while a wise man, as well as a just man and the rest, needs the necessaries of life, when they are sufficiently equipped with things of that sort the just man needs people towards whom and with whom he shall act justly, and the temperate man and the brave man and each of the others is in the same case, but the wise man, even when by himself, can contemplate truth, and the better the wiser he is; he can perhaps do so better if he has fellow-workers, but still he is the most self-sufficient. And *this activity alone would seem to be loved for its own sake; for nothing arises from it apart from the contemplating, while from practical activities we gain more or less apart from the action. And happiness is thought to depend on leisure; for we are busy that we may have leisure, and make war that we may live in peace.* Now the activity of the practical excellences is exhibited in political or military affairs, but the actions concerned with these seem to be unleisurely. Warlike actions are completely so (for no one chooses to be at war, or provokes war for the sake of being at war; *any one would seem absolutely murderous if he were to make enemies of his friends in order to bring about battle and slaughter*); but *the action of the statesman is also unleisurely,* and—apart from the political action itself—aims at despotic power and honors, or at all events happiness, for him and his fellow citi-

logical structure of teleological striving. But now a new conception of happiness is introduced in relation to which the political life, even at its best, is now revealed as "incomplete," as not *really* "self-sufficient."

Aristotle is explicit that now that the vista of a contemplative life has opened up, the life of practical virtue appears "second rate":

> But *in a secondary degree the life in accordance with the other kind of excellence is happy;* for the activities in accordance with this befit our human estate. Just and brave acts, and other excellent acts, we do in relation to each other, observing what is proper to each with regard to contracts and services and all manner of actions with regard to passions; and all of these seem to be human.... The excellence of the intellect is a thing apart; we must be content to say this much about it, for to describe it precisely is a task greater than our purpose requires. It would seem, however, also to need external equipment but little, or less than moral excellence does. Grant that both need the necessaries, and do so equally, even if the statesman's work is the more concerned with the body and things of that sort; for there will be little difference there; but in what they need for the exercise of their activities there will be much difference. The liberal man will need money for the doing of his liberal deeds, and the just man too will need it for the returning of services (for wishes are hard to discern, and even people who are not just pretend to wish to act justly); and the brave man will need power if he is to accomplish any of the acts that correspond to his excellence, and the temperate man will need opportunity; for how else is either he or any of the others to be recognized? It is debated, too, whether the choice or the deed is more essential to excellence, which is assumed to involve both; it is surely clear that its completion involves both; *but for deeds many things are needed, and more the greater and nobler the deeds are.* But *the man who is contemplating the truth needs no such thing, at least with a view to the exercise of his activity;* indeed they are, one may say, even hindrances, at all events to his contemplation; but in so far as he is a man and lives with a number of people, he chooses to do excellent acts; he will therefore need such aids to living a human life.
>
> But that *complete happiness is a contemplative activity* will appear from the following consideration as well. We assume the gods to be above all other beings blessed and happy; but what sort of actions must we assign to them? Acts of justice? Will not the gods seem absurd if they make contracts and return deposits, and so on? Acts of a brave man, then, confronting dangers and running risks because it is noble to do so? Or liberal acts? To whom will they give? It will be strange if they are really to have money or anything of the kind. And what would their temperate acts be? Is not such praise tasteless, since they have no bad appetites? If we were to run through them all,

the circumstances of action would be found trivial and unworthy of gods. Still every one supposes that they *live* and therefore that they are active; we cannot suppose them to sleep like Endymion. Now *if you take away from a living being action, and still more production, what is left but contemplation?* Therefore the activity of God, which surpasses all others in blessedness, must be contemplative, therefore that which is most akin to this must be most the nature of happiness. (*E.N.* X.8, 1178a9–b22; my emphasis)

If one looks at the overall movement of thought (and emotion) from the beginning of the *Nicomachean Ethics* up until this moment, one can see the structure of a trauma. According to Freud, trauma has a retrospective structure.[36] In the typical scenario that Freud first envisaged, a child has an experience—a seduction—that at the time she cannot understand. Nevertheless, a trace of the event is laid down in memory. Only later, as the child develops, is there another experience that triggers a retrospective understanding of the meaning of the earlier experience. But this new understanding cannot be assimilated: it wounds the mind that was on the verge of understanding it. On this model, neither of the two experiences is traumatic in and of itself. The earlier experience need not have been traumatic when it occurred because it was registered, but not understood. The later experience, for its part, can be innocent in itself—as, for instance, the experience of mild sexual arousal in a situation that triggers a reminiscence of the earlier occasion. What becomes explosive is the cocktail of both those experiences.

Now the beginning of the *Nicomachean Ethics* is like the stage of childhood seduction. Ethically speaking, we are children when we begin. As the intended audience, we have been well brought up and are, so to speak, well disposed toward virtue. But we do not yet understand the meaning of our ethical habits and dispositions. We do not yet really understand our own character. In this sense, the *Nicomachean Ethics* is the beginning of an ethical reflection on who we are. It is at this point that Aristotle installs a number of enigmatic messages to us: that our lives as a whole are directed toward "happiness," that there is "*the* good," "the end of all the things we do," and that happiness is "complete" and "self-sufficient." There is no way at the beginning of inquiry that we can understand what these messages mean. And thus they must have a cer-

---

[36] See the *Project for a Scientific Psychology* (*S.E.* I.350–59); Laplanche, *Life and Death in Psychoanalysis*, ch. 2. See also J. Laplanche and J.-B. Pontalis, *The Language of Psychoanalysis* (London: Hogarth Press, 1983): "Deferred Action," pp. 111–14.

tain oracular appeal for us: drawing us into this inquiry, yet puzzling and intriguing us.

The bulk of the book is then taken up with an exploration of the ethical life—the life organized around and giving expression to the traditional ethical virtues. Aristotle sometimes calls this the "political life" because the highest expression of such a life would be that of the statesman organizing, legislating, and running the polis. This is our ethical adolescence. And it is here that the trauma occurs. Aristotle said in book I that the proper statesman would have to have his eye on *the* good, for it is his job to organize the polis so as to promote it. Indeed, as we have seen, Aristotle rather preposterously claims that we should look to the actual activities of statesmen to get some idea what he means by *"the* good." But if the highest expression of ethical life is the statesman actually legislating for *the* good, he has to know what he is legislating for. And it is at this point of reflection that ethical life suffers a trauma. For we find that the "meanings" laid down in ethical childhood come to acquire meaning in the course of ethical development that the ethical life can no longer contain.

Aristotle has seduced us into discontent with the ethical life as such. It is now seen as yielding, at best, a kind of "second-rate" happiness. This is what Freud would call a compromise-formation. We are told that the ethical life is still a happy one, but there is now a discontent-inducing qualification. At the beginning of the *Ethics,* as he delineates the marks and features of "happiness," Aristotle says, "but we must add: in a complete life"—and he takes up the problem of reversals and misfortunes in life. The consolation he offered was that the virtuous person was the best equipped to keep his balance—he better than anyone else would be able to tolerate the reversal without losing his happiness. But now what we have at the end of the *Ethics* is a kind of intellectual reversal. If the ethically virtuous person really is good at keeping his balance, then he ought to take this occasion to shift his life from an ethical life to a contemplative one. If he cannot do so, he will be able to retain his happiness, but he cannot help but realize that it is second-rate.

In effect, Aristotle is recommending a different level of homeostasis for the best human life. That is, instead of living one's entire life at the level of a practical engagement with the world, that engagement should now be seen as aiming at producing a surplus that makes leisure possible—and thus makes possible the activities appropriate to leisure. This transformation, in which practical activity is now seen as aiming beyond itself, turns practical activity into busyness. Again, it is familiar to give a political critique of this move: a theorist of the master-class will try to valorize leisure activity. But from a psychoanalytic point of view, there is a deeper, inchoate urge that is getting expressed in a specific formulation. Psychoanalytically speaking, any form of life will tend to generate a fantasy of what it is to get outside that life. This is because life is experienced, consciously and unconsciously, as being lived under pressure—and it is correlative to that experience that there is a fantasy of release. Thus it is to be expected that as soon as ethical life gets conceptualized as such—as soon as we can experience such a life as forming *a life*—there will tend to be fantasies about what it would be like *to get outside.* Aristotle formulates a specific instance of such a fantasy—filling it out in teleological and aristocratic terms—but the fantasy has the general structure of promising true happiness just outside the "confines" in which we ordinarily live. In this sense, "the wise" have returned at a theoretical level to the view of "the many." The many, you will recall, thought, when they were sick, that happiness lay in health, when they were poor, that happiness lay in wealth. Now we find that the ethically virtuous think that *real* happiness lies in contemplation.

The idea of a contemplative life is a powerful organizing fantasy—one that tends to hide its fantastic status. After all, one might think, the contemplative life is a real possibility—indeed, Aristotle must have thought that he was living such a life. Why, then, call this a fantasy? This is an important question, and it deserves a layered response. But, in the first instance, I want to claim that this question itself helps to cover over the fantastic nature of the contemplative life. That is, the very fact that a contemplative life could actually be lived makes it seem like it is not a fantasy. But the question of whether or not something is a fantasy is not answered by whether one can act on it. Some fantasies one can act on, others not. The real issue is what motivations get organized and expressed by the fantasy. What we need to look at is how life gets reorganized by the insertion into it of the ideal of a contemplative life.

The ideal of a contemplative life involves, as we have already seen, a reorientation of the meaning of that life. Consider an ethically virtuous person, in the midst of his life, who has just sat through Aristotle's lectures. That is, someone who has just gotten to the point where we are now. What he must realize at the end of the semester that he could not realize at the beginning is that there is now a completely transformed meaning to " . . . in a complete life." At the beginning of the semester he could think: "I am already living a virtuous life. If I can *just* keep this up throughout my life I will have led a complete, happy life. And there is no better guarantee that I will be able to continue to lead such a life than that I already am leading such a life. Already being virtuous is the best guarantee I could have that I will be able to go on in the same way." But by the end of the semester, he has to think: "If I *only* go on living in this way, I will have achieved at most second-rate happiness." So a source of discontent has been injected into the ethical life. He now will reorient his life so as to aim for contemplation. Before he achieves the leisure time in which to contemplate, he cannot know for sure that the occasion will ever arise. Thus his ethically virtuous life must be lived with a certain amount of hope, expectation, and uncertainty. Of course, being virtuous, he will experience these emotions in moderation, but they will be there. And even when he achieves the leisured occasion for contemplation—and experiences the highest form of pleasure and happiness—he must recognize that such occasions as these will be short-lived compared to the rest of his life.

To be sure, Aristotle is talking about the happy life. And a contemplative life is a contemplative life even during the stretches within it that one is not contemplating. It is the entire life that is the happiest life. Fine. The real issue, though, is the lived content of this happiest life. Aristotle explicitly says that the lived moments of contemplation are both more pleasant and overall better than the noncontemplative moments of a contemplative. life. So even in the best and happiest human life, most of the moments of that life will be lived with the realization that what ultimately makes that life the happiest and the best are passing moments within that life. And even in those best and happiest moments of the best and happiest life there is room for the thought that this is a fleeting part of one's life.

From a psychoanalytic point of view, this is all just as well. If contemplation were a state that one could achieve and just stay there indefinitely and unproblematically, then Aristotle would have been led to feel discontent within it—and he would start to fantasize a *real* happiness that lies just outside. The beauty of contemplation as a candidate for occupying a special place of longing is, first, that, for Aristotle, it is the teleologically highest form of activity. Second, it is all but inaccessible for most people, even the ethically virtuous. Third, those few who do manage to find time to contemplate will experience that time as precious and short-lived. As if to drive the point home, Aristotle emphasizes that even if one is living the best and happiest human life it falls short of the gods, who get to contemplate endlessly and eternally.

> But [the contemplative] life would be too high for man; for it is not in so far as he is man that he will live so, but in so far as something divine is present in him; and by so much as this is superior to our composite nature is its activity superior to that which is the exercise of the other kind of excellence. If intellect is divine, then, in comparison with man, the life according to it is divine in comparison with human life. But we must not follow those who advise us, being men, to think of human things, and being mortal, of mortal things, but must, so far as we can, make ourselves immortal and *strain every nerve to live in accordance with the best thing in us,* for even if it be small in bulk, much more does it in power and worth surpass everything. This would seem, too, to be each man himself, since it is the authoritative and better part of him. It would be strange, then, if he were to choose not the life of himself but that of something else. And what we said before will apply now; that which is proper to each thing is by nature best and most pleasant for each thing; for man, therefore, *the life according to intellect is best and pleasantest, since intellect more than anything else is man. This life therefore is also the happiest.* (E.N. X.7, 1177b26–78a8; my emphasis)

I don't think it takes much imagination to see Aristotle saying that the happiest life has a smidge of disappointment built into it. Again there are the two sides of the same message. In contemplating we join in the activity of the gods; in contemplating we fall short of their activity.[37] That we must "strain every nerve" suggests it is a real effort to get outside the ordinary conditions of life—even the ethically virtuous life. And in the very process we are reminded of our own mortality. In relation to the gods, we do not have a sense of glorified participation with them (or: do not only have a sense of that) but also of the overwhelming distance that separates our contemplative activities from theirs. In achieving the ultimate human happiness we thereby become aware of the finite and limited nature of that happiness.

There is, though, at least the guarantee that within life we will always have something to strive for. In this way, the contemplative ideal gives meaning and shape to our experiences of discontent. It gives a shape to desire: and a guarantee that we will always stay at a certain distance from the ultimate object of our desire. Thus the basic experience of pressure in being alive is given a certain kind of shape and meaning.

---

[37] See also *E.N.* X.8. 1179a22–32: the double-edged message continues.

It has a shape that promises some escape from the pressure of life, while at the same time ensuring that the fantasy will always be in place to explain the continuing experience of discontent that is life itself.

All this would suggest that Aristotle implicitly recognizes that the true human happiness involves keeping happiness at a safe distance. It shouldn't be too far away or we'll get discouraged, but if it gets too close we'll start to feel some discontent with it and fantasize another happiness, lying just beyond the current horizon. And in placing true happiness just beyond the horizon of the ethical life, Aristotle introduces a lack into that life. Something is now experienced as missing from it. So the function of the idea of a contemplative life, from a psychoanalytic point of view, is not, as presented, to give us an end state that when achieved will finally give us true happiness. Rather it is to give us a fantasy for our present use: something we can aim for from a distance. Notice that we began the *Ethics* with Aristotle introducing a gap into ethical life. Ethical reflection is inaugurated with Aristotle's injection of the enigmatic signifier "happiness." An inquiry was then launched into what that "happiness" could be. By the end of the inquiry, though, we close that gap with a gap. The answer to the question "what is happiness?" is that it is a "something" that lies outside the ethical life itself. Now the point of the ethical life is to get outside it. And given that contemplation is praised for being the most solitary and ultimate self-sufficient human activity, it is hard to resist the conclusion that, for Aristotle, *the fundamental good of ethics is to get as far away from one's neighbors as possible.* The less one has to do with them the better! Even in the midst of ethical life, its real value, when correctly understood, is that someday it will allow one to get away from it.

8.

But what is this getting away from it all? Looked at from a certain angle, it looks as though Aristotle is valorizing death. At least, among the activities of life, he valorizes the one that comes closest to a fantasy of being in a deathlike state. First, it is an image of an escape from the pressures of ordinary practical life. It is what we would do in our best leisure time, and as such it is the ideal of what one does in a kind of existential Sabbath.[38] It is a higher form of activity than that of the

[38] Cp. *E.N.* X.7, 1177b5.

nonleisurely practical life—and thus it is what we would do when we have gotten beyond life (as it is ordinarily lived). Second, contemplation is the activity of the gods: thus it is in itself a deathless activity. But deathless activity is precisely what the dead do: only the living engage in activities that come to an end. When Aristotle tries to think through what the gods do, he immediately eliminates all practical activities: all the fulfilling of needs or desires, all busywork. But for gods to be gods they must be active: so Aristotle needs to focus on an activity that isn't itself the practical filling of a need. in other words, if one wants to hold onto the bare idea of liveliness and activity but take away from that idea as many marks and features of actual life as lived, one ends up with contemplation.[39] Contemplation is the most deathlike form of life. Thus it is that, imaginatively speaking, immortality is a form of death: it is what death would be like if death were a form of life. For death is our immortal condition. Note that Aristotle stresses that contemplation is our most "continuous" activity, allowing the least interruption, that it is our most solitary and self-sufficient activity, and that it is complete in and of itself. If death were an activity, it would be like that.

At just this point in the argument, Aristotle reiterates a point he has made earlier: that other animals cannot be happy.[40] These are creatures who cannot take their lives as a whole into account, and thus cannot reason practically about the happiness of their lives. In other words, they cannot take their deaths into account: and their inability to take their death into account is intimately tied to their inability to be happy.

This, I think, sheds light on the value of our values. By this stage of reflection, it seems that, for Aristotle, the value of our reflection on the best life is that it induces a kind of being-unto-death. It creates a fantasy of a release from the ordinary pressures of ethical life, a fantasy of sharing with the gods the greatest, stressless pleasure. This is a fantasy that carries within it an experience of lack, an experience of being at a distance from this wonderful goal. It is a fantasy of release that helps us organize and direct our ordinary practical lives. Those who know most about human life know that what is best is to organize life so as to escape its ordinary conditions—even the conditions of excellence within it. What is best about being human is the opportunity to break out of being human. Or: to be most human is to break out of the ordinary conditions of human life.

[39] See, e.g., *E.N.* X.8, 1178b20ff.
[40] *E.N.* X.8, 1178b24.

9.

If Aristotle were the Aristotle with whom we think we are familiar, we would expect the *Ethics* to end with a summing up of all that has been accomplished in the text. We find no such thing: "are we to suppose that our program has reached its end? Surely, as is said, where there are things to be done, the end is not to survey and recognize the various things, but rather to do them . . . ."[41] In fact, we find an Aristotle who seems somewhat irritated, saying that the real work is only about to begin.

As book X, chapter 8, ends, we are in a position to draw the following conclusions. First, most people are not and will never be happy; second, even the elite who lead an ethically virtuous life achieve only second-rate happiness; third, those few who are able to lead a contemplative life will at best be able to contemplate for relatively short periods of their lives. In brief, happiness by and large eludes the human condition. Humans may long for it in the way they long to win the lottery—and, in fact, the mass of humankind has a better chance of winning the lottery. At least with the lottery every ticket has an equal chance; for the mass of humankind the very possibility of happiness is ruled out at birth (or shortly thereafter). Those who are not lucky enough to be born into a situation in which they can be well brought up have no chance.

All the rest of animal nature is basically able to fulfill its nature unproblematically. There will be occasional mutants and occasions when the environment doesn't cooperate, but, for the most part, each species is able to flourish in its distinctive way. It is only humans who have a characteristic problem of failing to thrive. For humans, happiness *is* human flourishing, yet happiness by and large eludes them. Thus by injecting "happiness" as the organizing goal of human teleology Aristotle manages to disrupt the teleological structure itself. For he has made it virtually impossible for humans to fulfill their nature. Although the teleological worldview is used to give content to what happiness consists in, once the picture is filled out it puts pressure on the teleological worldview itself.

Aristotle tries to save his teleology by a flight to aristocracy. "The many," he says, are not swayed by good arguments[42]—this is to be expected by now—but Aristotle now suggests that even if they had

[41] *E.N.* X.9, 1179a34–b2.
[42] *E.N.* X.9, 1179b10–80a5.

been brought up under good laws, they would still need to be tightly controlled by law throughout their lives. In other words, it is not simply a matter of their not having been well brought up to begin with.

> But it is surely not enough that when they are young they should get the right nurture and attention; since they must, even when they are grown up, practice and be habituated to them, we shall need laws for this as well, and generally speaking to cover the whole of life; for most people obey necessity rather than argument, and punishments rather than what is noble. (*E.N.* X.9, 1180a1–5)

This is the teleological irony of aristocracy. On the surface it looks like the expression of a teleological worldview that only the best should live in the best way. Yet this position also expresses, as it covers over, an anomaly in the system: namely, that the human race is the only species in nature where almost all of its members are failing to flourish. This disruption of the harmonious order is caused precisely by the introduction of "happiness" as the purported concept by which we should evaluate our lives. It is usually assumed that it is because Aristotle was an aristocrat that he was attracted to such a teleological worldview. The question now arises whether to hold onto his teleology he had to be an aristocrat.

But even the aristocratic ploy no longer seems to be able to contain his doubts.

> ...if (as we have said) *the man who is to be good* must be well trained and habituated, and go on to spend his time in worthy occupations and neither willingly nor unwillingly do bad actions, and if this can be brought about if men live in accordance with a sort of intellect and right order, *provided this has force—if this be so, the paternal command indeed has not the required force or compulsive power* (nor in general has the command of one man, unless he be a king or something similar), but the law *has* compulsive power, while it is at the same time an account proceeding from a sort of practical wisdom and intellect. And while people *hate* men who oppose their impulses, even if they oppose them rightly, *the law in its ordaining of what is good is not burdensome.* (*E.N.* X.9, 1180a14–24; my emphasis)

The suggestion here seems to be that the compulsive power of law is needed *even for the good.* One reason is to contain the hatred a son would otherwise feel for his father. According to Aristotle, if a son's impulses were not inhibited by an impersonal law, but by his father's prohibition, the son would come to hate the father. It no longer seems like happiness is unproblematically available even for those who already are good.

So even those who are constitutionally prepared for happiness, those who have been born into the right circumstances and well brought up—even they would have problems without the law. And yet, the law doesn't yet exist!

In the Spartan state alone, or almost alone, the legislator seems to have paid attention to questions of nurture and occupations; in most states such matters have been neglected, and each man lives as he pleases, Cyclops-fashion, "to his own wife and children dealing law."[43] Now it is best that there should be a public and proper care for such matters; but if they are neglected by the community it would seem right for each man to help his children and friends towards excellence, and that they should be able or at least choose to do this. (*E.N.* X.9, 1180a24–32)

And surely he who wants to make men, whether many or few, better by his care must try to become capable of legislating, if it is through laws that we can become good. . . .

Must we not, then, next examine whence or how one can learn how to legislate? Is it, as in all other cases, from statesmen? Certainly it was thought to be a part of statesmanship. Or is a difference apparent between statesmanship and the other sciences and faculties? In the others the same people are found offering to teach the faculties and practicing them, e.g. doctors and painters; but while the sophists profess to teach politics, it is practiced not by any of them but by the politicians, who would seem to do so by dint of a certain faculty and experience rather than of thought; for they are not found either writing or speaking about such matters (though it were a nobler occupation perhaps than composing speeches for the law-courts and the assembly), nor again are they found to have made statesmen of their own sons or any other of their friends. But it was to be expected that they should if they could; for there is nothing better than such a skill that they could have left to their cities, or could choose to have for themselves, or therefore, for those dearest to them. Still, experience seems to contribute not a little; else they could not have become politicians by familiarity with politics; and so it seems that those who aim at knowing about the art of politics need experience as well.

But those of the sophists who profess the art seem to be very far from teaching it. For, to put the matter generally, they do not even

[43] The reference is to *Odyssey* IX.114.

know what kind of thing it is nor what kinds of thing it is about . . . .
(*E.N.* X.9, 1180b23–81a14)

Now our predecessors have left the subject of legislation to us
unexamined; it is perhaps best, therefore, that we should ourselves
study it, and in general study the question of the constitution, in order to complete to the best of our ability the philosophy of human
nature . . . . Let us make a beginning of our discussion. (*E.N.* X.9,
1181b12–23)

In other words: we need proper laws to be good and become happy,
but such laws do not exist. No one has really thought about this seriously; and neither politicians nor sophists know what they are talking
about. At the beginning of the *Nicomachean Ethics* we were given confidence that *the* good existed by pointing to political science. The good
was purportedly that which legislators legislate. But at the very end of
the book this reassurance is taken away. The original appeal was to the
actual practice of statesmen in the actual world, but now there is the admission that no one in the actual world knows what he is doing.

From this perspective the beginning of the *Ethics* looks especially seductive. We were lured into a false sense of confidence about *the* good:
even if we didn't know what it was, there were purportedly experts—
those in the know—and they were the masters of political science. But
now that the argument has already secured the conclusion that the truly
happy life is contemplative not political, Aristotle can kick away the
ladder. For him the question now becomes how to formulate legislation
for a polis in ways that will keep most people on the right track practically speaking while making room for philosophy among the few.

At this point, a certain question becomes irresistible: does Aristotle's
entire ethical system as it reaches this closing moment finally show itself
to be an expression of mourning for Socrates? For in this pessimistic-
hopeful vision, society is to be legislated in a way that preserves traditional values but makes room for philosophy instead of killing it off.

For the moment, I should like to take stock of where we have been.
We began with a hope—and an approach to an ethical system that is at
once attractive and self-satisfied. The original hope was that we might
expand this character- and psychology-based ethics to include an understanding of the unconscious. But as we start to look at the system from a
psychoanalytic point of view, we find that instead of being able to add to
it, the system itself starts to fall apart. The *Ethics* presents itself as part of

a larger teleological system in which everything has its place and every-thing is in its place. What could be more existentially reassuring than to learn that the ethically virtuous life is the happiest? But now it appears that, for humans to be placed in the teleological order, Aristotle had to disturb the order in which they had been living. Following Socrates and Plato, Aristotle disturbs the universe by injecting "happiness" as a pur-ported concept in terms of which one's entire life can and should be eval-uated. It is only when "happiness" is in place that humans can be said to occupy a place in the teleological order—but the teleological order can-not account for its own inauguration. The establishment of a teleologi-cal principle—"happiness"—by which to evaluate human life itself lies beyond the teleological principle.

And while it appears on the surface that "happiness" is a profound organizing principle for human life, just under the surface we begin to see that its injection into life has a profoundly disturbing effect. For al-though it was originally deployed to show that the ethical life was a happy one, by encouraging us to think about the value of our lives taken as a whole, Aristotle creates the conditions in which it is possible to for-mulate the fantasy of real happiness lying just outside. In this way, "happiness" creates its own discontent. Now Aristotle is too deep and honest a thinker simply to ignore this pressure, and he tries to contain it within the overall framework of his teleological system. But, as I think I have shown, it just doesn't work. The teleological system cannot con-tain the expression of discontent and breaking-out that it itself gener-ates. The question then becomes: how should we understand this dis-content?

Rhetorics of Value

GEOFFREY HILL

THE TANNER LECTURES ON HUMAN VALUES

Delivered at

Brasenose College, Oxford
March 6 and 7, 2000

GEOFFREY HILL is University Professor, professor of literature and religion, and co-director of the Editorial Institute at Boston University. He is a fellow of the American Academy of Arts and Sciences and of the Royal Society of Literature, and an honorary fellow of both Keble College, Oxford, and Emmanuel College, Cambridge. His scholarly and critical works include *The Lords of Limit: Essays on Literature and Ideas* (1984); *The Enemy's Country: Words, Contexture, and Other Circumstances of Language* (1991); and *Style and Faith* (forthcoming). He is also the author of numerous volumes of poetry, including *Mercian Hymns* (1971), *The Mystery of the Charity of Charles Péguy* (1983), *Canaan* (1997), *The Triumph of Love* (1998), and *Speech! Speech!* (2000).

I. INTRINSIC VALUE: MARGINAL OBSERVATIONS ON A CENTRAL QUESTION

It has never been easy to define the nature of value; nonetheless forms of discourse have been designed and devoted—over many centuries—to such an attempt. Monetary theorists have created cogent descriptions, but individual cogency has not prevented general confusion even over the real nature of *intrinsic value* in relation to coins of the realm: although this term, on first acquaintance, carries a convincing air of authority.

I have deliberately restricted myself, at this point of the discussion, to the noun in the singular. To undertake any assessment of the meaning of value is to risk appearing a fool. To pronounce upon human values may expose one as an ethical charlatan. "Human values" can, at any time and on any occasion, become vulnerable to the harsh dismissal that Dietrich Bonhoeffer gave to "cheap grace."[1]

Two inferences may be drawn from what I have said thus far. It may be wiser to speak in terms of value rather than of values. It may be useful to restrict a discussion of the singular, "value," to statements regarding the nature of *intrinsic value.* The matter of intrinsic value carries a distinct referential weight in two particular areas or spheres of activity and discourse: coinage, where it can be assayed, and moral philosophy, where it cannot. In most cases the crux of the problem is the intersection of the material and the symbolic, if intersection can be said actually to take place. If there is no intersection there is likely to be hiatus, a "gap," somewhat in Gillian Rose's sense of *aporia.*[2] The suspect nature of much general discourse on the nature and quality of that mystical entity or aura called "human values" can be traced, I suggest, to a variety of attempts to claim continuity where none exists. This is particularly the case with the type of value-discourse that is a simple trope of monetary values. I shall say more on this aspect in my seminar-presentation, in relation to currency reforms advocated and in part supervised by Isaac

[1] Dietrich Bonhoeffer, *The Cost of Discipleship,* translated by R. H. Fuller from *Nachfolge,* 1937 (London: SCM Press, 1948), pp. 37–49.

[2] Gillian Rose, *Mourning Becomes the Law* (Cambridge: Cambridge University Press, 1996), pp. 8, 10.

Newton and John Locke,[3] and in further relation to the symbolic application of monetary value to ethical and aesthetic values by various writers. If asked to name the major proponent of that form of rhetoric in which intrinsic currency value is somehow understood as underpinning and validating intrinsic ethical or aesthetic value, I would reply: John Ruskin, especially in *Unto This Last, Essays on Political Economy, Munera Pulveris,* and sections of *Fors Clavigera.* As is readily apparent from Letters 12 and 58 of *Fors,* Ruskin's own rhetorical currency can prove less than stable: in the first instance, debased with vituperation; in the second, sounding Puginesque in its insistence on purity of design. In the instance of Letter 12, it seems to me a mark of futility to project an exhausted rage against a largely unspecified and unrealizable enemy whom one chooses to name "Judas." There are examples enough of this self-stultifying rhetoric among the major Victorian moralists and their immediate successors: in Thomas Carlyle especially, but also in Matthew Arnold and Ruskin; as, later, in T. S. Eliot, who took his cue from Arnold, and in Ezra Pound, who, to some extent, derived his ethical aesthetics from Ruskin.[4]

The history of ideas is a respectable genre to which I am as indebted as any educated or self-educated man or woman of our time. It has to be said, however, that one cannot profitably debate the substance and issue of intrinsic value from the standpoint of the historian of ideas; the difficulty is revealed to be with the minting and assaying of ideas as themselves; with the transformation of ideas of quality into inherently qualitative statements. In arguments of this kind, direct quotation rather than paraphrase, therefore, must figure prominently within the texture of one's own presentation.

I begin with a sentence from David Hume's essay "Of Refinement in the Arts":

> Knowledge in the arts of government naturally begets mildness and moderation, by instructing men in the advantages of humane maxims above rigour and severity, which drive subjects into rebellion,

[3] *The Correspondence of Isaac Newton,* 7 vols. (Cambridge: Cambridge University Press for the Royal Society, 1959–77), vols. 4–7; P. H. Kelly, ed., *Locke on Money,* 2 vols. (Oxford: Clarendon Press, 1991).

[4] Hugh Witemeyer, "Ruskin and the Signed Capital in Canto 45," *Paideuma* 4, no. 1 (Spring 1975): 85–88, acknowledging Hugh Kenner, *The Pound Era* (1971), pp. 323–26; Guy Davenport, *The Geography of the Imagination* (San Francisco: North Point Press, 1981), pp. 44–48.

and make the return to submission impracticable by cutting off all hopes of pardon.[5]

To set Hume on the arts of government against a characteristic turn of phrase from one of the several sets of Tudor injunctions to the reformed clergy—"that this damnable device of despair may be clearly taken away and firm belief and steadfast hope surely conceived of all their parishioners"[6]—is to detect, even in this small compass, significant differences and similarities. Each quotation tunes its effect by the correspondence between two given but indeterminate values: political value and English word value. In the Edwardian Injunctions of 1547, drawn up and set down with the authority and approval of Archbishop Cranmer and Lord Protector Somerset,[7] "despair" has a double valency, at once spiritual and temporal: it is doubly "damnable." Those who despair are desperate. As Thomas More wrote: "The devil is desperate and hath not nor cannot have faith and trust in gods promises" (*OED: desperate,* sense 1). A man in despair re-enacts the political as well as the spiritual desperation of the arch-fiend: he is ready for all manner of treasons, plots, and stratagems. Correlatively, a quiet conscience in respect to God, within the terms set by the archbishop, signifies a compliant citizen, obedient to the government of the lord protector, mindful of the interests of the commonweal above his own.

That which stays implicated in the words authorised by Cranmer and Somerset is explicated in Hume. I remark, here, his word "advantages"—understood, in 1752 as in 1547, as advantages to the ruler rather than to the ruled. Each example is addressing the matter of convenience. In the Tudor injunctions, convenience is spelled out as a magisterial rigour of supervision. The concern manifested in the distribution of such instructions to the parish clergy is less with the diffusion of intrinsic value supposedly emanating from the boy-king—and which his fine profile portrayed on gold coins of fluctuating bullion value seems designed to suggest—than with the threat of contagion by real or imagined evil. Hume's "Of Refinement in the Arts" is also focused on convenience, which surfaces (supposing there to be depth) in such

[5] *Essays, Moral, Political, and Literary,* ed. E. F. Miller (Indianapolis: Liberty Fund, 1985), pp. 273–74.

[6] Gerald Bray, *Documents of the English Reformation* (Minneapolis: Fortress Press, 1994), p. 253.

[7] Ibid., p. 247.

words as "diffuse" (vb), "advantageous," "naturally begets," "render," "beneficial":

> But industry, knowledge, and humanity, are not advantageous in private life alone: They diffuse their beneficial influence on the *public,* and render the government as great and flourishing as they make individuals happy and prosperous.[8]

The significance of the verb "diffuse" should not be overlooked in this genial sequence of politic *congés* to private and public equity. Hume structures his sentences with such economy of syntax as to inhibit our sense of the pervading indeterminacy of his critical terms. We have to recall that diffusion means "wide and general distribution" (*OED*): this is the substance of the piece, though "substance" on reflection is not the right word. The grammar floats an insubstantiality—"and render the government as great and flourishing as they make individuals happy and prosperous." Consider the question of clauses introduced by "as." English literary syntax, at the time when Hume was composing his *Essays, Moral, Political, and Literary,* was the beneficiary of various strong and weak forms of the "as . . ." clause. The first I will term the clause of simple indemnity: "as good as gold"; it is a weak form dependent upon a strong sense, at the proverbial level, of intrinsic value. The *OED* calls it the *comparative of equality.* The second, which I name the comparative of commonweal, is well demonstrated in the "King James" rendering of Isaiah 24:2: "And it shall be as with the people, so with the priest, as with the servant, so with his master, as with the maid, so with her mistresse, as with the buyer, so with the seller, as with the lender, so with the borrower, as with the taker of vsurie, so with the giuer of vsurie to him." This is the strong form of the *OED*'s comparative of equality: Isaiah is in fact threatening that the people will be made equal in desolation and destruction, but such threats of "levelling" would be without effect if there were not the ever-present sense of the hierarchic and stratified commonweal as a divine propriety.

The apocalyptic pseudo-logic of such admonitions, in the English of 1611, I would count—together with the archaisms of *Euphues* that were novelties in Thomas Hobbes's childhood—among the stylistic influences discernible in *Leviathan,* even while that monster is swallowing whole the old power of the English prophetic voice:

[8] Hume, *Essays,* p. 272.

> For as that stone which by the asperity, and irregularity of Figure, takes more room from others, than it selfe fills; . . . is by the builders cast away as unprofitable, and troublesome: so also, a man that by asperity of Nature, will strive to retain those things which to himselfe are superfluous, and to others necessary; and for the stubbornness of his Passions, cannot be corrected, is to be left, or cast out of Society, as combersome thereunto.[9]

No more of that nonsense, observe, concerning the stone that the builders rejected having become the "head of the corner":[10] though the resonance of that great *sententia* is not without its value to Hobbes. The formulation "as the stone which/so also a man that" is decorative rather than substantial; but Hobbes is skilled at making the inconsequential appear to be of consequence. In this respect he anticipates David Hume, or at least the Hume of *Essays, Moral, Political, and Literary.* It has been well said that "Hume's final authority is opinion: see his essay 'Of the Original Contract' for the equivocating use of 'really' in the statement that there is *really* no other standard of morality but opinion."[11] If that is so, Hobbes is his master in points of detail, in particular the knack of using fashions of syntax so as to make opinion appear to be genuine ratiocination.

There is, however, more to be said of *Leviathan* even if not—at least for the time being—of Hume's thoughts on matters literary and social. *Leviathan,* whatever else it is or is not, is a tragic elegy on the extinction of intrinsic value. None of Hobbes's opponents understood this, with the possible exception of Clarendon, himself a tragic elegist of no mean power, and except, possibly, Joseph Butler, in the *Fifteen Sermons* of 1726/29 and the two Dissertations, "Of Personal Identity" and "Of the Nature of Virtue" (both 1736). Hobbes's despair, in *Leviathan,* arises from the extinction of personal identity, which he in turn identifies with intrinsic value in the person of the young Royalist Sidney Godolphin, killed in the Civil War. The three sentences from Hobbes's "A Review and Conclusion" beginning "Nor is there any repugnancy between fearing the Laws, and not fearing a publique enemy . . ." are among the greatest English examples of "high sentence"—the equal of Browne's *sententiae* in *Urne Buriall* or Ralegh's in the preface to his *The History of*

---

[9] *Leviathan,* ed. C. B. MacPherson (Harmondsworth: Penguin Books, 1968), p. 209.

[10] Acts 4:11, 1 Pet. 2:7, King James Bible, 1611.

[11] Dr. Kenneth Haynes, private communication, January 25, 2000.

the World. The question that follows upon my acknowledgment is this: if Hobbes is seriously of the opinion that intrinsic value in the English commonweal perished when Godolphin was killed, how does he read his own elegiac tribute to his dead friend? The three sentences I am here considering end with a splendid *traductio* " . . . who hating no man, nor hated of any, was unfortunately slain in the beginning of the late Civill warre, in the Publique quarrell, by an undiscerned and an undiscerning hand."[12] If it can be granted that such sentences resonate as I here claim, may I conclude that Hobbes, with his impeccable sense of timing and upstaging, is here upstaging his own pretended cynicism of despair? How far is he implying that the intelligence that created *Leviathan* is the true heir in an untrue world, and witness for an unwitnessing future, to the magnanimity of Godolphin, Falkland, and the Great Tew "symposium," whatever arguments to the contrary might be drawn from the theses of the work itself?

Nothing that I have so far said with regard to Godolphin's significance, for Hobbes the man as also for his *Leviathan,* adds one iota to the assessment made by Irene Coltman in *Private Men and Public Causes: Philosophy and Politics in the English Civil War* (London: Faber, 1962). And I move into the next, and perhaps more contentious, stage of my argument by glancing at the final sentence of her study of Godolphin's posthumous endowment to late seventeenth century political thought, a sentence that she takes from Clarendon's *Brief View and Survey*—a bitter attack on Hobbes's abandonment of the spirit and principles of Great Tew: "I cannot forbear to put him [Hobbes] in mind, that I gave him for an expiation of my own defects, and any trespasses which I may have since committed against him, the Friendship of that great Person."[13] "That great Person" is Sidney Godolphin; and "Friendship" between Hobbes and Godolphin was initiated, so Clarendon avers, by his introducing them to each other at a time when all three were fellow-members of the Great Tew symposium. The phrase to which I return is "gave him for an expiation." This is a *mea culpa* that does not mitigate—indeed it may exacerbate—the severity of Clarendon's indictment of Hobbes's book. Though "expiation" is a singularly powerful word, Clarendon cannot be said to surrender any of the indignation to which he clearly feels entitled: the word stands in the guise of a word now for-

[12] *Leviathan,* p. 718.

[13] Coltman, *Private Men,* pp. 191–92; Edward Hyde, Earl of Clarendon, *A Brief View and Survey* . . . (London, 1676; photo facsimile reprint, London: Routledge Thoemmes Press, 1996), p. 320.

eign to Hobbes, the meaning of which needs to be given him clearly and slowly, even while its implication (tempting old friends to the sin of wrath) is laid at his door. For Clarendon, then, it is as if "intrinsic value" is something tightly knit that treachery and ingratitude cause to unravel. It is easier to say what "intrinsic" value is in defeat than in victory. Intrinsic value, for the loser, is sealed into enduring qualities of the life that was; the price paid by the victor is the inevitable lifelong penalty of compromise and corruption. This, I believe, is how writers as different as Andrew Marvell (in the "Horatian Ode") and Clarendon (in the *Brief View and Survey*) reflected upon these issues.

"Reflection" is a word entirely characteristic of Joseph Butler's *Fifteen Sermons Preached at the Rolls Chapel*. Unlike Clarendon, Hobbes, or Marvell, Butler's experience of the Civil War and the first thirty or so years of its aftermath was gained at second hand. It is clear, however, that for him, as much as for Clarendon and John Bramhall, one of the more dreadful legacies of the mid-century anarchy was the publication and success of *Leviathan.* Nonetheless, where Bramhall and Clarendon struggle to uproot the new, Butler reassesses the tried and tested: for him the essay is an assay; and reflection is at the heart of it. In this he so anticipates the significance that Coleridge attaches to the word *reflection* that the relative sparsity of references to him throughout the *Marginalia,* and elsewhere in Coleridge's writings, is surprising.[14]

There is a significant early letter written by George Eliot in 1842, when she was in her twenty-third year, at a time when even the earliest of her published fiction had still to be written; it is significant as anticipating the kind of self-correcting speculative rumination that characterizes the authorial commentary in *Middlemarch.* The letter in question is her response to an acquaintance, an Independent clergyman and professor of theology, who was attempting to lead her back to the intense Evangelical faith from which she had recently turned away. She is here commenting on a course of corrective reading which the Reverend Francis Watts had prescribed for her:

> You have well stated one of my sources of doubt: still I am aware that *with adequate evidence* Bishop Butler's little phrase 'for aught we

---

[14] Samuel Taylor Coleridge, *Collected Works,* Bollingen Series, 75, part 12, *Marginalia,* 5 vols. (Princeton: Princeton University Press, 1980), vol. 1 [12:1], p. 867: George Whalley, "considering . . . that in Feb. 1801 [Coleridge] regarded Butler as one of the 'the three greatest, nay, only three *great* Metaphysicians which this Country *has* produced' . . . it is surprising how few references [he] makes to Joseph Butler."

know' must silence objections, for, the existence of evil being allowed, and the solution adopted that all partial evil is universal good, then as a certain amount of temporal evil is to the whole amount of temporal good, so in an infinitely surpassing proportion would be the eternal woe of a limited number to the eternal bliss of a larger multitude and to *possible* moral results co-extensive with the Divine Government.[15]

The two phrases to which I draw particular attention are the quotation of Butler's own locution "for aught we know" and Eliot's own words (underlined in the autograph) *"with adequate evidence."* In Butler's *Analogy* (1736), as Eliot's editor Gordon Haight observes, "the phrase ['for aught we know'] appears repeatedly." Haight conjectures that the particular instance George Eliot has in mind occurs in chapter seven of Butler's treatise: "The natural government of the world is carried on by general laws. For this there may be wise and good reasons: the wisest and best, for aught we know to the contrary."[16]

Of all George Eliot's writings, I would suggest, it is in *Middlemarch*, in the final redirecting toward redemption of the book's burden of particular and manifold error and waste, that she stays closest to the substance of Butler's Christian ethics. *Middlemarch* is a novel whose general ethos is in the *Analogy's* "for aught we know," while its structuring of plot and character seems determined by Eliot's own caveat that *"with adequate evidence"* Butler's "little phrase" "must silence objections":

> But the effect of [Dorothea's] being on those around her was incalculably diffusive: for the growing good of the world is partly dependent on unhistoric acts; and that things are not so ill with you and me as they might have been, is half owing to the number who lived faithfully a hidden life, and rest in unvisited tombs.[17]

In some mysterious way, then, some "infinitely surpassing proportion," nothing of real worth is irretrievably lost. In a novel so powerfully attentive to humanity's perverse gift for supplanting things of value with things that are worthless, the "incalculably diffusive" nature of the benefaction is made to seem equal with foresight and moral deliberation.

---

[15] *Letters of George Eliot*, ed. G. Haight, 6 vols. (New Haven: Yale University Press, 1954), vol. 1, p. 135.

[16] Ibid., p. 135 n. 9.

[17] *Middlemarch*, World's Classics ed. (Oxford: Oxford University Press, 1988), p. 682.

Eliot saw herself as a meliorist[18] and initially, in such a passage as that with which she concludes *Middlemarch,* may be thought of as carrying some way further Locke's connection of intrinsic value and "improvement." As he argues that intrinsic value is only latent, dormant even, in a piece of land until or unless human labour develops it by work of hand[19]—manures it, that is to say—so she seems able, in the closing paragraphs of her novel, to suggest that human worth itself may lie deep and dormant and unrealized if it is not thoroughly worked by the "manifold wakings of men to labour and endurance."[20]

I say "able to suggest" to characterize degrees of relative success and failure. Also, I wish to anticipate that familiar style of incredulity (familiar, I mean, to ancient readers—like myself—of E. P. Thompson's *The New Reasoner*) that one can be so indulgent toward the rhetoric of political quietism. The success I would describe as Eliot's capacity to represent that actuality of reflection and endurance by an achieved style that, in its own reflective power and in its demands upon both author's and reader's sustained powers of attention, shows itself the moral equivalent of those very qualities it describes. It seems to me that, for the author of *Middlemarch,* intrinsic value is not so much in things, or even in qualities, as in a faculty: the faculty of sustained attention; attention conceived of, moreover, as a redemptive power. Coleridge, who comprehended this faculty better than any of his contemporaries, and whose comprehension is exemplified in the title of a major work, *Aids to Reflection,* left nothing that so embodied this comprehension as do George Eliot's *Middlemarch* and Wordsworth's *The Prelude.* Coleridge's most radically creative ideas and perceptions are sustained, in *The Prelude,* with Wordsworth's ideas and perceptions engrafted upon them, as they are not sustained even in *Aids to Reflection.*

I referred a few moments ago to degrees of relative success and failure. The faculty of attention in George Eliot's work is indisputable: to praise this is not to deny that on major issues, both particular and general, she finds herself attending to a self-projected impasse; nor to deny that, at such points, she is capable of dissolving the frame as calculatingly as an equivocating politician in his memoirs. My term "dissolving" refers

[18] B. J. Paris, *Experiments in Life: George Eliot's Quest for Values* (Detroit: Wayne State University Press, 1965), p. 48.

[19] John Locke, *Two Treatises of Government,* ed. P. Laslett (Cambridge: Cambridge University Press, 1988), p. 298 (from *The Second Treatise*).

[20] *Middlemarch,* p. 644.

back, in the first instance, to the final paragraph of *Middlemarch,* in the second, to the paragraph in Hume's essay "Of Refinement in the Arts," which I also quoted earlier. The word the two passages have in common is "diffuse"/"diffusive." Hume: "They [industry, knowledge, and humanity] diffuse their beneficial influence on the *public,* . . ."; Eliot: "But the effect of [Dorothea's] being on those around her was incalculably diffusive. . . ." Taken phrase against phrase I would be hard put to say that Eliot is ethically more reliable than Hume. They are both lobbyists: Hume for his own pleasures and satisfactions; Eliot for her self-stabilizing compensations of "partly dependent" and "half-owing"—little drawn breaths and exhalations of scruple that compare badly with Keats's "I have been half in love with easeful Death,"[21] a phrase that has the capacity to cut short and cauterize the unlovely aspects of Keats's self-absorption: a failing that he was well able to combat (though it was never easy) in the poems of 1819.

Set Eliot's *Middlemarch* in its entirety against Hume's *Essays, Moral, Political, and Literary* in its entirety, and I have more confidence in putting the case. Eliot writes with sufficient command of detail (of both plot and style) over some hundreds of pages that the body of her detailed accuracies is able to ride the shock of her special pleading and evasiveness. In this, George Eliot is very like Wordsworth; in both of them quantity, taken overall, enhances quality. There is enough evidence, in context, of stubborn attentiveness over a broad and varied range of a given world that reflective language itself becomes a redemptive agent of the author's self-deceptions, willed and unconscious evasions, ethical sentimentality and political shape-shifting. It is the ability to recognize, and to realize in the arduous process of writing itself, the nature of the redemptive faculty or agency that characterizes the major writer. Judged by these standards, *Middlemarch* is a great work, *Essays, Moral, Political, and Literary* a set of accomplished personal and social amusements.

I might hesitate to call Butler's *Fifteen Sermons* a great work in the sense that *Middlemarch* is great; I would not hesitate to attest that Butler's work is more than an amusement. I mean by amusement what Joseph Addison meant by it in the *Spectator* of March 30, 1711, recalling how often "amus[ed himself] with the tombstones and inscriptions" in Westminster Abbey. At this date "to amuse" could mean both "to divert

---

[21] *The Poems of John Keats,* ed. J. Stillinger (London: Heinemann, 1978), p. 371.

with pleasant trifles" and "to engage in sober reflection." It is worth pointing out that Butler cannot be contained by either definition, whereas a polished amenability to both is a characteristic of many successful sermons and periodical essays of the period. In such a context, Hume's *Essays, Moral, Political, and Literary* can be understood as a collection of urbane and amusing lay-sermons.

In Butler's tenth sermon, "Upon Self-Deceit," we find the following:

> Truth, and real good sense, and thorough integrity, carry along with them a peculiar consciousness of their own genuineness: there is a feeling belonging to them, which does not accompany their counterfeits, error, folly, half-honesty, partial and slight regards to virtue and right, so far only as they are consistent with that course of gratification which men happen to be set upon.[22]

It is certainly possible to challenge both the premises and delivery of this argument. If we object to Hume's equivocation in his statement that there is "really" no standard of morality other than that imposed by opinion, should we not also object to Butler's "Truth, and real good sense, and thorough integrity"? Or to his "peculiar consciousness," or to that "feeling . . . which does not accompany . . . counterfeits"?

One has to recall here that Butler is the older man and that Hume was able to record the bishop's approval and general recommendation of the two volumes of *Essays, Moral, Political and Literary* when they appeared in 1741 and 1742 (*DNB,* "Hume"). The diction employed by both Butler and Hume is the common diction of eighteenth-century rational theology and moral philosophy. One has to fine-tune the language of criticism in order to reveal the distinction between them; but, as the language of criticism ought in any case to be fine-tuned, this requirement should not be unexpected or unwelcome. Distinctions within broadly similar forms of idiom may indicate differences in basic premise. Butler, I believe, retained a sense of the Fall and its consequences, if not in the deep-set Augustinian sense, then in some form sufficiently marked to differentiate his view from that of Hume and the Deists:

> *Lastly,* the various miseries of life which lie before us wherever we turn our eyes, the frailty of this mortal state we are passing through,

---

[22] *Fifteen Sermons Preached at the Rolls Chapel,* ed. W. R. Matthews (1914; London: G. Bell, 1949), p. 159.

may put us in mind that the present world is not our home; that we are merely strangers in it, as our fathers were. (*Fifteen Sermons,* p. 106).

Such a passage is profoundly Pauline (or profoundly "pseudo-Pauline," since the reference is to Hebrews) as Hume never is. And so, for Butler, I would say, "our ignorance, the imperfection of our nature, our virtue and our condition in this world" are intrinsic to our creatureliness:[23] notice, in the words I have just quoted (from the beginning of Sermon XIV), how "virtue" is not lacking but is found together *with* "our ignorance" and "the imperfection of our nature." At the heart of his thinking, that is to say, the author of *The Analogy of Religion Natural and Revealed, to the Constitution and Course of Nature* does not rely on analogy—our own philosophy's resistance to Butler and preferral of Hume rests on the assumption that it does and is thereby outdated as Hume is not—but on the intervention of incarnated Grace in our carnal perplexity: our "imbecility or weaknes" as Hooker called the natural condition.[24] It is to be remarked that the phrase "for aught we know," upon which George Eliot placed emphasis and which Haight confirms as characteristically recurrent throughout Butler's *Analogy,* is found earlier, in the preface to *The Lawes of Ecclesiasticall Politie,* where Hooker remarks that "the staines and blemishes found in our State" as "springing from the root of humaine frailtie and corruption, not only are, but have been alwaies more or lesse, yea and (for any thing we know to the contrary) will be to the worlds end complained of, what forme of government soever take place."[25] In such writing—and here I place Hooker and Butler together—the "root" is at once our frailty and our conscience. A single root, it yet performs a double function: as aboriginal frailty, it transforms gifts into penalties and is itself further disfigured; as aboriginal grace, it remains within the density of fallen nature, transforming frailty and corruption into redemptive self-knowledge, and is itself finally transfigured. Hooker's name does not feature in the index to the excellent volume of *Tercentenary Essays, Joseph Butler's Moral and Religious Thought;*[26] neither does that of Donald MacKinnon, who gave con-

[23] *Fifteen Sermons,* p. 217.

[24] Richard Hooker, *Tractates, and Sermons,* vol. 5 of the Folger Library Edition of *The Works of Richard Hooker,* (Cambridge, Mass.: Harvard University Press, 1990), p. 73.

[25] *Works* (Folger), vol. 1, pp. 15–16.

[26] Ed. Christopher Cunliffe (Oxford: Clarendon Press, 1992).

centrated attention to Butler's ethics and whose own affirmation that "the language of repentance is not a kind of bubble on the surface of things" reestablishes the proper *gravitas* of Butler for the mid-twentieth century.[27] John Henry Newman's name is noted, and rightly; for he several times acknowledged his indebtedness to Butler, referring to him as "the greatest name in the Anglican Church" (*Tercentenary Essays*, 8). I myself used (*supra*) the word "aboriginal" to recall that link by alluding to Newman's phrase for the inheritance of Original Sin—"the human race is implicated in some terrible aboriginal calamity."[28] Butler, in what Newman elsewhere calls "his grave and abstract way,"[29] might demur at "terrible" and "calamity" but that he grasps the full nature of *implication* I do not doubt. His strength—and in this he stands in the direct line: Hooker-through-Newman—is to comprehend and accept the intrinsic value of our self-realization in and through conscience as stemming directly from the implicated nature of our strength and frailty.

I am aware that allusions—or even precise references—to the nature of the intrinsic do not of themselves guarantee intrinsicality. I am undertaking in these Tanner Lectures, I remind myself, a double task: to offer as succinctly as I am able, within the formally prescribed limits, a natural history of the term "intrinsic value"; and to try to determine if there is any way in which intrinsic value can be proven in a context or contexts other than that of the assay office at the Mint. One can put a gold or silver coin to the "assay"; it is conceivable, though this may be merely a conceit, that one could assay with equivalent precision the intrinsic value of Shakespeare's sixty-sixth sonnet or Keats's "Ode to a Nightingale."

Ben Jonson entered in his commonplace book—published posthumously as *Timber, or, Discoveries: Made upon Men and Matter*—ideas given to him by his wide and deep reading, particularly in Classical Latin authors and in such Humanist authorities as Erasmus: "Wheresoever, manners, and fashions are corrupted, Language is, It imitates the publicke riot. The excesse of Feasts, and apparell, are the notes of a sick State; and the wantonnesse of language, of a sick mind."[30] The intelli-

---

[27] D. M. MacKinnon, *A Study in Ethical Theory* (London: A. & C. Black, 1957), p. 138.

[28] *Apologia Pro Vita Sua,* ed. M. J. Svaglic (Oxford: Clarendon Press, 1967), p. 218.

[29] Ibid., p. 463: "Answer in Detail to Mr Kingsley's Accusations."

[30] *Ben Jonson,* ed. C. H. Herford, P. Simpson, and E. Simpson, 11 vols. (Oxford: Clarendon Press, 1925–52), vol. 8, p. 593.

gence that believes in these words, from wheresoever derived, and seals that belief by giving them this cogent stability, affirms also its acceptance of a doctrine of intrinsic value, albeit tacitly. The tacit understanding here is that language does not universally descend into corruption in company with a sick mind, or the mind of a sick state. Jonson had no doubt that his own times were sick; but he never doubted the capacity of language, his own language in particular, to retain its sanity and to guard the sanity of those who gave it their assent. Giving assent to one of Jonson's moral axioms is not necessarily an exercise for the prudent: he requires of his readers the full *yea, yea!* Failing that, I think he would prefer the full *nay, nay!* to "maybe" or "just possibly" or "perhaps." If you do answer with *yea, yea!*—as I admit that I do—you are henceforward committed to a course of thought and statement that accepts opposition as a part of the common lot, which can hardly avoid controversy, and which will be, or from some points of vantage will appear to be, narrowly constrained and constraining.

Toward, and into, this matter of constraint, however, more than one way of approach is open. Peter Geach has observed that "if you opt for virtue, you opt for being the sort of man who *needs* to act virtuously . . . . And if you opt for chastity, then you opt to become the sort of person who *needs* to be chaste."[31] Geach credits the philosopher Philippa Foot with this neo-Aristotelianism; but she would not have claimed that the retrieval began with her. It is more than likely that she found it in Butler's *Fifteen Sermons,* in the Third Sermon, "Upon Human Nature":

> But allowing that mankind hath the rule of right within himself, yet it may be asked, "What obligations are we under to attend to and follow it?" . . . The question . . . carries its own answer along with it. Your obligation to obey this law, is its being the law of your nature. That your conscience approves of and attests to such a course of action, is itself alone an obligation. (p. 64)

Obligation. Attestation. If I conclude that the condition of language— the language of imaginative attestation—in relation to the conditions laid down by the world is very much as Ben Jonson depicts it; and if I further conclude that a paradigm of ethical self-evaluation and affective

---

[31] Peter Geach, *God and the Soul* (New York: Schocken Books, 1969), p. 123.

acceptance is in being as Bishop Butler describes it; and that this paradigm in its bearing upon the world (as also in the world's bearing upon it) is essentially the same today as it was in 1726: I have put myself in the position of being obligated to speak somewhat as I have spoken throughout this paper. I resume my chain of hypothesis, as follows: If I am constrained to choose not to be a part of the "public riot," and if I abide by Ben Jonson's analogy, State health/sickness: Language health/sickness, or if I propose to push the issue deeper than analogy into interrelationship or even interpenetration (State-into-language/language-into-State), then Butler's argument offers more serrations and striations, more toe-hold and hand-hold for the resistant conscience of our imagination, than can be found in the arguments of any other eighteenth-century author—not excluding such a triumph of the moral imagination as Samuel Johnson's *Life of Richard Savage.* My language is in me and is me; even as I, inescapably, am a minuscule part of the general semantics of the nation; and as the nature of the State has involved itself in the nature that is most intimately mine. The nature that is most intimately mine may by some be taken to represent my intrinsic value. If it is so understood, it follows that intrinsic value, thus defined, bears the extrinsic at its heart.

A crucial issue remains. In so framing the matter, do I confuse intrinsic with mediated value? Here again I believe that Butler has shown that, in some if not all circumstances, intrinsic and mediated value cannot, may not, be separated. It is my "obligation to obey this law [in] its being the law of [my] nature"; that is, in and of itself, the intrinsic being that I mediate.

The rest is paradox. For the poem to engage justly with our imperfection, so much the more must the poem approach the nature of its own perfection. It is simply not true to say that the intrinsic value of a line or phrase cannot be assayed and proven in close and particular detail. For the intrinsic value of the entire poem so to be established would require the significant detail to illumine and regulate the whole. I am left with no other course but to say that the great poem moves us to assent as much by the integrity of its final imperfection as by the amazing grace of its detailed perfection. But of one thing I am sure: at those points where the intrinsic value of the formal structure, by whatever means, is revealed to us, that value is on the instant mediated.

II. POETRY AND VALUE

Joseph Butler and Gottfried Wilhelm Leibniz had a friend in common, although they never met. Each was the mentor and friend of Caroline, queen-consort of George II. Leibniz's friendship with her was closer and of a longer duration; even so, her devotion to Butler's *Analogy of Religion* was such that he owed his public rise and acclaim to her interest perhaps as much as to his own distinction of intellect and spiritual *savoir-faire.*

Butler and Leibniz were more closely related, however, than such biographical marginalia might indicate. It has been observed of the author of the *Analogy* that his "metaphysic of personal being as radically active *and* sentient is profoundly pluralistic as well as profoundly relational, and has more affinities with Leibniz (that most Anglican of continental philosophers) than with either Spinoza or Descartes: he is troubled by neither of their characteristic problems—maintaining individual distinctness or genuine interaction, respectively."[1] I have now to decide what "profoundly pluralistic" means in this—or any—context; and what, if anything, terms and phrases such as "radically active *and* sentient," "profoundly relational," "maintaining individual distinctness [and] genuine interaction" have to do with the topic of this lecture: "Poetry and Value."

I remarked in my previous paper that students of Coleridge's philosophical, theological, and political writings have found surprisingly little reference to Butler in those pages, and astonishingly little in the *Marginalia* and *Table Talk.* I came to Coleridge long before I came to Butler and until quite recently if asked with which English thinker I associate the terms "radically active *and* sentient," "maintaining individual distinctness [and] genuine interaction," I would have named the author of *Aids to Reflection, Biographia Literaria,* "This Lime-Tree Bower my Prison" and "Dejection: an Ode." One of the "lost" great books of the past two hundred years is *Aids to Reflection* as it might have been if Coleridge had chosen to reflect upon the axioms of Joseph Butler rather than the aphorisms of Archbishop Leighton.[2] But one must avoid sophistication. The fact is that the name of Leibniz features more promi-

---

[1] C. Cunliffe, ed., *Joseph Butler's Moral and Religious Thought* (Oxford: Clarendon Press, 1992), p. 146.

[2] Hazlitt, in the essay "My First Acquaintance with Poets," records Coleridge's praise of Butler's *Fifteen Sermons Preached at the Rolls Chapel:* noted by John Beer in his edition of Coleridge's *Aids to Reflection* (Princeton, N.J.: Princeton University Press, 1993), p. lxxxix. See also Lecture I, note 14.

nently than that of Butler in the indices to Coleridge's major works. Butler and Coleridge show strong affinity in areas of thought relating to individual distinctness and genuine interaction because each—Butler by affinity, Coleridge by derivation—shares Leibniz's awareness of particular forms of potentiality and realization, and perhaps also of loss. In my own autodidactic inquiry into the nature of intrinsic value and the questionable relationship of value-theory to the spoken and written word, especially as this is formalized in the art of poetry, they exist as a triumvirate of moral assessors. I should add that, attached as I am to a form of belief in Original Sin, one that is probably not too far removed from the orthodox, I expect my assessors to be in some respects compromised, though this in no way lowers them in my estimation. I should say further that however evasive I may be on the question, the fact that I do have such a strong attachment to Newman's "terrible aboriginal calamity" makes particularly difficult my attempts to give some kind of priority to the status of intrinsic value as an ethical referent. As I observed in my previous lecture, Hobbes, in *Leviathan,* presents us with an enduring vision of "inhaerent," or intrinsic, value, but in the person of a dead man and in the body of a vanished society. In this respect, *Leviathan* is a powerfully elegiac work; and when I praise the "inhaerent"—meaning the "intrinsic"—in an elegiac context, the term must carry a different kind of inference from the specific weight of the word "intrinsic" as applied to precious metals employed in the manufacture of coins. I am conscious, also, that what initially draws me to the idea of intrinsic value is a set of expectations and presuppositions that are themselves attached to interest and thereby compromised. I find that I am here presenting two interinvolved—but not indivisible—categories as if each confronted us with issues identical to those of the other: I mean questions relating to the nature of language and questions relating to poetics. The status of language in relation to the speakable and the unspeakable is less problematic than that of poetics so situated: it is with particular reference to the latter ganglion of energy, *techne,* belief, and opinion that I am self-committed to address you on this occasion. Let me here present—briefly, since I shall be considering them more fully in the closing stages of my discussion—the degrees of significance attached to language by two major European figures of the last sixty years, Dietrich Bonhoeffer and Helmuth James von Moltke. As their last recorded words indicate, language did not in the end forsake them, nor did they finally surrender language to some existential brute force such as that evoked by Czeslaw

Milosz in his parable of "a man threatened with instant death." My strong impression is that neither Bonhoeffer nor von Moltke would have concluded in his final hours or moments that what "*judge{s}* all poets and philosophers" is the "very amusing sight" of machine-gun bullets upending cobblestones "on a street in an embattled city." Milosz's observation,[3] like much of the late twentieth century poetry on which he has made his mark, is suspended between vitalism and nihilism essentially as Bonhoeffer in his *Ethics* foresaw the condition of an overridingly post-Christian world: "Vitalismus endet zwangsläufig im Nihilismus, im Zerbrechen alles Natürlichen."[4] The spirit that motivated Bonhoeffer and von Moltke was grounded in its own recognition of intrinsic value, which was neither the semantic irreducibility of Mallarmé nor the zero-apprehension of Milosz's man under machine-gun fire. There is a significant similarity between Ezra Pound's belief in the absolute authority of poetics—"all values ultimately come from our [i.e., the poets'] judicial sentences"[5] and Milosz's belief in the absolute supremacy of the corrida and its "moment of truth." This likeness of opposites stems from the fact that the provenance of both is *symboliste,* or, one might say, Romantic-confrontational. This is not the situation in which Bonhoeffer and von Moltke find themselves and find language adequate to their particular witness. Poetry is ruled out of their form of witness only if one forgets the Psalms and the kenotic hymn of Paul's Epistle to the Philippians. As this lecture is inescapably confessional, I am bound to offer myself as a child of our time who, forced to respond to the disputatious "relevance of poetry after Auschwitz" question, would think immediately of Paul Celan's "Todesfuge" but only belatedly of the Psalms and the Prophets.

I say "inescapably confessional," but is there not also something artificial or engineered in the premise and mannerism of modern confession, something at once arbitrary and highly convenient in so presenting the issues as being exclusively, to use my term, Romantic-confrontational? To read Bonhoeffer's *Ethics* or the last letters of Helmuth James von Moltke is to discover that they have more in common with Butler's *Fifteen Sermons* than with the poetics of existential crisis. In his "Preface" to the second edition (1729) of the sermons Butler writes:

---

[3] *The Captive Mind,* trans. Jane Zielonko (Harmondsworth: Penguin Books, 1980), p. 41.

[4] *Ethik,* in *Werke,* vol. 6 (Munich: Christian Kaiser Verlag, 1992), p. 171.

[5] *The Letters of Ezra Pound,* ed. D. D. Paige (New York: Harcourt Brace, 1950), p. 181: letter to F. E. Schelling, July 8, 1922.

If the observation [i.e., that benevolence is no more disinterested than any of the common particular passions] be true, it follows, that self-love and benevolence, virtue and interest are not to be opposed, but only to be distinguished from each other; in the same way as virtue and any other particular affection, love of arts, suppose, are to be distinguished.[6]

Given the climate of confrontation and exclusiveness within which the particular manners and mannerisms of modern poetics have evolved, Butler's suggestion that, in order to distinguish, you do not absolutely have to draw up things *in extremis* or antagonistically comes as a moment of surprising grace; and, indebted as I am to Blake's *The Marriage of Heaven and Hell,* I would nonetheless offer the structure of Butler's comment as a form of critical observation upon the explicit strategies of that powerfully isolationist yet powerfully influential work: "Without Contraries is no progression. Attraction and Repulsion, Reason and Energy, Love and Hate, are necessary to Human existence."[7]

There is, I concede, a view contrary to mine: this is, that in the passage that I took from Butler's 1729 "Preface" we have the grammar of a sceptic and hedonist; and that the impacted antithetical syntax of Blake's sentences reveals the extremes to which a radical moralist must go to disrupt the easy flow of self-serving parlance. It is quite true that there is a marked absence of tension in Butler's argument. It is equally the case that Blake's language of radical opposition does our simple thinking for us less straightforwardly than at first appears. If attraction and repulsion are demonstrably contraries, does it necessarily follow that reason and energy are similarly opposed, on any grounds other than Blake's say so? I would claim that there is an energy of reason, a reason in energy, which Blake's own work embodies in itself and for itself, and which is not of its own volition demeaned to the level of marketable slogan, though such a process can be forced through by others, as Allen Ginsberg and his British counterparts made evident when they took up Blake forty or so years ago. In part, what I am attempting to define as "intrinsic value" is a form of technical integrity that is itself a form of common honesty. Believing, as I have admitted I do, in the radically flawed nature of humanity and of its endeavours entails an acceptance of

[6] Joseph Butler, *Fifteen Sermons Preached at the Rolls Chapel,* ed. W. R. Matthews (1914; London: Bell, 1969), p. 23.

[7] *The Poems and Prophecies of William Blake,* ed. M. Plowman (London: Dent, 1927), p. 43.

the fact that, in one way or another, our integrity can be bought; or our honesty can be maimed by some flaw of *techne;* at the same time, however, our cynicism can be defeated, our defeatism thwarted, by processes within the imagination that, as processes, are scarcely to be distinguished from those that discover and betray some flaw in our conceptual structure or hypothesized ideal. There are, indeed, various terms—"discover" and "betray" are two of them, "reduce" and "invent" are others— that in themselves reveal this to be so. That is to say, they are descriptive of *techne* and also imply moral deductions having to do with technicalities. The supporting evidence is preserved in and by the *Oxford English Dictionary.*

Another way of stating the claim is to say that the ethical and the technical are reciprocating forces and that the dimension in which this reciprocation may be demonstrated is the contextual. If context is the arena of attention, it is also the arena of inattention. Crucial nodes of discourse *are* crucial precisely because they bring attention and inattention together in a specific crux, as here in a passage from an early letter of Leibniz: "Pilate is condemned. Why? Because he lacks faith. Why does he lack it? Because he lacks the will to attention. Why this? Because he has not understood the necessity of the matter.... Why has he not understood it? Because the causes of understanding were lacking."[8]

It has been suggested that Leibniz "was aware that 'an inevitable necessity...would destroy the freedom of the will, so necessary to the morality of action.'"[9] That being so, Pilate is condemned, according to Leibniz, by a mechanics of inner necessity that has the appearance of intimate mimesis, of being an accurate slow-motion exposure of Pilate's psychological incapacity and moral illogicality in the process of *becoming* "inevitable necessity," that is to say, "the necessity of the matter."

I associated the names of Leibniz and Butler at the start of this discussion because I think that Butler's method in *Fifteen Sermons* is similar to that aspect of Leibniz's method as revealed in the letter to Magnus Wedderkopf. He appears as a sceptic and a hedonist because he apprehends the mental rhythms of scepticism and hedonism rather as Leibniz apprehends the inertia of Pilate's logical illogic. There is certainly vanity, in more than one sense of the term, in Leibniz's presentation of Pilate's hypothetical thought-process in the shape of a psychological,

[8] *Philosophical Papers and Letters,* ed. L. E. Loemker (Dordrecht: D. Reidel, 1969), p. 146.

[9] Leibniz, *Political Writings,* ed. P. Riley (Cambridge: Cambridge University Press, 1972), p. 11.

metaphysical, and semantic *fait accompli;* it is perhaps vain of Butler to display before us, in so steady a fashion, the inner workings of self-deceit, cant, and hypocrisy and to show an equal certitude in charting their acceptable opposites. I believe, on the grounds of a close reading of *Fifteen Sermons,* that he recognizes such tendencies as comprising several facets of that human nature within which his own nature is implicated. From evidence both internal and historical, we have a basis from which to project his likely answer to the question: *Where do you stand?*—"between Ecclesiasticus and Shaftesbury's *Characteristics."* That, if you like, describes the general terrain within which his moral sensibility moves most freely; but "freely" does not accurately define Butler's capacity for making distinctions, which, although they derive from the standard figures of eloquence, nonetheless attest to a reflectively working mind.

> It is manifest [a] great Part of common Language, and of common Behaviour over the World, is formed upon Supposition of . . . a Moral Faculty; whether called Conscience, moral Reason, moral Sense, or divine Reason; whether considered as a Sentiment of the Understanding, or as a Perception of the Heart, or, which seems the Truth, as including both.[10]

It was my recollection of this passage especially—it is from the "Dissertation of the Nature of Virtue," 1736—that caused me to cavil at Blake's opposing Reason to Energy. Each clause in Butler's sentence is a modifier or qualifier; there is an immediate connection here between his *referral* to a "Faculty, or practical discerning Power within us" and the demonstration of that power of discernment in the structure of the sentence.[11] It is in the light of this example also that I take further a suggestion made by one of Butler's editors, W. R. Matthews, in 1914:

> Perhaps the most original part of Butler's teaching is his treatment of the "particular passions." He observes that all desires for particular objects are, in the strict sense, disinterested, since they seek their external object as their end and rest in that.[12]

I would need to be persuaded that, considered as "teaching," there is much actual originality here: it seems to me thoroughly in line with

---

[10] *The Analogy of Religion . . . to Which Are Added Two Brief Dissertations,* 5th ed. (London: Robert Horsfield, 1765), p. 452.

[11] Ibid., p. 453.

[12] *Fifteen Sermons,* pp. xxii–xxiii.

that form of modified Thomism that Hooker diffused into the body of
Anglican thought and that one finds cropping up in various unlikely
places. The originality is in the active shaping of the reflective voice;
and the quality of that voice itself is effective in conveying to the reader
a sense of what it means to take the measure of one's own thought
through the common medium of language.

I would take this speculation a step further by suggesting a modifi-
cation to the sense in which we understand "disinterested" in relation
both to Butler's intentions and to the nature of language itself. Language, whatever else it is and is not, can be understood historically as a
form of seismograph: registering and retaining the myriad shocks of humanity's interested and disinterested passions. One may not be always
alert to this characteristic in daily conversation, and it is probably better
for us that this is so; but no one, I believe, could consult the great *Oxford
English Dictionary* and fail to appreciate that my term "seismograph,"
crude as it is, at least registers something of that seemingly illimitable
capacity. If I am even approximately right, one must conclude that a
reflective grasp of language will necessarily involve more than an easy
familiarity with the surface conventions for conveying "intelligence"
(i.e., information), conventions that, by and large, do not interfere with
one's self-possession or the possessiveness of one's own interested passions. Reflection—certainly as Butler and Coleridge would understand
the term—is the faculty or activity that draws the naturally interested
sensibility in the direction of disinterestedness. It is not necessary to
my argument to suppose or suggest that some hypostatic condition of
perfect disinterest is attainable within the usages, whether ordinary or
extraordinary, of the English language. The particular quality of our humanity that I am attempting to describe, on this occasion in terms of
poetry and value, is best revealed in and through the innumerable registrations of syntax and rhythm, registrations that are common to both
prose and poetry and to which as writers and as readers we attend or fail
to attend.

At the start of this lecture I coupled the names of Butler and
Coleridge, and associated both with that of Leibniz. I did so, having in
mind a passage from *Nouveaux essais sur l'Entendement Humain* (1703), in
which Leibniz challenges Locke's interpretation of the understanding or
intellective soul (Leibniz's term for it is "l'âme"), a passage to which Coleridge returned more than once in his own philosophical writings:[13]

---

[13] Notably in *Biographia Literaria,* ch. 9, first paragraph; *Logic,* ch. 12, second paragraph; *Aids to Reflection,* 2nd ed., Aphorism 6 (Comment).

You [Philalèthe = Locke, the Lockeans] oppose to me this axiom received by the philosophers, that there is nothing in the soul which
does not come from the senses [que rien n'est dans l'âme qui ne vi-
enne des sens]. But the soul itself must be excepted and its affections
[Mais il faut excepter l'âme même et ses affections]. *Nihil est in intellectu, quod non fuerit in sensu, excipe: nisi ipse intellectus.*[14]

Coleridge seized on this Leibnizian redirecting of Aristotle's maxim
as if he saw in it the possibility of encrypting the very nature of intrinsic
value: such value would be held permanently to attention within the
clause itself, *nisi ipse.* Coleridge thus expatiated on his understanding of
Leibniz's modifier: "the act of comparing supposes in the comparing
Faculty, certain inherent forms, that is, Modes of reflecting, not referable
to the Objects reflected on, but pre-determined by the Constitution and
(as it were) mechanism of the Understanding itself."[15] I do not find this
any advance on Butler's discourse on the "Moral Faculty" to which I have
already referred. In fact in requiring the locution "and (as it were) mechanism" Coleridge's definition is retrograde. I would not wish, even so, to
underrate the significance of this endeavour, a significance that is enhanced by his capacity of attuning conceptual hypotheses to his semantic perceptiveness, his immediate sense of language as mediator in the
struggle toward a grasp of intrinsic natures (one of several ways in which
he anticipates Hopkins's search for instress and inscape).

Gerard M. Hopkins's poetry, as also in certain instances his prose, is
both material evidence of and expert witness to the precise nature of the
activity of reflection that we see adumbrated in Butler and developed by
Coleridge. Hopkins simultaneously clarifies and complicates these issues: first, because his mastery of the essential techniques is such that he
reduces to a bare minimum the distance between the mediate and the
immediate characteristics of language; second, because, in his profound-
est theological allegiance, he is totally committed to mediation. At the
same time, therefore, he is both innovative, finding radically new ways
of compounding the intellective with the sensuous elements of language, and also reactionary: devoted to those beliefs and practices that,
in severe opposition to the liberalising inclinations of the century, concentrated a worshipper's attention upon Mary as Mediatrix and upon the
saints as intercessors. Hopkins at Oxford was a pupil of both Walter
Pater, for whom intrinsic value was signified—irrespective of context I

[14] *Nouveaux essais,* ed. J. Brunschwig (Paris: GF-Flammarion, 1990), p. 88.

[15] Samuel Taylor Coleridge, *Collected Works,* Bollingen Series 75, part 9, *Aids to Reflection,* ed. J. Beer (Princeton, N.J.: Princeton University Press, 1993), p. 225.

would say—by the "hard gemlike flame," and T. H. Green, who felt able to criticize Butler for being "content to leave the moral nature a cross of unreconciled principles,"[16] and whose own sense of intrinsic value was, like that of Locke and George Eliot, inseparable from ideas of improvement, of the moral imperative to bring to fulfillment within society, as much as within the individual life, latent qualities and virtues that would otherwise remain dormant or, worse, in a condition of torpor.

If I say that these are artificial distinctions I am evading the issue. The most refined forms of artifice, brought to bear upon the conditions of our natural life, lose something of their artificiality even as they infiltrate and complicate spontaneous activity. Green's objection to Butler's "cross of unreconciled principles" is brusque and inappropriately theatrical, though less so than Ruskin's choice of the name "Judas" for the national betrayal of the values of a true commonweal by estimating wealth as commodity values, that is to say, assessing national wealth in terms of what is more truly "illth."[17]

Ruskin in fact acknowledged that the "use of substances of intrinsic value as the materials of a currency, is a barbarism"[18] but maintained nonetheless its utility as a "mechanical check" and as an instrument of exchange with "foreign nations."[19] In short, intrinsic value, understood in terms of bullion value, was demanded by the conditions of life: to which Ruskin reacted in the mid to late nineteenth century very much as Hobbes had understood anarchy and arbitrary force in the mid seventeenth century. I began the research for these lectures essentially an adherent of "intrinsic value" as delineated by Ruskin. I am now much less sure of my position, partly because I am no longer confident that I can discern the point at which Ruskin himself crosses an indeterminate line between, on the one hand, regarding money as "an expression of right,"[20] or entitlement, or as a "sign" of "relations," and, on the other hand, using a monetary trope in which "intrinsic value" is by sleight of will substituted as the vital referent. In the first instance, Ruskin concedes that, if received as a "sign," money is "Always and necessarily . . . imperfect. . . ; but capable of approximate accuracy if rightly ordered";[21]

[16] T. H. Green, *Works,* 3 vols. (London: Longmans Green, 1888), vol. 3, p. 104.

[17] *Unto this Last and Other Essays* (London: Dent, 1970), p. 216.

[18] Ibid., p. 209.

[19] Ibid.

[20] Ibid., p. 208.

[21] Ibid., note 1.

in the second instance, the "expression of right" itself takes on a mysterious intransitive quality that is thereafter to be received—and not
questioned—by us as "intrinsic value." Any acknowledgment of "approximate accuracy" is dissolved and Ruskin's real authority of eloquence is devoted, as here in *Essays on Political Economy,* to the creation
and promulgation of an idea of the intrinsic that is scarcely to be distinguished from the intransitive:

> It does not in the least affect the intrinsic value of the wheat, the air,
> or the flowers, that men refuse or despise them. Used or not, their
> own power is in them, and that particular power is in nothing else.[22]

This has an undeniable eloquent beauty; but to what is it applied?
Ruskin is devoting the same degree of intensity to his subject that
Wordsworth in "Michael" or "Resolution and Independence" or "The
Female Vagrant" or Book XII of *The Prelude* devotes to the unrecognized
and publicly unfulfilled powers of men and women forced to live in var-
ious kinds of straitened circumstance.

What Wordsworth and Ruskin have in common, in these passages
at least, is the eloquence of mourning. They are essentially elegists
when they write of the intrinsicality of the despised and rejected
among the common people and the common things of the earth, as
Hobbes was an elegist when he wrote of the "inhaerent" virtues of the
dead Royalist soldier-poet Sidney Godolphin. As such points, I would
add, Wordsworth and Ruskin seem to me to spring from common
seventeenth–eighteenth century roots: from Locke's association of intrinsic value with potentiality for improvement and from the philosophy of individuation made axiomatic in Butler's "Preface" to *Fifteen Sermons:* "Everything is what it is, and not another thing."[23] The crucial
difference is that whereas in 1690 (Locke) and 1729 (Butler) the tone is
optimistic or at least melioristic, by the first decade of the nineteenth
century (*The Prelude,* Book XII) it is, at best, stoical.

The great exception, and the major challenge, to these conclusions I
take to be John Henry Newman. It is in Newman's pastoral theology
that Butler's teaching finds its nineteenth-century fulfillment. And
Newman is no more an elegist—in the central body of his writing—
than is Butler. Fr. Sillem, the editor of Newman's *Philosophical Notebook,*

[22] Ibid., p. 204.
[23] *Fifteen Sermons,* p. 23.

implies that Newman read Butler in the same spirit as that in which he read St. Athanasius and St. John Chrysostom, whose writings "expressed the inner unity of their own minds rather than that of an abstract system."[24] My reason for choosing this particular observation will be apparent in the general context of our discussion of intrinsic value. Sillem's particular choice of words makes emphatic the difference between the intransitive and the transitive. If, as is true of Newman (according to Sillem), the intrinsic value, the "inner unity," is in the mind's conduct and disposition of its own best qualities, there is no arbitrary limit to, or restriction upon, the burgeoning of such estimation. Our notion of intrinsic value does not inevitably make us *laudatores temporis acti*. Our grasp of intrinsic value is transitive in its implications. What I have termed the elegiac celebration of "intrinsic value" understands the value as being in some sense isolated from current degradation, and therefore as being inviolate, held securely within the sphere of the intransitive. With Ruskin, more than with Wordsworth, the result is loss of proportion: it is surely disproportionate when Ruskin claims: "It does not in the least affect the intrinsic value of the wheat, the air, or the flowers, that men refuse or despise them." Locke would have said, and here he would be cogent as Ruskin is not, that the intrinsic value of a bushel of wheat cannot be isolated from the value of the human labour that contributed to its growth and harvesting. The idea, then, that some other human act, i.e., of "refusing" the bushel of wheat, preserves a mysterious integrity of its "own power" within the rejected grain is a sentiment little short of the absurd. One is put in mind of the fate of certain elderly authors who, rescued from oblivion by côteries and the editors of small-circulation journals, are invariably described as having been hitherto "strangely" or "unaccountably" neglected. The "neglect" by some kind of imaginative fiat is simultaneously held to be both their "documentary claim" to present notice and an intrinsic part of the "neglected" author's newly proclaimed value.

The title of this lecture, I remind myself, is "Poetry and Value." It seems fitting, therefore, that I should now make explicit a number of conclusions that have been implicit, or in suspension, during the earlier part of my paper. To do so, I need to return to the question "What is the constitution of the activity we call 'reflection'?" In the chapter of "Pru-

---

[24] John H. Newman, *The Philosophical Notebook*, ed. E. J. Sillem, 2 vols. (Louvain: Nauwelaerts, 1969–70), vol. 1, p. 94.

dential Aphorisms," in the second edition of *Aids to Reflection* Coleridge advised his reader: "Whether you are reflecting for yourself, or reasoning with another, make it a rule to ask yourself the precise meaning of the word, on which the point in question appears to turn;"[25] and, in the same section of his book, he noted: "At the utmost [the moral philosopher as opposed to "the botanist, the chemist, the anatomist, &c."] has only to rescue words, already existing and familiar, from the false or vague meanings imposed on them by carelessness, or by the clipping and debasing misusage of the market."[26] He is referring to the misusage of such words as "happiness," "duty," "faith," "truth," and, by implication, of the word "reflection" itself. "Reflection" is not here identifiable as a "passive attending upon the event"[27] or even as a "wise passiveness"[28] but in metaphors of, and associations with, energy conceived as a "co-instantaneous yet reciprocal action"[29] of the individual "will" and an "empowering" law; of "THE WORD, as informing; and THE SPIRIT, as actuating."[30] Language, that is to say, does not issue from reflection but is an inherent element within the activity of reflection itself; it is an integral part of the body of reflection.

The issue here, for Coleridge as for Butler and Leibniz and, albeit less happily, for Ruskin also, is whether the intrinsicality of value can be, ought to be, made viable in and for the contingent world, the domain of worldly power and circumstance. In each case the answer—in principle—is yes; in practice the resolution is, in varying degrees and for various reasons, less than perfect. The toll is most severe in the case of Ruskin and is the effect of a cause that Coleridge precisely anticipated, in *Aids to Reflection,* when defining sophistry: "For the juggle of sophistry consists, for the greater part, in using a word in one sense in the premiss, and in another sense in the conclusion."[31] I read this as a prescient description of that flaw in Ruskin's argument, to which I earlier drew attention, and which I now attribute to the term "intrinsic" occurring in

[25] Coleridge, *Aids to Reflection,* p. 47.

[26] Ibid.

[27] T. S. Eliot, "Tradition and the Individual Talent," part 2, final paragraph, in T. S. Eliot, *Selected Essays* (London: Faber, 1934), p. 21.

[28] Wordsworth, "Expostulation and Reply," line 24, in *Wordsworth: Poetry and Prose,* ed. W. M. Merchant (London: Hart-Davis, 1969), p. 123.

[29] *Aids to Reflection,* p. 75.

[30] Ibid., p. 77.

[31] Ibid., p. 46.

one sense in the premise and in another sense in the conclusion. One may balk at the word "sophistry," if sophistry can be understood only as intentional juggling to deceive. I do not believe that Ruskin intentionally misleads; nor do I say that we have here the broken or jumbled threads of an inattentive weaver of platitudes. Ruskin's was a great and scrupulous mind. He is overcome, in this particular area of discourse, as we are all overcome, at some time or another in our particular areas of discourse, by a kind of neutral, or indifferent, or disinterested force in the nature of language itself: a force that Coleridge describes incomparably well in the sudden blaze of a sentence at the beginning of *Aids to Reflection:* "For if words are not THINGS, they are LIVING POWERS, by which the things of most importance to mankind are actuated, combined, and humanized."[32] As much weighs here upon that plural present indicative of the verb *to be*—the verb substantive—as weighs upon the verbs "discover," "betray," "reduce," "invent" in other contexts, or upon the locutions "excipe" and "nisi ipse" in Leibniz's modifying of Aristotle's axiom, "nihil est in intellectu, quod non fuerit in sensu." And certainly no less weighs upon the grammar of a sentence in Helmuth James von Moltke's farewell letter before his execution in January 1945, rejoicing that, in the end, the Third Reich could find no justification for killing him other than the fact of his Christianity: "nicht als Grossgrundbesitzer, nicht als Adliger, nicht als Preusse, nicht als Deutscher . . . sondern als Christ und als gar nichts anderes."[33]

Syntax such as we find here, in this context, establishes the *Grundbass* (as we would speak of the ground-bass in a Bach *continuo*) in the midst of the *Abgrund:* the abyss, the deep, in the psalms of penitence and lamentation. I do not say, however, that with von Moltke's words we move into a dimension unique to him and unperceived or unanticipated by such a thinker as Joseph Butler. Coleridge and Newman seem especially able to comprehend and to take further the implications and resonances of certain of Butler's phrases of adumbration. Newman's *An Essay in Aid of a Grammar of Assent* builds upon the sense of Butler's "full intuitive conviction"[34] as much as upon the distinction between *"mere power and authority,"*[35] a distinction that Butler says "everybody is ac-

---

[32] Ibid., p. 10.

[33] *Briefe an Freya, 1939–1945,* ed. B. R. von Oppen (Munich: Beck, 1988), p. 60.

[34] *Fifteen Sermons,* p. 12.

[35] Ibid., p. 57.

quainted with,"[36] though he refrains from adding "but which not everybody understands." Newman also works to ensure that "full intuitive conviction" is not confused with or supplanted by "blind propension."[37] Coleridge's achievement is to show how "full intuitive conviction," "blind propension," the tendency to mistake power for authority; above all, perhaps, how a sense of "the moral rule of action interwoven in [our] nature,"[38] as Butler calls it, can without arbitrariness of analogy, be extended into the nature of human language itself, in such a way that language becomes, not a simple adjunct or extension of "the moral rule of action" but rather a faculty of reflective integration.

Invited (or self-appointed) to put, as succinctly as I can, my views regarding the nature and responsibility of "poetry" in the field, or court, of "value," I offer the following response.

A poem issues from reflection, particularly but not exclusively from the common bonding of reflection and language; it is not in itself the passing of reflective sentiment through the medium of language. The fact that my description applies only to a minority of poems written in English or any other language, and to the poetry written in this country during the past fifty years scarcely if at all, does not shake my conviction that the description I have given of how the uncommon work moves within the common dimension of language is substantially accurate.

[36] Ibid.
[37] Ibid., p. 197.
[38] Ibid., p. 255.

I. Human Rights as Politics

II. Human Rights as Idolatry

MICHAEL IGNATIEFF

THE TANNER LECTURES ON HUMAN VALUES

Delivered at

Princeton University
April 4–7, 2000

MICHAEL IGNATIEFF is a London-based commentator with the BBC and CBC. He was educated in Canada at Upper Canada College and Trinity College, Toronto, and received his Ph.D. from Harvard University. He has been a fellow at King's College, Cambridge; École des Hautes Études, Paris; and St. Antony's College, Oxford; and Visiting Carr Professor of Human Rights Practice at Harvard. His academic publications include *Wealth and Virtue: The Shaping of Political Economy in the Scottish Enlightenment* (1984); *The Needs of Strangers: An Essay on the Philosophy of Human Needs* (1985); *The Warrior's Honor: Ethnic War and the Modern Conscience* (1997); *Isaiah Berlin: A Life* (1999); and, most recently, *Virtual War: Kosovo and Beyond* (2000). His non-academic work includes *The Russian Album* (1987), which won both Canada's Governor General's Award and the Heinemann Prize of Britain's Royal Society of Literature; and *Scar Tissue* (1993), which was short-listed for the Booker Prize in 1993. He is currently serving as a member of the independent international commission on Kosovo, chaired by Judge Richard Goldstone of South Africa.

I. HUMAN RIGHTS AS POLITICS

1. HUMAN RIGHTS AND MORAL PROGRESS

In *If This Is a Man,* Primo Levi describes being interviewed by Dr. Pannwitz, chief of the chemical department at Auschwitz.[1] Securing a place in the department was a matter of life or death: if Levi could convince Pannwitz that he was a competent chemist, he might be spared the gas chamber. As Levi stood on one side of the doctor's desk, in his concentration camp uniform, Dr. Pannwitz stared up at him. Levi later remembered:

> That look was not one between two men; and if I had known how completely to explain the nature of that look, which came as if across the glass window of an aquarium between two beings who live in different worlds, I would also have explained the essence of the great insanity of the third German [reich].

Here was a scientist, trained in the traditions of European rational inquiry, turning a meeting between two human beings into an encounter between different species.

Progress may be a contested concept, but we make progress to the degree that we act upon the moral intuition that Dr. Pannwitz was wrong: our species is one and each of the individuals who compose it is entitled to equal moral consideration. Human rights is the language that systematically embodies this intuition, and to the degree that this intuition gains influence over the conduct of individuals and states, we can say that we are making moral progress. Richard Rorty's definition of progress applies here: "an increase in our ability to see more and more differences among people as morally irrelevant."[2] We think of the global diffusion of this idea as progress for two reasons: because if we live by it, we treat more human beings as we would wish to be treated

---

[1] Primo Levi, *If This Is a Man,* translated by Stuart Woolf (London: Abacus, 1987), pp. 111–12. The significance of the passage was pointed out to me by Alain Finkielkraut's *L'Humanité perdue: essai sur le 20ième siecle* (Paris: Seuil, 1996), pp. 7–11.

[2] Richard Rorty, *Truth and Moral Progress: Philosophical Papers* (Cambridge: Cambridge University Press, 1998), p. 11.

ourselves and in so doing help to reduce the amount of unmerited cruelty and suffering in the world. Our grounds for believing that the spread of human rights represents moral progress, in other words, are pragmatic and historical. We know from historical experience that when human beings have defensible rights—when their agency as individuals is protected and enhanced—they are less likely to be abused and oppressed. On these grounds, we count the diffusion of human rights instruments as progress even if there remains an unconscionable gap between the instruments and the actual practices of states charged to comply with them.

Calling the global diffusion of Western human rights a sign of moral progress may seem Eurocentric. Yet the human rights instruments created after 1945 were not a triumphant expression of European imperial self-confidence but a reflection on European nihilism and its consequences, at the end of a catastrophic world war in which European civilization very nearly destroyed itself. Human rights was a response to Dr. Pannwitz, to the discovery of the abomination that could occur when the Westphalian state was accorded unlimited sovereignty, when citizens of that state lacked criteria in international law that could oblige them to disobey legal but immoral orders. The Universal Declaration represented a return by the European tradition to its natural law heritage, a return intended to restore *agency,* to give individuals the juridical resources to stand up when the state ordered them to do wrong.

2. The Juridical, Advocacy, and Enforcement Revolutions

Historically speaking, the Universal Declaration is part of a wider reordering of the normative order of postwar international relations, designed to create fire-walls against barbarism. The juridical revolution included the UN Charter of 1945, outlawing aggressive war between states; the Genocide Convention of 1948, protecting religious, racial, and ethnic groups against extermination; the revision of the Geneva Conventions of 1949, strengthening noncombatant immunity; and finally the international convention on asylum of 1951 to protect the rights of refugees.

Before the Second World War, only states had rights in international law. With the Universal Declaration of Human Rights of 1948, the rights of individuals received international legal recognition.[3] For the first time, individuals—regardless of race, creed, gender, age, or any other status—were granted rights that they could use to challenge unjust state law or oppressive customary practice.

The juridical revolution should not be seen apart from the struggle for self-determination and national independence among the colonies of Europe's empires and, just as important, the battle for full civil rights by black Americans, culminating in the Civil Rights Act of 1965.[4] The international rights revolution was not led by states that already practiced what they preached. America and the European nations had not completed the juridical emancipation of their own citizens or subject peoples. Indeed, many of the states that contributed to the drafting of the Universal Declaration saw no apparent contradiction between endorsing international norms abroad and continuing oppression at home. They thought that the Universal Declaration would remain a pious set of clichés more practiced in the breach than in the observance. Yet once articulated as international norms, rights language ignited both the colonial revolutions abroad and the civil rights revolution at home.

Fifty years on, most modern states have ratified the international human rights conventions and some countries have incorporated their rights and remedies into the structure of their constitutions. The European Court of Human Rights, established in 1953, now affords citizens of European states the capacity to appeal against injustices in civil and state administration to the European Court in Strasbourg.[5] European states, including Britain, now accept that decisions taken by their courts or administrative bodies can be overturned by a human rights court independent of their national parliament and court systems.[6] New nations seeking entry into the European Union accept that they

[3] A. H. Robertson and J. G. Merrills, *Human Rights in the World,* 4th ed. (London: Manchester University Press, 1986), ch. 1; Johannes Morsink, *The Universal Declaration of Human Rights: Origins, Drafting and Intent* (Philadelphia: University of Pennsylvania Press, 1998).

[4] Paul Gordon Lauren, *The Evolution of International Human Rights: Visions Seen* (Philadelphia: University of Pennsylvania Press, 1998), p. 269; also Yael Danieli et al. (eds.), *The Universal Declaration of Human Rights: Fifty Years and Beyond* (New York: Baywood, 1998).

[5] Geoffrey Robertson, *Crimes against Humanity: The Struggle for Global Justice* (London: Allen Lane, 1999), pp. 51–54.

[6] Luke Clements and James Young (eds.), *Human Rights: Changing the Culture* (Oxford: Blackwell, 1999); see also Andrew Moravcsik, "The Origins of Human Rights Regimes: Democratic Delegation in Postwar Europe," *International Organization* 54, no. 2 (Spring 2000): 217–53.

must align their domestic law in accordance with the European Convention, even jettisoning capital punishment, since it falls foul of European human rights standards.

In the developing world, ratifying international human rights covenants has become a condition of entry for new states joining the family of nations. Even oppressive states feel obliged to engage in rhetorical deference toward human rights instruments. While genuflection toward human rights is the homage that vice pays to virtue, the fact that wicked regimes feel so obliged means that vice can now be shamed and even controlled in ways that were unavailable before 1945.

The worldwide spread of human rights norms is often seen as a moral consequence of economic globalization. The U.S. State Department's annual report for 1999 on human rights practice around the world describes human rights and democracy—along with "money and the Internet"—as one of the three universal languages of globalization.[7] This implies too easily that human rights is a style of moral individualism that has some elective affinity with the economic individualism of the global market, and that both advance hand in hand. Actually, the relation between human rights and money, between moral and economic globalization, is more antagonistic, as can be seen, for example, in the campaigns by human rights activists against the labor and environmental practices of the large global corporations.[8] Human rights has gone global not because it serves the interests of the powerful but primarily because it has advanced the interests of the powerless. Human rights has gone global by going local, imbedding itself in the soil of cultures and world views independent of the West, in order to sustain ordinary people's struggles against unjust states and oppressive social practices.

We can call this global diffusion of human rights culture a form of moral progress even while remaining skeptical of the motives of those who helped to bring it about. The states who signed the Universal Declaration never actually believed that it would constrain their behavior. After all, it lacked any enforcement mechanism. It was a declaration only, rather than a state treaty or a convention requiring national ratifi-

---

[7] United States Department of State, *1999 Country Reports on Human Rights* (Washington, D.C., 1999), introduction.

[8] T. F. Homer-Dixon, *Environment, Scarcity and Violence* (Princeton: Princeton University Press, 1999); O. Mehmet, E. Mendes, and R. Sinding, *Towards a Fair Global Labour Market: Avoiding a New Slave Trade* (London: Routledge, 1999); see also Amnesty International, *Human Rights: Is It Any of Your Business?* (London: Amnesty, 2000); Carnegie Council on Ethics and International Affairs, *Human Rights Dialogue* 2, no. 4 (Fall 2000), "Who Can Protect Workers' Rights?"

cation. The drafters—men and women like Eleanor Roosevelt, René
Cassin, and John Humphrey—were willing to live with a mere declaration because they believed that it would raise human rights consciousness around the world and in so doing restrain potential perpetrators of
abuse.[9] We can respect their achievement while remaining skeptical
about their faith. We have good reason to be doubtful about the preven-
tive impact of human rights codes. Yet if human rights has not stopped
the villains, it certainly has empowered bystanders and victims. Human
rights instruments have given bystanders and witnesses a stake in abuse
and oppression both within and beyond their borders, and this has
called forth an advocacy revolution, the emergence of a network of non-
governmental human rights organizations—Amnesty International
and Human Rights Watch being only the most famous—to pressure
states to practice what they preach.[10] Because of this advocacy revolution, victims have gained historically unprecedented power to make
their case known to the world.[11]

The advocacy revolution has broken the state's monopoly on the conduct of international affairs, enfranchising what has become known as
global civil society. Here too we can believe in progress even while remaining dubious about some of the achievement. The phrase "global
civil society" implies a cohesive moral movement when the reality is
fierce and disputatious rivalry among nongovernment organizations.
Global human rights consciousness, moreover, does not necessarily imply that the groups defending human rights actually believe the same
things. Many of these NGOs espouse the universalist language of human rights, but actually use it to defend highly particularist causes: the
rights of particular national groups or minorities or classes of persons.
There is nothing wrong with particularism in itself. Everyone's universalism ultimately anchors itself in a particular commitment to a spe-
cially important group of people whose cause is close to one's heart or
convictions. The problem is that particularism conflicts with universalism at the point at which one's commitment to a group leads one to

[9] René Cassin, *La Pensée et l'action* (Paris: Lalou, 1972); John P. Humphrey, *Human Rights
and the United Nations: A Great Adventure* (Dobbs Ferry, N.Y.: Transnational, 1984); Eleanor
Roosevelt, *On My Own* (London: Hutchinson, 1959), ch. 8; Mary Ann Glendon, *A World
Made New: Eleanor Roosevelt and the Universal Declaration of Human Rights* (New York: Random House, 2000).

[10] William Korey, *NGO's and the Universal Declaration of Human Rights* (New York: St.
Martin's Press, 1998); see also Margaret Keck and Kathryn Sikkink, *Activists beyond Borders:
Advocacy Networks in International Politics* (Ithaca: Cornell University Press, 1998).

[11] See, for example, Irina Ratushinskaya, *Grey Is the Colour of Hope* (New York: Knopf,
1988).

countenance human rights violations toward another group. Persons who care about human rights violations committed against Palestinians may not care so much about human rights violations committed by Palestinians against Israelis, and visa versa.

Human rights activism likes to portray itself as an antipolitics, in defense of universal moral claims designed to delegitimize "political," i.e., ideological or sectarian, justifications for the abuse of human beings. In practice, impartiality and neutrality are just as impossible as universal and equal concern for everyone's human rights. Human rights activism means taking sides, mobilizing constituencies powerful enough to force abusers to stop. As a consequence, effective human rights activism is bound to be partial and political. Yet at the same time, human rights politics is a politics disciplined or constrained by moral universals. The role of moral universalism is not to take activists out of politics, but to get activists to discipline their partiality—their conviction that one side is right—with an equal commitment to the rights of the other side.

Because human rights activists take it for granted that they represent universal values and universal interests, they have not always taken as much care as they might about the question of whether they truly represent the human interests they purport to defend. They are not elected by the victim groups they represent, and in the nature of things they cannot be. But this leaves unresolved their right to speak for and on behalf of the people whose rights they defend. A more acutely political, as opposed to moral, activism might be more attentive to the question of who activists represent and how far the right to represent extends. Few mechanisms of genuine accountability connect NGOs and the communities in civil society whose interests they seek to advance.[12]

Yet even if we grant that many NGOs are more particularist, and less accountable than they claim, many others perform an essential function. By monitoring human rights abuses and bringing these abuses to light, they keep state signatories of human rights conventions up to the mark, or at least expose the gap between promise and practice, rhetoric and reality. Without the advocacy revolution of the NGOs, in other words, it is likely that the passage of so many human rights instruments since 1945 would have remained a revolution on paper.

Extraterritorial moral activism predates the Universal Declaration,

---

[12] Kenneth Anderson, "After Seattle: NGO's and Democratic Sovereignty in an Era of Globalization," unpublished essay, Harvard Law School, autumn 2000. I am grateful to Ken Anderson for letting me see this paper.

of course. All human rights activism in the modern world properly traces its origins back to the campaigns to abolish the slave-trade and then slavery itself.[13] But the catastrophe of European war and genocide gave impetus to the ideal of moral intervention beyond national borders and to the moral proposition that a network of international activists could pressure and shame their own states into intervening in delinquent states in the name of universal values. Thanks to human rights advocacy international politics has been democratized, and the pressure that human rights advocates can bring to bear on state actors—witness the campaigns on behalf of Soviet Jewry, or the international struggle against apartheid—has forced most states to accept that their foreign policy must at least pay rhetorical attention to values, as well as interests. Indeed, human rights considerations are now increasingly used to make the claim that in cases where values point one way and interests the other, values should trump. The United Nations system itself is beginning to reflect this new reality. Until the 1960s, UN bodies were wary of criticizing the human rights behavior of member states.[14] The apartheid regime of South Africa was the first exception, and after this breach in the wall there came others: the denunciation of the Greek junta in the 1970s, and the critique of repression in the Eastern bloc in the 1980s. After forty years of deference toward the sovereignty of states, the United Nations decided in the 1990s to create its own cadre of human rights activists under the leadership of the High Commissioner for Human Rights.[15] The commissioner's office still lacks financial resources and real support from UN member states, and the commissioner only has the power to name and shame defaulting governments. Still, every time a state is denounced for its human rights record, it becomes harder for it to secure international loans or political and military help when it is in danger. Naming and shaming for human rights abuses now have real consequences.

Beyond the power to name and shame governments (and also private corporations) who violate human rights covenants, the international

---

[13] Lauren, *Evolution of International Human Rights,* p. 32; P. M. Kielstra, *The Politics of Slave Trade Suppression in Britain and France, 1814–48* (London: Macmillan, 2000).

[14] Korey, *NGO's and the Universal Declaration of Human Rights,* ch. 3.

[15] United Nations High Commissioner for Human Rights, Reports and Statements, Geneva, Switzerland, 1999. See also Tom Farer and Felice Gaer, "The UN and Human Rights: At the End of the Beginning," in Adam Roberts and Benedict Kingsbury, *United Nations, Divided World: The UN's Role in International Relations* (Oxford: Clarendon Press, 1993), pp. 240–96.

community has also created new instruments to punish violators. This is the enforcement revolution in human rights. The International Tribunal at Arusha secured the first convictions under the Genocide Convention since its promulgation in 1948. The prosecutors at the Hague have secured the first international convictions for war crimes since Nuremberg. The first international warrant for the arrest of a sitting head of state has been issued. The first forensic investigation of war crimes sites, immediately following a violation, was undertaken in Kosovo. These are important steps by any measure. The tribunal has done much to break the cycle of impunity in Rwanda, Bosnia, and now Kosovo. Each arrest of a suspect and each conviction by a tribunal help to substantiate the reality of a universal jurisdiction for crimes against humanity.[16] These tribunals, however, are temporary instruments created to respond to contingent catastrophes. The next step is the creation of a permanent International Criminal Tribunal. The statute for such a tribunal has been agreed on in Rome; and once ratified by a majority of states, it may finally be established, admittedly with its powers diluted and diminished, chiefly as a result of objections by the United States.

3. AMERICAN EXCEPTIONALISM

It is at this point, of course, that uncomfortable aspects of the human rights revolution reveal themselves, at least insofar as the United States is concerned. America's insistence on watering down the powers of the International Criminal Tribunal has opened up a significant rift between the United States and allies, like Britain and France, who can claim descent from the same family of rights traditions.[17] What bothers the American administration is not merely the prospect of seeing American military personnel brought before tendentious tribunals. Nor is American resistance to international human rights merely "rights narcissism"—the conviction that the land of Jefferson and Lincoln has nothing to learn from international rights norms.[18] It is that Americans

[16] Michael Ignatieff, *Virtual War: Kosovo and Beyond* (London: Chatto and Windus, 2000), pp. 115–37; Sara Sewall and Carl Kaysen (eds.), *The United States and the International Criminal Court* (New York: Rowman and Littlefield, 2000).

[17] Kenneth Roth, "The Court the US Doesn't Want," *New York Review,* November 19, 1998; see also David Rieff, "Court of Dreams," *New Republic,* September 7, 1998; and Geoffrey Robertson, *Crimes against Humanity: The Struggle for Global Justice* (London: Allen Lane, 1999), pp. 300–341.

[18] The phrase "rights narcissism" is my own and figures in my "Out of Danger," *Index on Censorship* 3 (1998): 98.

believe their rights derive their legitimacy from their own consent, as embodied in the U.S. Constitution. International rights covenants lack this element of national political legitimacy.[19] As a result, since the early 1950s, the American Congress has been reluctant to ratify international rights conventions. This ratification process—which, after all, is intended to vest these conventions with domestic political legitimacy—has often delayed full international implementation of the conventions or has introduced so many qualifications and reservations about American participation as to leave them weakened.

America's reluctant participation places it in a highly paradoxical relation to an emerging international legal order based on human rights principles. Since Eleanor Roosevelt chaired the committee that produced the Universal Declaration, America has promoted human rights norms around the world, while also resisting the idea that these norms apply to American citizens and American institutions. The utopia to which human rights activism aspires—an international legal order with the capacity to enforce penalties against states—is inimical to the American conception that rights derive their legitimacy from the exercise of national popular sovereignty.

Europeans and Canadians, for example, may feel that American death penalty statutes are a violation of the right to life in Article 3 of the UDHR, but a majority of Americans believe that such statutes are the expression of the democratically expressed will of the people.[20] Hence international human rights objections are both irrelevant and intrusive.[21]

4. HUMAN RIGHTS AND NATIONALISM

American congressional objections to international human rights instruments may seem to be an expression of American "exceptionalism" or "imperialism," depending on one's point of view. Yet Americans are hardly the only people to believe that their own civil and political rights

---

[19] Paul Kahn, "Hegemony," unpublished paper, Yale Law School, January 2000. I am indebted to Paul Kahn for letting me see this essay in advance of publication.

[20] David Rieff, "Death Row," *Los Angeles Times Book Review*, February 13, 2000; also H. A. Bedau (ed.), *The Death Penalty in America: Current Controversies* (New York: Oxford University Press, 1999); Amnesty International, *The Death Penalty: List of Abolitionist and Retentionist Countries* (London: Amnesty, 1999).

[21] Amnesty International, *Rights for All: Country Report, The USA* (London: Amnesty, 1998).

are both more legitimate and more valuable than the rights enshrined in international covenants. In most liberal democracies, citizens look first to their domestic rights and remedies, and only when these are exhausted or denied do they turn to human rights conventions and international bodies. National groups who do not have states of their own—Kurds, Kosovar Albanians, and Tamils—certainly make use of human rights language to denounce their oppression, but for ultimate remedy they seek statehood for themselves and the right to create a framework of political and legal protection for their people.

International human rights has furthered the growth of nationalism, since human rights covenants have endorsed the core claim of nationalist movements to collective self-determination. But colonial groups and oppressed minorities have put more faith in obtaining a state of their own than in the protection of international human rights regimes. The classic case of this preference for national rights rather than human rights is, of course, the state of Israel. The Universal Declaration was, in large measure, a response to the torment of the Jewish people. Yet the survivors' overwhelming desire to create a Jewish state, capable of defending Jews everywhere against oppression, reveals that they trusted more to the creation of a state of their own than to the uncertain benefits of universal human rights protection within other people's national states.

Those who stand most in need of human rights protection in the modern world—homeless, stateless peoples, minorities at the mercy of other ethnic or religious majorities—tend to seek collective self-determination, preferably in the form of a defensible state of their own or, if the situation allows, self-rule within an autonomist or federal association with another people. Collective self-government provides defensible rights, legitimized by popular sovereignty and enforced by local courts, police, and punishments. No wonder nationalist movements that promise this solution seem attractive to stateless, homeless, rightless peoples around the world.

Yet nationalism solves the human rights problems of the victorious national groups while producing new victim groups, whose human rights situation is made worse. Nationalists tend to protect the rights of majorities and deny the rights of minorities. Even if one grants that collective self-determination on nationalist lines is going to be the preference of most persecuted groups seeking rights protection in the modern world, there still remains an important place for universalist human rights regimes. Minorities need the right to appeal against particularist and unjust rights rulings by the ethnic majorities they live beside. This is especially the case—as in the example of Israel—where ethnic majorities rule peoples who are not citizens and who do not come under full constitutional protection of national laws. In places like the occupied territories of the West Bank, Palestinian subjects of Israeli military rule stand in need of international rights monitoring and domestic human rights scrutiny.

Even societies that do fully incorporate minorities into national rights regimes need the remedies provided by international human rights. All societies need a juridical source of legitimacy for the right to refuse legal but immoral orders. Human rights is one such source. The most essential message of human rights is that there are no excuses for the inhuman use of human beings. In particular, there is no valid justification for the abrogation of human rights on the grounds of national security, military necessity, or states of siege and emergency. At most, rights protections can be suspended in cases of ultimate necessity, but these suspensions of rights must be justified before legislatures and courts of law, and they must be temporary.

Another essential function of international human rights covenants, even in societies with well-ordered national rights regimes, is to provide a universalist vantage point from which to criticize and revise particularistic national law. The European Convention on human rights has provided this vantage-point for the national rights regimes of European states since 1952, and comparison between its standards and those of national states has worked to improve and advance the rights protection afforded by national legislation.

So this is where we are after fifty years of a human rights revolution. Most human beings depend for their rights on the states they live in; those who do not have states of their own aspire to one and in some cases are fighting for one. Yet even though the nation state remains the chief source of rights protection, international human rights movements and covenants have gained significant influence over national rights regimes. Although the "default settings" of the international order continue to protect state sovereignty, in practice the exercise of state sovereignty is conditional, to some degree, on observance of proper human rights behavior. When states fail in this regard, they render themselves subject to criticism, sanction, and, as a final resort, intervention.

5. Establishing the Limits of Human Rights

As international human rights has gained power and authority, its scope and remit have become increasingly blurred. What precise balance is to be struck between international human rights and state sovereignty? When is intervention justified to reverse human rights abuses in another state? Failure to provide coherent answers to these problems has resulted in an enduring uncertainty as to how far the writ of international human rights should run.

The juridical, advocacy, and enforcement revolutions have dramatically raised expectations, and it is unsurprising that the reality of human rights practice should disappoint. The rights and responsibilities implied in the discourse of human rights are universal, yet resources—of time and money—are finite. When moral ends are universal, but means are limited, disappointment is inevitable. Human rights activism would be less insatiable, and less vulnerable to disappointment, if activists could appreciate the degree to which rights language itself imposes—or ought to impose—limits upon itself.

The first limit is a matter of logic and formal consistency. Because the very purpose of rights language is to protect and enhance individual agency, rights advocates must, if they are to avoid contradicting their own principles, respect the autonomy of those agents. Likewise, at the collective level, rights language endorses the desire of human groups to rule themselves. If this is so, human rights discourse must respect the right of those groups to define the type of collective life they wish to lead, provided that this life meets the minimalist standards requisite to the enjoyment of any human rights at all.

Human rights activists accept this limit in theory—but tend to soften it into the necessarily vague requirement to display cultural sensitivity in the application of moral universals. In reality, the limit is something more. If human rights principles exist to validate individual agency and collective rights of self-determination, then human rights practice is obliged to seek consent for its norms and to abstain from interference when consent is not freely given. Only in strictly defined cases of necessity—where human life is at risk—can coercive human rights interventions be justified. These norms of informed consent operate inside liberal democratic states to protect human subjects from well-intentioned but potentially harmful medical interventions. The same rules of informed consent need to govern human rights interventions.

If, for example, religious groups determine that women should occupy a subordinate place within the rituals of the group, and this place is accepted by the women in question, there is no warrant to intervene on the grounds that human rights considerations of equality have been violated.[22] Human rights principles themselves imply that groups that do not actively persecute others or actively harm their own members should enjoy as much autonomy as the rule of law allows.[23]

Establishing the limits of human rights as a language of moral intervention is all the more important because at least one source of power that held Western human rights in check is now in ruins. There were two human rights cultures after 1945, not just one. The Communist rights tradition—which put primacy on economic and social rights—kept the capitalist rights tradition—emphasizing political and civil rights—from overreaching itself. Since the Helsinki Final Act of 1975, in which the Soviet bloc conceded the right of its citizens to have human rights organizations, there has been one global human rights culture. The collapse of communism leaves the West freer than before to undertake interventions in the affairs of delinquent or collapsed states. But these interventions have served to blur rather than clarify the proper line between the rights of states and the rights of citizens who may be oppressed within these states. The West has got ahead of itself, and it is time to redraw the balance. We may need less intervention, not more; more respect for state sovereignty, not less. This is the political dimension of the problem. But a cultural dimension ensues. As the West intervenes ever more frequently but ever more inconsistently in the affairs of other societies, the legitimacy of its rights standards is put into question. Human rights is increasingly seen as the language of a moral imperialism just as ruthless and just as self-deceived as the colonial hubris of yesteryear.

Activists who suppose that the Universal Declaration of Human Rights is a comprehensive list of all the desirable ends of human life fail to understand that these ends—liberty and equality, freedom and security, private property and distributive justice—conflict and, because they do, the rights that define them as entitlements are also in conflict. If rights conflict and there is no evident order of moral priority in rights

---

[22] Avishai Margalit and Moshe Halbertal, "Liberalism and the Right to Culture," *Social Research* 61, no. 3 (Fall 1994).

[23] Will Kymlicka, *Multicultural Citizenship* (Oxford: Clarendon Press, 1995), pp. 107–31.

claims, we cannot speak of rights as trumps.[24] The idea of rights as trumps implies that when rights are introduced into a political discussion, they serve to resolve the discussion. In fact, the opposite is the case. When political demands are turned into rights claims, there is a real risk that the issue at stake will become irreconcilable, since calling a claim a right is to call it non-negotiable, at least in popular parlance.[25] Compromise is not facilitated by the use of rights claim language. So if rights are not trumps, and if they create a spirit of non-negotiable confrontation, what is their use? At best, rights create a common framework, a common set of reference points that can assist parties in conflict to deliberate together. Common language, however, does not necessarily facilitate agreement. In the American abortion debate, for example, both sides agree that the inhuman use of human life should be prohibited and that human life is entitled to special legal and moral protections.[26] Yet this is hardly common ground at all, since the two sides disagree as to when human life commences and as to whether the claims of the mother or the unborn child should prevail. This example suggests that it is an illusion to suppose that the function of human rights is to define a higher realm of shared moral values that will assist contending parties to find common ground. Broad evaluative consensus about human rights may be a necessary condition for deliberative agreement, but it is not a sufficient one. Other political factors are essential for closure: shared exhaustion with the conflict, dawning mutual respect, joint mutual recognition—all these must be present, as well as common commitment to moral universals, if agreement is to be reached.

The larger illusion I want to criticize is that human rights is above politics, a set of moral trump cards whose function is to bring political disputes about competing claims to closure and conclusion. Shared human rights talk can do something to engender mutual respect and foster mutual recognition, provided that each side listens with respect to the other's particularist inflection of universal claims. Beyond that, rights language raises the stakes. It reminds disputants of the moral nature of their claims. When two sides recognize that the other side has a claim of

---

[24] Ronald Dworkin, *Taking Rights Seriously* (Cambridge, Mass.: Harvard University Press, 1977).

[25] Mary Ann Glendon, *Rights Talk: The Impoverishment of Political Discourse* (New York: Free Press, 1991).

[26] Ronald Dworkin, *Life's Dominion: An Argument about Abortion, Euthanasia, and Individual Freedom* (New York: Knopf, 1993).

right, the dispute ceases to be—in their eyes—a conflict between right and wrong and becomes a conflict between competing rights. The resolution of these competing rights claims never occurs in the abstract kingdom of ends, but in the kingdom of means. Human rights is nothing other than a politics, one that must reconcile moral ends to concrete situations and must be prepared to make painful compromises not only between means and ends, but between ends themselves.

But politics is not just about compromise and deliberation. Human rights language is also there to remind us that there are some abuses that are genuinely intolerable, and some excuses for these abuses that are insupportable. Rights talk, therefore, helps us to know when deliberation and compromise have become impossible. Hence, human rights talk is sometimes used to assemble the reasons and the constituencies necessary for the use of force. Given the conflictual character of rights, and given the fact that many forms of oppression will not answer to argument and deliberation, there are occasions, which must be strictly defined, when human rights as politics becomes a fighting creed, a call to arms.

6. Human Rights and Self-Determination

From being the insurgent creed of activists during the Cold War, human rights has become "main-streamed" into the policy framework of states, multilateral lending institutions like the World Bank, and the UN itself. The foreign policy rhetoric of most Western liberal states now repeats the mantra that national interests must be balanced by due respect for values, chief of which is human rights. But human rights is not just an additional item in the policy priorities of states. If taken seriously, human rights values put interests into question, interests such as sustaining a large export sector in a nation's defense industry, for example. It becomes incoherent for states like Britain and the United States to condemn Indonesia or Turkey for their human rights performance while providing their military with vehicles or weapons that can be used for the repression of civilian dissent. When values do not actually constrain interests, an "ethical foreign policy"—the self-proclaimed goal of Britain's Labour government—becomes a contradiction in terms.

This is not the only practical problem in reconciling values and interests in dealing with states that violate human rights. There is the additional conflict between furthering the human rights of individuals and maintaining the stability of the nation-state system. Why should stability be of concern to human rights activists? Simply because stable states provide the possibility for national rights regimes, and these remain the most important protector of individual human rights.

Democratic governments in the age of human rights have to reconcile dealing both with governments in power and with a dissident or oppressed opposition or an ethnic minority seeking self-determination. Many of these states face secessionist challenges, often backed up by terrorism. Other states face minority rights challenges that jeopardize the unity of the state. To be sure, oppressive states, faced with these challenges, usually exaggerate them and defend their repression on the grounds of ultimate necessity: *salus populi primus lex.* China, for example, justifies human rights abuses as the price required to maintain the unity of a continental nation state subject to many regional, ethnic, religious, and tribal pressures. Whenever human rights complaints are aired within earshot of the Chinese leadership, they are quick to waive the specter of civil war—in other words, to argue that furthering human rights and maintaining state stability are ultimately incompatible.

Much of this is special pleading in defense of the privileges and political monopoly of the party in power. Chinese human rights activists correctly reply that the best long-term guarantee of Chinese national unity is a democratic regime that guarantees human rights.[27] They are also correct to point out that trade liberalization and free markets do not necessarily bring human rights and democracy in their wake. It is quite conceivable to combine authoritarian politics with free markets, despotic rule with private property. When capitalism enters the gates of a closed society, it does not necessarily function as a Trojan horse for human rights. Human rights will come to authoritarian societies when activists risk their lives and create a popular and indigenous demand for these rights and when their activism receives consistent and forthright external support from influential nations.

We need not be detained by the special pleading of authoritarian, one-party regimes, but there is much more of a conflict between human rights and state stability when the regime in question is not oppressively authoritarian and when the human rights demands come in the form of a collective demand for territorial autonomy, self-rule, or secession. In these situations, Western states want to promote human rights,

---

[27] Wei Jing Sheng, "The Taste of the Spider," *Index on Censorship* 3 (1998): 30–38; see also U.S. Department of State, *1999 Country Reports on Human Rights: China.*

but not at the price of dismembering viable democracies and adding to the number of failed, collapsed, or disunited states in the world system. Most states in the post–Cold War era skate around this tension in the fundamental goals of their policy: both supporting human rights and propping up states whose stability is deemed to be essential.

Some human rights activists deny this conflict between state stability and human rights. They claim that the best guarantee of state stability has to be democracy, human rights, and fairness in the states in question. In the long run this may be true; but in the short term—where most governments actually live—democracy and human rights often conflict, and popular sovereignty for a majority is often achieved at the cost of ethnic cleansing for a minority. Sometimes the conflicts unleashed by the coming of democracy shatter the state altogether, plunging all human groups into a war of all against all.

The overwhelming problem of the post–Cold War world system has been the collapse of state order in three key sectors of the globe—the Balkans, the Great Lakes region of Africa, and the southern Islamic frontier of the former Soviet Union.[28] Obviously these regions have fragmented in part because of the flagrant human rights abuses committed by ethnic majority tyrannies that tried—and failed—to create stable nation states. But in part fragmentation also results from the destructive impact of demands for territorial autonomy and independence on the part of secessionist groups. Western governments watching the slide of these regions into endemic civil war are justified in concluding that restoring stability—even if it is authoritarian and undemocratic—matters more than either democracy or human rights. Stability, in other words, may count more than justice.

Most Western states are finessing this moral triage between rights and stability. They proclaim human rights as their goal, while aiding or investing in states with derisory human rights records. While this is usually seen as a problem of hypocrisy—not matching words to deeds—in fact it represents a fundamental conflict of principle.

The issues at stake can be illustrated by looking at the case of the Kurds. Promoting the human rights of Kurds and maintaining the territorial integrity of Turkey are not obviously compatible. For Kurds are not campaigning simply to improve their civic position as individuals,

---

[28]See Mary Kaldor, *New and Old Wars: Organized Violence in a Global Era* (London: Polity, 1999); see also Michael Ignatieff, *Blood and Belonging: Journeys into the New Nationalism* (London: Vintage, 1993).

but to achieve self-determination as a people. Kurdish human rights campaigns are not essentially individual and apolitical in character. They represent a demand for collective self-determination that challenges the governmental authority of Turkey, Syria, Iran, and Iraq. It is by no means obvious how autonomy for the Kurds can be reconciled in practice with the territorial integrity of these states. Because the West fails to face this conflict in its own principles, its interventions satisfy no one. The Turks regard Western human rights criticism as meddling in their internal affairs, while the Kurds regard our support for their struggle as false and disingenuous.

The Kurdish case also illustrates the political naiveté that so often diminishes the effectiveness of human rights advocacy. For too long human rights has been seen simply as a form of apolitical humanitarian rescue for oppressed individuals. Thus human rights advocates campaign on behalf of groups or individuals imprisoned or oppressed by the states in the region without squarely facing up to the political issue—which is how to find a constitutional framework in the four states that have a Kurdish minority that will guarantee their rights, without creating a dynamic toward independence that would drive the region into civil war. Such a framework would require the Security Council to convene a conference to redefine the constitutions and boundaries of four states. None of the states in question will submit to such interference. The only viable option is a long and persistent negotiation between Western governments and the nations in the region, aiming at relaxing the unitary national ideologies of the countries concerned so that minority groups like the Kurds can find ways to protect their own linguistic and historical heritage with forms of autonomy and constitutionally protected devolution.[29] At this point, of course, human rights values and state interests conflict, since Western states have a stronger interest in conciliating Turkey as a trusted ally in a volatile region than they do in pushing it to change its constitution. A further alibi for Western inaction is intense and debilitating Kurdish factionalism. It is difficult to represent the interests of a victim community when its elites waste their energies fighting among themselves, yet neither independent human rights organizations nor Western governments have much capacity to put an end to the Kurdish power struggle.

Since large-scale constitutional reordering in the Kurdish region is

---

[29] On Kurdistan, see Ignatieff, *Blood and Belonging,* pp. 176–212; P. G. Kreyenbroek and S. Sperl, *The Kurds* (London: Routledge, 1991).

rightly seen as an illegitimate interference in the sovereignty of established states, Western states with human rights agendas are forced back to a strategy of quiet diplomacy that places two-way bets: one on the government in power, another, smaller bet on the oppressed minority. It discretely aids both, while undermining each, with consequences that actually devalue the legitimacy of its own moral language.

The same inability to reconcile human rights values with maintaining state stability has bedeviled Western policy toward Indonesia. Since 1975 journalists and human rights activists have denounced the Indonesian seizure and occupation of the former Portuguese colony of East Timor. But as long as Indonesia was regarded as a bulwark of the East Asian security system of the United States, as long as the territorial integrity of the huge island archipelago was seen as the overriding objective of Western policy, nothing was done to stop Indonesian oppression of the East Timorese. How then are we to explain why in 1998 the West suddenly began to take a sustained interest in the human rights situation in East Timor? With the collapse of the Soviet regime, there was no longer a credible Communist threat in East Asia to justify further appeasement of the Indonesian military. Secondly, the overthrow of Suharto by the students and the East Asian economic crisis weakened the Indonesian regime so that it could no longer resist human rights pressure. Finally, an indigenous human rights movement, championed by able and courageous individuals, was making the Indonesian human rights record a matter of real embarrassment in the international arena, at a time when Indonesia needed international credits and diplomatic support. This confluence of pressures led Indonesia to accede to demands for a referendum in East Timor, which Western observers duly supervised. But the UN Security Council supposed that it could help the East Timorese achieve self-determination, while doing nothing to protect them from the wrath of the pro-Indonesian militias. In effect, the Security Council granted their claim to self-determination without respecting their need for security. The consequences were easy to predict: the massacre of civilians, the destruction of an already poor country, and finally the inevitable dispatch of a peace-keeping force onto what remains the sovereign territory of Indonesia.

Have we sufficiently attended to the probable consequences of this intervention for the territorial integrity of Indonesia? If East Timor successfully secedes, how many other parts of a complex multiethnic, multilingual, multiconfessional state will also seek independence? It may prove impossible to reconcile self-determination for the East Timorese with the long-term territorial integrity of Indonesia as it now exists. Even accepting that East Timor is a special case—a former colony illegally annexed—we seem not to understand that human rights advocacy is contributing to the possible disintegration, at high human cost, of the state of Indonesia. If it is said that its disintegration is inevitable anyway, then it still follows that we need a policy that prevents such disintegration from jeopardizing what we intervened to safeguard in the first place, namely the human rights of ordinary people. For we can be sure that the Indonesian military will not go without a bloody struggle, and we can be certain that self-determination for some groups will be purchased with the blood of the minorities in their midst.

To repeat, the problem in Western human rights policy is that by promoting ethnic self-determination we may actually endanger the stability that is a precondition for protecting human rights. Having started the ball rolling in Indonesia, we need to help Indonesians decide where it should stop: whether secessionist claims by other minorities can be contained within a devolved Indonesian democracy, or whether some of these claims will have to result, one day, in statehood.

Beyond the specifics of the Indonesian case, human rights activists need to face up to the fact that human rights advocacy can set in train secessionist pressures that do threaten existing states and may make the human rights situation of ordinary people worse rather than better in the short term. The painful truth is that national self-determination is not always favorable to individual human rights, and democracy and human rights do not necessarily advance hand in hand.

7. Human Rights, Democracy, and Constitutionalism

In order to reconcile democracy and human rights, Western policy will have to put more emphasis not on democracy alone but on constitutionalism, the entrenchment of a balance of powers, judicial review of executive decisions, and enforceable minority rights guarantees.[30] Democracy without constitutionalism is simply ethnic majority tyranny.

In the face of secessionist claims, which threaten the territorial in-

---

[30] Fareed Zakaria, "The Rise of Illiberal Democracy," *Foreign Affairs* (November/December 1997): 22–43; Louis Henkin, *Constitutionalism, Democracy and Foreign Affairs* (New York: Columbia University Press, 1990); see also Anthony Lewis, "Yes to Constitutions and Judges That Enforce Them," *International Herald Tribune,* January 7, 2000.

tegrity of nation states, human rights activists will have to do more than merely champion arrested human rights activists. Nor can they remain neutral in the face of secessionist claims. They will have to develop criteria for understanding which secessionist claims deserve full independence and statehood and which ones can be solved by means of regional autonomy and political devolution. Where groups have sound historical reasons for believing that they cannot live in security and peace alongside another group inside a state, they may have a necessary claim to secession and statehood, based on their right to self-defense. But such claims are not justified everywhere. Where there is no such history of bad blood, no recent history of intercommunal violence, as for example between Canada and the Québecois, between the English and the Scots, secessionist claims may best be met with devolution and autonomy within the existing nation state. Devolutionist solutions tend to protect minority rights more effectively than separationist ones. In a territory where an ethnic majority has self-government, it remains bound by the federal constitution signed with the other ethnic majority to respect its own minorities. When outright separation occurs, this pattern of mutual rights supervision no longer takes place within shared institutions.

Where a state is democratic, secessionist demands for self-determination should be contained within the framework of that state wherever possible; but where a state is not democratic, where it opposes all devolution to minorities and denies them protection of their educational, linguistic, and cultural rights, secession and independence become inevitable.[31]

Yet the case of Sri Lanka, where there has been a secessionist movement among the minority Tamil population since 1983 against the Singalese-dominated government, indicates just how difficult it is to get the balance right between minority rights, state sovereignty, and individual human rights. The two populations did not have a long history of intercommunal violence before or after national independence in 1947. There was substantial, and deeply resented, discrimination against the Tamil language together with denial of access to state employment. But violence—in which both sides then took part—did not begin until the 1980s. To reward a secessionist claim with independence now would be

---

[31] Robert McCorquodale, "Human Rights and Self-Determination," in Mortimer Sellers (ed.), *The New World Order: Sovereignty, Human Rights and the Self-Determination of Peoples* (Oxford: Berg, 1996), pp. 9–35; see also Hurst Hannum, *Autonomy, Sovereignty and Self-Determination: The Accommodation of Conflicting Rights* (Philadelphia: University of Pennsylvania Press, 1996).

to reward a terrorist movement with a great deal of blood on its hands. It would also transfer political control over the Tamil people to the hands of a group with no democratic credentials. In so doing, secession might confer collective self-determination on the Tamils in the form of single party dictatorship, and this would achieve self-determination for the Tamils as a people, while delivering them up as individuals to tyranny. In these circumstances, the best guarantee of individual Tamil rights and of collective protection of their language and culture would not be the separate statehood demanded by the Tigers, but instead substantial self-government and autonomy for the Tamil people within the framework of a democratic Sri Lankan state no longer dominated by the Singala majority.[32]

This example should indicate, first, that there are substantial dangers for human rights of individuals if the international community were to concede statehood to secessionist groups who back their campaign with terror; second, that any resolution of these minority rights claims requires more supple, less unitary and intransigent states. Indeed, the problem is not just getting the state and the insurgent minority to respect human rights. A long-term solution requires an institutional setting in which the state is no longer communalized, no longer seen as the monopoly of any particular confessional, ethnic, or racial group, in which the state is reinvented as the arbiter of a civic pact between ethnic groups. Constitutionalism and the civic state are the institutional sine qua non of effective human rights protection.

Constitutionalism implies loosening up the unitary nation state— one people, one nation, one state—so that it can respond adequately to the demands of minorities for protection of their linguistic and cultural heritage and for their right to self-government. But communalization becomes inevitable in poor countries where the state—with its resources, perquisites, and privileges—remains the major source, not merely of political power, but of social and economic prestige as well. As long as economic, social, and political power is concentrated in the state, states will become the monopoly of the ethnic majority that holds democratic power. Ethnic conflict is at its most intense in societies, like the former Communist state of Yugoslavia or a desperately poor state like Rwanda, where control of state power is the unique source of all social, political, and economic privilege. Breaking the zero-sum game of

---

[32] International Center for Ethnic Studies, *Sri Lanka: The Devolution Debate* (Colombo: ICES, 1998); Robert Rotberg (ed.), *Creating Peace in Sri Lanka: Civil War and Reconciliation* (Washington, D.C.: Brookings, 1999).

ethnic competition for state power requires enlarging social and eco-nomic sources of privilege independent of the state, so that even if mi-nority groups can never prevail democratically against majorities, they can secure independent sources of wealth, privilege, and prestige. If so, they do not need to seek secession and can remain within a state demo-cratically dominated by another ethnic group. The South African white minority, for example, has a secure place within the institutions of the economy and society of a black South Africa. Their power in the econ-omy effectively protects them from the adverse effects of majority rule. An independent civil society, therefore, is the essential economic basis for multiethnic pluralism, but also for constitutionalism. Being com-mitted to constitutionalism and human rights, therefore, means a com-prehensive strategy of economic and social development as well, aimed at creating an independent and plural civil society. Only then can states create the checks and balances that protect minorities against ethnic majority tyranny.

Beyond making the nation state more flexible toward minority rights claims, the international order needs to strengthen multinational and regional organizations so that they can grant rights of participation to nations and autonomist regions. This allows nations who do not have states on their own to enter the international arena and advance their in-terests without having to insist on full sovereignty and further fragment the state system. The European Community allows Catalans, Scots, Basques, and other nonstate peoples to participate in fora promoting the development of their regions. The Organization for Cooperation and Se-curity in Europe (OSCE) helps substate groups and national minorities to find representation and protection in the international arena. The OSCE's minority rights commissioner has done pioneering work with the Baltic states, helping them to revise their citizenship and language laws in order to protect the rights of the Russian minority.[33] In this way, three small states maintain their national independence without creat-ing a *casus belli* with their former imperial occupier, while minorities in-side these states know that powerful European institutions are keeping watch on their interests.[34]

In the world now emerging, state sovereignty will become less

[33] Walter Kemp (ed.), *Quiet Diplomacy in Action: The OSCE High Commissioner on Na-tional Minorities* (Amsterdam: Kluwer, 2000).

[34] John Packer, "Problems in Defining Minorities," in D. Fottreell and B. Bowring (eds.), *Minority and Group Rights in the New Millennium* (Amsterdam: Kluwer, 1999), pp. 223–74; see also *The Oslo Recommendations Regarding the Linguistic Rights of National Minorities* (The Hague: Foundation on Inter-Ethnic Relations, 1998).

absolute and national identity less unitary. As a result, human rights within states will be protected by overlapping jurisdictions. Regional rights bodies—like the OSCE—will have more oversight over minority rights problems in member states, and they will do so simply because emerging states conclude that surrendering some of their sovereignty on these issues is worth the price of full admission to the European club. As sovereignty is more permeable and more controlled, minorities will feel less afraid, and therefore less responsive to secessionist appeals.

Yet it is utopian to look forward to an era beyond state sovereignty. Instead of regarding state sovereignty as an outdated principle, destined to pass away in the era of globalization, we need to appreciate the extent to which state sovereignty is the basis of order in the international system and that national constitutional regimes represent the best guarantee of human rights. This is an unfamiliar, even controversial principle within a human rights community that for fifty years has looked on the state as the chief danger to the human rights of individuals. And so it proved in the age of totalitarian tyranny. Today, however, the chief threat to human rights comes not from tyranny alone, but from civil war and anarchy. Hence, we are rediscovering the necessity of state order as a guarantee of rights. It can be said with certainty that the liberties of citizens are better protected by their own institutions than by the well-meaning interventions of outsiders.

So human rights might best be strengthened in today's world not by weakening already weak and overburdened states but by strengthening them wherever possible. State failure cannot be rectified by human rights activism on the part of NGOs. What is required when states fail is altogether more ambitious: regional powers brokering peace accords between factions; peace-keeping forces to ensure that truces stick; multilateral assistance to build national institutions, like tax-collection, police forces, courts, and basic welfare services. The aim of the exercise is to create states strong enough and legitimate enough to recover their monopoly over the means of violence, to impose order and create the rule of law. Authoritarian rule usually endangers human rights less than anarchy and civil war do. Societies that accord their citizens a degree of personal security are preferable to no government at all.

It is not merely that democracy may not be possible; there may also be an objection in principle as to our right to insist on it. In *The Law of Peoples,* John Rawls argues that liberal states do not have a right to impose their idea of constitutional democracy on others. There may be other nondemocratic, but hierarchical and ordered states whose internal orders do provide the rule of law and some elementary respect for human rights. Rawls imagines a society called Kazanistan that debars full political participation for those not of Muslim faith but tolerates the religious and private rights of other religious and ethnic minorities. Such a state lives at peace within the international system, even if it does not meet all criteria of human rights equality. There is nothing in Rawls's view—or mine—that would mandate interference in the domestic affairs of this state. Liberal democrats, Rawls argues, need to accept that state forms other than their own may provide adequate procedural fairness and minority rights protection.[35]

This is not the only lesson that human rights activists from Western liberal democracies may need to learn. The other lesson is that universality properly implies consistency. It is inconsistent to impose international human rights constraints on other states unless we accept the jurisdiction of these instruments on our own. Canadians have no business telling Latvia, Lithuania, and Estonia what to do about Russian minority rights unless they accept an obligation to subscribe to OSCE standards in their own treatment of French and aboriginal minorities. Americans have no business lecturing other countries about their human rights performance unless they are prepared to at least enter into dialogue with international rights bodies about sensitive areas—capital punishment and the conditions in American prisons, for example—which may be in contravention of international rights norms. The obligation to at least engage in dialogue is clear, and the obligation that nations actually practice what they preach is the minimum requirement for a legitimate and effective human rights policy.

8. HUMAN RIGHTS AND MILITARY INTERVENTION

Where all order in a state has disintegrated and its people have been delivered up to a war of all against all, or where a state is engaging in gross, repeated, and systematic violence against its own citizens, the only effective way to protect human rights is direct military intervention. Since 1991, this "right of humanitarian intervention" has been asserted, most loudly by the French, but also by other governments seeking to

[35] John Rawls, *The Law of Peoples* (Cambridge, Mass.: Harvard University Press, 1999), pp. 75–78.

justify interventions in Iraq, Bosnia, and Kosovo.[36] The armed forces of
the Western powers have been busier since 1989 than they ever were
during the Cold War, and the legitimizing language for this activity has
been the defense of human rights. Yet the juridical status of a right of
intervention is exceedingly unclear.[37] While the UN Charter calls on
states to proclaim human rights, it also prohibits the use of force against
other states and forbids internal interference. The human rights
covenants that states have signed since 1945 have implied that state
sovereignty is conditional on adequate human rights observance. The
gulf in international law between the nonintervention language of the
charter and the interventionist implications of human rights covenants
has never been bridged.

Drafters of the Universal Declaration explicitly assumed that the
Declaration would warrant interventions where human rights abuse was
flagrant. As René Cassin, one of the drafters of the Declaration, put it in
1946, "when repeated or systematic violation of human rights by a
given state within its borders results in a threat to international peace
(as was the case of the Third Reich after 1933), the Security Council has
a right to intervene and a duty to act."[38]

In practice, of course, states have been exceedingly wary of the right
of intervention, and when they have intervened, they have done so as a
temporary measure. Thus where a state fails in its elementary obligations—maintaining physical security and an adequate food supply for
its population—or where its army and police are engaged in sustained
violence against minority or dissident political groups, it may temporarily forfeit its rights of sovereign immunity within the international system. But the forfeiture is temporary. Northern Iraq remains
under the formal jurisdiction of the government in Baghdad, while in
practice Allied aircraft patrolling overhead prevent any effective exercise of Iraqi sovereignty in the Kurdish enclave. Kosovo, for example, is
under UN protectorate, but UN Security Council Resolution 1244 explicitly reaffirms that the territory remains under Yugoslav sovereignty.

[36] Bernard Kouchner, *Le Malheur des autres* (Paris: Grasset, 1993); Kofi Annan, *The Question of Intervention* (New York: United Nations, 1999).

[37] Gerry J. Simpson, "The Diffusion of Sovereignty: Self-Determination in the Post-
Colonial Age," in Sellers, *The New World Order*, p. 55; Christopher Greenwood, "International Law, Just War and the Conduct of Modern Military Operations," in Patrick Mileham
and Lee Willet (eds.), *Ethical Dilemmas of Military Interventions* (London: RIIA, 1999),
pp. 1–9.

[38] M. G. Johnson and Janusz Symonides, *The Universal Declaration of Human Rights: A
History of Its Creation and Implementation, 1948–1998* (Paris: UNESCO, 1998), p. 32.

This idea that interventions do not eradicate or supersede the sovereignty of the defaulting party, merely suspend it, is our attempt to provide universal human rights protection to endangered groups within states without abrogating the sovereignty of that state. We hold onto the importance of state sovereignty for another reason, which is to prevent intervention from becoming imperial. Both our human rights norms and the UN Charter outlaw the use of military power for territorial aggrandizement or occupation. Hence our military interventions are intended to be self-limiting. We are not intervening to take over territory, but to bring peace and stability and then get out; our mandate is to restore self-determination, not to extinguish it. Managing these conflicting tensions has not been easy. We are now firmly ensconced in long-term protectorates in Bosnia, Kosovo, and East Timor, behaving like imperial police with imperial obligations and no exit in sight.

Looking at the interventions we have undertaken since the end of the Cold War, who can say that we have been successful? In Bosnia, the intervention has not created a stable self-governing society. Instead we have frozen an ethnic civil war in place. We have not succeeded in anchoring a human rights culture in shared institutions.

Intervention, instead of reinforcing respect for human rights, is consuming their legitimacy, both because our interventions are unsuccessful and because they are inconsistent. And we cannot solve our problem by not intervening at all. In 1994, the UN Security Council stood by and did nothing while hundreds of thousands of Tutsis were massacred by a concerted, organized, and centrally directed plan of genocide organized by the Hutu-dominated government of Rwanda. Failing to intervene in Rwanda has proved even more damaging to the standing and credibility of human rights principles than late and partial interventions in Iraq, Bosnia, and Kosovo.

So what are we to do? If human rights are universal, human rights abuses everywhere are our business. But we simply cannot intervene everywhere. If we do not ration our resources, how can we possibly be effective? Rationing is both inevitable and necessary, yet there needs to be a clear basis to justify these decisions.

Three criteria have emerged in the late 1990s to ration interventions: (1) the human rights abuses at issue have to be gross, systematic, and pervasive; (2) they have to be a threat to international peace and security in the surrounding region; and (3) military intervention has to stand a real chance of putting a stop to the abuses.

In practice, a fourth criterion comes into play: the region in question must be of vital interest, for cultural, strategic, or geopolitical reasons, to one of the powerful nations in the world. Most states abide by the rough and ready rule that military intervention is only warranted when a gross and persistent human rights crisis is simultaneously a threat to their own national security interests or those of their most important allies. Intervention in Kosovo was justified on this mixture of human rights and national interest grounds: the human rights violations endured by the Kosovars threatened to destabilize Albania, Macedonia, and Montenegro and constituted a threat to the peace and security of the region.

The national interest criterion is supposed to limit the ambit of moral concern, in fact, to trump values. But in Kosovo and Bosnia, values and interests were nearly indistinguishable. The NATO powers intervened to make values prevail, to safeguard the territorial integrity of neighboring states, and, most important of all, to demonstrate the credibility of NATO when faced with a challenge from a defiant leader of a small state.

But values and interests do not always point policy in the same direction. The idea of national interest implies that where gross human rights abuses do *not* threaten the peace and security of a region, military intervention is not warranted. Burma's repression of civilian dissent may be a clear violation of international human rights norms, but so long as its military rulers do not constitute a threat to their neighbors, they run no risk of military intervention.

There are cases, however, where purely domestic repression rises to such a level that while interests say: "Stay out," values cry: "Go in." The Rwandan genocide ought to have been such a case, but since Western countries could not articulate a pressing national interest to undertake the risks involved in military action, they stood by and watched 800,000 people die, leaving many Africans to conclude that our supposed commitment to universal values was fatally compromised by racial partiality. In reality, Rwanda was never a purely internal genocide, and our failure to stop it is a direct cause of the widening collapse of state order in the whole of central Africa.

The Rwandan case illustrates that the line between internal and external conflict is hard to draw; that the national interest criterion that keeps us from interfering is not so clear as its defenders claim it to be;

and, finally, that atrocities may be so terrible that we are bound to intervene even when they do not impinge on any direct national interest.

Even when a state's domestic behavior is not a clear and present danger to the international system, it is a reliable predictor that it is likely to be so in the future. Consider the example of Hitler's regime, 1933–38, or Stalin's in the same period. In hindsight, there seems no doubt that Western governments' failure to sanction or even condemn their domestic policies encouraged both dictators to believe that their international adventures would go unpunished and unresisted.

So the line between purely domestic human rights abuses and those that threaten international peace and security is unclear, and the deferred or future costs of remaining silent about domestic abuses can be terrible indeed. Yet the rule against intervening in other people's states protects weak states against stronger ones and guarantees a minimum degree of equality between national communities in the world arena. Moreover, the nonintervention rule acts as a restraint on intemperate, premature, and ill-judged forms of coercion. It gives time for sanctions, diplomacy, and negotiation to work. But if they fail, what then? There are no peaceful diplomatic remedies when we are dealing with a Hitler, a Stalin, a Saddam, or a Pol Pot.

If force is an inescapable feature of human rights protection, the question then becomes whether we need to change the default setting of the international system, which is currently set against intervention. Most small states believe that any formalized right of intervention would constitute an encouragement to intervention that would in turn erode the sovereignty of rights-observing and rights-violating states alike. But those in favor believe that the international system needs to formalize in words what it already believes in practice: that state sovereignty is conditional on human rights performance and that, where this performance threatens international peace and security, the Security Council should have the right to mandate a graduated set of coercive responses ranging from sanctions to full-scale military intervention. The failure to formalize a right of intervention under the UN system simply means that coalitions of the willing who wish to intervene will do so by bypassing the authorizing process of the UN altogether.[39]

[39] Advisory Council on International Affairs, "Humanitarian Intervention" (Amsterdam, 2000; see www.aiv-advice.nl); also Danish Institute of International Affairs, "Humanitarian Intervention: Legal and Political Aspects" (Copenhagen, 1999).

Changing the default of the international system may or may not be desirable. In practice, there is as little chance of a change in the UN Charter language on intervention as there is of substantive Security Council veto reform or enlargement. We are thus stuck with enforcing human rights in the twenty-first century with an international system drafted by the victors of 1945. As a result, interventions will rarely command international consensus because the institutions do not exist to create such consensus. Human rights may be universal, but support for coercive enforcement of their norms will never be universal. Because interventions will lack full legitimacy, they will have to be limited and partial, and because they will have to be limited and partial, they will only be partially successful.

9. MEANS AND ENDS

The legitimacy of human rights standards in the new century will be further compromised by the gulf that has opened up between the universalistic values we proclaim and the risk-averse means we choose to defend them. Since the end of the Cold War, Western nations, acting through the Security Council, have repeatedly promised to protect civilians caught in the middle of civil wars or menaced by rogue regimes. Such promises were made by the UN military mission to Rwanda, by the UN peace-keepers in Srebrenica.[40] In both cases, large populations trusted our moral promises, and their trust was horribly betrayed. I do not need to rehearse the Srebrenica catastrophe here.[41] A comprehensive UN report to the Secretary General has already drawn the necessary lessons: if the UN offers to protect civilians in safe havens, its member states must provide heavy armor and air-cover and issue robust rules of engagement that allow attacking forces to be engaged and repulsed. This is not a job for lightly armed peace-keepers. Indeed, peace-keeping itself is out of date. It has a limited role in the supervision of truce and border lines established after conflicts between states. Most of the wars

---

[40] On the UN military role in Rwanda, see Romeo Dallaire, "The End of Innocence: Rwanda, 1994," in Jonathan Moore (ed.), *Hard Choices: Moral Dilemmas in Humanitarian Intervention* (New York: Rowman and Littlefield, 1998), pp. 71–87.

[41] UN Office of the Secretary General, "Srebrenica Report," pursuant to UNGA Resolution 53/35 (1998), November 15, 1999; see also "Report of the Panel on UN Peace Operation," UN General Assembly, August 21, 2000.

since 1989 are internal conflicts between crumbling or disintegrating state armies and a variety of insurgent militias. Both sides use ethnic cleansing as a weapon of war in the drive to create defensible territories with ethnically homogenous populations. In these conditions, there is not only no peace to keep, but no credible position of neutrality either. In these situations, human rights protection can only be undertaken as part of peace-enforcement operations in which the international community aligns with the side more nearly in the right and uses military force robustly to stop human rights abuse and create conditions for the reestablishment of stable state order in the region.

Any military or humanitarian intervention amounts to a moral promise to persons in need. If we make promises of this sort, we owe it ourselves and those we intend to help to devise the military strategy, rules of engagement, and chain of command necessary to make good on our promises. Our failure to do so—in Rwanda and in Bosnia—has undermined the credibility of human rights values in zones of danger around the world. Innocent civilians now have no good reason to trust any moral promise made by UN agencies, especially its peace-keepers.

10. INTERVENTION AS A REWARD FOR VIOLENCE

Intervention is also problematic because we are not necessarily coming to the rescue of pure innocence. Intervention frequently requires us to side with one party in a civil war, and the choice frequently requires us to side with parties who are themselves guilty of human rights abuses.

The early warning systems of our democracies only sound the alarm when victims turn to terror and reprisal. For all the earnest talk about the importance of early intervention and prevention, the international community rarely commits resources to a problem before violence has broken out. But this in turn compromises the legitimacy of human rights interventions, for they appear to require violations of human rights for them to occur. The Kosovo Liberation Army committed human rights abuses against Serbian civilians and personnel in order to trigger reprisals, which would in turn force the international community to intervene on their behalf.[42] The KLA's success between 1997 and

[42] See Michael Ignatieff, "The Dream of Albanians," *New Yorker,* January 11, 1999; see also Michael Ignatieff, "Balkan Physics," *New Yorker,* May 10, 1999; and Human Rights

1999 was a vintage demonstration of how to exploit the human rights conscience of the West in order to incite an intervention that resulted eventually in guerrilla victory.

For several years, the West hesitated before the choice it had to make. It could either sit by and watch Kosovo descend into full-scale civil war, which threatened to destabilise Albania, Macedonia, or Montenegro, or it could intervene and attempt to control the roll-out of Kosovan self-determination. Gradually, it chose the second option. But this military intervention, when it came in March 1999, then unleashed a genuine human rights disaster: the forcible eviction of 800,000 Kosovan citizens to Albania and Macedonia, followed by the massacre of up to 10,000 of those who remained.

The Western allies said they were waging a war for the sake of human rights. In reality, they were dragged into a war by an oppressed ethnic majority whose guerrilla army itself committed human rights abuses. Having been dragged into a war, the West then found itself unable to stop a flood of human rights abuses unleashed as a response to intervention. And even now, the West hesitates over the ultimate question of whether Kosovo should achieve full status as an independent state. Kosovan Albanians who feel that the human rights abuses they have suffered at the hands of the Serbs validate their claim to statehood now feel betrayed by the West; while the West feels equally betrayed by the human rights abuses—the wholesale eviction of Serbs—that have followed the liberation of Kosovo. This enormously complicates the issue of Kosovo's final status, for granting Kosovars full independence appears to reward a secessionist movement that used terror. An indefinite UN protectorate in Kosovo seems the only solution, since it postpones the necessity of deciding Kosovo's final status.[43]

Some human rights activists profess to be untroubled by the West's assumption of an unlimited and indefinite "human rights protectorate" in the whole Balkan region. They believe a profound and long-term shift of the balance of power away from nation states is underway. For many human rights activists, state sovereignty is an anachronism in a global

Watch, *Human Rights Abuses in Kosovo* (New York: Human Rights Watch, 1993); *Humanitarian Law Violations in Kosovo* (New York: Human Rights Watch, 1998); *A Week of Terror in Drenica: Humanitarian Law Violations in Kosovo* (New York: Human Rights Watch, 1999).

[43] Independent International Commission on Kosovo, *The Kosovo Report* (New York: Oxford University Press, 2000).

world. They wish to see ever more global oversight, ever more power to the international human rights community, ever more human rights protectorates. But is this wise? All forms of power are open to abuse, and there is no reason why power that legitimizes itself in the name of human rights should not end up as open to abuse as any other. Those who will end up with more power may only be those who have power already: the coalitions of the willing, the Western nations with the military might necessary for any successful "human rights" intervention.

The only outcome in Kosovo consistent with our principles is one that moves the province toward effective self-government by its own people and away from administration by UN, NATO, and European Community personnel. Either we believe in self-determination or we don't. A prolonged imperial administration of the south Balkans, justified in the name of human rights, will actually end up violating the very principles it purports to defend.

So, to summarise the political dimensions of the human rights crisis: we are intervening in the name of human rights as never before, but our interventions are sometimes making matters worse. Our interventions, instead of reinforcing human rights, are slowly consuming their legitimacy as a universalistic basis for foreign policy.

The crisis of human rights relates first of all to our failure to be consistent—to apply human rights criteria to the strong as well as to the weak; second, to our related failure to reconcile individual human rights with our commitment to self-determination and state-sovereignty; and third, to our inability, once we intervene on human rights grounds, to successfully create the legitimate institutions that alone are the best guarantee of human rights protection.

These problems of consistency have consequences for the legitimacy of human rights standards themselves. Non-Western cultures look at the partial and inconsistent way we enforce and apply human rights principles and conclude that there is something wrong with the principles themselves. The political failure, in other words, has cultural consequences. It has led the cultures of the non-Western world to view human rights as nothing more than a justification for Western moral imperialism. Failure to be consistent in enforcement and clear about the boundaries of state sovereignty has led to an intellectual and cultural challenge to the universality of the norms themselves. This will be the subject of my second lecture.

II. HUMAN RIGHTS AS IDOLATRY

Fifty years after its proclamation, the Universal Declaration of Human Rights has become the sacred text of what Elie Wiesel has called a "world-wide secular religion."[1] UN Secretary General Kofi Annan has called the Declaration the "yardstick by which we measure human progress." Nobel Laureate Nadine Gordimer has described it as "the essential document, the touchstone, the creed of humanity that surely sums up all other creeds directing human behavior."[2] Human rights has become the major article of faith of a secular culture that fears it believes in nothing else. It has become the lingua franca of global moral thought, as English has become the lingua franca of the global economy.

The question I want to ask about this rhetoric is this: if human rights is a set of beliefs, what does it mean to believe in it? Is it a belief like a faith? Is it a belief like a hope? Or is it something else entirely?

Human rights is misunderstood, I shall argue, if it is seen as a "secular religion." It is not a creed; it is not a metaphysics. To make it so is to turn it into a species of idolatry: humanism worshipping itself. Elevating the moral and metaphysical claims made on behalf of human rights may be intended to increase its universal appeal. In fact, it has the opposite effect, raising doubts among religious and non-Western groups who do not happen to be in need of Western secular creeds.

It may be tempting to relate the idea of human rights to propositions like the following: that human beings have an innate or natural dignity, that they have a natural and intrinsic self-worth, that they are sacred. The problem with these propositions is that they are not clear and they are controversial. They are not clear because they confuse what we wish men and women to be with what we empirically know them to be. On occasion, men and women, for example, behave with inspiring dignity. But that is not the same thing as saying that all human beings have an innate dignity or even a capacity to display it. Because these ideas about dignity, worth, and human sacredness appear to confuse what is with what ought to be, they are controversial, and because they are controversial they are likely to fragment commitment to the practical responsibilities entailed by human rights instead of strengthening them. Moreover, they are controversial because each version of them

---

[1] Elie Wiesel, "A Tribute to Human Rights," in Y. Danieli et al. (eds.), *The Universal Declaration of Human Rights: Fifty Years and Beyond* (Amityville, N.Y.: Baywood, 1999), p. 3.

[2] Nadine Gordimer, "Reflections by Nobel Laureates," in Danieli et al., *Universal Declaration of Human Rights*, p. vii.

must make metaphysical claims about human nature that are intrinsically contestable. Some people will have no difficulty thinking human beings are sacred, because they happen to believe in the existence of God the Father and believe He created Mankind in His likeness. People who do not believe in God must either reject that human beings are sacred or believe they are sacred on the basis of a secular use of religious metaphor that a religious person will find unconvincing. Foundational claims of this sort divide, and these divisions cannot be resolved in the way humans usually resolve their arguments, by means of discussion and compromise. Far better, I would argue, to forego these kinds of foundational arguments altogether and seek to build support for human rights on the basis of what such rights actually *do* for human beings.

While the foundations for human rights belief may be contestable, the prudential grounds for believing in human rights protection are much more secure. People may not agree why we have rights, but they can agree that they need them. Such grounding as modern human rights requires, I would argue, is based on what history tells us: that human beings are at risk of their lives if they lack agency; that agency itself requires protection in internationally agreed standards; that these standards should entitle individuals to oppose and resist unjust laws and orders within their own states; and, finally, that when all other remedies have been exhausted, these individuals have the right to appeal to other peoples, nations, and international organizations for assistance in defending their rights. These facts may have been demonstrated most clearly in the catastrophic history of Europe in the twentieth century, but there is no reason in principle why non-European peoples cannot draw the same conclusions from them or why in ages to come the memory of the Holocaust and other such crimes will not move future generations to support the universal application of human rights norms.

A prudential—and historical—justification for human rights need not make appeal to a philosophical anthropology of human nature. Nor should it seek its ultimate court of appeal in an articulation of the human good. Human rights are an account of what is right, not an account of what is good. People may enjoy full human rights protection and still believe that they lack essential features of a good life. If this is so, shared belief in human rights ought to be compatible with diverging attitudes to what constitutes a good life. A universal regime of human rights protection ought to be compatible with moral pluralism. That is, it should be possible to maintain regimes of human rights protection in a wide variety of civilizations, cultures, and religions, each of which happens to disagree with the other as to what a good human life should be. Another way of putting the same thought is that people from different cultures may continue to disagree about what is good, but nevertheless agree about what is insufferably, unarguably wrong.

The universal commitments implied by human rights can only be compatible with a wide variety of ways of living if the universalism implied is self-consciously minimalist. Human rights can command universal assent only as a decidedly "thin" theory of what is right, a definition of the minimum conditions for any kind of life at all. Even then it may not be minimal enough to command universal assent. No authority whose power is directly challenged by human rights regimes is likely to concede their legitimacy. The bias of human rights advocacy must be toward the victim, and the test of legitimacy—and hence of universality—is what might be termed the victim's consent. If victims do freely seek human rights protection, rights language applies. The objections of those who engage in oppression can be heard—as to facts about whether oppression is or is not occurring. If victims seek protection, those in power will obviously refuse to admit the jurisdiction of rights, but they have no legitimacy in doing so. The claims of victims should count more than the claims of oppressors. Still, victims cannot enjoy unlimited rights in the definition of what constitutes an abuse. A human rights abuse is something more than an inconvenience, and raising human rights claims is something more than drawing attention to yourself and your people and engaging in a competitive battle for recognition. Seeking human rights redress is distinct from seeking recognition. It is about protecting an essential exercise of human agency. Hence, while it is the victim's claim of abuse that sets a human rights process moving, a victim remains under an obligation to prove that such an abuse genuinely occurred, and it must be an abuse, not just an inconvenience.

In these lectures, my definition of "minimal" will be focused on agency. By agency, I mean more or less what Isaiah Berlin meant by "negative liberty," the capacity of each individual to achieve rational intentions without let or hindrance. By rational, I do not necessarily mean sensible or estimable, merely those intentions that do not involve obvious harm to other human beings. Human rights is a language of individual empowerment, and empowerment for individuals is desirable because when individuals have agency they can protect themselves against injustice. Equally, when individuals have agency they can define for themselves what they wish to live and die for. In this sense, to emphasize agency is to empower individuals, but also to impose limits on human rights claims themselves. To protect human agency necessarily requires us to protect all individuals' right to chose the good life as they see fit. The usual criticism of this sort of individualism is that it imposes a Western conception of the individual on other cultures. My claim is the reverse: that moral individualism protects cultural diversity, for an individualist position must respect the diverse ways individuals choose to live their lives. In this way of thinking, human rights is only a systematic agenda of "negative liberty," a tool-kit against oppression, a tool-kit that individual agents must be free to use as they see fit within the broader frame of cultural and religious beliefs that they live by.

Why should this "minimalist" justification for human rights be necessary? Why should it matter that we find a way to reconcile human rights universalism with cultural and moral pluralism? Since 1945 human rights language has become a source of power and authority. Inevitably, power invites challenge. Human rights doctrine is now so powerful, but also so confused, so unthinkingly imperialist in its claims that it has begun to invite serious intellectual attack on the legitimacy of its standards and claims. These challenges have raised important questions about whether human rights deserves the authority it has acquired; whether its claims to universality are justified, or whether it is just another cunning exercise in Western moral imperialism.

There are three distinct sources of the cultural challenge to the universality of human rights. Two come from outside the West: one from resurgent Islam, the second from East Asia; and the third, from within the West itself. Each of these is independent of the others; but taken together, they have raised substantial questions about the cross-cultural validity and hence legitimacy of human rights norms.

1. THE ISLAMIC CHALLENGE

The challenge from Islam has been there from the beginning.[3] When the Universal Declaration was being drafted in 1947, the Saudi Arabian delegation raised particular objection to Article 16, relating to free marriage choice, and Article 18, relating to freedom of religion. On the

---

[3] Katerina Dalacoura Islam, *Liberalism and Human Rights* (London: I. B. Tauris, 1998); F. Halliday, "The Politics of Islamic Fundamentalism," in A. S. Ahmed and H. Donnan (eds.), *Islam, Globalization and Post-Modernity* (London: I. B. Tauris, 1994); A. A. An-Naim (ed.), *Human Rights in Cross-Cultural Perspectives* (Philadelphia: University of Pennsylvania Press, 1992), ch. 1; see also Mehdi Amin Razavi and David Ambuel (eds.), *Philosophy, Religion and the Question of Tolerance* (New York: SUNY Press, 1997), ch. 4.

question of marriage, the Saudi delegate to the committee examining the draft of the Universal Declaration made an argument that has resonated ever since through Islamic encounters with Western human rights:

> The authors of the draft declaration had, for the most part, taken into consideration only the standards recognized by western civilization and had ignored more ancient civilizations which were past the experimental stage, and the institutions of which, for example, marriage, had proved their wisdom through the centuries. It was not for the Committee to proclaim the superiority of one civilization over all other or to establish uniform standards for all countries of the world.[4]

This was simultaneously a defence of the Islamic faith from Western secular standards and a defence of patriarchal authority. The Saudi delegate in effect argued that the exchange and control of women is the very *raison d'être* of traditional cultures and that the restriction of female choice in marriage is central to the maintenance of patriarchal property relations. On the basis of these objections to Articles 16 and 18, the Saudi delegation refused to ratify the Declaration.

There have been recurrent attempts, including Islamic Declarations of Human Rights, to reconcile Islamic and Western traditions by putting more emphasis on family duty and religious devotion and by drawing on distinctively Islamic traditions of religious and ethnic toleration.[5] But these attempts at syncretic fusion between Islam and the West have never been entirely successful: agreement is reached by actually trading away what is vital to each side. The resulting consensus is bland and unconvincing.

Since the 1970s the Islamic relation to human rights has grown more hostile. Ever since the Islamic Revolution in Iran rose up against the failed and tyrannical modernization of the shah, Islamic figures have questioned the universal writ of Western human rights norms. They have pointed out that the Western separation of church and state, secular and religious authority, is alien to the jurisprudence and political thought of the Islamic tradition. The freedoms articulated in Articles 18 and 19 of the Universal Declaration make no sense within the theo-

---

[4] Glen Johnson and Janusz Symonides, *The Universal Declaration of Human Rights: A History of Its Creation and Implementation, 1948–1998* (Paris: UNESCO, 1998), pp. 52–53.

[5] Paul Gordon Lauren, *The Evolution of International Human Rights: Visions Seen* (Philadelphia: University of Pennsylvania Press, 1998), p. 8.

cratic bias of Islamic political thought. Likewise, the right to marry and found a family, to freely choose one's partner, is a direct challenge to the forces in Islamic society that enforce the family choice of spouse, polygamy, and the keeping of women in purdah. In Islamic eyes, universalizing rights discourse implies a sovereign and discrete individual, which is blasphemous from the perspective of the Holy Koran.

In assessing this challenge, the West has made the mistake of assuming that fundamentalism and Islam are synonymous. Islam of course speaks in many voices and variants, some more anti-Western than others, some more theocratic than others. National contexts may be much more important in defining local Islamic reactions to Western values than broad theological principles in the religion as a whole. Where Islamic societies have managed to modernize, create a middle-class, and enter the global economy—Egypt and Tunisia being examples—a constituency in favor of basic human rights can emerge. Egypt, for instance, is in the process of passing legislation to give women the right to divorce; and although dialogue with Egypt's religious authorities has been difficult and the law has made compromises with Islamic conceptions of female duty that human rights activists may find objectionable, women's rights will be substantially enhanced by the new legislation.[6] In Algeria, where a secularizing elite who rode to power after a bloody anticolonial revolution failed to modernize their country, the opposition, led by Islamic militants, has taken an anti-Western, anti–human rights direction. And in Afghanistan, where the state itself has collapsed and Western arms transfers have only aggravated the nation's decline, the Taliban movement has arisen, explicitly rejecting all Western human rights standards. Again, the critical variant is not Islam itself— a protean, many-featured religion—but the fateful course of Western policy and economic globalization itself.

But there is another Western reaction to the Islamic challenge that is equally ill-conceived. There is a style of cultural relativism that concedes too much to the Islamic challenge and in the process trades away the universality of human rights standards. For the last twenty years, an influential current in Western political opinion has faced the challenge to the universality of human rights language by maintaining, in the words of Adamantia Pollis and Peter Schwab, that human rights are a "Western construct of limited applicability," a twentieth-century

---

[6] *New York Times,* March 3, 2000.

fiction, dependent on the rights traditions of America, Britain, and France and therefore inapplicable in cultures that do not share this historical matrix of liberal individualism.[7]

This current of thought has complicated intellectual origins: the Marxist critique of the rights of man, the anthropological critique of the arrogance of late nineteenth century bourgeois imperialism, and the postmodernist critique of the universalizing pretensions of European Enlightenment thought.[8] All of these tendencies have come together in a critique of Western intellectual hegemony as expressed in the language of human rights. Human rights is seen as an exercise in the cunning of Western reason: no longer able to dominate the world through direct imperial rule, Western reason masks its own will to power in the impartial, universalizing language of human rights and seeks to impose its own narrow agenda on a plethora of world cultures who do not actually share the West's conception of individuality, selfhood, agency, or freedom. This postmodernist relativism began as an intellectual fashion in Western campuses, but it has seeped slowly into Western human rights practice, causing all activists to pause and consider the intellectual warrant for the universality they once took for granted.

2. ASIAN VALUES

This challenge within has been amplified by a challenge from without: the critique of Western human rights standards by some political leaders in the tiger economies of East Asia. While the Islamic challenge to human rights can be explained in part by the failure of Islamic societies to benefit from the global economy, the Asian challenge is a response to Asia's staggering economic success. Malaysia's leaders, for example, feel confident enough to reject Western ideas of democracy and individual rights in favor of an Asian route to development and prosperity—which depends on authoritarian government and authoritarian family structures—because Malaysia has enjoyed such demonstrable economic success in the 1980s and 1990s. The same can be said about Singapore, which combined political authoritarianism with market capitalism in a

---

[7] A. Pollis and P. Schwab (eds.), *Human Rights: Cultural and Ideological Perspectives* (New York: Praeger, 1979), pp. 1, 4; see also Amitai Etzioni, "Cross-Cultural Judgments: The Next Steps," *Journal of Social Philosophy* 28, no. 3 (Winter 1997).

[8] For a Marxist critique of human rights as bourgeois ideology, see Tony Evans (ed.), *Human Rights Fifty Years On: A Reappraisal* (Manchester: Manchester University Press, 1998).

spectacularly successful synthesis. Singapore's Lee Kuan Yew has been quoted as saying that Asians have "little doubt that a society with communitarian values where the interests of society take precedence over that of the individual suits them better than the individualism of America." This Singaporean model cites rising divorce and crime rates in the West in order to argue that Western individualism is subversive of the order necessary for the enjoyment of rights themselves.[9] An "Asian model" puts community and family ahead of individual rights and order ahead of democracy and individual freedom. In reality, of course, there is no single Asian model: each of these societies has modernized in different ways, within different political traditions, and with differing degrees of political and market freedom. Yet it has proven useful for Asian authoritarians to argue that they represent a civilizational challenge to the hegemony of Western models.[10]

Let it be conceded at once that these three separate challenges to the universality of human rights discourse—two from without, one from within the Western tradition—have had a productive impact. They have forced human rights activists to question their assumptions, to rethink the history of their commitments, and to realize just how complicated intercultural dialogue on rights questions actually becomes when all cultures enter the dialogue on grounds of moral and intellectual equality.

3. HUMAN RIGHTS AND INDIVIDUALISM

Having said this, however, I would argue that Western defenders of human rights have traded too much away. In the desire to find common ground with Islamic and Asian positions and to purge their own discourse of the imperial legacies uncovered by the postmodernist critique, Western defenders of human rights norms risk compromising the very universality they ought to be defending. They also risk rewriting their own history.

Many traditions, not just Western ones, were represented at the drafting—the Chinese, Middle Eastern Christian, but also Marxist,

---

[9] For a mordant critique of the Singaporean argument, see Ian Buruma, "The King of Singapore," *New York Review,* June 10, 1999. Lee Kuan Yew quoted in the *International Herald Tribune,* November 9–10, 1991.

[10] W. T. De Bary, *Asian Values and Human Rights: A Confucian Communitarian Perspective* (Cambridge, Mass.: Harvard University Press, 1998), pp. 1–16.

Hindu, Latin American, Islamic—and the drafting committee members explicitly construed their task not as a simple ratification of Western convictions, but as an attempt to define a delimited range of moral universals from within their very different religious, political, ethnic, and philosophic backgrounds.[11] This helps to explain why the document makes no reference to God in its preamble. The Communist delegations would have vetoed any such reference and the competing religious traditions could not have agreed on the wording of the terms that would make human rights derive from our common existence as God's creatures. Hence the secular ground of the document is not a sign of European cultural domination so much as a pragmatic common denominator designed to make agreement possible across the range of divergent cultural and political viewpoints.

It remains true of course that Western inspirations—and Western drafters—played the predominant role in the drafting of the document. Even so, their mood in 1947 was anything but triumphalist. They were aware, first of all, that the age of colonial emancipation was at hand: Indian independence was proclaimed while the language of the Declaration was being finalised. Although the Declaration does not specifically endorse self-determination, its drafters clearly foresaw the coming tide of struggles for national independence. Because it does proclaim the right of people to self-government and freedom of speech and religion, it also concedes the right of colonial peoples to construe moral universals in a language rooted in their own traditions. Whatever failings the drafters of the Declaration may be accused of, unexamined Western triumphalism is not one of them. Key drafters like René Cassin of France and John Humphrey of Canada knew the knell had sounded on two centuries of Western colonialism.[12]

They also knew that the Declaration was not so much a proclamation of the superiority of European civilization as an attempt to salvage the remains of its Enlightenment heritage from the barbarism of a world war just concluded. The Universal Declaration is written in full awareness of Auschwitz and dawning awareness of Kolyma. A consciousness of European barbarism is built into the very language of the Declaration's preamble: "whereas disregard and contempt for human rights

[11] Johannes Morsink, *The Universal Declaration of Human Rights: Origins, Drafting and Intent* (Philadelphia: University of Pennsylvania Press, 1999).

[12] René Cassin, "Historique de la déclaration universelle en 1938," in his *La Pensée et l'action* (Paris: Editions Lalou, 1972), pp. 103–18; J. P. Humphrey, *Human Rights and the United Nations: A Great Adventure* (Dobbs Ferry, N.Y.: Transnational, 1984), pp. 46–47.

have resulted in barbarous acts which have outraged the conscience of mankind . . ."

The Declaration may still be a child of the Enlightenment, but it was written when faith in the Enlightenment faced its deepest crisis of confidence. In this sense, human rights is not so much the declaration of the superiority of European civilization as a warning by Europeans that the rest of the world should not seek to reproduce its mistakes. The chief of these was the idolatry of the nation state, causing individuals to forget the higher law commanding them to disobey unjust orders. The abandonment of this moral heritage of natural law, the surrender of individualism to collectivism, the drafters believed, led to the catastrophe of Nazi and Stalinist oppression. Unless the disastrous heritage of European collectivism is kept in mind, as the framing experience in the drafting of the Universal Declaration, its individualism will appear to be nothing more than the ratification of Western bourgeois capitalist prejudice. In fact, it was much more: a studied attempt to reinvent the European natural law tradition in order to safeguard individual agency against the totalitarian state.

It remains true, therefore, that the core of the Universal Declaration is the moral individualism for which it is so much reproached by non-Western societies. It is this individualism for which Western activists have become most apologetic, believing that it should be tempered by greater emphasis on social duties and responsibilities to the community. Human rights, it is argued, can only recover universal appeal if it softens its individualistic bias and puts greater emphasis on those parts of the Universal Declaration, especially Article 29, which says that "everyone has duties to the community in which alone the free and full development of his personality is possible." This desire to water down the individualism of rights discourse is driven by a desire both to make human rights more palatable to less individualistic cultures in the non-Western world and also to respond to disquiet among Western communitarians at the supposedly corrosive impact of individualistic values on Western social cohesion.[13]

But this tack mistakes what rights actually are and misunderstands why they have proven attractive to millions of people raised in non-Western traditions. Rights are only meaningful if they confer entitlements and immunities on individuals; they only have force and bite if

---

[13] Michael Sandel, *Democracy's Discontents* (Cambridge, Mass.: Harvard University Press, 1996).

they can be enforced against institutions like the family, the state, and the church. This remains true even when the rights in question are collective or group rights. Some of these rights—like the right to speak your own language or practice your own religion—are essential preconditions for the exercise of individual rights. The right to speak a language of your choice won't mean very much if the language has died out. For this reason, group rights are needed to protect individual rights. But the ultimate purpose and justification of group rights is not the protection of the group as such, but the protection of the individuals who compose it. Group rights to language, for example, must not be used to prevent an individual from learning a language besides the language of the group. Group rights to practice religion should not cancel the right of individuals to leave a religious community if they choose.[14]

Rights are inescapably political because they tacitly imply a conflict between a rights holder and a rights "withholder." Rights presume an individual rights holder and some authority against which the rights holder can make claims. To confuse rights with aspirations, and rights conventions with syncretic syntheses of world values, is to wish away the conflicts that define the very content of rights. There will always be conflicts between individuals and groups, and rights exist to protect individuals. Rights language cannot be parsed or translated into a non-individualistic, communitarian framework. It presumes moral individualism and is nonsensical outside that assumption.

Moreover, it is precisely this individualism that renders it attractive to non-Western peoples and explains why human rights has become a global movement. Human rights is the only universally available moral vernacular that validates the claims of women and children against the oppression they experience in patriarchal and tribal societies; it is the only vernacular that enables dependent persons to perceive themselves as moral agents and to act against practices—arranged marriages, purdah, civic disenfranchisement, genital mutilation, domestic slavery, and so on—that are ratified by the weight and authority of their cultures. These agents seek out human rights protection, not because it ratifies their culture, but precisely because it legitimizes their protests against its oppression.

If this is so, then we need to rethink what it means when we say that rights are universal. Rights doctrines arouse powerful opposition be-

[14] Michael Ignatieff, *The Rights Revolution* (Toronto: Anansi, 2000), ch. 3; Will Kymlicka, *Multicultural Citizenship* (Oxford: Clarendon Press, 1995).

cause they challenge sources of power: religions, family structures, authoritarian states, and tribes. It would be a hopeless task to attempt to persuade these holders of power of the universal validity of rights doctrines, since if these doctrines prevailed they would necessarily abridge and constrain their exercise of authority. Thus universality cannot imply universal assent, since in a world of unequal power, the only propositions that the powerful and powerless would agree on would be entirely toothless and anodyne ones. Rights are universal because they define the universal interests of the powerless, namely that power be exercised over them in ways that respect their autonomy as agents. In this sense, human rights is a revolutionary creed, since it makes a radical demand of all human groups, that they serve the interests of the individuals who compose them. This then implies that human groups should be, insofar as possible, consensual, or at least that they should respect an individual's right to exit when the constraints of the group become unbearable.

The idea that groups should respect an individual's right of exit is not easy to reconcile with what groups actually are. Most human groups—the family, for example—are blood groups, based on inherited kinship or ethnic ties. People do not choose to be born into them and do not leave them easily, since these collectivities provide the frame of meaning within which individual life makes sense. This is as true in modern secular societies as it is in religious or traditional societies. Group rights doctrines exist to safeguard the collective rights—for example, to language—that make individual agency meaningful and valuable. But individual and group interests inevitably conflict. Human rights exist to adjudicate these conflicts, to define the irreducible minimum beyond which group and collective claims must not go in constraining the lives of individuals.

Even so, defending individual agency does not necessarily entail adopting Western ways of life. Believing in your right not to be tortured or abused need not mean adopting Western dress, speaking Western languages, or approving of the Western way of life. To seek human rights protection is not to change your civilization; it is merely to avail yourself of the protections of "negative liberty."

Human rights doesn't have to delegitimize traditional culture as a whole. The women in Kabul who come to Western human rights agencies seeking their protection from the Taliban militias do not want to cease being Muslim wives and mothers; they want to combine respect for their traditions with the right to an education or professional health care provided by a woman. They hope the agencies will defend them against being beaten and persecuted for claiming such rights.[15]

The legitimacy of these claims to rights protection depends entirely on the fact that the people who are making them are the victims themselves. In Pakistan, it is local human rights groups, not international agencies, who are leading the fight to defend poor country women from "honor killings," being burned alive when they disobey their husbands; it is local Islamic women who are criticizing the grotesque distortion of Islamic teaching that provides justification for such abuse.[16] Human rights has gone global, but it has also gone local because it empowers the powerless, gives voice to the voiceless.

It is simply not the case, as Islamic and Asian critics contend, that human rights forces the Western way of life upon their societies. For all its individualism, human rights does not require adherents to jettison their other cultural attachments. As Jack Donnelly argues, human rights "assumes that people probably are best suited, and in any case are entitled, to choose the good life for themselves."[17] What the Declaration does mandate is the right to choose, and specifically the right to *leave* when choice is denied. The global diffusion of rights language would never have occurred had these not been authentically attractive propositions to millions of people, especially women, in theocratic, traditional, or patriarchal societies.

Critics of this view of human rights diffusion would argue that it is too "voluntaristic": it implies that traditional societies are free to choose the manner of their insertion into the global economy; free to choose which Western values to adapt and which to reject. In reality, these critics argue, people are not free to choose. Economic globalization steamrolls over local economies, and moral globalization—human rights— follows behind as the legitimizing ideology of global capitalism. "Given the class interest of the internationalist class carrying out this agenda," Kenneth Anderson writes, "the claim to universalism is a sham. Universalism is mere globalism and a globalism, moreover,

---

[15] See Michael Ignatieff, *The Warrior's Honour: Ethnic War and the Modern Conscience* (London: Vintage, 1995), pp. 55–69.

[16] See *Murder in Purdah,* BBC Television Correspondent Special, January 23, 1999, directed by Giselle Portenier, produced by Fiona Murch.

[17] Jack Donnelly, "Human Rights and Asian Values: A Defense of Western Universalism," in Joanne R. Bauer and Daniel A. Bell (eds.), *The East Asian Challenge for Human Rights* (Cambridge: Cambridge University Press, 1999), p. 86.

whose key terms are established by capital."[18] This idea that human rights is the moral arm of global capitalism falsifies the insurgent nature of the relation between human rights activism and the global corporation.[19] The NGO activists who devote their lives to challenging the employment practices of global giants like Nike and Shell would be astonished to discover that their human rights agenda has been serving the interests of global capital all along. Anderson conflates globalism and internationalism and mixes up two classes, the free market globalists and the human rights internationalists, whose interests and values are in conflict.

While free markets do encourage the emergence of assertively self-interested individuals, these individuals often want human rights precisely to protect them from the indignities and indecencies of the market. Moreover, the dignity such individuals are seeking to protect is not necessarily derived from Western models. Anderson writes as if human rights is always imposed from the top down by an international elite bent on "saving the world." He ignores the extent to which the demand for human rights is issuing from the bottom up.

The test of human rights legitimacy, therefore, is take-up from the bottom, from the powerless. Instead of apologizing for the individualism of Western human rights standards, activists need to attend to another problem, which is how to create conditions in which individuals are genuinely free to avail themselves of such rights as they want. Increasing the freedom of people to exercise their rights depends on close cultural understanding of the frameworks that often constrain choice. The much debated issue of genital mutilation illustrates this point. What may appear as mutilation in Western eyes is simply the price of tribal and family belonging to women; if they fail to submit to the ritual, they no longer have a place within their world. Choosing to exercise their rights, therefore, may result in a social ostracism that leaves them no option but to leave their tribe and make for the city. Human rights advocates have to be aware of what it really means for a woman to abandon traditional practices. But, equally, activists have a duty to

---

[18] Kenneth Anderson, "Secular Eschatologies and Class Interests," in Carrie Gustafson and Peter Juviler (eds.), *Religion and Human Rights: Conflicting Claims* (Armonk, N.Y.: M. E. Sharpe, 1999), p. 115.

[19] Richard Falk, "The Quest for Human Rights," in *Predatory Globalization: A Critique* (London: Polity, 1999), ch. 6.

334 The Tanner Lectures on Human Values

inform women of the medical costs and consequences of these practices and seek, as a first step, to make them less dangerous for women who wish to undergo them. Finally, it is for women themselves to decide how to make the adjudication between tribal and Western wisdom. The criteria of informed consent that regulate patient choice in Western societies are equally applicable in non-Western settings, and human rights activists are under an obligation, inherent in human rights discourse itself, to respect the autonomy and decision-making power of agents. An activist's proper role is not to make the choices for the women in question, but to enlarge their sense of what the choices entail. In traditional societies, harmful practices can only be abandoned when the whole community decides to do so. Otherwise, individuals who decide on their own face ostracism and worse. Consent in these cases means collective or group consent.

Sensitivity to the real constraints that limit individual freedom in different cultures is not the same thing as deferring to these cultures. It does not mean abandoning universality. It simply means facing up to a demanding intercultural dialogue in which all parties come to the table under common expectations of being treated as moral equals. Traditional society is oppressive to individuals within it not because it fails to afford a Western way of life, but because it does not accord them a right to speak and be heard. Western activists have no right to overturn traditional cultural practice, provided that practice continues to receive the assent of its members. Outsiders have the right to argue—not to insist—that all individuals within the group have a right to express their opinion about a tradition's continuance and to exit freely if they cannot give their assent. Human rights is universal not as a vernacular of cultural prescription but as a language of moral empowerment. Its role is not in defining the content of culture but in trying to enfranchise all agents so that they can freely shape that content.

Empowerment and freedom are not value-neutral terms: they have an unquestionably individualistic bias, and traditional and authoritarian societies will resist these values because they aim a dart at the very premises that keep patriarchy and authoritarianism in place. But how people use their freedom is up to them, and there is no reason to suppose that if they adopt the Western value of freedom they will give it Western content. Furthermore, it is up to victims, not outside observers, to define for themselves whether their freedom is in jeopardy. It is entirely

possible that people whom Western observers might suppose are in oppressed or subordinate positions will seek to maintain the traditions and
patterns of authority that keep them in this subjection. Women are
placed in such subordinate positions in many of the world's religions,
including ultra Orthodox Judaism and certain forms of Islam. Some
will come to resent these positions, others will not, and those who do
not cannot be supposed to be trapped inside some form of false consciousness that it is the business of human rights activism to unlock. Indeed adherents may believe that the forms of participation provided by
their religious tradition enable them to enjoy forms of belonging that
are more valuable to them than the negative freedom of private agency.
What may be an abuse of human rights to a human rights activist may
not be seen as such by those whom human rights activists construe to be
victims. This is why consent ought to be the defining constraint of human rights interventions in all areas where human life itself or gross and
irreparable physical harm is not at stake.

Human rights discourse is universal precisely because it supposes
that there are many differing visions of a good human life, that the
West's is only one of them, and that, provided agents have a degree of
freedom in the choice of that life, they should be left to give it the content that accords with their history and traditions.

To sum up at this point, Western human rights activists have surrendered too much to the cultural relativist challenge. Relativism is the
invariable alibi of tyranny. There is no reason to apologize for the moral
individualism at the heart of human rights discourse: it is precisely this
that makes it attractive to dependent groups suffering exploitation or
oppression. There is no reason, either, to think of freedom as a uniquely
Western value or to believe that advocating it then unjustly imposes
Western values on them. For it contradicts the meaning of freedom itself to attempt to define for others the use they make of it.

The best way to face the cultural challenge to human rights—coming from Asia, Islam, and Western postmodernism—is to admit its
truth: rights discourse *is* individualistic. But that is precisely why it has
proven an effective remedy against tyranny, and why it has proven attractive to people from very differing cultures. The other advantage of
liberal individualism is that it is a distinctly "thin" theory of the human
good: it defines and proscribes the "negative," i.e., those restraints and
injustices that make any human life, however conceived, impossible; at

the same time, it does not prescribe the "positive" range of good lives that human beings can lead.[20] Human rights is morally universal because it says that all human beings need certain specific freedoms "from"; it does not go on to define what their freedom "to" should consist in. In this sense, it is a less prescriptive universalism than many world religions: it articulates standards of human decency without violating rights of cultural autonomy.

Certainly, as Will Kymlicka and many others have pointed out, there are some conditions of life—the right to speak a language, for example—that cannot be protected by individual rights alone. A linguistic minority needs to have the right to educate its children in the language in order for the linguistic community to survive, and it can only do this if the larger community recognizes its collective right to do so. At the same time, however, all collective rights provisions have to be balanced with individual rights guarantees, so that individuals do not end up being denied substantive freedoms for the sake of the group. This is not an easy matter, as any English-speaking Montrealer with experience of Quebec language legislation will tell you. But it can be done, provided individual rights have an ultimate priority over collective ones, so that individuals are not forced to educate their children in a manner that is not freely chosen.[21] Even granting, therefore, that groups need collective rights in order to protect shared inheritances, these rights themselves risk becoming a source of collective tyranny unless individuals retain a right of appeal. To repeat, it is precisely the individualism of human rights that makes it a valuable bulwark against even the well-intentioned tyranny of linguistic or national groups.

The conflict over the universality of human rights norms is a political struggle. It pits traditional, religious, and authoritarian sources of power against human rights advocates, many of them indigenous to the culture itself, who challenge these sources of power in the name of those who find themselves excluded and oppressed. Those who seek human rights protection are not traitors to their culture, and they do not necessarily approve of other Western values. What they seek is protection of their rights as individuals within their own culture. Opposition to their

---

[20] These distinctions—negative liberty, positive liberty, freedom from, freedom to—are suggested by Isaiah Berlin, "Two Concepts of Liberty," in Henry Hardy (ed.), *The Proper Study of Mankind* (London: Chatto and Windus, 1997), pp. 191–243; on "thin" theories of the good, see John Rawls, *A Theory of Justice* (Cambridge, Mass.: Harvard University Press, 1970).

[21] Kymlicka, *Multicultural Citizenship,* pp. 2–6.

demands invariably takes the form of a defense of the culture as a whole against intrusive forms of Western cultural imperialism, when in reality this relativist case is actually a defense of local political or patriarchal power. Human rights intervention is warranted not because traditional, patriarchal, or religious authority is primitive, backward, or uncivilized by *our* standards, but because it oppresses specific individuals who themselves seek protection against these abuses. The warrant for intervention derives from *their* demands, not from ours.

4. The Spiritual Crisis

Whereas the cultural crisis of human rights has been about the intercultural validity of human rights norms, the spiritual crisis of human rights concerns the ultimate metaphysical grounds for these norms. Why do human beings have rights in the first place? What is it about the human species and the human individual that entitles them to rights? If there is something special about the human person, why is this inviolability so often honored in the breach rather than in the observance? If human beings are special, why exactly do we treat each other so badly?

Human rights has become a secular article of faith. Yet the faith's metaphysical underpinnings are anything but clear. Article 1 of the Universal Declaration cuts short all justification and simply declares: "All human beings are born free and equal in dignity and rights. They are endowed with reason and conscience and should act towards one another in a spirit of brotherhood." The Universal Declaration enunciates rights; it doesn't explain why people have them.

The drafting history of the Declaration makes clear that this silence was deliberate. When Eleanor Roosevelt first convened a drafting committee in her Washington Square apartment in February 1947, a Chinese Confucian and a Lebanese Thomist got into a stubborn argument about the philosophical and metaphysical bases of rights. Mrs. Roosevelt concluded that the only way forward lay in West and East agreeing to disagree.[22]

There is thus a deliberate silence at the heart of human rights culture. Instead of a substantive set of justifications explaining why human rights are universal, instead of reasons that go back to first principles—

---

[22] See Morsink, *The Universal Declaration of Human Rights.*

as in Thomas Jefferson's unforgettable preamble to the American Declaration of Independence—the Universal Declaration of Human Rights simply takes the existence of rights for granted and proceeds to their elaboration.

Pragmatic silence on ultimate questions has made it easier for a global human rights culture to emerge. As the philosopher Charles Taylor puts it, the concept of human rights "could travel better if separated from some of its underlying justifications."[23] The Declaration's vaunted "universality" is as much a testament to what the drafters kept *out* of it, as to what they put *in.*

The Declaration envisioned a world where, if human beings found their civil and political rights as citizens were taken away, they could still appeal for protection on the basis of their rights as human beings. Beneath the civil and political, in other words, stood the natural. But what exactly is the relationship between human rights and natural rights, or between the human and the natural? What is naturally human?

Human rights is supposed to formalize in juridical terms the natural duties of human conscience in cases where civil and political obligations either prove insufficient to prevent abuses or have disintegrated altogether. Human rights doctrines appear to assume that if the punishments and incentives of governed societies are taken away, human rights norms will remind people of the requirements of natural decency. But this assumes that the capacity to behave decently is a natural attribute. Where is the empirical evidence that this is the case? A more likely assumption is that human morality in general and human rights in particular represent a systematic attempt by human communities to correct and counteract the natural tendencies they discovered in themselves as human beings. The specific tendency they were seeking to counteract is that while we may be naturally disposed, by genetics and history, to care for those close to us—our children, our family, our immediate relations, and possibly those who share our ethnic or religious origins—we may be naturally indifferent to all others outside this circle. Historically, human rights doctrines emerged to counteract this tendency toward particularist and exclusivist ethical circles of concern and care. As Avishai Margalit has put it, "we need morality to overcome our natural indifference for others."[24]

[23] Charles Taylor, "Conditions of an Unforced Consensus on Human Rights," in Bauer and Bell, *The East Asian Challenge for Human Rights,* p. 126.

[24] Avishai Margalit, "The Ethics of Memory," the Horkheimer Lectures, May 1999, Goethe University, Frankfurt. I am grateful to Avishai Margalit for letting me see these lectures in manuscript.

The history immediately antecedent to the Universal Declaration of Human Rights provides abundant evidence of the natural indifference of human beings. The Holocaust showed up the terrible insufficiency of all the supposedly natural human attributes of pity and care in situations where these duties were no longer enforced by law. Hannah Arendt argued in *Origins of Totalitarianism* that when Jewish citizens of European states were deprived of their civil and political rights, when, finally, they had been stripped naked and could only appeal to their captors as plain, bare human beings, they found that their nakedness did not even awaken the pity of their tormentors. As Arendt put it, "it seems that a man who is nothing but a man has lost the very qualities which make it possible for other people to treat him as a fellow man."[25] The Universal Declaration set out to reestablish the idea of human rights at the precise historical moment in which they had been shown to have had no foundation whatever in natural human attributes.

All that one can say about this paradox is that it defines the divided consciousness with which we have lived with the idea of human rights ever since. We defend human rights as moral universals in full awareness that they must counteract rather than reflect natural human propensities.

So we cannot build a foundation for human rights on natural human pity or solidarity. For the idea that these propensities are natural implies that they are innate and universally distributed among individuals. The reality—as the Holocaust and countless other examples of atrocity make clear—is otherwise. We must work out a basis for belief in human rights on the basis of human beings as they are, working on assumptions about the worst we can do, instead of hopeful expectations of the best. In other words, we do not build foundations on human nature but on human history, on what we know is likely to happen when human beings do not have the protection of rights. We build on the testimony of fear, rather than on the expectations of hope. This, it seems to me, is how human rights consciousness has been built since the Holocaust. Human rights is one of the achievements of what Judith Shklar once called "the liberalism of fear."[26] Likewise, in 1959, Isaiah Berlin argued that in the post-Holocaust era awareness of the necessity of a moral law is no longer sustained by belief in reason but by the memory of horror. "Because

[25] Hannah Arendt, *The Origins of Totalitarianism* (New York: Harcourt and Brace, 1973), p. 300.

[26] Judith N. Shklar, "The Liberalism of Fear," in Stanley Hoffman (ed.), *Political Thought and Political Thinkers* (Chicago: University of Chicago Press, 1998), pp. 3–21.

these rules of natural law were flouted, we have been forced to become conscious of them."[27] And what, in his view, were these rules?

> We know of no court, no authority, which could, by means of some recognized process, allow men to bear false witness, or torture freely or slaughter fellow men for pleasure; we cannot conceive of getting these universal principles or rules repealed or altered.

The Holocaust laid bare what the world looked like when pure tyranny was given free rein to exploit natural human cruelty. Without the Holocaust then, no Declaration. Because of the Holocaust, no unconditional faith in the Declaration either. The Holocaust demonstrates both the prudential necessity of human rights and their ultimate fragility.

If one end product of Western rationalism is the exterminatory nihilism of the Nazis, then any ethics that takes only reason for its guide is bound to be powerless when human reason begins to rationalize its own exterminatory projects. If reason rationalized the Holocaust, then only an ethics deriving its ultimate authority from a higher source than reason can prevent a Holocaust in the future. So the Holocaust accuses not just Western nihilism, but Western humanism itself and puts human rights in the dock. For human rights is a secular humanism: an ethics ungrounded in divine or ultimate sanction and based only in human prudence.

It is unsurprising, therefore, that in the wake of the Holocaust human rights should face an enduring intellectual challenge from a range of religious sources, Catholic, Protestant, and Jewish, all of whom make the same essential point: that if the purpose of human rights is to restrain the human use of power, then the only authority capable of doing so must lie beyond humanity itself, in some religious source of authority.

Michael Perry, a legal philosopher at Wake Forest University, argues, for example, that the idea of human rights is "ineliminably religious."[28] Unless you think, he says, that human beings are sacred, there seems no persuasive reason to believe that their dignity should be protected with rights. Only a religious conception of human beings as the handiwork of God can sustain a notion that individuals should have in-

---

[27] Isaiah Berlin, "European Unity and Its Vicissitudes," in *The Crooked Timber of Humanity* (London: Chatto and Windus, 1991), pp. 204–5.

[28] M. J. Perry, *The Idea of Human Rights: Four Inquiries* (New York: Oxford University Press, 1998), pp. 11–41.

violable natural rights. Max Stackhouse, a Princeton theologian, argues that the idea of human rights has to be grounded in the idea of God, or at least the idea of "transcendent moral laws." Human rights needs a theology in order to explain, in the first place, why human beings have "the right to have rights."[29]

Secular humanism may indeed be putting human beings on a pedestal when they should be down in the mud where they belong. If human rights exists to define and uphold limits to the abuse of human beings, then its underlying philosophy had better define humanity as a beast in need of restraint. Instead human rights makes humanity the measure of all things, and from a religious point of view this is a form of idolatry. Humanist idolatry is dangerous for three evident reasons: first, because it puts the demands, needs, and rights of the human species above any other and therefore risks legitimizing an entirely instrumental relation to other species; second, because it authorizes the same instrumental and exploitative relationship to nature and the environment; and finally, because it lacks the metaphysical claims necessary to limit the human use of human life, in such instances as abortion or medical experimentation.[30]

What, exactly, is so sacred about human beings? Why, exactly, do we think that ordinary human beings, in all their radical heterogeneity of race, creed, education, and attainment, can be viewed as possessing the same equal and inalienable rights? If idolatry consists in elevating any purely human principle into an unquestioned absolute, surely human rights looks like an idolatry.[31] To be sure, humanists do not literally worship human rights, but we use the language to say that there is something inviolate about the dignity of each human being. This is a worshipful attitude. What is implied in the metaphor of worship is a cultlike credulity, an inability to subject humanist premises to the same critical inquiry to which humanist rationalism subjects religious belief. The core of the charge is that humanism is simply inconsistent. It criticizes all forms of worship, except its own.

To this humanists must reply, if they wish to be consistent, that

---

[29] Max Stackhouse, "Human Rights and Public Theology," in Gustafson and Juviler, *Religion and Human Rights,* pp. 13, 16.

[30] Peter Singer, *Animal Liberation* (New York: Random House, 1990); J. M. Coetzee, *The Lives of Animals* (Princeton, N.J.: Princeton University Press, 1999).

[31] Moshe Halbertal and Avishai Margalit, *Idolatry* (Cambridge, Mass.: Harvard University Press, 1992).

there *is* nothing sacred about human beings, nothing entitled to worship or ultimate respect. All that can be said about human rights is that they are necessary to protect individuals from violence and abuse and if it is asked why, the only possible answer is historical. Human rights is the language through which individuals have created a defense of their autonomy against the oppression of religion, state, family, and group. Conceivably, other languages for the defense of human beings could be invented, but this one is what is historically available to human beings here and now. Moreover, a humanist is required to add, human rights language is *not* an ultimate trump card in moral argument. No human language can have such powers. Indeed, rights conflicts and their adjudication involve intensely difficult tradeoffs and compromises. This is precisely why rights are not sacred, nor are those who hold them. To be a rights-bearer is not to hold some sacred inviolability, but to commit oneself to live in a community where rights conflicts are adjudicated through persuasion, rather than violence. With the idea of rights goes a commitment to respect the reasoned commitments of others and to submit disputes to adjudication. The fundamental moral commitment entailed by rights is not to respect, and certainly not to worship. It is to deliberation.[32] The minimum condition for deliberating with another human being is not necessarily respect, merely negative toleration, a willingness to remain in the same room, listening to claims one doesn't like to hear, for the purpose of finding compromises that will keep conflicting claims from ending in irreparable harm to either side. That is what a shared commitment to human rights entails.

This reply is not likely to satisfy a religious person. From a religious perspective, to believe, as humanists do, that nothing is sacred—although what others hold to be sacred is entitled to protection—is to remove any restraining limits to the exercise of human power.

The idea of the sacred—the idea that there is some realm that is beyond human knowing or representation, some Mount Sinai forever withheld from human sight—is supposed to impose a limit on the human will to power. Even as metaphor—divorced from any metaphysical claim—the sacred connotes the idea that there must be a moral line that no human being can cross. The ideology of human rights is clearly an attempt to define that line. But, from a religious point of view, any attempt to create any strictly human limit to the exercise of human power

---

[32] Amy Gutmann and Dennis Thompson, *Democracy and Disagreement* (Cambridge, Mass.: Belknap Press, 1996).

is bound to be self-defeating. Without the idea of the nonhuman divine, without the idea of the sacred and the idea of impassable limits, both to reason and power, there can be no viable protection of our species from ourselves. The dispute comes down to this: the religious side believes that only if humans get down on their knees can they save themselves from their own destructiveness; a humanist believes that they will only do so if they stand up on their own two feet.

This is an old dispute, and each side has powerful historical arguments. The strongest aspect of the religious case is the empirical evidence that men and women, moved by religious conviction, have been able to stand up against tyranny when those without such convictions did not. In the Soviet labor camps, religious people, from convictions as various as Judaism and Seventh Day Adventism, gave inspiring examples of indestructible dignity. Similarly, it was religious conviction that inspired some Catholic priests and laypersons to hide Jews in wartime Poland. Finally, the black movement for civil rights in the United States is incomprehensible unless we remember the role of religious leadership, metaphors, and language in inspiring individuals to risk their lives for the right to vote. These examples carry more weight than metaphysical argument. But secularism has its heroes too. The lyric poet Anna Akhmatova's writing gave voice to the torments of all the women like herself who lost their husbands and children in the Gulag. Primo Levi, a secular Jew and a scientist, gave witness on behalf of those who perished at Auschwitz. His work is exemplary testimony to the capacity of secular reason to describe the enormity of evil. Moral courage draws its resources where it can, and both secular and religious sources have inspired heroes.

If we turn from the sources of heroism to the sources of villainy, the religious cannot claim that the fear of God has prevented humans from doing their worst. The idea that a sense of the sacred is necessary to keep humans moral stands on weak empirical grounds, to say the least. Indeed, sacred purposes have often been pressed into the service of iniquity. Religion after all is a foundational doctrine, making claims that it regards as incontestable. The belief that one possesses unassailable grounds of faith has been one of the most powerful justifications for torture, forced conversion, the condemnation of heresy, and the burning of heretics. Foundational beliefs, unmixed with humility, have been a longstanding menace to the human rights of ordinary individuals.

On the other hand, it is hard to deny the force of the religious counterargument—that the abominations of the twentieth century were an expression of secular hubris, of human power intoxicated by the means at its disposal and unrestrained by any sense of ethical limit. To the extent that history is a relevant witness in metaphysical matters, its testimony corroborates neither the believer nor the unbeliever. Before radical evil, both secular humanism and ancient belief have been either utterly helpless victims or enthusiastic accomplices.

So how are we to conclude? A humanist will point out that religions make anthropomorphic claims about the identity of their God while simultaneously claiming that He cannot be represented. This contradiction is idolatrous, but it may be a necessary idolatry; believers must worship something. Their devotions must fall upon some image or object that can give a focus to their prayers. Hence the unavoidable necessity of graven images or representations of divinity in most of the world religions. Idolatry may therefore be a necessary component on any belief. If this is true of religion, it may also be true of humanism. We may not be entitled to worship our species, but our commitment to protect it needs sustaining by some *faith* in our species. Such faith, needless to say, can only be conditional, reasserted in the face of the evidence that we are, upon occasion, worse than swine.

The idea of idolatry calls all believers, secular or religious, to sobriety; it asks them to subject their own enthusiasm, their overflowing sense of righteousness or correctness, to a continual scrutiny. Religious persons aware of the dangers of idolatry scrutinize their worship for signs of pride, zeal, or intolerance toward other believers; nonbelievers ought to scrutinize their beliefs for signs of Voltairian contempt for the convictions of others. Such contempt presumes that human reason is capable of assessing and dismissing the truth content of a competing form of religious belief. For both a religious and a secular person, the metaphor of idolatry acts as a restraint against both credulity and contempt. For secular unbelievers radically misread the story of Exodus if they think it is a warning merely against religious credulity. Surely it is the great mythic warning against human fallibility, both secular and religious, our weakness for idols of our own making, our inability to cease worshipping the purely human. A humanism that worships the human, that takes pride in being human, is surely as flawed as those religious beliefs that purport to *know* God's plans for humans. A humanism that is not idolatrous is a humanism that refuses to make metaphysical claims that it cannot justify; it is a humanism that justifies itself only on the grounds that we have good reason to fear our delusional attachment to violence. In short, it is a humanism with the wisdom to respect the dire warnings of Exodus.

Yet even a humble humanism should have the courage to ask why human rights needs the idea of the sacred at all. If the idea of the sacred means that human life ought to be cherished and protected, why does such an idea need theological foundations? Why do we need an idea of God in order to believe that human beings are not free to do what they wish with other human beings; that human beings should not be beaten, tortured, coerced, indoctrinated, or in any way sacrificed against their will? These intuitions derive simply from our own experience of pain and our capacity to imagine the pain of others. Believing that humans are sacred does not necessarily strengthen these injunctions. The reverse is often true: acts of torture or persecution are frequently justified in terms of some sacred purpose. Indeed the strength of a purely secular ethics is its insistence that there are no "sacred" purposes that can ever justify the inhuman use of human beings. An antifoundational humanism may seem insecure, but it does have the advantage that it cannot justify inhumanity on foundational grounds.

A secular defense of human rights depends on the idea of moral reciprocity: that we judge human actions by the simple test of whether we would wish to be on the receiving end. And since we cannot conceive of any circumstances in which we or anyone we know would wish to be abused in mind or body, we have good reasons to believe that such practices should be outlawed. That we are capable of this thought experiment—i.e., that we possess the faculty of imagining the pain and degradation done to other human beings as if it were our own—is simply a fact about us as a species. Because we are all capable of this form of limited empathy, we all possess a conscience, and because we do, we wish to be free to make up our own minds and express those justifications. The fact that there are many humans who remain indifferent to the pain of others does not prove that they do not possess a conscience, merely that this conscience is free. This freedom is regrettable: it makes human beings capable of freely chosen acts of evil, but this freedom is constitutive of what a conscience is. Such facts about human beings—that they feel pain, that they can recognize the pain of others, and that they are free to do good and abstain from evil—provide the basis by which we believe that all human beings should be protected from cruelty. Such a minimalist conception of shared human capacities—

empathy, conscience, and free will—essentially describes what is required for an individual to be an agent of any kind. Protecting such an agent from cruelty means empowerment with a core of civil and political rights. Those who insist that civil and political rights need supplementing with social and economic ones make a claim that is true—that individual rights can only be exercised effectively within a framework of collective rights provision—but they may be obscuring the priority relation between the individual and the collective. Individual rights without collective rights may be difficult to exercise, but collective rights without individual ones means tyranny.

Moreover, rights inflation—the tendency to define anything desirable as a right—ends up eroding the legitimacy of a defensible core of rights. That defensible core ought to be those that are strictly necessary to the enjoyment of any life whatever. The claim here would be that civil and political freedoms are the necessary condition for the eventual attainment of social and economic security. Without the freedom to articulate and express political opinions, without freedom of speech and assembly, together with freedom of property, agents cannot organize themselves to struggle for social and economic security.

As Amartya Sen argues, the right to freedom of speech is not, as the Marxist tradition maintained, a lapidary bourgeois luxury, but the precondition for having any other rights at all. "No substantial famine has ever occurred," Sen observes, "in any country with a democratic form of government and a relatively free press." The Great Leap Forward in China, in which between 23 and 30 million people perished as a result of irrational government policies implacably pursued in the face of their obvious failure, would never have been allowed to take place in a country with the self-correcting mechanisms of a free press and political opposition.[33] So much for the argument so often heard in Asia that a people's "right to development," to economic progress, should come before their right to free speech and democratic government. Such civil and political rights are both an essential motor of economic development in themselves and also a critical guarantee against coercive government schemes and projects. Freedom, to adapt the title of Sen's latest book, *is* development.[34]

Such a secular defense of human rights will necessarily leave religious thinkers unsatisfied. For them secular humanism is the contin-

[33] Amartya Sen, "Human Rights and Economic Achievements," in J. R. Bauer and D. A. Bell (eds.), *The East Asian Challenge for Human Rights,* pp. 92–93.

[34] Amartya Sen, *Development as Freedom* (New York: Oxford University Press, 1999).

gent product of late European civilization and is unlikely to command assent in non-European and nonsecular cultures. Accordingly, a lot of effort has been expended in proving that the moral foundations of the Universal Declaration are derived from the tenets of all the world's major religions. The Universal Declaration is then reinterpreted as the summation of the accumulating moral wisdom of the ages. Paul Gordon Lauren begins his history of the idea of human rights with an inventory of the world's religions, concluding with the claim that "the moral worth of each person is a belief that no single civilization or people or nation or geographical area or even century can claim uniquely as its own."[35]

This religious syncretism is innocuous as inspirational rhetoric. But as Lauren himself concedes, only Western culture turned widely shared propositions about human dignity and equality into a working doctrine of rights. This doctrine didn't originate in Jeddah or Peking, but in Amsterdam, Sienna, and London, wherever Europeans sought to defend the liberties and privileges of their cities and estates against the nobility and the emerging national state.

To point out the European origins of rights is not to endorse Western cultural imperialism. Historical priority doesn't confer moral superiority. As Jack Donnelly points out, the Declaration's historical function was not to universalize European values, but actually to put certain of them—racism, sexism, and anti-Semitism for example—under eternal ban.[36] Non-Western foes of human rights take its proclamations of "universality" as an example of Western arrogance and insensitivity. But universality properly means consistency: the West is obliged to practice what it preaches. This puts the West, no less than the rest of the world, on permanent trial.

5. THE WEST AGAINST ITSELF

In the moral dispute between the "West" and the "Rest," both sides make the mistake of assuming that the other speaks with one voice. When the non-Western world looks at human rights, it assumes— rightly—that the discourse originates in a matrix of historical traditions shared by all the major Western countries. But the non-Western world

---

[35] Paul Gordon Lauren, *The Evolution of International Human Rights* (Philadelphia: University of Pennsylvania Press, 1999), p. 11.

[36] Donnelly in Bauer and Bell (eds.), *The East Asian Challenge for Human Rights,* p. 68.

should begin to notice how differently nations with the same rights traditions interpret its core principles. A common tradition does not necessarily result in common points of view on rights matters. All of the formative rights cultures of the West—the English, the French, and the American—give a different account of privacy, free speech, incitement, and the right to life. In the fifty years since the promulgation of the Universal Declaration, these disagreements within the competing Western rights traditions have become more salient. Indeed, the moral unanimity of the West—always a myth more persuasive from the outside than from the inside—is breaking up and revealing its incorrigible heterogeneity. American rights discourse once belonged to the common European natural law tradition and to the British common law. But this sense of a common anchorage now competes with a growing sense of American moral and legal exceptionalism.

American human rights policy in the last twenty years is increasingly distinctive and paradoxical: a nation with a great national rights tradition that leads the world in denouncing the human rights violations of others but that refuses to ratify international rights conventions itself. The most important resistance to the domestic application of international rights norms comes not from rogue states outside the Western tradition or from Islam and Asian societies. It comes, in fact, from within the heart of the Western rights tradition itself, from a nation that, in linking rights to popular sovereignty, opposes international human rights oversight as an infringement on its democracy. Of all the ironies in the history of human rights since the Declaration, the one that would most astonish Eleanor Roosevelt is the degree to which her own country is now the odd one out.

In the next fifty years, we can expect to see the moral consensus that sustained the Universal Declaration in 1948 splintering still further. For all the rhetoric about common values, the distance between America and Europe on rights questions—like abortion and capital punishment—may grow, just as the distance between the West and the Rest may also increase. There is no reason to believe that economic globalization entails moral globalization. Indeed, there is some reason to think that as economies have unified their business practices, ownership, languages, and networks of communication, a countermovement has developed to safeguard the integrity of national communities, national cultures, religions, and indigenous and religious ways of life.

This does not mean the end of the human rights movement, but its belated coming of age, its recognition that we live in a plural world of cultures that have a right to equal consideration in the argument about what we can and cannot, should and should not, do to human beings. Indeed, this may be the central historical importance of human rights in the history of human progress: it has abolished the hierarchy of civilizations and cultures. As late as 1945, it was normative to think of European civilization as inherently superior to the civilizations it ruled. Many Europeans continue to believe this, but they know that they have no right to do so. More to the point, many non-Western peoples also took the civilizational superiority of their rulers for granted. They no longer have any normative reason to continue believing this. One reason why this is so is the global diffusion of human rights. It is the language that most consistently articulates the moral equality of all the individuals on the face of the earth. But to the degree that it does, it simultaneously increases the level of conflict over the meaning, application, and legitimacy of rights claims. Rights language says: all human beings belong at the table, in the essential conversation about how we should treat each other. But once this universal right to speak and be heard is granted, there is bound to be tumult. There is bound to be discord. Why? Because the European voices that once took it upon themselves to silence the babble with a peremptory ruling no longer believe in their right to do so, and those who sit with them at the table no longer grant them the right to do so. All this counts as progress, as a step toward a world imagined for millennia in different cultures and religions: a world of genuine moral equality among human beings. But if so, a world of moral equality is a world of conflict, deliberation, argument, and contention.

To repeat a point made earlier: We need to stop thinking of human rights as trumps and begin thinking of them as a language that creates the basis for deliberation. In this argument, the ground we share may actually be quite limited: not much more than the basic intuition that what is pain and humiliation for you is bound to be pain and humiliation for me. But this is already something. In such a future, shared among equals, rights are not the universal credo of a global society, not a secular religion, but something much more limited and yet just as valuable: the shared vocabulary from which our arguments can begin and the bare human minimum from which differing ideas of human flourishing can take root.

Tradition without Convention:

The Impossible Nineteenth-Century Project

CHARLES ROSEN

THE TANNER LECTURES ON HUMAN VALUES

Delivered at

University of Utah
April 11, 2000

CHARLES ROSEN is professor emeritus in the Committee on Social Thought and in music at the University of Chicago. He studied piano and general music at Juilliard School and was educated at Princeton University, where he received his Ph.D. in 1951. He made his New York debut at Town Hall in 1951, the same year that he made the first complete recording of the Debussy études. He has concertized throughout the United States and Europe and in South Africa, New Zealand, Brazil, and Israel. His diverse discography of more than fifty recordings includes "The Last Keyboard Works of Johann Sebastian Bach" and "The Last Six Beethoven Sonatas"; his recording of Beethoven's *Diabelli Variations* was nominated for a Grammy Award. Igor Stravinsky invited him to record his Movements for Piano and Orchestra, and Elliott Carter his Double Concerto. His many books include *The Classical Style: Haydn, Mozart, Beethoven* (1971), which won the National Book Award; *Romantic Poets, Critics, and Other Madmen* (1999), awarded the Truman Capote Prize for literary criticism; and *Critical Entertainments: Music Old and New* (2000).

Some years ago, when I was practicing a difficult passage in the Concerto in B-flat Major, K. 450 by Mozart (Example 1), I found that I had absentmindedly strayed into a similar virtuoso phrase from another B-flat Concerto, the last one, K. 595 (Example 2).

Example 1. K. 450, I bars 65–68

Example 2. K. 595, I bars 97–102

Both these phrases represent typical Mozartean virtuosity in B-flat major. We can find other examples in the finale of the Sonata in B-flat Major, K. 333 (this movement, indeed, is written like a concerto rondo arranged for solo piano and mimics the relation of orchestra to soloist throughout) (Example 3):

Example 3.

and in the Sonata for Piano and Violin K. 454, also in B-flat major (finale, bars 259ff.) (Example 4):

Example 4.

These passages are formed out of the basic elements of tonality: placing them well requires a certain mastery, but the invention of material here may be said to be almost at the zero degree. It is easy to see how any one of these passages may conveniently be replaced by a similar one from another work. The kind of mistake I made, however, is unlikely to happen with a later concerto. During the nineteenth century an important change took place in the history of musical style in the West—a progressive change, and we are still living with it.

Late eighteenth century music depended on a repertoire of conventional formulaic phrases that might be transferred at will from one work to another. Of course, almost all musical styles depend on some sort of conventional repertoire of motifs: in most periods the main body of this repertoire generally consists of cadence formulas, ways of ending or rounding off individual phrases or complete works. These cadence formulas, in fact, may often be said to define the style.

What is striking, however, about the second half of the eighteenth century is the grand dimension of these formulas, their imposing length—how long they last and what a large role they play temporally in the structure. They are not simply, as in other periods, motifs or short sequential sets of harmonies, but elaborate phrases lasting several bars, sometimes, indeed, a succession of several phrases. They act within large forms as a kind of stuffing. They fill out the work.

They also articulate the form, occurring most often at cadences. In concertos (and sometimes in sonatas), these formulas are virtuoso arabesques woven out of scales and arpeggios: for the most part they are derived from the coloratura passage-work developed at that time for the operatic stage, and the technique is transferred to the keyboard concerto and sonata or, less often, to the violin concerto. It is essential to the tradition that these conventional passages of virtuosity be executed with grace and ease. In symphonies and quartets, the conventional phrases tend to be elaborate and lengthy flourishes or fanfares. They mark the spaces between the end of one melody and the beginning of another, or between two playings of the same theme. We may take an example from one of the more symphonic of Mozart's piano sonatas, the A minor, K. 310. The rounding-off of the main theme is marked by a lengthy but conventional half cadence (Example 5).

Later, the end of the exposition is articulated by an equally conventional phrase. Here there is standard virtuoso figuration in the left hand and a military fanfare in the right (Example 6).

Example 5.

Example 6.

These banal phrases are a stumbling block today to critics of Mozart, who prefer to gloss over, or even forget, the conventional aspects of his work and concentrate on the more original inspirations, which are often very radical indeed. This modern prejudice, however, does a disservice to Mozart's accomplishment, as his handling of the most conventional material reveals an easy mastery denied to almost all his contemporaries, and we therefore fail to see how the more eccentric aspects of his style depend on a purely conventional context to make their effect. I have written elsewhere that when there is a convention of form, it is always found completely and elaborately fulfilled and even nakedly revealed in Mozart, while Haydn deals with the conventions as quickly as possible, even sometimes attempting to disguise or skate over them. This explains why the amount of "stuffing" is so much greater in Mozart's work than in Haydn's, where, nevertheless, it still plays an important role.

One might speculate that the expansive treatment of the traditional filling material has made Mozart an easier composer for today's audiences to listen to than Haydn with his more summary way of dealing with it, now that we have absorbed, and are no longer disconcerted by, the radical innovations in Mozart that made him such a difficult composer for his contemporaries. The conventional passages functioned as an aid to intelligibility, and still work as such today.

It is worth considering briefly one of the most radical passages in Mozart to see how it depends on the most conventional setting. The most routine procedure for rounding out a development section in the last quarter of the eighteenth century is a cadence on the relative minor—or a half cadence on its dominant (V of vi)—followed by a return to the tonic. The second solo, or development, of Mozart's Concerto in B-flat Major, K. 595 begins with his most astonishing modulation—from F major to B minor—and continues with a series of surprises (Example 7).

The progression, perhaps the most extreme in all of Mozart, goes from B minor to C major, C minor, E-flat minor, V of B major, V of A-flat major, V of F minor, and finally V of G minor, the relative minor. The last three moves are accomplished with conventional passagework, and, indeed, with the arrival at G minor, we reach another convention of the second solo of concerto form during Mozart's lifetime, the use of arpeggios.

These arpeggios begin the retransition, and the harmonic progression is a strikingly conventional ascent to the subdominant: g, c, f, B-flat, E-flat. Then Mozart reaffirms the conventional relative minor by its dominant (D major), and then, with a set of arpeggios, accomplishes the return to the opening theme and the tonic. The conventional detail is as exquisitely handled as the unprecedented and eccentric harmonic progressions. In this extraordinary work, the conventional elements of structure, the banal figuration, and the arpeggios help Mozart to solve the problem of an expansive form. They allow the composer to slow down the momentum as the development section reaches its end after the disconcertingly swift changes of the opening, and the endow the return to the opening theme with the necessary breadth. They announce the resolution while suspending the movement toward it.

The passages of conventional filler—arpeggios, virtuoso figuration, or fanfares—are essential to the late eighteenth century's project of

Example 7.

enlarging the shorter binary forms of the first half of the century into the more imposing sonata forms. The growth of public concerts at that time made the larger forms desirable, and what was wanted were forms more tightly organized than the relatively loose sectional forms of the *da capo* aria or the *concerto grosso,* in which the dramatic climax cannot be focused as successfully and as lucidly as in the later symphonic structures, where the moments of extreme dramatic tension are far more clearly articulated than they could have been with early eighteenth century style.

On the lowest level, the long passages of stuffing in the late eighteenth century simply helped to pass the time, to extend the dimensions of the form, to make it more imposing. However, the emphasis they added at cadences had powerful consequences for the large-scale harmonic structure as well: they enabled the composer to transform with ease the standard half-cadence on V at the end of the first part of an early eighteenth century binary form into a full cadence that affirmed the dominant in what would later be called a modulation, raising the long-range power of the harmony to a higher level. The conventionality was, in fact, an asset; it made the form more easily intelligible in public performance. The audience did not have to strain to understand something original or eccentric.

In concerto and aria, the conventional virtuoso figuration may be said paradoxically to have combined physical excitement with intellectual relaxation. They made it possible for the audience to admire the performers without having to strain to admire the composition. The moments of purely conventional material that essentially resolved any previous harmonic and even melodic tension were basic to the style we call classical, which required, at a point about three-quarters of the way through the movement, an emphatic and lengthy resolution of any form of structural dissonance, a resolution that could not, as later in Chopin and Liszt, be postponed to the last page.

The conventionality is also derived from improvisation, which in general is dependent on a repertory of standard figures. For example, in the keyboard concertos of the third quarter of the eighteenth century by Wagenseil and others, the second solo (or what, in a sonata form, we would later call the development section) was sometimes notated only as a series of harmonies that were to be arpeggiated at will in any way the soloist pleased. Later in the century these arpeggios were written out and specified by the composer. The standard formulas did not disappear. A page of sketches by Beethoven once puzzled experts, as it consisted entirely of a series of these standard figures, all relatively banal. It was realized that this was a repertory of figures that Beethoven could use in improvisation—he was, in fact, famous for his extempore powers, and he had his collection of formulas just as the poets who improvised oral epic poetry had their repertory of standard phrases, images, metaphors, and epithets. Beethoven was, however, to effect a profound change in the use of conventional material.

2.

The aethestics of the late eighteenth century developed a fixed prejudice against the conventional as part of the widespread and even fashionable contemporary speculation on the nature of language, a prejudice extending into our own time. There is a double significance to the word "conventional," and the two meanings cannot be completely separated in eighteenth-century aesthetics. The conventional is both commonplace (that is, familiar and banal) and arbitrary (that is, imposed by an act of will). A convention is accepted by everyone precisely because it is arbitrary, because it is imposed. There can be no disagreement because there is no argument. For the eighteenth-century critic, the signs of painting are "natural": that is, the painted image of a tree signifies a tree because it looks like a tree. The arbitrary nature of language, however, has been acknowledged at least since Aquinas: a word signifies its meaning by convention, not because it sounds like, or imitates, its meaning—even when it does, as with onomatopoeia (words like "buzz" and "gargle"), the meaning is still fixed and imposed by arbitrary convention. That is why language is essentially social, not personal, and makes available only the meanings that society has agreed upon, not the inimitably individual significance that each of us might like in order to express something absolutely unique.

The most famous eighteenth-century discussion of the arbitrary character of linguistic signs is G. E. Lessing's *Laokoon,* written in 1766, in which it is maintained that the arbitrary signs of language can only describe in temporal succession those qualities in Nature that coexist simultaneously:

> Es ist wahr; da die Zeichen der Rede willkührlich sind, so ist es gar wohl möglich, daß man durch sie die Teile eines Körpers eben so wohl auf einander folgen lassen kann, als sie in der Natur neben einander befindlich sind. Allein dieses ist eine Eigneschaft der Rede und ihrer Zeichen überhaupt, nicht aber in so ferne sie der Absicht der Poesie am bequemsten sind. Der Poet will nicht bloß verständlich werden, seine Vorstellungen sollen nicht bloß klar und deutlich sein; hiermit begnügt sich der Prosaist. Sondern er will die Ideen, die er in uns erwecket, so lebhaft machen, daß wir in der Geschwindigkeit die wahre sinnlichen Eindrücke ihrer Gegenstände zu empfinden glauben, und in diesem Augenblicke der Täuschung, uns der Mittel, die er dazu anwendet, seiner Worte bewußt zu sein aufhören.

[It is true, the signs of speech are arbitrary, so it is indeed possible that through them one can let the parts of a body follow each other when they are to be found contiguous in Nature. But this is, above all, a characteristic of speech and its signs, not, however, insofar as they are most convenient for poetry. The poet does not want simply to be understood, his representations should not be simply clear and intelligible: that would content the writer of prose. But the poet wants the ideas that he awakens in us to be made so lively that we immediately believe that we feel the real sensuous impressions of his objects, and, in this moment of illusion, gives us the means to cease to be conscious of his words.]

In short, poetry transcends the arbitrary nature of language. Ideally, the words in the poem do not merely signify the meanings established by convention; they make the reader seem to experience the meaning sensuously and directly. The words are transformed from arbitrary signs into natural ones: the words of a poem, if the poet is successful, appear to convey their meaning by their sound and rhythm and by the way they are ordered. The significance arises not only by the conventions of meaning recorded in a dictionary but out of the poem itself, which gives the illusion of newly inventing or recreating the meanings of the words.

In his essay, Lessing was influenced by Denis Diderot's *Lettre sur les sourds et muets* of 1751, which asserted that in poetry, sound, rhythm, and word order are all so many "hieroglyphics" (or symbols) that combine to remove the arbitrary character of meaning. For Diderot, language in poetic discourse takes on a kind of organic life:

Il passe alors dans le discours du poëte un esprit qui en meut & vivifie toutes les syllabes. Q'est-ce que cet esprit? j'en ai quelquefois senti la présence; mais tout ce que j'en sais, c'est que c'est lui qui fait que les choses sont dites & représentées tout à la fois; que dans le même temps que l'entendement les saisit, l'ame en est émue, l'imagination les voit, & l'oreille les entend; & que le discours n'est plus seulement un enchaînement de termes energiques qui expose la pensée avec force & noblesse, mais que c'est encore un tissu d'hiéroglyphes entassées les uns sur les autres qui la peignent. Je pourrais dire en ce sens que toute poésie est emblématique.

[There takes place in the poet's discourse a spirit that activates and enlivens all the syllables. What is this spirit? sometimes I have felt its presence, but all I know is that it causes things to be both said and represented at once, that at the same time that the understanding

grasps them, the soul is moved, the imagination sees them, and the
ear hears them, and that the discourse is no longer only a series of energetic terms that display the thought with force and nobility, but
also paint it by a web of hieroglyphics piled on top of each other. I
might say that in this sense all poetry is emblematic.]

This astonishingly early proclamation of symbolist theory implies that
poetry transforms the signs of language, the words, from arbitrary into
natural symbols. The poetic technique breathes life into the words: they
no longer signify by simple convention, but by stimulating and awak-
ening the listener to their meaning. For Diderot, this poetic sophistication is a sign of an advanced state of civilization, and he also proposes to
carry his analysis of the effects of poetry and its hieroglyphic character
into the arts of painting and music. But not everyone, he claims, is capable of appreciating the subtleties of poetry: those who are sensitive to
them form an elite (although not, it must be said hastily, an elite defined
by class). As Diderot remarks, the symbolic nature of poetic discourse
makes even the easiest poet hard to read if we wish to understand him
fully, and impossible to translate.

3.

The identification of the commonplace with the arbitrary is profound,
but it obscures the dynamic process of stylistic development: a convention only becomes commonplace when it loses its logical reason for existing—when, in short, it becomes arbitrary, when its justification
becomes dubious. A convention remains alive when it seems inevitable;
but when we become aware that we can do without it, it begins to be
tiresome, and even to seem vulgar. It is not frequency that makes repetition appear commonplace, but the lack of evident necessity. A slice of
bread at every meal will not seem tiresome to those who find it unthinkable to go without it. When the classical conventions were still
vigorous, they were felt to be as indispensable as bread or potatoes.
When, for example, the convention of the final cadence in tonal music
or the modulation to the dominant in an exposition went unchallenged,
it did not then feel banal or commonplace.

   In the final quarter of the eighteenth century, however, the demand
for originality, perhaps imperceptibly at first, stimulated musicians to

question certain aspects of the tonal language. It has sometimes been claimed that composers like Haydn and Mozart thought of themselves as craftsmen writing only for their contemporaries rather than as original and even radically innovative artists with at least one eye on posterity. This will not hold water, however. Connoisseurs insisted on originality—and of course, as they do today, resisted it when it came along. One sign of this was the despairing sense that the conventions of tonality had now been exhausted. Charles Burney's conversation in 1770 with the Roman opera composer Rinaldo di Capua is instructive in this respect:[1] music was finished, the Italian composer asserted—all possible beautiful melodies had already been invented, all the beautiful modulations discovered. The best one could do was to create an ugly modulation to set the beautiful one in relief.

The modern dogma that the shock of the ugly is the inevitable and only road to original creation has begun to rear its head. Even more instructive is the comment of critic Johann Friederich Reichardt in 1782 on the rising reputation of Johann Sebastian Bach. Reichardt was not entirely comfortable with the new vogue: technically, he felt, Bach was one of the greatest masters, but he was deficient in his rendering of sentiment. If Bach and Handel had only understood the human heart, he claimed, "a great genius who would not be satisfied today only with equaling them would have to overthrow our entire tonal system in order to create a new field for himself" (*Musikalisches Kunstmagazin*). This astonishing foreboding of the arrival of atonality is a witness to the importance attached to radical originality.

Only a decade or so later, however, Novalis was to be even more incisive when he wrote:

> Alles Ausgezeichnete verdient den Ostrazism. Es ist gut, wenn es ihn sich selbst gibt.

> [All excellence merits ostracism. It is well when it ostracizes itself.]

This is one of the fundamental tenets of modernism. By 1828, the Italian poet Giacomo Leopardi was to claim that any truly original melody was bound inevitably to displease a public that was content only with the familiar.

---

[1] See my *The Frontiers of Meaning* (New York: Hill and Wang, 1994), Lecture 2.

4.

In the process of the destruction of conventional material, Beethoven is a pivotal but ambiguous figure. The conventional material does not disappear from his music—on the contrary, there is perhaps even more of it in his work than in Mozart's. But it loses some, or even most, of its conventional aspect. The traditional, conventional use of arpeggios in the second solo of the concerto will give us a good example: they are present in every one of Beethoven's concertos. Ostentatiously present, in fact, and that makes all the difference. The clearest example is the "Emperor" concerto, bars 273–301 (Example 8).

Following Haydn rather than Mozart, Beethoven arrives at the relative minor early in the development instead of waiting for the more traditional end of the section, and the soloist accompanies the melody in the orchestra for sixteen bars with varied arpeggios. With bar 289, the arpeggios are no longer an accompaniment but have taken over the texture aggressively. Fragments of the main theme in the orchestra now become the accompaniment to the relentless and energetic arpeggios of the soloist. The arpeggios have ceased to appear conventional: they have become thematic, the principal motif, the bearer of meaning on which we concentrate all our attention. In short, the "arbitrary" has been "naturalized"—that is, given an immediately perceptible meaning unforeseen by the tradition and independent of it. It now sounds as if Beethoven had created the idea of arpeggios specifically for his concerto: with that, the existence of a tradition has been made irrelevant. Beethoven does not simply employ the traditional stuffing with the mastery of Mozart: he reinvents it.

In the development of a Mozart concerto, the standard arpeggios may be played with an improvisatory quality—for example, the opening of the development in the first movement of the Concerto in G Major, K. 453. Mozart recalls the origin of this convention. In the "Emperor" concerto, however, all sense of improvisation must be left behind. These arpeggios are no longer improvised; they are composed. They must be played strictly as part of a symphonic texture.

It has often been remarked, furthermore, how much of Beethoven's thematic material is not merely derived from the conventional filling of the classical technique but reproduces it nakedly, generally in his most important works. The opening themes of the Ninth Symphony, the "Eroica," and the "Appassionata" all start as simple unadorned arpeg-

Example 8.

gios, as if the basic building blocks of tonality were enough of a stimulus to create a form. The conventional cadence is similarly remodeled
under his hands. The opening of the Sonata in E-flat Major, op. 31 no. 3,
juxtaposes the radical and the banal in a new way (Example 9).

The opening six bars are among Beethoven's most eccentric inspirations, harmonically, melodically, and rhythmically. Opening with a
question that expresses a powerful yearning by an intense chromatic rise

Example 9.

and a gradual and dramatic slowing down, these bars are answered by a cadence of the utmost conventionality. It is, in fact, the banal aspect of the cadence that gives it an ironic air and makes a witty and deflating contrast to the strange opening. Using the commonplace for ironic purposes was, I think, new in music at that time, unless we count the exaggeratedly simple minuet that accompanies Susanna's appearance from the closet in the second act finale of *The Marriage of Figaro,* when she obviously enjoys the discomfiture of the count and the countess. The irony is certainly new in pure instrumental music: Beethoven's cadence sounds exaggeratedly conventional, coming as it does after the extraordinary opening, and it enhances by contrast the intense lyricism of the opening. In any case, the conventional cadence is no longer conventional as it now speaks with an individual voice, and adds a note of comedy to the lyrical atmosphere. We might say that the conventional has become a special effect essential to the representation of sentiment in this work, and has consequently been naturalized.

I might add, parenthetically, that a theme of such contrasting character is inherited from the classical technique of Mozart, and was about to become impossible in the music of the 1830s and after. In Mozart's work, these contrasting themes are generally replayed at once with the contrast now resolved into a synthetic whole, as in the "Jupiter" Symphony, where the opening opposition is restated, now united by a flute solo (Example 10).
In Beethoven's Opus 31, no. 3, the synthesis or resolution of the contradictory character of the main theme is postponed to the end of the exposition, where a condensed and laconic version of both the opening motif and its witty conclusion closes the section (Example 11).

This postponement is an adaptation of the scheme learned from Mozart, but employed in a way that reinforces the effectiveness of the larger structure. The tension created by the opposition within the main theme is left unresolved by Beethoven until the final cadence of the

Example 10a.

Example 10b.

Example 11.

exposition. The need for resolution even on this small scale is extended
to the entire exposition. It should be observed that in this sonata the
conventionality of the simple cadence that always resolves the intense
and eccentric opening of the principal theme is only partly ironic: it is
also a sign of grace. A difficult and puzzling motif is succeeded by a gesture of sociability. The conventionality here is clearly a virtue and a
pleasure, a form of relief from the more complex experience of the previous bars: we are expected to welcome and appreciate the cadence precisely for its conventionality.

It is easy to find examples of Beethoven's rethinking the major conventions in order to give the impression that they have been invented
for the particular work; and, as I have implied, this is a sign that the
conventions were beginning to lose their authority for the musical
imagination. I mention only one further example here—briefly, as I have
written about it elsewhere.[2] Perhaps the dreariest of academic conventions is the use in fugue of the devices of inversion, augmentation, and
diminution. In the finale of Opus 110, Beethoven employs these devices
as if each had been invented specifically for this one work. After the
exhausted character of the second Adagio arioso (*ermattet*), the rising
theme of the fugue is inverted, now descending and so losing its force;
the return to life (*poi a poi di nuovo vivente*) is signified by the augmentation of the theme in a tempo twice as slow that gradually accelerates
back into the original tempo, and by the diminution of the theme, now
three times as fast, giving the sense of new vigor. These old-fashioned
and banal devices are here given a meaning within a dramatic scenario
for, as far as I know, the first time in the history of music. The conventions of the fugue are naturalized, and this would have been unnecessary
if they had not been felt to be in need of justification, to have outlived
their usefulness.

_____

[2] See *The Classical Style: Haydn, Mozart, Beethoven,* revised and enlarged edition (New
York: Norton, 1998), penultimate chapter.

5.

The generation that followed Beethoven—Chopin, Schumann, Liszt, Mendelssohn, Berlioz, Wagner[3]—was torn between the need to master the classical conventions and the desire to ignore them. Liszt's one attempt at the classical sonata is clearly a reformulation and deformation of the conventions for the purpose of constructing a new type of dramatic form. It is not program music like some of the sonatas by Clementi or Dussek or like Beethoven's "Pastoral" Symphony, all of which work by mimesis: the now conventional structure of sonata-form is reworked by Liszt from within, to create a progressive scenario of despair, consolation, Satanism, triumph, and death (for the layout of the work, he followed in the steps of Beethoven and Schubert, using the finale of the Choral Symphony and the "Wanderer" Fantasy as models). Neither Schumann nor Mendelssohn created his most successful works with full respect for, or obedience to, the classical sonata conventions: Schumann almost always displays a certain awkwardness with them, and Mendelssohn an inevitable blandness. Both achieved their most distinguished and popular achievements in large forms when these appear to be invented with relative freedom, as in their recasting of the concerto or the program overture. Chopin's two mature sonatas have always been brilliantly effective in public, but the principal movements are idiosyncratic and even eccentric. The large works of Chopin and Schumann that have had the greatest prestige evade classical sonata modules: the Ballades, Scherzos, and Polonaises, the F Minor Fantasy and the Barcarolle, the *Davidsbündlertänze,* the *Carneval,* the C Major Fantasy, *Dichterliebe, Frauenliebe und Leben,* etc.

More significant, however, is the disappearance from the music of both Chopin and Schumann of the conventional passagework still found in Beethoven and Hummel, an almost total disappearance in Schumann after opus 1, and a drastic reduction in Chopin after the Andante Spianato and Grande Polonaise. Any virtuoso "filling" that remains in mature Chopin is no longer simply cadential in nature (with rare exceptions, like the end of the E Major Scherzo), but is either thematic or reworked with astonishing originality, above all in the final sections of the Ballades.

The late 1840s betrayed a new musical conservatism, a desire to return to the past already evident in the work of Liszt and Schumann.

---

[3] I do not have the space here to consider the important intermediate figures of Schubert and Weber.

Even Wagner and the so-called Music of the Future did not remain untouched by this change in musical ideology: we can see this not only in *Die Meistersinger* and *Parsifal,* but also in parts of *Der Ring des Nibelungen.* The leading figure in the reaction is, of course, Brahms: the reminiscence of Beethoven's Opus 106 in Brahms's Opus 1 and the allusion to Beethoven's Choral Symphony in Brahms's Symphony No. 1 were manifestos, and were understood as such at the time. Chrysander even shrewdly interpreted the reference to the Choral Symphony as a signal that Brahms intended to lead music back to a pure instrumental style.

We are beginning today, however, to understand how radically Brahms reinterpreted classical forms and technique, how he attempted to revive and preserve the style while getting rid of many of its most conventional aspects. The basis of classical triadic tonality is the relation between tonic and dominant. This was considerably weakened by the composers of the 1830s, who were more interested in mediants than in a classical tonic/dominant polarity. The diatonic purity of triadic tonality was attacked from the beginning by the minor mode, which always introduces chromatic elements. In the eighteenth century the minor mode is essentially an exception, an agent of trouble. It is therefore significant that all the sonatas for piano, or for violin and piano, or for cello and piano by Chopin and Schumann are in the minor mode, which uses the mediant as an immediate secondary key instead of the dominant (although the dominant minor can turn up later in the exposition in a succeeding tonicization). What is essential to triadic tonality, however, is the major dominant.[4]

In a number of works, Brahms goes farther than anyone to weaken the tonic/dominant polarity by substituting the dominant *minor* for the major.[5] The dominant minor lacks precisely the sharpened leading tone necessary to the strong tonal cadence. The exposition of the first movement of the third string quartet in B-flat major mixes the major and minor modes of F major very ambiguously, and this removes some of the power of the dominant. (The theme of the variations in the last movement uses D minor instead of the dominant F: the exotic harmonic

---

[4] Beethoven's occasional substitution of a mediant for the dominant is always preceded by an elaborate preparation on the dominant of the mediant chosen. This is largely evaded by Chopin, who prefers a rapid change using a pivot note (e.g., shifting from A flat major to E major by holding the tonic note of A-flat and simply putting an E-natural under it). For an elaborate form like the first movement of the B minor sonata, he moves in the exposition from B minor to the relative major D major by first shifting astonishingly to D minor and then changing the mode.

[5] See my *Sonata Forms* (New York: Norton, 1980), final chapter.

structure is B-flat major/D minor :‖: D major/B-flat major.) The solo exposition of the D major violin concerto goes to A minor, and the solo exposition of the B-flat major piano concerto goes to F minor (this makes
a problem for the opening ritornello, since returning directly to B flat
major from F minor is not possible, but it is cleverly solved by Brahms's
placing of the secondary material at first in D minor). Brahms also uses
the mediant minor instead of the major in the Cello Sonata in F Major,
where the exposition of the opening movement goes to A minor. In a
study of the proportions of Brahms's sonata forms, James Webster found
the coda to be anomalous for its length: there was, however, no way to
avoid a long coda, as logic forced Brahms to end his recapitulation correctly in D minor, and it was necessary to find the way back to F major.
In short, these are all, superficially, classical eighteenth-century forms,
but the harmonic structures are profoundly subversive of the traditional
stylistic language: the procedures weaken the foundations of the style
by adding an anomalous chromatic emphasis at odds with the very tradition that Brahms was claiming to revive. Carl Dahlhaus has cogently
remarked that in Wagner's *Die Meistersinger* the frequent diatonic pages
presuppose a basic chromatic background.[6] In spite of the opposition of
Brahms and Wagner, we may say the same of Brahms.

And we should go further: with both composers, the purely diatonic
in their music has come to sound exotic, the chromaticism normal. In
one respect Brahms goes more radically in the direction of twentieth-
century modernism than Wagner does: the dissonant contours of his
melodic shapes are insistent and spiky, and the dissonances carry more
weight than their release and resolution into consonance, which are always correct but for the most part deliberately underplayed. The interior cadences are generally weak (this is a characterization, not in the
least a value judgment), rarely decisive: moreover, the cadences in the
melodies are often out of phase with the cadences in the bass, which
serves to increase their weakness.

By softening the force of the cadence, Brahms attacked the principal
conventional element of the classical system while, at the same time, he
reproduced with extraordinary cunning the proportions, the procedures, and many of the lineaments of the style. He studied the composers of the past and recreated their techniques with material or
procedures that would have been previously rejected or would have been
unthinkable. The transition to the opening of the recapitulation of the

[6] See his article "Wagner" in *Grove 2* (1981).

Example 12.

first movement of the B-flat concerto is an example of his sophistication (Example 12).

A V-I cadence that prepares the return of the tonic and the main theme depends traditionally for its effect on the sense of a strong down-beat on the tonic chord. Brahms reproduces here the standard dominant preparation, even at great length, but the arrival of the tonic is placed as if it was still part of the dominant harmony and the articulation is

blurred. The blurring continues with the replaying of the two phrases of the opening theme, originally heard in the horn with echoes from the soloist: here, theme and echoes are merged, the antiphonal clarity of the opening of the movement becomes complex, the contours fluid. (In what follows, Brahms seems to have taken to heart Donald Francis Tovey's observation that in the concertos of Mozart the recapitulation is a synthesis of the first ritornello and the first solo.) The reentry of the main theme at the beginning of a recapitulation is the most important tonic cadence in the classical scheme next to the final cadence itself, and Brahms's treatment affects the structure of the movement as a whole. His attempt to evade the most conventional effect here can be compared to Wagner's treatment of the tonic cadences in the most diatonic of his works, *Die Meistersinger:* a very large number of these all-too-numerous cadences avoid the final tonic chord for a surprise resolution into V7 of V—or what would be a surprise if it did not occur so often in this work that it almost hardens into a new convention.

What is most remarkable about the return in this concerto of Brahms is the lack of forward drive and the sense of suspended rhythm. The end of the development appears to dissolve into the recapitulation. The tension of the lengthy dominant preparation of a return in the classical manner is not so much grounded as dispersed. Perhaps Brahms was influenced here by Mendelssohn's lyrical technique of ending a development with an air of exhaustion, but he has transferred that effect here to the return itself. The classical resolution on the tonic midway in the second part of the sonata is achieved on paper, but the dramatic scenario is completely subverted. Brahms seems to me far more radical in this instance than Beethoven in the "Appassionata," where the tension of the development is prolonged into the recapitulation by a dominant pedal. The recapitulation of Brahms's second piano concerto is very much like the recapitulation of his Symphony no. 4, where the opening theme returns in a stillness marked *dolce,* with the rhythm arrested and even suspended by the augmentation. This extraordinary passage is often performed with an unnecessary *ritenuto,* spoiling the subtle effect of the pianissimo arpeggios in the strings, which create two written-out four-bar fermatas.[7]

Brahms may seem to be preserving the classical conventions, but in fact he reformulates their function in ways that attack the foundations of the style. Perhaps Haydn was equally revolutionary for his period, but Beethoven's works never altered the premises of the musical lan-

---

[7] The aesthetic implied by these striking moments lies behind the even more unclassical return of the opening movement of Symphony no. 3: not only is there no dominant preparation of the return of the tonic F major (except at the last possible and very brief moment), but any sense of a dominant is contradicted by a repeated emphasis on an E flat over an E flat pedal and then a brief tonic pedal. Perhaps this derived from a study of Beethoven's Symphony no. 4, where the return of the tonic had been prepared paradoxically by a long tonic pedal, but Brahms has subverted the essentially classical aspects of Beethoven's device. In any case, introducing the tonic through an emphasis on the flatted seventh must have been unprecedented when Brahms did it here.

guage to the extent that Brahms does in many of the large works. But then Brahms had the radical experience of the generation of Schumann as part of his equipment, to say nothing of the contemporary challenge of Wagner, for whom Brahms had a grand but suitably nuanced admiration.

The second piano concerto makes more use of conventional virtuoso figuration than, for example, Schumann did in his piano concerto, from which it was virtually eliminated. Nevertheless, Brahms's use is idiosyncratic and, we might say, fundamentally unconventional. He does, naturally, follow Beethoven in naturalizing the conventional by making it thematic. The arpeggios that begin the cadenza right after the opening of the concerto provide an example (Example 13):

Example 13.

This makes the opening page of the "Emperor," on which it is clearly modeled, seem by contrast extremely conventional, and the free tempo of Beethoven's cadenza has yielded to a much stricter tempo.

Not all of the conventional elements, however, are given a similar thematic character. In this concerto, which is famous for its exacerbation of the virtuoso element, the conventional arpeggios, scales, and figuration of the concertos of Mozart are not absent. Nevertheless, one essential character of the conventional filling in a classical concerto is canceled by Brahms: the grace and ease with which it should be performed. Almost without exception, the conventional material is slightly altered by Brahms so that it sounds awkward as well as difficult; the pianist not only has trouble playing it, but—against the grain of the convention, contradicting its purpose—clearly appears to everyone to be having difficulty. The tradition demanded that the difficulties of display be solved with an apparent ease of execution: the virtuosity was an impersonal or neutral element of the composition; the ease of the performer allowed the admiration of the spectators to be concentrated entirely on the execution of the purely mechanical. Our consciousness of the deliberate awkwardness of the passages of display in Brahms, by contrast, adds an impure element that partially blocks the audience's surrender to the interests of the performer; the awkward alterations divert attention to the composer, even in passages of almost completely mechanical content (Example 14):

Example 14. Bar 154, B flat Concerto, I

The extra note A-natural in this arpeggio of the dominant seventh of F minor makes this bar horrendously difficult to perform, and impossible to execute with any sense of ease. The most difficult passages in a concerto by Rachmaninov or Tchaikovsky allow the soloist an appearance of facility and grace refused by Brahms. This imposed awkwardness oddly transforms the mechanical into the expressive—or, in other words, the arbitrary sign into a natural signifier. Similarly with the famous parallel thirds in the final movement (Example 15):

Eample 15. Bars 32–36

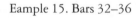

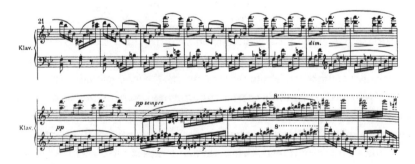

This reproduces part of the scheme of the opening strain of the finale of Beethoven's Concerto no. 3 in C Minor that Brahms followed almost slavishly as a model for the finale of both his piano concertos and is a substitute for Beethoven's brief cadenza, except that Beethoven's trill precedes the scale, and his scale is only a single line, not in parallel thirds. Brahms later reinforces the new complexity by demanding that the parallel thirds be played by one hand alone. Even if the soloist plays all the notes *leggiero* as marked, this never sounds like the more free-wheeling cadenza style of the Beethoven concerto. It is only when we compare this with the model, in fact, that we realize that these bars actually function as a cadenza written out in strict time and that Brahms, as he did with the first concerto, has adhered faithfully to the Beethoven scheme, with a motif repeated several times followed by a cadenza leading directly back to the opening phrase of the main theme (Example 16):

Example 16. Bars 20–28

In short, Brahms has rewritten the classical cadenza so as to remove the basic convention and function of a cadenza, its sense of free improvisation.

One idiosyncratic employment of convention should be mentioned: the use of a convention so old-fashioned, so archaic, that it had ceased to be conventional, but had become an original and almost exotic effect. In Brahms's Violin Sonata no. 2 in A Major, the development section begins by playing the main theme at the dominant and then replaying it at the tonic. Beginning a development with the main theme at the

dominant was a convention that was still alive; beginning with the
main theme at the tonic was an experiment of Beethoven in Opus 31,
nos. 1 and 3. But playing the main theme at the dominant and immediately after at the tonic is a form so archaic that, as far as I know, it had
not been practiced by anyone since the 1760s, when it was commonplace and almost standard. Derived from the mid-century opera aria, it
can be found frequently in works of Haydn from that early period
(Oliver Strunk called it a "premature recapitulation" and thought it a
banal device, which it was), but Haydn later abandoned the scheme,
perhaps not only because it was banal but also because it inconveniently
reduced the tension of the development. Brahms revives it, but with
great originality (Example 17):

Example 17.

He exploits the inconvenience, as the relaxation of harmonic tension
increases the lyricism. It is also the fruit of a musicological study—a
convention so buried in the past that it has been forgotten and is no
longer conventional. Brahms is not only continuing a classical tradition,
but amusing himself here, I think, by resuscitating the dead.

6.

The project of purging art music of its conventions continues after Brahms into the twentieth century, and is still active today. Debussy almost always used only compound arpeggios, complicating the triadic nature of the device, and consented to write simple scales only ironically, as in the Etude for five fingers "in the style of Mr. Czerny." (As far as I can remember, Ravel wrote scales only *glissando* on either the white or black keys, which changes them from a witness to the harmonic language of tonality into examples of pure sonority.) The disappearance of scales and arpeggios is a great hardship for performers today, causing much misery above all perhaps for pianists, as the arrangement of the black and white keys of the keyboard was specifically designed to facilitate their execution and to make anything else more onerous. With instruments constructed for tonality, the loss of conventional material has made music harder to play, and, as we all know, harder to listen to. In the general development in the nineteenth century of all the arts—music, literature, and painting—the attempt to rid the arts of the standard conventions is the villain in the wicked creation of a difficult style and the consequent alienation of that large part of the public that resents any heavy demands made upon its attention.

The difference between art music and popular music is, in fact, largely a question of how much close attention is required or demanded for appreciation. Of course, when so-called classical music is familiar enough so that it no longer makes us uncomfortable, we can listen to it happily without paying much attention to it and think about more pressing and more practical considerations. The once controversial work of Wagner or Stravinsky can now be transformed into Muzak and performed in elevators without inspiring a public outcry.

Sustaining the classical tradition while weakening, or even dispensing with, so many of its conventions was a paradoxical activity. The classical language of music was largely dependent on these conventions: getting rid of them attacked the musical tradition and injured it almost beyond repair—at least, the music language was radically and systematically altered in the process in ways that were probably not completely understood, the consequences certainly not clearly foreseen. That the greatest and most durable masterpieces from 1750 to the present were composed through this project is not enough to make the fundamental loss of eighteenth-century tonality less poignant. Musicians were vaguely and intermittently aware of the danger of this loss of the tradition long before the present day: how wonderful it would be, Brahms once observed, to be a composer at the time of Mozart when it was easy to write music. The demand for innovation, the prejudice against convention, has made music not only harder to play and harder to listen to but also harder to compose.

In the twentieth century, a reaction against the sensuous delights of unlimited chromaticism and atonality brought an attempt to return to diatonic tonality in the work of composers as disparate as Virgil Thomson, Samuel Barber, and Philip Glass, to name only a few. But the tonal system they employ is by no means that of the eighteenth century: the symmetry of dominant and subdominant directions has disappeared, and there is no longer any of the rigor with which chromatic tonal relations were regulated in Haydn and his contemporaries. It is not that the eighteenth-century conventions are infringed or violated: on the contrary, they are ignorantly or innocently disregarded. In general, tonal relations are loosely conceived by neoconservatives and neoromantics today, and their laxity has not permitted a renaissance or revival of the structural richness of the classical tradition. Exceptionally, the most astonishingly effective use of a diatonic language in the last century has been that of Stravinsky after *Les Noces,* who exploited the conventions and formulas of tonality ironically. The main theme of his piano sonata shows his method (Example 18).

The harmonies are all tonic and dominant, but their function has been subverted: every melody note of the tonic triad after the first is harmonized by a dominant, every melody note from the dominant is harmonized by a tonic chord. Here there is a direct and consistent violation of the tonal significance, a systematic destruction of the conventions of tonality that undercuts any nostalgia or sentimentality that might arise from the composition of a sonata in C major. In *The Poetics of Music,* Stravinsky observed that in the 1920s he used the formulas of classical tonality the way he had previously employed the motifs of folk music. The technique in both cases was fundamentally one of alienation. The trill at the opening of the melody of the sonata reveals this as clearly as the harmony: a classical trill prepares the resolution of the cadence as the leading-tone goes into the tonic; transforming the trill into a *tremolo* on the interval of a ninth blocks resolution, as the dissonance of the ninth hangs over unresolved (above all because the composer has incorporated

Example 18.

the dissonance into a semblance of resolution). The technique of alienation is basic to Romanticism (defined succinctly by Novalis as "making
the strange familiar and the familiar strange") and the neoconservative
Stravinsky, like the neoconservative Brahms, continued the revolutionary development initiated by the late eighteenth century. Both subverted the conventions as they transformed them.

How is a convention established? Clearly by repetition. Of course,
the conventions that have been most firmly set in place are those that are
consonant with the basic nature of the musical language and style—but
that, too, is established by familiarity achieved through repetition. Perhaps the most profound aspect of serious music today is its disdain for
repetition. This is not a new phenomenon but the end of a long and
gradual development: the essential difference between an early eighteenth century *da capo* and a late eighteenth century sonata form is that
the *da capo* is structurally a literal repeat sometimes with added orna-
mentation improvised on the spot or planned by the soloist, while the
return of the opening section in the sonata has to be completely rewritten with an altered harmonic structure. Simple repetition (even with
improvised decoration) no longer satisfied the new sensibility.

The prejudice against unvaried repetition became firmly ingrained
during the nineteenth century. By the early twentieth, Strauss, Debussy,

and others have renounced the repetition of even short sections, unless they were completely rethought and reformulated. With the second half of the twentieth century, the avant-garde foreswore even the repetition of a theme. In the music of Luciano Berio, Karl-Heinz Stockhausen, Pierre Boulez, Elliott Carter, and others, we come upon the return of textures and even the return of certain kinds of harmonic configurations, but there is no return of a theme and even no simple recurrence of a motif. It would seem that the most interesting composers of our day have determined to block what might result in the creation of new conventions for future generations. We can be sure, however, that convention will find itself a way back by stealth, and it is probably already doing so.

Ecological Collapses of Pre-industrial Societies

JARED DIAMOND

THE TANNER LECTURES ON HUMAN VALUES

Delivered at

Stanford University
May 22–24, 2000

JARED M. DIAMOND is professor of physiology at the University of California at Los Angeles (UCLA) Medical School. He is also a research associate in ornithology at the American Museum of Natural History (New York) and the Los Angeles County Museum of Natural History. He was educated at Harvard University and received his Ph.D. from the University of Cambridge. He is a fellow of the American Academy of Arts and Sciences, a member of the National Academy of Sciences and the American Philosophical Society, and is director of the World Wildlife Fund, U.S.A. His evolutionary studies have been recognized by, among others, the Burr Award of the National Geographic Society and the Coues Award of the American Ornithologists' Union. He is the author of a number of books and monographs, including *The Third Chimpanzee* (1992), which won Britain's Science Book Prize (Rhône-Poulenc Prize), and most recently *Guns, Germs, and Steel: The Fates of Human Societies* (1997), which won both the Rhône-Poulenc Prize and the Pulitzer Prize for general nonfiction. He is the recipient of a MacArthur Foundation Fellowship, and in 1999 he was awarded the National Medal of Science.

Historians often justify the study of history on the grounds that it gives us the opportunity to learn from human errors in the past. Until recently, though, it seemed that we had nothing to learn from the past about how to avoid the environmental predicament in which human societies find themselves today. The greatest risk to humanity in coming decades is the risk that we may continue to damage our environment to a degree incompatible with our current standard of living, or even incompatible with our existence. That risk has seemed a unique one in human history, a consequence of our uniquely high modern numbers coupled with our uniquely potent destructive modern technology. There has been a widespread belief that pre-industrial peoples, unlike us moderns, respected Nature and lived in harmony with their environment and were wise stewards of natural resources.

But, in fact, many pre-industrial societies did collapse. Let us define "collapse of a society" as a local drastic decrease in human population numbers and/or in political, economic, or social complexity. Collapse can even proceed to the point that the human population completely disappears over a large area. By those definitions, the long list of victims of pre-industrial collapses includes the Anasazi of the U.S. Southwest, Angkor Wat, Cahokia outside St. Louis, Classic Lowland Maya, Easter Island and some other Polynesian societies, Fertile Crescent societies, Great Zimbabwe, the Greenland Norse, Harappan Indus Valley civilization, Mycenean Greece, and the Western Roman Empire. These vanished civilizations have fascinated us for a long time, as romantic mysteries.

Recent overwhelming evidence from archaeology and other disciplines is now demonstrating that some of those romantically mysterious

The ideas discussed in this paper arose from discussions with many friends and colleagues, whom I thank for their generosity and patience, and whom I absolve of responsibility for my errors. They include Julio Betancourt, Alfred Crosby, Jeffrey Dean, Anne and Paul Ehrlich, Eric Force, Patrick Kirch, Kristian Kristiansen, Barry Rolett, Stephen Schneider, Peter Vitousek, R. Gwinn Vivian, and Marshall Weisler. For generous encouragement and support I thank Eve and Harvey Masonek, Peter Myers, Vicki and Roger Sant, Doron Weber, Alan Weeden, Wren Wirth, and the following foundations: the Guggenheim Foundation, W. Alton Jones Foundation, Eve and Harvey Masonek and Samuel F. Heyman and Eve Gruber Heyman 1981 Trust Undergraduate Research Scholars Fund, Sloan Foundation, Summit Foundation, Weeden Foundation, and Winslow Foundation. I thank my research assistants Michelle Fisher-Casey, Laura Kim, and Lori Rosen, who have always been ready to track down yet another article or to type yet another draft.

collapses actually were self-inflicted ecological disasters, similar to the ecological suicide that we risk committing today. Those pre-industrial suicides unfolded despite the fact that past societies had much smaller populations and much less potent destructive technology than we possess today. We really can learn from the past. But this proves to be a very complicated problem. This is not a problem for anyone who likes simple answers or one-factor explanations, just as life itself is not an enterprise for anyone who likes simple answers or one-factor explanations.

What are some of the complications? First of all, it is certainly not the case that all pre-industrial societies were doomed to collapse. There are many parts of the world, like Japan and Java and Tonga and Tikopia, where human societies have existed continuously for thousands of years without any signs of collapse. Is this just because some environments are ecologically robust and other environments are ecologically fragile, and is it that the societies that collapsed were the ones in the fragile environments?

Second, environments may deteriorate not only as a result of human impacts, but also as a result of external climate changes, such as drought or cooling or an El Ninõ event. It is hard enough to distinguish internally from externally caused environmental change when it happens under our eyes today. How do we distinguish them in the past? Isn't it likely that societies that damaged their environments were most likely to collapse at a time of some added external stress like a drought, causing the two types of explanations to be inextricably linked?

Third, most human societies are connected to and dependent on other human societies through trade. Isn't it possible that societies in robust environments might be dragged down by collapses of neighboring societies in fragile environments?

Fourth, this same fact that most societies don't exist in a vacuum causes an obvious further problem. When a society that has neighbors disintegrates for any reason, the usual result is conquest or absorption by an intact neighboring society with which the failing society has been chronically at war for a long time anyway. Hence it is regularly difficult to decide whether the basic cause of collapse was "purely" military reasons or whether the conquest was just the coup-de-grace to a society already fatally weakened for fundamentally ecological reasons. For example, remember the long-standing debate over the fall of the Western Roman Empire: were those barbarian invasions the real cause, or was it instead the case that Rome's internal problems, such as environmental problems, merely allowed the barbarians chronically at Rome's borders to prevail at last?

Finally, people are not just helpless, ignorant victims of events. There is no doubt that many or most traditional societies were far more knowledgeable about their natural environments than most of us moderns are, if only because they were living much closer to their natural environments than we do today. People look around, they notice things, they are capable of very complex reasoning and planning, and they are motivated to act in their own self-interests. Why didn't people see obvious environmental disaster looming, and why didn't they take precautions to avert disaster? Sometimes they did take precautions that succeeded, like replanting of forests, or terracing to prevent erosion, or agricultural intensification. Why did they sometimes fail? Is it more likely that societies in some environments than in other environments will succeed in developing responses capable of mastering environmental problems?

I shall not attempt to review the fate of every pre-industrial society that ever did or did not collapse and to apportion the causes of collapse in every case. Instead, I shall discuss just two sets of cases, which nevertheless illustrate many or most of the problems involved in pre-industrial collapses. The first set consists of collapses and non-collapses of Polynesian and other societies on islands in the Pacific Ocean between about 1600 B.C. and A.D. 1800. The second set is much closer to home for Americans and consists of the collapses of most Native American farming societies in the U.S. Southwest between about A.D. 1100 and 1500.

The clearest examples of collapses of isolated societies involve remote Polynesian islands. Polynesia was settled by canoe voyagers, originating ultimately from the islands of the Bismarck Archipelago north of New Guinea, between about 1600 B.C. and A.D. 1000 (Bellwood 1987; Kirch 1997a; Kirch 2000; Spriggs 1997). Many Polynesian islands lie hundreds or even thousands of miles from the nearest other land. Hence many Polynesian societies, once they were founded by canoe voyagers, eventually lost contact with their ancestral source population and became totally cut off from other peoples for a thousand years or more, so we can be certain that the fates of those societies were not due to military conquest by neighbors, and we can thereby exclude one set of potential causes of collapses.

Among such isolated Polynesian societies, different ones experienced very different fates. Some, such as the Tongan Archipelago, are socially stratified kingdoms that have persisted uninterruptedly for about 3,600 years from their founding until the present, without any signs of a marked decline in population or in societal complexity (Kirch 1984). Others, such as the societies of Easter Island and New Zealand's South Island, did decline drastically in human numbers and complexity but continued to exist. A dozen other Polynesian societies, including those of Henderson Island and Necker Island and pre-*Bounty*-mutineer Pitcairn Island, collapsed so completely that no human remained alive.

The most spectacular collapse is also the one best documented archaeologically (Bahn and Flenley 1992; Flenley 1979; Flenley and King 1984; Steadman et al. 1994). Easter Island, the most remote habitable scrap of land in the world, lies in the Pacific Ocean about 2,000 miles west of South America and almost an equal distance east of the nearest inhabited Polynesian island. Easter is famous for its hundreds of giant stone statues, weighing up to 80 tons, that were carved, dragged miles overland, and erected on platforms by a people with stone tools but no metal tools, and without sources of power except for their own muscles. When Europeans "discovered" Easter in A.D. 1722, the carving of statues had already ceased, and the statues were being pulled down by the islanders themselves. But the ultimate cause of that collapse, which inspired an expedition by Thor Heyerdahl, invocations of extraterrestrial astronauts by Erich Von Däniken, and much wild speculation by others, was for a long time in doubt.

The ecological origins of Easter's collapse became clear only within the last twenty years, when palynological evidence for Easter's former vegetation began to be uncovered. That evidence has now been fleshed out by archaeological and paleontological excavations, which are still ongoing. The following picture of Easter's history has emerged.

Today, Easter Island is barren, eroded, devoid of native trees, devoid of native land birds, and with just a few species of breeding seabirds confined to offshore rock stacks. But when discovered by Polynesians around A.D. 300, Easter was covered with tropical forest, including the world's largest palm tree (Dransfield et al. 1984). In that forest lived at least six species of land birds, including herons, rails, parrots, and owls. The breeding seabirds, which included albatrosses, boobies, frigate birds, petrels, shearwaters, storm petrels, terns, and tropic birds, numbered about thirty species, more than are known from any other single

Polynesian island. The first Polynesian settlers began to clear the forest for agriculture. They used the trees for firewood and to build canoes with which they went to sea to catch porpoises and deep-water fish. They ate the native land birds, the seabirds, and the fruits of the palm tree. They also used the trunks of the palm trees as rollers and levers to transport and erect their giant statues.

In this initially rich environment, Easter's human population exploded to about 10,000 people, living at a population density of about 160 people per square mile. Eventually, the forest was cleared so completely that all of the tree species, all of the land bird species, and most of the seabird species became extinct. Without logs as rollers and levers, it became impossible to transport and erect statues. Without tree cover, the topsoil eroded, agricultural yields fell, and fuel sources other than weeds and crop wastes disappeared. Without canoes, deep-sea fishing became impossible, porpoises disappeared from the diet, and the sole remaining large animal source of protein became—other humans. The tree and bird extinctions and the soil erosion eliminated much of Easter's resource base and left no possibility of rebuilding Easter society. While humans themselves did not become extinct on Easter, three-quarters of the human population did die out in an orgy of cannibalism, starvation, and warfare. What had been one of the world's most remarkable civilizations self-destructed.

The fate of Easter Island society seizes hold of our imagination, because the parallel between Easter Island isolated in the Pacific Ocean and Planet Earth isolated in our own galaxy is so obvious. When the Easter Islanders got into serious difficulties encompassing their entire island, they had nowhere to flee, no one to whom to turn for help—just as would be true for all of us humans today if we should face a similar worldwide crisis. I can't stop wondering what were the words of the Easter Islander who cut down the last palm tree. Did he shout "jobs, not trees"? Did he invoke private property rights, a plea to keep big government of the chiefs off his back, the uncertainties behind the extrapolations of fear-mongering environmentalists, and technology's power somehow to solve all problems?

I mentioned at the outset that history, like life itself, is complicated. That was true also in Polynesia, where history on different islands ran very different courses. On some islands, including Tonga, Tikopia, Tahiti, Rarotonga, and the high Marquesan islands, human populations continued to flourish for thousands of years, from the arrival of ancestral Polynesians until European arrival in the seventeenth or eighteenth centuries. On other islands there were environmental degradation and population declines as on Easter Island; those other islands included Mangaia, Mangareva, Rapa, low Marquesan islands, parts of New Caledonia, and parts of Fiji. On still other islands, including Henderson, pre-*Bounty* Pitcairn, the Line Islands, Necker, and Nihoa, the trajectory of Polynesian history ended before European arrival with complete abandonment or die-off: not a single person was left alive. How can we account for these very different courses of Polynesian history?

Numerous environmental factors as well as numerous cultural factors appear to have played a role. Among environmental factors, a leading one was rainfall: low-rainfall islands like Easter were more likely to become deforested than higher-rainfall islands like Tahiti and Tonga, for the obvious reason that rates of regrowth of vegetation after cutting increase with rainfall. Deforestation tended to be more extensive on low islands than on high islands because of so-called orographic rain: rainfall above an elevation of 3,000 feet on high Marquesan islands fed streams carrying nutrients leached from mountain soils and descending to the drier lowlands of those islands. Deforestation tended to increase with latitude, for the obvious reason that vegetation regrowth is slower at the cooler temperatures of high latitudes, as on Easter and New Zealand's South Island. Young or active volcanoes, such as Tikopia and Tonga and Hawaii's Big Island, were less likely to become deforested than old weathered islands because of higher levels or rates of replenishment of soil nutrients (cf. Chadwick et al. 1999).

Those are some of the environmental factors, but there were also cultural factors, i.e., different cultural responses. People on some islands limited deforestation by abandoning slash-and-burn shifting cultivation in favor of intensive agriculture on fixed garden plots, relying either on tree orchards as on Tikopia and the Marquesas (Rolett 1998) or else on irrigated taro fields as on Rarotonga and Rapa. P. V. Kirch (1997b) has pointed out that small islands, such as Tikopia, had the potential for developing bottoms-up conservation measures, because everyone could see what was happening to the whole island; large islands with centralized political leadership, such as Tonga, had the potential for developing top-down centrally imposed conservation measures; and medium-sized islands might fall between those two stools and fail to develop either set of conservation measures. Very isolated islands, such as Easter and Rapa, were prone to deforestation because their inhabitants were unlikely to resort to immigration as an escape valve for population buildup. But, conversely, societies on some islands with larger neighbors, such as Pitcairn and Henderson, whose Polynesian populations depended on trade with Mangareva 300 miles distant, were fatally destroyed when that neighbor became deforested (Weisler 1994).

Does this mean that we shall never arrive at real explanations, but only at a long laundry list of possible explanations why some islands were abandoned, other island societies declined but did not disappear, and still other societies continued to thrive? Clearly, this is a complicated problem, but I think that we shall eventually succeed in achieving a more satisfying synthesis than a mere laundry list. There are probably fewer than ten major explanatory factors, and possibly considerably fewer than ten because some of the cultural factors really were not independent variables but instead arose only in certain environments. Our available database will consist of different outcomes of human history on dozens of different islands. Hence I hope that we shall eventually be able to answer the question which are the most fragile Pacific island environments, in which pre-industrial societies were most likely to collapse.

My other set of examples is the collapse of Anasazi and other Native American societies in the U.S. Southwest in the centuries before Columbus's arrival (Cordell 1994, 1997; Crown and Judge 1991; Gumerman 1998; Hegmon 2000; Lister and Lister 1981; Plog 1997; Sebastian 1992; Vivian 1990). While agriculture reached the Southwest from Mexico around 1800 B.C., it was not until around A.D. 500 that people began living in settled villages. Thereafter, populations exploded in numbers and spread over the landscape, only to collapse in regional abandonments or drastic reorganizations at different times in different areas: in the middle or late twelfth century for Chaco Canyon, Mimbres, North Black Mesa, and the Virgin Anasazi; around A.D. 1300 for Kayenta, Mesa Verde, and Mogollon; and in the middle of the fifteenth century for the Hohokam. What accounts for these abandonments, collapses, or reorganizations? Favorite single-factor explanations invoke environmental damage, drought, or warfare and cannibalism.

Actually, the field of U.S. southwestern pre-history is a graveyard for single-factor explanations. Multiple factors have operated, but they all go back to the fundamental problem that the U.S. Southwest is a fragile and marginal environment for agriculture. It has low and unpredictable rainfall, quickly exhausted soils, and very low rates of forest regrowth. External environmental problems, especially major droughts and episodes of arroyo-cutting, tend to recur at intervals much longer than a human lifetime or oral memory span, so people without writing could not possibly plan for such events. Given those fundamental problems, it is impressive that Native Americans in the Southwest developed such complex farming societies, large villages, and large populations as they did. Testimony to their success is that most of this area now supports a much sparser population growing their own food than it did in Anasazi times. It is an unforgettable experience to drive through areas dotted with the remains of former Anasazi stone houses, dams, and irrigation systems and to see now a virtually empty landscape with only the occasional occupied modern house.

Today our attention is drawn to a few large and famous archaeological sites that were occupied continuously for several centuries, such as Pueblo Bonito in New Mexico's Chaco Canyon. In reality, most southwestern archaeological sites were occupied for only a few decades until its people moved on, probably compelled to move by problems of deforestation and soil nutrient exhaustion. They could practice that shifting settlement strategy as long as human population numbers were so low that there were large unoccupied areas or that each area was left unoccupied for sufficiently long after occupation that vegetation and soil nutrients had time to recover. Eventually, though, once human populations had increased to fill up the landscape, people could no longer escape their problems by moving.

Multiple environmental problems and cultural responses contributed to abandonments in the U.S. Southwest, and different factors were of different importance in different areas. For example, deforestation was a problem for the Anasazi, who required trees to supply the roof beams of their houses, but not for the Hohokam, who did not use beams in their houses. Salinization resulting from irrigation agriculture was a problem for the Hohokam, who had to irrigate their fields, but not for the Mesa Verdeans, who did not have to irrigate. Other southwestern peoples were done in by dropping water tables or by soil nutrient exhaustion. Despite these varying proximate causes of abandonments, all were ultimately due to the same fundamental problem: people living in fragile environments, adopting solutions that were brilliantly successful and understandable in the short run, but that failed or else created fatal problems in the long run when confronted with external environmental changes or human-caused environmental changes that people without written histories or archaeologists could not have anticipated.

Our understanding of pre-history in the U.S. Southwest is exceptionally detailed because of two advantages that archaeologists in this area enjoy. First, rather than having to date sites by the radiocarbon method used by archaeologists elsewhere, with its inevitable errors of 50–100 years, they date sites to the nearest year by the tree rings of the site's wood construction beams (Dean and Robinson 1978; Dean et al. 1996; Windes and Ford 1996). The widths of the rings vary from year to year, depending on rainfall and drought conditions each year. Tree rings thus provide southwestern archaeologists with uniquely exact dating and uniquely detailed year-to-year environmental information. Second, the Southwest is infested with small rodents called packrats, which have the virtue for archaeologists that they shelter themselves in structures called middens made of vegetation gathered within a few dozen yards. The packrats urinate in their own middens, their urine dries out and crystalizes, and the midden becomes a solidified dry mass of vegetation that the animals abandon after a decade or two. Thus, the midden is in effect a high-resolution time capsule of the local vegetation: a paleoecologist can return there up to 40,000 years later, identify the plant remains in the midden, radiocarbon-date the midden, and state what plants were growing in the vicinity at that date in the past (Betancourt 1984; Betancourt and Van Devender 1981).

As I mentioned, different southwestern sites were abandoned or transformed at different times for different specific reasons (Dean et al. 1985). The most intensively studied abandonment was of the most spectacular and largest set of sites, the Anasazi sites in Chaco Canyon of northwestern New Mexico (Lister and Lister 1981; Sebastian 1992; Vivian 1990). Chaco Anasazi society flourished from about A.D. 600 for more than five centuries until it disappeared sometime between 1150 and 1200. It was a complexly organized, geographically extensive, regionally integrated society whose stone buildings were the largest buildings erected in North America until the Chicago skyscrapers of the 1880s. Even more than the barren treeless landscape of Easter Island, the barren treeless landscape of Chaco Canyon today, with its deep-cut arroyos and sparse low vegetation of salt-tolerant bushes, astonishes us, because Chaco Canyon is now completely uninhabited except for a few National Park Service ranger houses. Why would anyone have built the most advanced city in North America in that wasteland,

and why, having gone to all that work of building it, did they then abandon it?

When Native American farmers moved into the Chaco Canyon area around A.D. 600, they initially lived in underground pithouses, as did other contemporary Native Americans in the Southwest. Around A.D. 700 the Chaco Anasazi, completely out of contact with Native American societies building structures of stone a thousand miles to the south in Mexico, invented for themselves the techniques of stone construction. Initially, those structures were only one story high, but around A.D. 920 what eventually became the largest Chacoan site of Pueblo Bonito went up to two stories, then over the next two centuries rose to five stories with 600 rooms whose roof supports were logs up to 16 feet long and weighing up to 700 pounds.

Why, out of all the Anasazi sites, was it at Chaco Canyon that construction techniques and political and societal complexity reached their apogee? Likely reasons are some environmental advantages of Chaco Canyon, which initially represented a favorable environmental oasis within northwestern New Mexico. The narrow canyon caught rain runoff from a large upland area, which resulted in high alluvial groundwater levels permitting farming independent of local rainfall in some areas and also high rates of soil renewal from the runoff. The Chaco area has a high diversity of wild plant and animal species and a relatively low elevation that provides a long growing season for crops. Nearby pinyon and juniper woodlands supplied wood for construction timber and firewood. The earliest roof beams identified by their tree rings are of locally available pinyon pines, and firewood remains in early hearths are of locally available pinyon and juniper. Anasazi diets were heavily dependent on growing corn, plus some squash and beans, but early archaeological levels also show much consumption of wild plants such as pinyon nuts, and much hunting of deer.

One environmental problem caused by the growing population developed by around A.D. 1000, when packrat middens show that the pinyon and juniper woodland initially in the vicinity of the large Chaco Canyon settlements had been completely cut down. The loss of the woodland not only eliminated pinyon nuts as a local food supply but also forced Chaco residents to turn to a different timber source for their fuel (Kohler and Matthews 1988) and construction needs. That source consisted of ponderosa pine, spruce, and fir trees growing in mountains up to fifty miles away at elevations several thousand feet higher than Chaco Canyon (Betancourt et al. 1986). With no draft animals available, logs weighing up to 700 pounds were transported in prodigious quantities to Chaco Canyon by human muscle power alone. Construction at Chaco Canyon used about 200,000 trees.

The other environmental problem that developed early involved hydrology (Bryan 1941). Initially, rain runoff would have been as a broad sheet over the canyon bottom, permitting floodplain agriculture watered by the runoff and also watered by a high alluvial groundwater table. When the Anasazi began diverting water into channels for irrigation, the concentration of water runoff in irrigation channels, and removal of vegetation, resulted by sometime before A.D. 1025 in the cutting of deep arroyos in which the water level was below field levels, making irrigation agriculture or agriculture based on groundwater impossible for people without pumps.

Despite the development of these two environmental problems that reduced crop production and virtually eliminated timber supplies within Chaco Canyon itself, the population of Chaco Canyon continued to increase, particularly in a big spurt of construction that began in A.D. 1029. A dense population is attested not only by the famous Great Houses (such as Pueblo Bonito) spaced about a mile apart on the north side of Chaco Canyon, but also by post holes indicating a continuous line of residences at the base of the cliffs between the Great Houses and by the remains of hundreds of small settlements on the south side of the canyon. This dense population was no longer self-supporting but became subsidized by outlying satellite settlements constructed in similar architectural styles and joined to Chaco Canyon in a regional network of hundreds of miles of roads. Chaco Canyon became a black hole into which goods were imported but from which nothing material was exported. Into Chaco Canyon came those tens of thousands of big trees for construction; pottery (all late-period pottery in Chaco Canyon was imported, probably because exhaustion of local firewood supplies precluded firing pots within the canyon itself); stone for making stone tools; turquoise for making ornaments, from other areas of New Mexico; macaws and copper balls from Mexico, as luxury goods; and probably food. Food remains in rubbish at archaeological sites attest to the growing problems of the canyon's inhabitants in nourishing themselves: deer declined in their diets, to be replaced by smaller game, especially rabbits and mice. Remains of complete headless mice suggest that people were catching mice in the fields, beheading them, and popping them into their mouths whole.

Why would outlying settlements have supported the Chaco center, dutifully delivering timber, pots, stone, turquoise, luxury goods, and food without receiving anything material in return? The answer is probably the same reason why outlying areas today support our cities such as Rome and Washington, D.C., which produce no timber or food but serve as religious and political centers. Chacoans were now irreversibly committed to living in a complex, interdependent society. They could no longer revert to their original condition of self-supporting mobile little groups, because the trees in the canyon were now gone, the arroyos were cut below field levels, and the growing population had filled up the region and left no unoccupied suitable areas to which to move. When the pinyon and juniper trees were cut down, the nutrients in the litter underneath the trees were flushed out. Today, more than 800 years later, there is still no pinyon/juniper woodland growing anywhere near the packrat middens that contain remains of the woodland before A.D. 1000.

The last construction beams at Pueblo Bonito, dating from the decade after 1110, are from a wall enclosing the plazas, which had formerly been open to the outside. That suggests strife: people were evidently now visiting Pueblo Bonito not just to participate in its religious ceremonies and to receive orders, but also to make trouble. The last tree-ring-dated roof beam at the nearby Great House of Chetro Ketl was cut in A.D. 1117, and the last roof beam anywhere in Chaco Canyon was put up in A.D. 1170. Other Anasazi sites show more abundant evidence of strife, including convincing evidence of cannibalism, plus settlements at the tops of steep cliffs at long distances from fields and water and understandable only as easily defended locations (Haas and Creamer 1993).

The last straw for Chacoans was a drought that tree rings show to have begun around A.D. 1130. There had been similar droughts previously, around A.D. 1090 and 1040, but the difference this time was that Chaco Canyon held more people, more dependent on outlying settlements, and with no unoccupied land to which to move. A drought that lasted more than three years would have been fatal, because modern Puebloans can store corn for only two or three years, after which it is too rotten or infested to eat. Sometime between A.D. 1150 and 1200, Chaco Canyon was abandoned and remained largely empty until Navajo sheepherders reoccupied it 600 years later. What actually happened to the thousands of Chacoan inhabitants? By analogy with historically witnessed abandonments of other pueblos during a drought in the 1670s (Vivian 1979), probably many people starved to death, some people killed each other, and the survivors fled to other settled areas in the Southwest.

We can now return to the question subject to longstanding debate: was Chaco Canyon abandoned because of human impact on the environment or because of drought? The answer is: it was abandoned for both reasons. Over the course of five centuries the human population of Chaco Canyon grew, their demands on the environment grew, their environmental resources declined, and people came to be living increasingly close to the margin of what the environment could support. That was the ultimate cause of abandonment. The proximate cause, the proverbial last straw that broke the camel's back, was a drought that finally pushed Chacoans over the edge.

That type of conclusion is likely to apply to many other collapses of past societies, and to our own destiny today. All of us today—houseowners, investors, politicians, university administrators, and others—can get away with a lot of waste when the economy is good. We forget that conditions fluctuate, and we may not be able to anticipate when conditions will change. By that time, we may already have become irreversibly committed to an expensive lifestyle, leaving bankruptcy as the sole out.

We have now considered pre-industrial collapses of societies in ecologically fragile environments, among Pacific Islanders and among Native Americans of the U.S. Southwest. The numerous other possible examples of collapses in fragile environments include those of Fertile Crescent societies, Great Zimbabwe, the Greenland Norse, Harappan Indus Valley civilization, and Mycenean Greece. There were also possible pre-industrial collapses in more robust environments, including Angkor Wat, Cahokia, Classic Lowland Maya, and Northwestern Europe. Hence pre-industrial societies can collapse for ecological reasons, not only because of problems in their own environments but also triggered by environmental collapses of neighbors (e.g., Weisler 1994). Can we extrapolate these historical findings to our prospects today?

There are obvious differences between past conditions and current conditions. Some of those differences make us less prone to collapse, while some of them make us more prone. Today we possess scientific ecological knowledge that past societies lacked. Offsetting that advantage, we have far more people today, wielding far more potent destructive technologies. Whereas ten thousand Easter Islanders wielding stone tools required many centuries to deforest their landscape, the Earth's six billion modern inhabitants, with their bulldozers and power machinery, deforest vast expanses in decades. In the past, societies could collapse in isolation without any effects elsewhere in the world. When Polynesian Easter Island society collapsed, nobody else in the world knew about it, nor was anybody affected. Today, no society, no matter how remote, can collapse without potential worldwide consequences. When distant Somalia collapsed, in went American troops; when the former Yugoslavia and Soviet Union collapsed, out went streams of refugees over all of Europe and the rest of world; and when changed conditions of society and settlement spread new diseases in Africa, those diseases spread over the world. Past societies faced frequent ecological crises of small amplitude over small areas. Modern global society faces less frequent but bigger crises over larger areas.

Is our situation hopeless? Of course not. We face big risks, but the biggest risks are not ones beyond our control, like a possible collision with an asteroid. Instead, the biggest risks are the ones that we are generating ourselves. Because we are the cause of our environmental problems, we are in control of them. The future is up for grabs, and it lies in our hands. We don't need new technologies to solve our problem; we just need the political will to apply solutions already available.

We tend to feel that our problems are so monumental that individuals can contribute nothing to solving them. In fact, there are many simple and cheap things that we can do as individuals. We can vote: many elections are decided by small margins, and the candidates often differ considerably in their environmental records and agendas. We can devote some time to causes that we think will help, such as population policy and environmental movements. We can work on fixing our local environment, which produces immediate benefits to us as individuals and also makes us citizens of the First World a credible example to other countries. We can contribute money: environmental organizations are so underfunded that a small contribution makes a big difference.

But our best hope is the media. When the Easter Islanders and the Anasazi were collapsing, they had no idea of the many other collapses going on elsewhere in the world around the same time (like those at

Angkor Wat, Cahokia, and Great Zimbabwe); nor had they any idea of the many similar collapses that had occurred in the past (like those of Fertile Crescent societies, Harappan society, and Mycenean Greece). We, in contrast, know of conditions in remote places and at remote times through books, newspapers, radio, television, movies, and other media. Most Americans have seen television footage of current conditions in Somalia and have seen TV documentaries about Easter Island or other vanished civilizations. We are the first societies in world history to have the opportunity of learning from the mistakes of many others. It's up to us to decide whether we choose to apply the obvious lessons.

REFERENCES

Bahn, P., and J. Flenley. 1992. *Easter Island, Earth Island.* London: Thames and Hudson.

Bellwood, P. 1987. *The Polynesians.* Revised ed. London: Thames and Hudson.

Betancourt, J. L. 1984. Late Quaternary Plant Zonation and Climate in Southeastern Utah. *Great Basin Naturalist* 44: 1–35.

Betancourt, J. L., J. S. Dean, and H. M. Hull. 1986. Prehistoric Long-Distance Transport of Construction Beams, Chaco Canyon, New Mexico. *Amer. Antiquity* 51: 370–75.

Betancourt, J. L., and T. R. Van Devender. 1981. Holocene Vegetation in Chaco Canyon, New Mexico. *Science* 214: 656–58.

Bryan, K. 1941. Pre-Columbian Agriculture in the Southwest as Conditioned by Periods of Alluviation. *Annals Assoc. Amer. Geographers* 31: 219–42.

Chadwick, O. A., L. A. Derry, P. M. Vitousek, B. J. Huebert, and L. O. Hedin. 1999. Changing Sources of Nutrients during Four Million Years of Ecosystem Development. *Nature* 397: 491–97.

Cordell, C. S. 1994. *Ancient Pueblo Peoples.* Washington, D.C.: Smithsonian.

Cordell, L. 1997. *Archaeology of the Southwest.* 2nd ed. San Diego: Academic Press.

Crown, P. L., and W. J. Judge (eds.). 1991. *Chaco and Hohokam.* Santa Fe: School of American Research.

Dean, J. S., R. C. Euler, G. J. Gumerman, F. Plog, R. H. Hevly, and T. N. V. Karlstrom. 1985. Human Behavior, Demography, and Paleoenvironment on the Colorado Plateaus. *Amer. Antiquity* 50: 537–54.

Dean, J. S., and W. J. Robinson. 1978. *Expanded Tree-Ring Chronologies for the Southwestern United States.* Tucson: University of Arizona.

Dean, J. S., M. C. Slaughter, and D. O. Bowden. 1996. Desert Dendrochronology: Tree-Ring Dating Prehistoric Sites in the Tucson Basin. *Kiva* 62: 7–26.

Dransfield, J., J. R. Flenley, S. M. King, D. D. Harkness, and S. Rapu. 1984. A Recently Extinct Palm from Easter Island. *Nature* 312: 750–52.

Flenley, J. R. 1979. Stratigraphic Evidence of Environmental Change on Easter Island. *Asian Perspectives.* 22: 33–40.

Flenley, J. R., and S. N. King. 1984. Late Quaternary Pollen Records from Easter Island. *Nature* 307: 47–50.

Gumerman, G. J. (ed.). 1998. *The Anasazi in a Changing Environment.* Cambridge: Cambridge University Press.

Haas, J., and W. Creamer. 1993. *Stress and Warfare among the Kayenta Anasazi of the Thirteenth Century A.D.* Chicago: Field Museum of Natural History.

Hegmon, M. (ed.). 2000. *The Archaeology of Regional Interaction.* Boulder: University Press of Colorado.

Kirch, P. V. 1984. *The Evolution of the Polynesian Chiefdoms.* Cambridge: Cambridge University Press.

———. 1997a. *The Lapita Peoples.* Oxford: Blackwell.

———. 1997b. Microcosmic Histories. *Amer. Anthropologist* 99: 30–42.

———. 2000. *On the Road of the Winds.* Berkeley: University of California Press.

Kohler, T. A., and M. H. Matthews. 1988. Long-term Anasazi Land Use and Forest Reduction: A Case Study from Southwest Colorado. *Amer. Antiquity* 53: 537–64.

Lister, R. H., and F. C. Lister. 1981. *Chaco Canyon.* Albuquerque: University of New Mexico Press.

Plog, S. 1997. *Ancient Peoples of the American Southwest.* London: Thames and Hudson.

Rolett, B. V. 1998. *Hanamiai: Prehistoric Colonization and Culture Change in the Marquesas Islands (East Polynesia).* New Haven: Yale University Press.

Sebastian, L. 1992. *The Chaco Anasazi.* Cambridge: Cambridge University Press.

Spriggs, M. 1997. *The Island Melanesians.* Oxford: Blackwell.

Steadman, D. W., P. V. Casanova, and C. C. Ferrando. 1994. Stratigraphy, Chronology, and Cultural Context of an Early Faunal Assemblage from Easter Island. *Asian Perspectives* 33: 79–96.

Vivian, G. 1979. *Gran Quivira.* Washington, D.C.: National Park Service.

Vivian, R. G. 1990. *The Chacoan Prehistory of the San Juan Basin.* San Diego: Academic Press.

Weisler, M. I. 1994. The Settlement of Marginal Polynesia: New Evidence from Henderson Island. *J. Field Archaeol.* 21: 83–102.

Windes, T. C., and D. Ford. 1996. The Chaco Wood Project: The Chronometric Reappraisal of Pueblo Bonito. *Amer. Antiquity* 61: 295–310.

THE TANNER LECTURERS

1976–77

OXFORD   Bernard Williams, Cambridge University

MICHIGAN   Joel Feinberg, University of Arizona
              "Voluntary Euthanasia and the Inalienable Right to Life"

STANFORD   Joel Feinberg, University of Arizona
              "Voluntary Euthanasia and the Inalienable Right to Life"

1977–78

OXFORD   John Rawls, Harvard University

MICHIGAN   Sir Karl Popper, University of London
              "Three Worlds"

STANFORD   Thomas Nagel, Princeton University

1978–79

OXFORD   Thomas Nagel, Princeton University
              "The Limits of Objectivity"

CAMBRIDGE   C. C. O'Brien, London

MICHIGAN   Edward O. Wilson, Harvard University
              "Comparative Social Theory"

STANFORD   Amartya Sen, Oxford University
              "Equality of What?"

UTAH   Lord Ashby, Cambridge University
              "The Search for an Environmental Ethic"

UTAH STATE   R. M. Hare, Oxford University
              "Moral Conflicts"

1979–80

OXFORD   Jonathan Bennett, University of British Columbia
              "Morality and Consequences"

CAMBRIDGE   Raymond Aron, Collège de France
              "Arms Control and Peace Research"

HARVARD   George Stigler, University of Chicago
              "Economics or Ethics?"

MICHIGAN   Robert Coles, Harvard University
              "Children as Moral Observers"

STANFORD   Michel Foucault, Collège de France
"*Omnes et Singulatim: Towards a Criticism of 'Political Reason'* "

UTAH   Wallace Stegner, Los Altos Hills, California
"*The Twilight of Self-Reliance: Frontier Values and Contemporary America*"

1980–81

OXFORD   Saul Bellow, University of Chicago
"*A Writer from Chicago*"

CAMBRIDGE   John Passmore, Australian National University
"*The Representative Arts as a Source of Truth*"

HARVARD   Brian M. Barry, University of Chicago
"*Do Countries Have Moral Obligations? The Case of World Poverty*"

MICHIGAN   John Rawls, Harvard University
"*The Basic Liberties and Their Priority*"

STANFORD   Charles Fried, Harvard University
"*Is Liberty Possible?*"

UTAH   Joan Robinson, Cambridge University
"*The Arms Race*"

HEBREW
UNIV.   Solomon H. Snyder, Johns Hopkins University
"*Drugs and the Brain and Society*"

1981–82

OXFORD   Freeman Dyson, Princeton University
"*Bombs and Poetry*"

CAMBRIDGE   Kingman Brewster, President Emeritus, Yale University
"*The Voluntary Society*"

HARVARD   Murray Gell-Mann, California Institute of Technology
"*The Head and the Heart in Policy Studies*"

MICHIGAN   Thomas C. Schelling, Harvard University
"*Ethics, Law, and the Exercise of Self-Command*"

STANFORD   Alan A. Stone, Harvard University
"*Psychiatry and Morality*"

UTAH   R. C. Lewontin, Harvard University
"*Biological Determinism*"

AUSTRALIAN
NATL. UNIV.   Leszek Kolakowski, Oxford University
"*The Death of Utopia Reconsidered*"

1982–83

OXFORD Kenneth J. Arrow, Stanford University
"The Welfare-Relevant Boundaries of the Individual"

CAMBRIDGE H. C. Robbins Landon, University College, Cardiff
*"Haydn and Eighteenth-Century Patronage in Austria and
Hungary"*

HARVARD Bernard Williams, Cambridge University
"Morality and Social Justice"

STANFORD David Gauthier, University of Pittsburgh
"The Incompleat Egoist"

UTAH Carlos Fuentes, Princeton University
"A Writer from Mexico"

JAWAHARLAL
NEHRU UNIV. Ilya Prigogine, Université Libre de Bruxelles
"Only an Illusion"

1983–84

OXFORD Donald D. Brown, Johns Hopkins University
"The Impact of Modern Genetics"

CAMBRIDGE Stephen J. Gould, Harvard University
"Evolutionary Hopes and Realities"

MICHIGAN Herbert A. Simon, Carnegie-Mellon University
"Scientific Literacy as a Goal in a High-Technology Society"

STANFORD Leonard B. Meyer, University of Pennsylvania
"Music and Ideology in the Nineteenth Century"

UTAH Helmut Schmidt, former Chancellor, West Germany
"The Future of the Atlantic Alliance"

HELSINKI Georg Henrik von Wright, Helsinki
"Of Human Freedom"

1984–85

OXFORD Barrington Moore, Jr., Harvard University
"Authority and Inequality under Capitalism and Socialism"

CAMBRIDGE Amartya Sen, Oxford University
"The Standard of Living"

HARVARD Quentin Skinner, Cambridge University
"The Paradoxes of Political Liberty"

Kenneth J. Arrow, Stanford University
"The Unknown Other"

MICHIGAN Nadine Gordimer, South Africa
"The Essential Gesture: Writers and Responsibility"

STANFORD Michael Slote, University of Maryland
"Moderation, Rationality, and Virtue"

1985–86

OXFORD   Thomas M. Scanlon, Jr., Harvard Univesity
"The Significance of Choice"

CAMBRIDGE   Aldo Van Eyck, The Netherlands
"Architecture and Human Values"

HARVARD   Michael Walzer, Institute for Advanced Study
"Interpretation and Social Criticism"

MICHIGAN   Clifford Geertz, Institute for Advanced Study
"The Uses of Diversity"

STANFORD   Stanley Cavell, Harvard University
"The Uncanniness of the Ordinary"

UTAH   Arnold S. Relman, Editor, *New England Journal of Medicine*
"Medicine as a Profession and a Business"

1986–87

OXFORD   Jon Elster, Oslo University and the University of Chicago
*"Taming Chance: Randomization in Individual and Social
Decisions"*

CAMBRIDGE   Roger Bulger, University of Texas Health Sciences Center,
Houston
*"On Hippocrates, Thomas Jefferson, and Max Weber: The
Bureaucratic, Technologic Imperatives and the Future of the
Healing Tradition in a Voluntary Society"*

HARVARD   Jürgen Habermas, University of Frankfurt
"Law and Morality"

MICHIGAN   Daniel C. Dennett, Tufts University
"The Moral First Aid Manual"

STANFORD   Gisela Striker, Columbia University
"Greek Ethics and Moral Theory"

UTAH   Laurence H. Tribe, Harvard University
"On Reading the Constitution"

1987–88

OXFORD   F. Van Zyl Slabbert, University of the Witwatersrand, South
Africa
"The Dynamics of Reform and Revolt in Current South Africa"

CAMBRIDGE   Louis Blom-Cooper, Q.C., London
"The Penalty of Imprisonment"

HARVARD   Robert A. Dahl, Yale University
"The Pseudodemocratization of the American Presidency"

MICHIGAN   Albert O. Hirschman, Institute for Advanced Study
*"Two Hundred Years of Reactionary Rhetoric: The Case of the
Perverse Effect"*

STANFORD	Ronald Dworkin, New York University and University College, Oxford *"Foundations of Liberal Equality"*
UTAH	Joseph Brodsky, Russian poet, Mount Holyoke College *"A Place as Good as Any"*
CALIFORNIA	Wm. Theodore de Bary, Columbia University *"The Trouble with Confucianism"*
BUENOS AIRES	Barry Stroud, University of California, Berkeley *"The Study of Human Nature and the Subjectivity of Value"*
MADRID	Javier Muguerza, Universidad Nacional de Educatión a Distancia, Madrid *"The Alternative of Dissent"*
WARSAW	Anthony Quinton, British Library, London *"The Varieties of Value"*

1988–89

OXFORD	Michael Walzer, Institute for Advanced Study *"Nation and Universe"*
CAMBRIDGE	Albert Hourani, Emeritus Fellow, St. Antony's College, and Magdalen College, Oxford *"Islam in European Thought"*
MICHIGAN	Toni Morrison, State University of New York at Albany *"Unspeakable Things Unspoken: The Afro-American Presence in American Literature"*
STANFORD	Stephen Jay Gould, Harvard University *"Unpredictability in the History of Life"* *"The Quest for Human Nature: Fortuitous Side, Consequences, and Contingent History"*
UTAH	Judith Shklar, Harvard University *"Amerian Citizenship: The Quest for Inclusion"*
CALIFORNIA	S. N. Eisenstadt, The Hebrew University of Jerusalem *"Cultural Tradition, Historical Experience, and Social Change: The Limits of Convergence"*
YALE	J. G. A. Pocock, Johns Hopkins University *"Edward Gibbon in History: Aspects of the Text in* The History of the Decline and Fall of the Roman Empire"
CHINESE UNIVERSITY OF HONG KONG	Fei Xiaotong, Peking University *"Plurality and Unity in the Configuration of the Chinese People"*

1989–90

OXFORD   Bernard Lewis, Princeton University
              "Europe and Islam"

CAMBRIDGE   Umberto Eco, University of Bologna
              "Interpretation and Overinterpretation: World, History, Texts"

HARVARD   Ernest Gellner, Kings College, Cambridge
              "The Civil and the Sacred"

MICHIGAN   Carol Gilligan, Harvard University
              "Joining the Resistance: Psychology, Politics, Girls, and Women"

UTAH   Octavio Paz, Mexico City
              "Poetry and Modernity"

YALE   Edward N. Luttwak, Center for Strategic and International
              Studies
              "Strategy: A New Era?"

PRINCETON   Irving Howe, writer and critic
              "The Self and the State"

1990–91

OXFORD   David Montgomery, Yale University
              *"Citizenship and Justice in the Lives and Thoughts of Nineteenth-
              Century American Workers"*

CAMBRIDGE   Gro Harlem Brundtland, Prime Minister of Norway
              *"Environmental Challenges of the 1990s: Our Responsibility
              toward Future Generations"*

HARVARD   William Gass, Washington University
              "Eye and Idea"

MICHIGAN   Richard Rorty, University of Virginia
              "Feminism and Pragmatism"

STANFORD   G. A. Cohen, All Souls College, Oxford
              "Incentives, Inequality, and Community"

              János Kornai, University of Budapest and Harvard
              University
              "Market Socialism Revisited"

UTAH   Marcel Ophuls, international film maker
              "Resistance and Collaboration in Peacetime"

YALE   Robertson Davies, novelist
              "Reading and Writing"

PRINCETON   Annette C. Baier, Pittsburgh University
              "Trust"

LENINGRAD   János Kornai, University of Budapest and Harvard
              University
              "Transition from Marxism to a Free Economy"

1991–92

OXFORD R. Z. Sagdeev, University of Maryland
"Science and Revolutions"

CALIFORNIA
 LOS ANGELES Václav Havel, former President, Republic of Czechoslovakia
(Untitled lecture)

 BERKELEY Helmut Kohl, Chancellor of Germany
(Untitled lecture)

CAMBRIDGE David Baltimore, former President of Rockefeller University
"On Doing Science in the Modern World"

MICHIGAN Christopher Hill, seventeenth-century historian, Oxford
"The Bible in Seventeenth-Century English Politics"

STANFORD Charles Taylor, Professor of Philosophy and Political Science,
  McGill University
"Modernity and the Rise of the Public Sphere"

UTAH Jared Diamond, University of California, Los Angeles
"The Broadest Pattern of Human History"

PRINCETON Robert Nozick, Professor of Philosophy, Harvard University
"Decisions of Principle, Principles of Decision"

1992–93

MICHIGAN Amos Oz, Israel
*"The Israeli-Palestinian Conflict: Tragedy, Comedy, and Cognitive
  Block—A Storyteller's Point of View"*

CAMBRIDGE Christine M. Korsgaard, Harvard University
"The Sources of Normativity"

UTAH Evelyn Fox Keller, Massachusetts Institute of Technology
"Rethinking the Meaning of Genetic Determinism"

YALE Fritz Stern, Columbia University
"Mendacity Enforced: Europe, 1914–1989"
"Freedom and Its Discontents: Postunification Germany"

PRINCETON Stanley Hoffmann, Harvard University
"The Nation, Nationalism, and After: The Case of France"

STANFORD Colin Renfrew, Cambridge University
"The Archaeology of Identity"

1993–94

MICHIGAN William Julius Wilson, University of Chicago
"The New Urban Poverty and the Problem of Race"

OXFORD Lord Slynn of Hadley, London
"Law and Culture—A European Setting"

HARVARD Lawrence Stone, Princeton University
"Family Values in a Historical Perspective"

CAMBRIDGE   Peter Brown, Princeton University
                "Aspects of the Christianisation of the Roman World"

UTAH   A. E. Dick Howard, University of Virginia
                "Toward the Open Society in Central and Eastern Europe"

                Jeffrey Sachs, Harvard University
                "Shock Therapy in Poland: Perspectives of Five Years"

                Adam Zagajewski, Paris
                *"A Bus Full of Prophets: Adventures of the Eastern-European
                    Intelligentsia"*

PRINCETON   Alasdair MacIntyre, Duke University
                *"Truthfulness, Lies, and Moral Philosophers: What Can We Learn
                    from Mill and Kant?"*

CALIFORNIA   Oscar Arias, Costa Rica
                "Poverty: The New International Enemy"

STANFORD   Thomas Hill, University of North Carolina at Chapel Hill
                "Basic Respect and Cultural Diversity"
                "Must Respect Be Earned?"

UC
SAN DIEGO   K. Anthony Appiah, Harvard University
                "Race, Culture, Identity: Misunderstood Connections"

1994–95

YALE   Richard Posner, United States Court of Appeals
                *"Euthanasia and Health Care: Two Essays on the Policy Dilemmas
                    of Aging and Old Age"*

MICHIGAN   Daniel Kahneman, University of California, Berkeley
                "Cognitive Psychology of Consequences and Moral Intuition"

HARVARD   Cass R. Sunstein, University of Chicago
                "Political Conflict and Legal Agreement"

CAMBRIDGE   Roger Penrose, Oxford Mathematics Institute
                "Space-time and Cosmology"

PRINCETON   Antonin Scalia, United States Supreme Court
                *"Common-Law Courts in a Civil-Law System: The Role of the
                    United States Federal Courts in Interpreting the Constitution
                    and Laws"*

UC
SANTA CRUZ   Nancy Wexler, Columbia University
                *"Genetic Prediction and Precaution Confront Human Social
                    Values"*

OXFORD   Janet Suzman, South Africa
                "Who Needs Parables?"

STANFORD   Amy Gutmann, Princeton University
                "Responding to Racial Injustice"

UTAH   Edward Said, Columbia University
                "On Lost Causes"

1995–96

PRINCETON   Harold Bloom, Yale University
I. *"Shakespeare and the Value of Personality,"* and
    II. *"Shakespeare and the Value of Love"*

OXFORD   Simon Schama, Columbia University
"Rembrandt and Rubens: Humanism, History, and the Peculiarity of Painting"

CAMBRIDGE   Gunther Schuller, Newton Center, Massachusetts
I. *"Jazz: A Historical Perspective,"* II. *"Duke Ellington,"* and
    III. *"Charles Mingus"*

UC
RIVERSIDE   Mairead Corrigan Maguire, Belfast, Northern Ireland
"Peacemaking from the Grassroots in a World of Ethnic Conflict"

HARVARD   Onora O'Neill, Newham College, Cambridge
"Kant on Reason and Religion"

STANFORD   Nancy Fraser, New School for Social Research
"Social Justice in the Age of Identity Politics: Redistribution, Recognition, and Participation"

UTAH   Cornell West, Harvard University
"A Genealogy of the Public Intellectual"

YALE   Peter Brown, Princeton University
"The End of the Ancient Other World: Death and Afterlife between Late Antiquity and the Early Middle Ages"

1996–97

TORONTO   Peter Gay, Emeritus, Yale University
"The Living Enlightenment"

MICHIGAN   Thomas M. Scanlon, Harvard University
"The Status of Well-Being"

HARVARD   Stuart Hampshire, Emeritus, Stanford University
"Justice Is Conflict: The Soul and the City"

CAMBRIDGE   Dorothy L. Cheney, University of Pennsylvania
"Why Animals Don't Have Language"

PRINCETON   Robert M. Solow, Massachusetts Institute of Technology
"Welfare and Work"

CALIFORNIA   Marian Wright Edelman, Children's Defense Fund
"Standing for Children"

YALE   Liam Hudson, Balas Copartnership
"The Life of the Mind"

STANFORD   Barbara Herman, University of California, Los Angeles
"Moral Literacy"

OXFORD   Francis Fukuyama, George Mason University
"Social Capital"

UTAH   Elaine Pagels, Princeton University
"The Origin of Satan in Christian Traditions"

1997–98

UTAH   Jonathan D. Spence, Yale University
                *"Ideas of Power: China's Empire in the Eighteenth Century and To-
                day"*

PRINCETON   J. M. Coetzee, University of Cape Town
                "The Lives of Animals"

MICHIGAN   Antonio R. Damasio, University of Iowa
                "Exploring the Minded Brain"

CHARLES
UNIVERSITY   Timothy Garton Ash, Oxford University
                "The Direction of European History"

HARVARD   M. F. Burnyeat, Oxford University
                "Culture and Society in Plato's Republic*"*

CAMBRIDGE   Stephen Toulmin, University of Southern California
                "The Idol of Stability"

UC IRVINE   David Kessler, Yale University
                "Tobacco Wars: Risks and Rewards of a Major Challenge"

YALE   Elaine Scarry, Harvard University
                "On Beauty and Being Just"

STANFORD   Arthur Kleinman, Harvard University
                *"Experience and Its Moral Modes: Culture, Human Conditions,
                and Disorder"*

1998–99

MICHIGAN   Walter Burkert, University of Zurich
                *"Revealing Nature Amidst Multiple Cultures: A Discourse with
                Ancient Greeks"*

UTAH   Geoffrey Hartman, Yale University
                "Text and Spirit"

YALE   Steven Pinker, Massachusetts Institute of Technology
                *"The Blank Slate, the Noble Savage, and the Ghost in the
                Machine"*

STANFORD   Randall Kennedy, Harvard University
                "Who Can Say 'Nigger'? . . . and Other Related Questions"

UC DAVIS   Richard White, Stanford University
                "The Problem with Purity"

OXFORD   Sidney Verba, Harvard University
                *"Representative Democracy and Democratic Citizens: Philosophical
                and Empirical Understandings"*

PRINCETON   Judith Jarvis Thomson, Massachusetts Institute of
                Technology
                "Goodness and Advice"

HARVARD   Lani Guinier, Harvard University
                "Rethinking Powers"

1999–2000

YALE	Marina Warner, London *"Spirit Visions"*
MICHIGAN	Helen Vendler, Harvard University *"Poetry and the Mediation of Value: Whitman on Lincoln"*
HARVARD	Wolf Lepenies, Free University, Berlin *"The End of 'German Culture'"*
CAMBRIDGE	Jonathan Lear, University of Chicago *"Happiness"*
OXFORD	Geoffrey Hill, Boston University *"Rhetorics of Value"*
PRINCETON	Michael Ignatieff, London *"Human Rights as Politics"* and *"Human Rights as Idolatry"*
UNIVERSITY OF UTAH	Charles Rosen, New York *"Tradition without Convention: The Impossible Nineteenth-Century Project"*
STANFORD	Jared Diamond, UCLA Medical School *"Ecological Collapses of Pre-industrial Societies"*